The New Russian Business Le

NEW HORIZONS IN LEADERSHIP STUDIES

Series Editor: Joanne B. Ciulla
Professor and Coston Family Chair in Leadership Ethics,
Jepson School of Leadership Studies, University of Richmond, USA
and UNESCO Chair in Leadership Studies,
United Nations International Leadership Academy

This important series is designed to make a significant contribution to the development of leadership studies. This field has expanded dramatically in recent years and the series provides an invaluable forum for the publication of high quality works of scholarship and shows the diversity of leadership issues and practices around the world.

The main emphasis of the series is on the development and application of new and original ideas in leadership studies. It pays particular attention to leadership in business, economics and public policy and incorporates the wide range of disciplines which are now part of the field. Global in its approach, it includes some of the best theoretical and empirical work with contributions to fundamental principles, rigorous evaluations of existing concepts and competing theories, historical surveys and future visions.

Titles in the series include:

The New Russian Business Leaders

Manfred F.R. Kets de Vries

Raoul de Vitry d'Avaucourt Chair of Leadership Development and Director, INSEAD Global Leadership Centre, Fontainebleau, France and Singapore

Stanislav Shekshnia

Adjunct Professor of Entrepreneurship, INSEAD, and Partner, Zest Leadership, Fontainebleau, France and Singapore

Konstantin Korotov

Ph.D. Candidate, INSEAD, Fontainebleau, France and Singapore

Elizabeth Florent-Treacy

Research Project Manager, INSEAD, Fontainebleau, France and Singapore

NEW HORIZONS IN LEADERSHIP STUDIES

Edward Elgar

Cheltenham, UK • Northampton, MA, USA

Published by
Edward Elgar Publishing Limited
The Lypiatts
15 Lansdown Road
Cheltenham
Glos GL50 2JA
UK

Edward Elgar Publishing, Inc.
William Pratt House
9 Dewey Court
Northampton
Massachusetts 01060
USA

Paperback edition 2005
Paperback edition reprinted 2009

This book has been printed on demand to keep the title in print.

A catalogue record for this book
is available from the British Library

ISBN 978 1 84376 499 1 (cased)
      978 1 84542 329 2 (paperback)

Printed and bound in Great Britain by
Marston Book Services Limited, Didcot

Contents

About the authors

Manfred F.R. Kets de Vries brings a different view to the much-studied subjects of leadership and the dynamics of individual and organizational change. Bringing to bear his knowledge and experience of economics (Econ. Drs, University of Amsterdam), management (ITP, MBA, and DBA, Harvard Business School), and psychoanalysis (Canadian Psychoanalytic Society and the International Psychoanalytic Association), Kets de Vries scrutinizes the interface between international management, psychoanalysis, psychotherapy, and dynamic psychiatry. His specific areas of interest are leadership development, career dynamics, executive stress, entrepreneurship, family business, succession planning, cross-cultural management, team building, coaching, and the dynamics of corporate transformation and change.

A clinical professor of leadership development, he holds the Raoul de Vitry d'Avaucourt Chair of Leadership Development at INSEAD, Fontainebleau, France. He is the Director of INSEAD Global Leadership Center. He is program director of INSEAD's top management seminar, 'The challenge of leadership: developing your emotional intelligence' and the program 'Consulting and coaching for change' (and has five times received INSEAD's distinguished teacher award). He has also held professorships at McGill University, the Ecole des Hautes Etudes Commerciales, Montreal, and the Harvard Business School, and he has lectured at management institutions around the world. He is a founding member of the International Society for the Psychoanalytic Study of Organizations. *The Financial Times*, *Le Capital*, *Wirtschaftswoche*, and *The Economist* have judged Manfred Kets de Vries one of world's leading thinkers on leadership.

Kets de Vries is the author, co-author, or editor of 20 books, including *Power and the Corporate Mind* (1975, new edition 1985, with Abraham Zaleznik), *Organizational Paradoxes: Clinical Approaches to Management* (1980, new edition 1994), *The Irrational Executive: Psychoanalytic Explorations in Management* (1984, editor), *The Neurotic Organization: Diagnosing and Changing Counter-Productive Styles of Management* (1984, new edition 1990, with Danny Miller), *Unstable at the Top* (1988, with Danny Miller), *Prisoners of Leadership* (1989), *Handbook of Character Studies* (1991, with Sidney Perzow), *Organizations on the Couch* (1991), *Leaders, Fools and Impostors* (1993), the prize-winning *Life and Death in the Executive Fast Lane: Essays on Irrational*

Organizations and their Leaders (1995) (the Critics' Choice Award 1995–96), *Family Business: Human Dilemmas in the Family Firm* (1996), *The New Global Leaders: Percy Barnevik, Richard Branson, and David Simon* (1999, with Elizabeth Florent), *Struggling with the Demon: Perspectives on Individual and Organizational Irrationality* (2001), *The Leadership Mystique* (2001), *The Happiness Equation* (2002) and *The Global Executive Leadership Inventory* (2003). His latest books are entitled *Are Leaders Born or are they Made: The Case of Alexander the Great,* and *Lessons on Leadership by Terror: Finding Shaka Zulu in the Attic* (both 2004). He is also the author of *The Global Executive Leadership Inventory* (2004), a widely used 360 degree leadership test.

In addition, Kets de Vries has published over 200 scientific papers as chapters in books and as articles in such journals as *Behavioral Science, Journal of Management Studies, Human Relations, Administration & Society, Organizational Dynamics, Strategic Management Journal, Academy of Management Journal, Academy of Management Review, Journal of Forecasting, California Management Review, Harvard Business Review, Sloan Management Review, Academy of Management Executive, The Psychoanalytic Review, Bulletin of the Menninger Clinic, Journal of Applied Behavioral Science, European Management Journal, International Journal of Cross Cultural Management, International Journal of Human Resource Management, Harper's* and *Psychology Today.* He has also written over a hundred case studies, including seven that received the Best Case of the Year award. He is a regular writer for a number of magazines. His work has been featured in such publications as *The New York Times, The Wall Street Journal, The Los Angeles Times, Fortune, Business Week, The Economist, The Financial Times* and *The International Herald Tribune.* His books and articles have been translated into 18 languages. He is a member of 17 editorial boards. He has been elected a Fellow of the Academy of Management.

Kets de Vries is a consultant on organizational design/transformation and strategic human resource management to leading US, Canadian, European, African and Asian companies. As a global consultant in executive development his clients have included ABB, Aegon, Air Liquide, Alcan, Alcatel, Accenture, Bain Consulting, Bang & Olufsen, Bonnier, BP, Ericsson, GE Capital, Goldman Sachs, Heineken, HypoVereinsbank, Investec, KPMG, Lego, Lufthansa, Lundbeck, Novartis, Nokia, NovoNordisk, Rank Xerox, Shell, SHV, SpencerStuart, Standard Bank of South Africa, Unilever and Volvo Car Corporation. As an educator and consultant he has worked in more than 30 countries.

The Dutch government has made him an Officer in the Order of Oranje Nassau. He was the first fly fisherman in Outer Mongolia and is a member of New York's Explorers Club. In his spare time he can be found in the rainforests or savannas of Central Africa, the Siberian taiga, the Pamir mountains, or within the Arctic circle.

Stanislav Shekshnia brings the perspective of a business executive and academic to strategy and organization. His specific areas of interest are leadership, entrepreneurship, leadership development and succession planning, cross-cultural management, organizational culture, and change management.

He has a master's degree in Economics and a Ph.D. from Moscow State University and an MBA from Northeastern University in Boston. In 1991–2002 Stanislav Shekshnia held positions of Director of Human Resources, Central and Eastern Europe of Otis Elevator; President and CEO, Millicom International Cellular, Russia and CIS; Chief Operating Officer of VimpelCom; and CEO of Alfa-Telecom. He served as Chairman of Vimpelcom-R and board member of a number of Russian companies.

In 2002 Stanislav Shekshnia co-founded Zest Leadership international consultancy. With Zest Leadership he concentrates on leadership, leadership development, organizational development and intercultural management. Dr Shekshnia provides personal coaching to business owners and corporate executives. His clients have included BP, TNK-BP, Ilim Pulp Enterprises, KAMAZ, Megatone and United Technologies.

Dr Shekshnia has over 15 years of graduate-level teaching experience in Russia, France and the United States. He is an Adjunct Professor of Entrepreneurship at INSEAD and has taught graduate courses in entrepreneurship, leadership, international mangement and people management and lectured at ESCP-EAP, HEC, Northeastern University, California State University at Hayworth, Stockholm School of Economics, Moscow State University and the International Management Institute in St. Petersburg.

Dr Shekshnia is the author, co-author or editor of five books, including Russian management bestseller *Managing People in Contemporary Organizations* (seven editions since 1995), *Group Focus* (2003, with M. Rousseau-Ovchinnikov), *Kak Eto Skazat Po-Russki: Western Management Methods in Russia* (2003), *Corporate Governance in Russia* (forthcoming, edited with S. Puffer and D. McCarthy). He has published book chapters, articles, executive commentaries, interviews and case studies on entrepreneurship, leadership, people management, intercultural management and business and management in Russia. His work has appeared in such journals as *Academy of Management Executive*, *European Management Journal*, *Journal of West–East Business*, *Case Research Journal*, *California Management Review*, *Compensation and Benefits Review*, *Journal of Management Inquiry*, *The International Executive*, *L'Expansion Management Review*, Russian business daily *Vedomosty*, *Expert*, *Management*, *Personnel Management*, *Personnel Mix*, *Kariera* and *Kompania* magazines.

Stanislav Shekshnia lives in Paris, but frequently travels to his motherland for business and hunting expeditions.

Konstantin Korotov is a pioneer of Western human resource development methods in Russia, and one of the first Western-trained Russian academics in the field of organizational behavior. With Master's degrees from INSEAD, New York University, and Moscow Linguistic University and experience of living and working in various parts of the world, he brings a multicultural perspective into his research, classroom and consulting. Having gained education and experience in design and delivery of management training programs in the United States, he brought his expertise to the Russian market in 1994 where he has since contributed to the accelerated development of human capital in many multinational and local companies. For many years he headed the Professional Development function of Ernst & Young in the Commonwealth of Independent States, being in charge of the skills and knowledge base of Ernst & Young professionals and development of employees of client companies. Bringing academic rigour to the world of professional services, Konstantin Korotov serves as a scientific director of Ernst & Young leadership development programmes in the Commonwealth of Independent States.

Intellectual curiosity and the drive to find answers to unresolved problems in leadership and management of people in organizations brought Konstantin Korotov to INSEAD where he is currently completing his doctoral research in organizational behavior. His research interests include identity and organizational identification, boundary-spanning in organizations, and leadership and leadership development. Part of his empirical research is conducted in Russia. Konstantin Korotov frequently speaks at academic and practitioner conferences and writes for scientific and business press on issues of identity, leadership, human resources management and development. He has written several case-studies illustrating leadership dilemmas. He has designed and delivered seminars and classes for Stockholm School of Economics, American Institute of Business and Economics, Moscow State University, Finance Academy under the Government of the Russian Federation, and Moscow Linguistic University. Constantly interested in being at the frontier of both academic and professional skills, Konstantin Korotov is also working on gaining change management and coaching expertise grounded in clinical organizational psychology under the scientific direction of Manfred Kets de Vries.

Fluent in English, Portuguese, Spanish, and French, in addition to his native Russian, Konstantin Korotov can often be found in Europe, Russia, the United States and Asia both doing research and helping executives and managers grow into successful leaders. His consulting clients include, among others, Ernst & Young, ABN-Amro Bank, Shell, Pepsi, Mars, Western-NIS Enterprise Fund, ISPAT, Edmund S. Muskie Program, AIESEC, and the Russian Presidential Program for Management Cadre Development.

Konstantin Korotov lives with his wife, Svetlana, and daughter, Anne-Sophie, in Paris and Moscow.

Elizabeth Florent-Treacy, Research Project Manager at INSEAD, Fontainebleau, France, is an American who has been living and working in France for nearly 20 years. She has conducted reseach in the following areas: global leadership; global organizations; corporate culture in European and global organizations; American, French and Russian business practices; family business issues; entrepreneurial leadership; cross-cultural management; women and global leadership; cultural aspects of mergers and acquisitions; transformational leadership; expatriate executives and families; and the psychodynamics of leadership. She holds a BA in Women's Studies with a specialization in Sociology, and an MA in Organization Development.

She has written 15 case studies, two of which won the European Case Clearinghouse award for best case in their category, *Banking on Change* (2001) and *British Petroleum: Transformational Leadership in a Transnational Organization* (2000). She has also taught seminars on case writing and teaching methods. She co-authored the following articles and book chapter with Professor Manfred Kets de Vries: 'Global leadership from A to Z', *Organizational Dynamics*, Spring 2002; 'Global Leadership', book chapter in Subir Chowdhury (ed.) *Organization 21C*, 2002; 'Roustam Tariko: Russian Entrepreneur', *Entrepreneurship Theory and Practice*, Spring 2003; and with Kets de Vries and Pierre Vrignaud 'The global leadership life inventory: Development and psychometric properties of a 360-degree feedback instrument', *The International Journal of Human Resource Management* (Spring 2004). She co-authored the following articles with Professor Randel Carlock: 'Work and love: finding one's role in the family firm', *Family Business Case Journal* (forthcoming); 'The HP–Compaq Merger' and 'Love and Work' in *Families in Business*, January 2003; and 'The HP–Compaq merger: a battle for the heart and soul of a company', *International Journal of Entrepreneurship Education*, Spring 2003. She has produced two business case videos: *Love and Work* and *FrogPubs*. She co-authored a book on global leadership with Professor Kets de Vries, *The New Global Leaders: Percy Barnevik, Richard Branson and David Simon and the Re-making of International Business* (April 1999), which has been translated into Dutch, Spanish, Chinese, Serbian, Croatian and Thai.

Elizabeth Florent-Treacy is 'only' fluent in English and French, but she is delighted that her sons are learning other languages in addition to their two native tongues. In particular, her younger son has decided to learn Russian. This brings her life full circle, from her own childhood in the United States overshadowed by the perceived menace of the Evil Empire, to a new reality in which the world rediscovers a nation and a people who largely merit respect and partnership.

Foreword

According to the 'Great Man' theory, leaders are born, not made. Some people have certain innate traits or qualities that make them leadership material. In his book, *On Heroes, Hero Worship, and the Historic in History*, Thomas Carlyle describes how Napoleon was born to change the face of human history. Carlyle says we have to search for the 'ablest' man to be our leader and then submit to him for our own good. Leo Tolstoy disagreed with Carlyle. In *War and Peace*, Tolstoy writes, 'It is incomprehensible that millions of Christian men killed and tortured each other because Napoleon was ambitious…' Tolstoy tells us that great men are nothing more than labels that give names to events. In other words, leaders are the right people, in the right place, at the right time. Fortunately, we do not have to choose between Carlyle's and Tolstoy's positions because both are right – leaders make history and history makes leaders. The study of leadership inevitably requires an understanding of that place where individuals interact with history and culture.

In this book, Manfred F. R. Kets de Vries, Stanislav Shekshnia, Konstantin Korotov and Elizabeth Florent-Treacy present an eloquent account of the new Russian entrepreneurs and the cultural and historical context in which they operate. Rarely do books on leadership provide both a rich description of cultural values and nuances *and* a grounded analysis of leaders' personalities and styles of leadership. Rarely do they offer such fascinating first-hand accounts from leaders who sound more as if they have stepped out of novels than the ashes of communism. Academics and business people will find this book an invaluable resource for understanding Russian attitudes towards business and leadership.

This book focuses on Russian entrepreneurs, but it offers lessons that apply to other cultures and other leadership contexts. The case studies in the book describe the psychological make-up of leaders, their family backgrounds, and their personalities. They illustrate some of the striking similarities of leaders across cultures. The book also describes the challenges of creating businesses in a culture that lacks the values associated with business in a free market, such as enlightened self-interest, adherence to rule of law, and a work ethic that includes the belief that hard work will pay off.

Changing ingrained cultural beliefs about work, leadership and business is not only a challenge for post-communist leaders but also business leaders in other societies and organizations. As the authors point out, the most important lessons in this book come from the ways in which these new Russian business leaders bring about radical change in their organizations and employees. For example, how do they build a productive workforce out of people raised in a 'we pretend to work, they pretend to pay us' culture? How do they provide quality service in a society where customer service is best summed up in the Russian novel *The Twelve Chairs*, by a sign in an office that reads, 'Finish Your Business and Leave'?

The New Russian Business Leaders is an exciting addition to the New Horizons in Leadership Studies Series. The series consists of scholarly interdisciplinary studies that enhance our understanding of leadership and the values and people that shape its practice. Cultural studies of leadership such as this one help us discover which aspects of leadership are universal and which ones are local.

Joanne B. Ciulla
Series Editor
7 December, 2003

Preface

I cannot forecast to you the action of Russia. It is a riddle wrapped in a mystery inside an enigma

Winston Churchill

The idea for a book about the new Russian business elite grew out of a preliminary study in 1998 of Russian business organizations and their leaders in the post-perestroika era. The introduction of radical political and economic reforms by Boris Yeltsin and market-oriented members of the Russian government resulted in a dramatic transformation of Russian society. The consequence of many of these changes has been mixed, however. Certain segments of industry have profited from the new situation – among them, oil companies, some high-tech firms, and selected financial institutions. Some entrepreneurial organizations have flourished, whereas other companies in other segments ceased to exist soon after inception. At that time, each of the authors of this book was following developments in the country from their own point of interest. We decided to pool our strengths and explore the enigma together.

It has proved to be a challenge. The fact that Russia is still in the middle of a radical transformation makes any attempt to decipher Russian business leadership styles an unnerving task. Every time we, the authors of this book, visit the country, we are tremendously impressed by the astonishing changes taking place there. Deciphering the enigma that is Russia becomes even more complex because the country is also extremely diverse – having long been a melting pot of different races, religions, languages, regions and cultures. The new Russian business leaders of the first perestroika wave came from different strata of the society – Communist Party and Komsomol, academia, industry, or the black economy. However, they often exhibited similar leadership styles rooted in traditional Russian culture, as reflected in power hoarding, the manipulation of employees, and the existence of multiple standards of behavior. In the ten-year period that began in 1993, on the other hand, we saw the emergence of another group of business leaders whose success draws on their own efforts and drive rather than simply political connections. In addition it is only recently that women have started to gain a visible presence as senior executives. It is becoming obvious that there is a new post-perestroika generation of business leaders in Russia. Given these various developments, this book looks at both traditional and more unconventional business leaders.

Over the past five years we studied these organizations in a society in transition, and collected our findings in seven case studies, focusing on Russian leaders in different industries. Some of the companies we visited still had visible and invisible traces of a Soviet-era infrastructure and mind-set. Others had a completely new organizational structure, inspired in some ways by Western business practices, and yet still uniquely Russian. The cases are presented with commentaries in this book in roughly chronological order, allowing the reader to follow the progression of the business paradigm within Russia over a ten year period.

As we studied Russian organizations, we realized we were seeing two kinds of leaders at the top of successful companies. In the first group were 'Russian' Russians, who retained a faintly xenophobic attitude toward Western organizations. These Russians were convinced that they should move into relationships with Western partners only with great caution. They sought to build 100 per cent Russian organizations. In the other group were the 'Global' Russians, leaders who have gained respect both within the Russian business community and internationally, as they build intangible bridges over which knowledge and products can travel both to and from the West. Many of them trade actively with foreign partners, acting as both vendors and buyers of goods and services. Some of the organizations led by new-generation executives are actively pursuing foreign investment, attracting shareholders globally. Some of them are even quite idealistic (perhaps too idealistic), believing that Western management practices are the answer to all ills – and they are very disappointed when this idea proves to be wrong.

We have also noticed significant changes in the Russian workforce. As Russian business practices mature, so has the Russian labor force. There are more and more individuals with Western business education and experience. Western business ideas and concepts are included in educational curricula at universities in Russia. As the challenges of organizations become more complex, the growing corps of talented young managers may become a blessing and a curse for top executives. New ways of managing talent become necessary, and the leaders of organizations that we have studied have different, sometimes totally opposite approaches to managing their human resources. Some treat them as almost disposable commodities, while others see their people as their most important capital and treat them accordingly by investing heavily in their training and development, both in financial and emotional terms. The concept of 'human resource management' is itself new, and it was quite interesting to hear about some of the mistakes made and lessons learned by the executives we talked to. Our cases cover a wide scope of leadership styles in Russian organizations, most of them with recognizable paternalistic (or maternalistic) roots.

Why did we write this book? As we move more into a global economy, the need to become familiar with executive behavior in Russia is increasingly apparent. In order to work effectively with Russian organizations, it is essential for potential Western partners and shareholders to understand fully the leadership style, organizational practices, and expectations typical of both 'Russian' and 'Global' Russian business leaders. Furthermore, the identification of salient management values and attitudes becomes very timely in predicting and obtaining shareholder value when dealing with Russian organizations. A comprehension of cross-cultural differences and the corollary institutional configurations will contribute to a greater success in doing business in Russia and/or with Russians, and by extension to many of the former Soviet-bloc countries in Eastern Europe.

KNOWLEDGE BASE

This book is the result of ten years of data collection and interviews in Russia, and personal experience of conducting business in the country. Two of the co-authors are Russian; one of them spent six years leading Russian organizations, while the other has been observing and training managers in Russia for nine years. Of the non-Russian authors, one is an American who has spent most of her adult life in France. The other non-Russian spent his formative years in Holland, but since then has lived the greater part of his life in other cultures. Furthermore, apart from the diversity in the authors' cultural backgrounds, there is also diversity in organizational *Weltanschauung* that will be reflected in the commentary to the cases. One of the authors has a strategic orientation to organizational analysis, another is more cognitive organizational oriented, while the fourth author's orientation is more of a cross-cultural nature. And not to forget, one of the authors has more of a clinical outlook to organizational analysis. Our view is that these different orientations contribute to the richness of the book.

The book includes a survey of the literature dealing with Russian national character and Russian history. Existing data gathered during frequent visits to Russia of the Western contributors are another source of information. The conceptual material also draws on Manfred Kets de Vries' two theoretical articles: 'The anarchist within' written for *Human Relations* and 'Journey into the wild East' written for *Organizational Dynamics*. These two articles explore the ways in which the Russian national character – including leadership style and organizational practices – is embedded in its culture: the ideals, values and assumptions about life that are widely shared among its people, and that guide specific behavior patterns. Comprehending the building blocks of culture in Russia and their similarities with Western culture and management philosophy will help to better understand the way business leaders develop in Russian organizations. This interplay of the idiosyncrasy of the Russian culture and modern Western management approaches makes up the theoretical framework within which we analyse the organizations in the book.

Our second source of data is our open-ended interviews and observations of Russian executives occupying influential positions in their respective organizations. Russian academics participated in the writing of all the case studies. These case studies, studying different parts of Russian enterprise, form the heart of this book. In writing these case studies we have had unprecedented access to the personal background and professional development of several very successful Russian leaders. We have interviewed powerful top executives, entrepreneurs and oligarchs, whose names are familiar to many Russians and Westerners. We have included leaders from a wide range of industries: banking, oil, high-tech software, and consumer goods. We also have been collecting shorter vignettes that illustrate additional leadership styles; these we have woven into the book. Thus the book covers the whole spectrum of Russian businesses from small entrepreneurial start-ups to huge companies that influence not only the economy but also the politics of the country.

INTENDED AUDIENCE

If Russians hope to be able to operate successfully in a global economy, as their recent societal transformations suggest that they do, they must identify and adopt the most appropriate forms of management and organization. Given the explosion of East–West strategic alliances, joint ventures, acquisitions and start-ups in what was the former Soviet Union, to make these ventures work (and many have been unsuccessful) – to create effective collaborative efforts – a deep understanding is needed of differences in leadership between Russians and people from other cultures. Russia has the potential to become one of the great economies of the world. The world cannot afford to stay away.

This book will be of interest to Russians, and people working in Russia, as well as in former Soviet-bloc member countries in Eastern Europe. This interest group will be made up of academics as well as practitioners. Because the case studies are first-hand, the book allows the reader to experience a Russian organization from the inside. Such exposure will be helpful in better understanding what it means to work with Russians. Consultants, HR professionals, venture capitalists, and other businesspeople who work with Russians, or are planning to invest in Russian businesses, will appreciate both the book's in-depth analysis of culture and character, as well as the practical advice and points of view offered by the executives we profile. In addition, the book can also be used in MBA classes and executive seminars in human resource management and leadership.

A ROAD MAP

The book is divided into three parts: 'Conceptual reflections', 'Case studies and commentaries', and 'Conclusions'. The first chapter highlights a number of salient aspects of the culture and character of Russia to facilitate an informed understanding of the way Russians deal with organizations and approach leadership style. This chapter starts with a number of contextual factors concerning Russia. The inference is made that these contextual factors contribute to a number of character traits. Subsequently, the implications of Russian child-rearing and educational practices are discussed. Attention is given to the development of a 'false self' – a public self that is split from the true private self – a phenomenon that was especially prevalent during the Soviet era. Other themes explored include the role of women in Russian society, emotional expressiveness, the particularistic outlook toward other people, and *Oblomovism* – the tendency toward apathy and inertia. The oscillation in Russia between order and disorder is also explored. The history of destructive bureaucracy in Russia is presented as a social defense. The Czarist legacy, with its contribution to a paranoid *Weltanschauung* and an anarchistic streak within the culture, is reviewed. The Russians' wish for strong leadership (and the existence of paternalistic practices) is analysed. Finally, Russian attitudes toward reality testing and time are looked at.

Chapter 2 is an East–West dialogue between the Western and Russian authors of the book. This opening dialogue is an accessible introduction to leadership in general, and to organizational leadership in Russia specifically. The dialogue covers a broad panorama of issues relevant to Russia. This dialogue sets the tone for the book: it is practical and draws on comments and insights offered by Russian executives themselves, while at the same time being grounded in theory and constructs that help the reader understand not only *what* Russian executives do, but also *why* they do it.

The second part of the book includes seven case studies. In Chapter 3, 'The Bolshevik evolution', a bi-cultural Russian executive returns to Russia after a 20-year exile in France to head Groupe Danone's transformation of a Soviet icon – the Bolshevik Biscuit Factory. Drawing on his experience of French and Russian culture, the new general manager brings Bolshevik into Danone's fold, and into the 21st century. This case study illustrates that privatized Soviet-era companies can be successfully integrated within a multinational organization – if certain precautions are taken. It shows that an *Anglo-Saxon-style* revolutionary change process is not always the best way to proceed in Eastern European organizations; that the commonly accepted goals of rapid change, employee empowerment and a flatter hierarchy are not necessarily appropriate in these organizations in the short-term; and that even the definitions of trust, strategy and leadership can differ according to cultural context. The challenge in this case lies in understanding the complexities – the lingering influence of the Soviet planned central economy, as well as the Russian culture and management systems.

Chapter 4, 'Russian Standard', is a case study about one of the first Russian entrepreneurs able to create a successful brand-management organization in the early 1990s, when entrepreneurship first became legal. It is the story of entrepreneurship in its purely Russian form, with lingering traces of the Soviet paternalism and a central command and control structure. The case describes Roustam Tariko's attempts to create a more Western organizational structure and create new businesses. It addresses issues that typically arise in new ventures and 'bricks to clicks' transformation, including: evolution from the messy start-up stage to a more professional organization; intrapreneurship and internal incubators; strategies for continued growth and diversification; and brand management and marketing – with a distinctly Russian flavor.

Chapter 5, 'Mikhail Khodorkovsky: man with a ruble', concerns the CEO of Yukos, Russia's largest oil company. This case describes the trials and tribulations of this business tycoon before he ran afoul of the state authorities. This oligarch, by 2003 the richest man in Russia and one of the richest people in the world, started his business career during Gorbachev's perestroika as a junior Komsomol (young Communists' organization) official. As head of Yukos Oil Company, Russia's largest oil and gas group, he oversaw the transformation of an unstructured asset portfolio – an amalgamation of traditional Russian organizations – into a world player in the oil markets. From the discussion he emerges as a mixture of the old-style leader, who believes that power should be concentrated at the top and tight control mechanisms should play a key role in managing his organization and, at the same time, a reborn, progressive businessman bringing transparency and Western expertise to Yukos – a company whose oil reserves now rival the largest Western organizations', making it a truly global player.

Chapter 6, 'Ice and flame: building a NYSE company in wild Russia' tells the story of a partnership between two polar opposites, a brash young American entrepreneur and a rumpled Russian academic. Together they built VimpelCom, a Russian cellular operator that grew in less than 10 years from a hypothetical concept, to a small family-like company, to a $35 billion NYSE-quoted corporation with 10 million subscribers on its nation-wide wireless networks. Each of the two founders made a unique contribution. Charismatic Dr Dmitry Zimin, the Russian scientist, transmitted the partners' vision to the organization, exciting employees with new challenges, and at the same time providing a comfort zone for them to absorb the rapid pace of growth and change in the organization. No less significantly, his knowledge of Russia's political system, contacts within the military, superior technical knowledge, and perseverance allowed him to build extremely valuable social networks outside of the company. American serial entrepreneur Augie K. Fabela II initially brought a knowledge base, which none of its competitors could match, and assumed the role of VimpelCom's link to the rest of the world, which later expanded to the growing Russian financial sector. Fabela was the driving force behind the audacious move to take the company public – the first Russian company to be quoted on the New York Stock Exchange.

Chapter 7, 'Frontstep Russia: a high-tech start-up and survival in a new "time of troubles"', describes a typical start-up, with three technically brilliant but rather naïve software specialists and computer programmers who wanted to test their entrepreneurial capabilities. After working for several months with Soviet factories, educational institutions and research organizations, the future entrepreneurs obtained Western-style management exposure working for one of the first Western–Russian joint ventures. Although this experience was an excellent learning opportunity, the entrepreneurs were left with a bitter after-taste of the authoritarian and despotic leadership style of their first Western boss. Ten years later, the company is in a successful partnership with an American organization. The case focuses on the charismatic general director, Maria Ilyina, who has some learning of her own to do as she changes her leadership style from that of 'Aunt Masha' of the early days, to become a leader who also fulfills an architectural role within her organization. This case study proves that 'garage-type' entrepreneurship is thriving in Russia.

The case study in Chapter 8, 'Troika Dialog', centers on the activities of Ruben Vardanian, President and a co-founder of Troika Dialog, Russia's oldest investment bank. This business leader is somtimes referred to as the 'Golden Boy of Russian Capitalism'. He joined Troika in 1991 as one of the company's original associates. Under Vardanian's leadership, Troika Dialog was transformed from an office with four unpaid employees into an organization with an enviable clientele and a worldwide reputation for fair practice. In 2001 he initiated an historic deal to acquire control of Rosgostrakh, one of the post-Soviet 'sleeping bears': a former insurance monopoly in the Russian Federation. After becoming president of Rosgostrakh, he was faced with the enormous challenge of transforming it into a modern financial services company.

The last case study in Chapter 9, 'World class heroes for Russia', focuses on Olga Sloutsker, the founder of WorldClass, a chain of fitness centers in Moscow. She has been described as 'one of the most colorful business women in Russia today'. The fitness industry in Russia started when Sloutsker and a partner opened a Moscow franchise of a Western fitness club. Sloutsker soon left her partners to open her own, 100 per cent Russian chain. The founding entrepreneur has created a totally Russian organization with no outside partners that has incorporated the best Western business practices. Her vision is unique: to encourage all Russians to be fit, and to make 'heroes' of them all.

In the third part of the book, in Chapter 10, we conclude by exploring a new leadership agenda for Russia. In this chapter we discuss the lessons learned.

It is suggested that management development takes on the role of catalyst to enhance a change of mind-set concerning leadership practices in Russia. A number of propositions are put forth to create more effective work behavior. To create high performance organizations, it is essential that the entrepreneurial spirit is cultivated. Finally, the prevalence of democratic centralism as a style of directing organizations is explored in the context of the desire for strong leadership. The argument is made that for Russian organizations to become more effective, this way of decision-making – a style that became perverted in Soviet times – needs to be reframed into truly empowering leadership. A number of propositions are put forth to create more effective work behavior and high performance organizations. Observations are made on how to cultivate the entrepreneurial spirit.

We hope that by reading this book non-Russians will acquire a greater understanding of Russian national character and leadership practices, and will be more effective in Russia. We also anticipate that Russians, by reflecting on how outsiders look at their behavior and business practices, may find better ways of making their organizations successful. To Russians, this book may help reconcile two worlds: the world of a new generation expectant of the future and the Soviet world of the bureaucrat with their old values and ideas. We realize that change is difficult. But we also recall the words of the French author François de la Rochefoucauld, 'The only thing constant in life is change'. The transformation of a country is embedded in the psychology of the people.

Acknowledgments

One of the best-known characters in Russian folklore and fairy tales is the deadly Baba Yaga. She is the archetype of the fearsome witch or sorceress, hideous to look at, with a mercurial nature, who cannibalistically devours those who naïvely stumble upon her domain. (Baba Yaga tales inspired the story of Hansel and Gretel.) She is also known as 'Baba Yaga Kostianaya Noga' (Baba Yaga Boney Leg), because in spite of her ferocious appetite, she remains as thin as a skeleton. She flies or rides in a mortar, using a pestle as a sort of paddle. (The womb-like vessel and the phallic pestle seem to represent her dualistic feminine and masculine nature.) Never one for leaving a trail behind her, she sweeps away all traces of her path with a broom.

Throughout the Slavic region, the term *baba* connotes an old woman, and the Russian word *yaga* means 'hag'. In addition to this name, this well-respected mythical elder is also referred to as the Guardian of the Underworld, the Mistress of the Forest, the Goddess of Death and Regeneration, the Wolf-Goddess, the Bone Mother, the Mistress of the Animals, and the Guardian Spirit of the Water of Life and Death. Baba Yaga rules over the elements, and her realms are the impenetrable forests of old Russia. She is the guardian of the frontier between the territory of mortals and the spirit world.

In the folk tales, Baba Yaga lives in a hut in the forest, a hut that seems to have a personality of its own. It can move about at will on its large chicken legs, and can even run after visitors who stumble into its domain. A fence made from the leftover bleached-white bones of Baba Yaga's victims, whose blazing eye sockets illuminate the darkness, surrounds the hut. This fence is a clear signal to anyone who would dare to pass through its gate that he or she must be prepared for an initiatory underworld experience, a trial that could end in sudden death or life-altering enlightenment, depending upon the wits and attitude of the initiate.

Baba Yaga is a very misunderstood figure. She is not merely a stereotypical wicked witch; she is much more labyrinthine than that. She represents a highly complex duality. Although she is mostly portrayed as a terrifying old crone and monster, she can also play the role of a helper and wise woman. She is not good, but she is not entirely evil; she does eat people and decorates her fence with their skulls, but like all forces of nature, though often wild and untamed, she can also be kind. She is an ugly old woman, but at times she turns into a young beauty. She sometimes gives advice and magical gifts to heroes and the pure of heart. Her home is at the same time a cemetery and also a place of divine magic.

Baba Yaga, this all-powerful Great Mother, is the giver of the gift of adulthood but also the giver of death. She is the Bone Mother who destroys but she is also the one who collects our white bones and pours the Water of Life and Death upon them, while singing her magic songs, helping us to be reborn. She is a magic symbol, the allegoric representation of a guide who helps people in their transition into adulthood, making young people responsible members of society. Her oven represents creation – the womb – a symbol of life and birth.

The heroes or heroines of the Baba Yaga tales often enter her domain searching for wisdom, knowledge and truth. Her hut is the place where these transmutations occur; it is the dark heart of the Underworld, the dwelling place of the dead ancestors who are symbolized by the grinning skulls around her hut. All who come to her hut ask to be fed or are eaten. She destroys and then she resurrects. In Baba Yaga stories, people symbolically experience a death, darkness, depression, or spiritual emptiness. They journey to Baba Yaga's hut, a place where they might, with skill and luck, be reborn.

The stories of Baba Yaga in a condensed form parallel the riddle that is Russia. Those who enter her domain – searching for wisdom, thirsting for knowledge, hungry for truth – do it at their own risk. But the journey will be worth it. Restoration, renewal, nourishment and enlightenment can only be found by taking this journey into Baba Yaga's underworld. In this book we make an effort to look for the truth and knowledge that such a journey can bring us.

Just as the people in the Baba Yaga tales look to the old woman for enlightenment, we, the authors of this book, have depended on the contribution and advice of others. Books are not written by authors in isolation. In developing the ideas for this book we talked to dozens of people in business, government and education. Their insights and recollections were invaluable. We learned something from their successes and their failures, and we tried to use that knowledge in our writing.

We gratefully acknowledge the contributions of all these people. Above all, however, we are extremely indebted to the leaders described in our case studies. We would like to thank Jacques Ioffé, Roustam Tariko, Mikhael Khodorkovsky, Dmitry Zimin, Augie Fabela II, Maria Ilynia, Ruben Vardanian, and Olga Sloutsker for their willingness to talk and to trust a group of strangers. Without their contributions, this book would not have been possible.

We would also like to thank the institutional supporters of this project, the members of INSEAD's Department of Research, in particular Landis Gabel, Anil Gaba and Alison James for their encouragement and support. We also gratefully acknowledge the work of two case writers, Pavel Pavlovsky and Irina Budrina, for their help in putting two of the case studies together. Robert

Treacy Ph.D., retired professor of American history, provided the historical analysis of the 19th century American robber barons. We would be remiss if we did not express our gratitude to Kathy Reigstad for her unfaltering enthusiasm and professionalism in editing the manuscript.

On a personal note Manfred Kets de Vries would like to thank Yuri Mattison and his team of guides, who live in the awesome mountains of the Pamir. Spending time with this group of very tough (but also very kind) men has been for him a catalyst to acquire a greater understanding of the Russian character, and also what makes for effective leader–follower relationships under extreme conditions.

Stanislav Shekshnia would like to thank his parents and God for bringing him into the world at the right time and the right place to be able to contribute an insider's view to this book; his Russian business partners and colleagues, especially one of the heroes in this book, Dr Zimin, for first-hand lessons in Russian leadership; and Professors Sheila Puffer and Daniel McCarthy for initial lessons in applying Western management theory to the study of Russian business leaders.

Konstantin Korotov would like to thank INSEAD and NYU academics who have equipped him with the research methodology and solid theoretical background indispensable to carrying out research in organizations. A special word of thanks is made to his parents who have always encouraged his stepping into uncharted waters and his family, which has been supportive and tolerant throughout his academic training and the process of working on this book.

Elizabeth Florent-Treacy has many thanks for Professor Manfred Kets de Vries, first author of this book, for having opened countless doors and learning opportunities to her. To borrow from Chaucer: 'Gladly wold he lerne, and gladly teche…He is a good felawe'. She also warmly thanks her father, Robert Treacy, who, when asked what time it is, always thoroughly explains how to build a clock, and her mother Carol, who took her to the library once a week without fail throughout her childhood.

Even though we gladly acknowledge the contributions of many others to this book, we, as authors, are fully responsible for its content and accept any and all of its faults. Our expectation is that by writing a book of this nature, we will make a small contribution in making Russia a better place. By presenting these various leaders – warts and all – as role models to the younger generation, we hope to contribute to the understanding of the way business people attain a heroic status – and the responsibilities that come with this status. By having made our own symbolic journey to Baba Yaga's hut, we hope that all of us will be more prepared to deal with what once was the Russian Wild East.

Fontainebleau, France
Spring, 2004

PART ONE

Conceptual reflections

1. The anarchist within

I don't know if it is the character of the Russian people that has created such dictators, or if the dictators themselves have given this character to the nation.

Baron Sigismund Von Harberstein,
ambassador of Emperor Frederick III to Russia

When Stalin says dance, a wise man dances.

Nikita Khrushchev, First Secretary of the Central Committee
of the Communist Party, Soviet Union (1953–1964)

We cannot understand the way Russians deal with organizations, or approach a discussion of their leadership style, without first looking at a number of salient aspects of Russian culture and character. In addition, if we want to make suggestions for change in leadership style and organizational practices, we need to explore Russian character and how it is shaped by contextual forces, and developmental and historical realities. Because Russian organizational practices are strongly influenced by Russian culture, we must take a preliminary detour into salient aspects of the Russian context.

As we move into an increasingly global economy, the need to become familiar with executive behavior in different cultures will grow ever more crucial, for two reasons:

- Managing people across cultures and in multicultural teams will be a primary challenge in the twenty-first century. Given the importance of global business, cross-cultural understanding is becoming a prerequisite to ensuring the effectiveness of multicultural teams. Future global leaders must adapt to the particularities of many regions and national cultures while at the same time meeting the expectations of followers in those different cultures.
- The identification of salient leadership values, attitudes and behavior around the world will facilitate the design and implementation of programs of organizational transformation and change. A comprehension of cross-cultural differences and the corollary institutional configurations will contribute to greater success in these ventures, making for competitive advantage.

Although these arguments in favor of cross-cultural understanding apply to all organizations everywhere, they have particular relevance to Russia and to organizations with connections to Russia. As Russia's potentially extensive participation in the global economy grows, making sense out of Russian leadership and organizational practices will be important to global management wherever it is based. Moreover, an inside–outside perspective concerning Russian behavior patterns will help the Russians themselves better understand the Russian way of doing things, illuminating the motives and rationale behind their behavior. Self-understanding will help Russians choose specific leadership styles that suit their national character while at the same time recognizing the converging success factors to be effective on a global scale.[1]

They have to recognize the delicate balance between the need to combine 'universal' and 'traditional' Russian values. Last but not least, many Russians are actively pursuing educational opportunities throughout the world and developing their careers in large and small companies on five continents. Some successful Russian businesses are expanding beyond the geographical boundaries of Russia, and Russians outside Russia are establishing new companies. Understanding the differences and commonalities between the Russian and other Western or Eastern leadership and management styles will be helpful to both Russians and non-Russians in their responsibilities as employers, employees, or business partners and advisors.

THE CLINICAL PARADIGM

The clinical paradigm, which underlies much of the thinking in this book, is based on a number of premises. The first premise argues that a rationale lies behind every form of irrationality. Though resistances may obscure interpretation, all types of behavior – ingrained behavior patterns, transference reactions (meaning a confusion in time and place in that we react towards people in the present *as if* they are important people from the past), and defensive mechanisms – no matter how strange, have an explanation. The second premise on which the clinical paradigm is based is the belief that much of people's motivation is unconscious; in other words, that many behavioral triggers that have an effect on human functioning lie outside of conscious awareness. The third premise of the clinical paradigm maintains that our behavior is very much a product of previously learned behavior patterns. Through experiences with significant people in childhood each of us develops preferred response patterns, and we tend to repeat these as adults. In a nutshell, then, the clinical paradigm refuses to take for granted what is directly observable.[2]

The clinical paradigm employs (primarily) constructs taken from psychoanalytic psychology in its various forms (particularly object relations theory), combined (when appropriate) with formulations from dynamic psychiatry, cognitive theory, family systems theory and developmental psychology. The aim behind relying on these various conceptualizations is to seek an understanding of the underlying motivations and behavior patterns that give rise to different values, beliefs and attitudes, all of which combine in the creation of specific organizational constructs.

BECOMING INFORMED ABOUT NATIONAL CHARACTER

The data on which this chapter is based is twofold. The first source of data was a review of the literature dealing with Russian national character and Russian history.[3] This material was complemented by open-ended, exploratory, in-depth interviews with (and observations of) Russian executives occupying influential positions in their respective organizations. Access to such executives occurred in two ways. Some of the executives participated in a number of leadership development workshops taught by Manfred Kets de Vries. These workshops gave an opportunity to engage in dialogue about Russian character and leadership practices. Additional material was obtained through visits to a number of companies operating in the financial services, trading and manufacturing sectors. Here the authors were present both in a consulting and a research role. Data gathering took place from 1993 to 2004.

These exploratory interviews were conducted in a semi-structured fashion. Each respondent was approached with a list of open-ended questions pertaining to Russian character, leadership style and organizational practices. Depending on the responses, revisions were made to the questions. Observational data consisted of notes taken by the authors while studying the various executives in meetings and during informal discussions. In engaging in this kind of fieldwork, the authors used 'grounded theory' to arrive at a set of hypotheses about Russian character and leadership practices; in other words, while engaged in the process of hypothesis formulation, we delineated connections, patterns and themes, continuously modifying the hypothesis depending on emerging material.[4] We also explored biases due to participant observation.[5] Through this ethnographic and clinical orientation, ideas were developed and 'thick' description emerged – description that involves, using Clifford Geertz's words, 'guessing at meanings, assessing the guesses, and drawing explanatory conclusions from the better guesses'.[6] We then integrated observed patterns of behavior with knowledge about the growth and development of human beings and the findings of developmental and clinical psychologists on the functioning of human personalities.

Using the clinical paradigm in doing ethnographic work implies the study of 'texts', which can be viewed as groupings of interrelated elements – all types of data containing various kinds of information that can be systematized into themes. In an organizational context, each 'text' presented is interpreted through the analysis of organizational artifacts: managerial statements, writings and observable behavior.[7] The 'text' implicit in a specific decision, a preference for a particular style of leadership, or a type of organizational design gives clues to what life in the organization is all about. In dealing with this 'text', any researcher relying on the clinical paradigm must be alert to underlying themes, meanings behind metaphors used, reasons underlying the selection of certain words, and the implication of certain activities. In decoding such 'texts', researchers extract significance from interrelated behavioral, cognitive and affective manifestations constructed out of experiences.

THE WHEEL OF CULTURE

The Russian national *character* (a concept here widely construed to include leadership style and choice of organizational practices) is embedded in its *culture*. *Character* implies 'deeply embedded, consistent, and relatively durable behavior patterns', that is, habitual ways in which a person deals with external and internal reality,[8] while *culture* embodies the ideals, values and assumptions about life that are widely shared among a population and that guide specific behavior patterns. Although the definition of *character* seems to be relatively straightforward, there is considerable disagreement about the precise definition of *culture*. Susan Schneider and Jean-Louis Barsoux argue that 'culture eludes precise definition or measurement'.[9] Scholars are fairly unanimous regarding its importance, however.

Margaret Mead, in her approach to the study of culture, refers to 'regularities in behavior that are shared'.[10] Clifford Geertz defines culture as 'webs of significance' in which people are suspended.[11] Geert Hofstede describes culture as 'the collective programming of the mind that distinguishes the members of one group or category of people from another'.[12] The ideals, values and assumptions represented by culture contribute to common norms, customs, rituals, ceremonies and perceptions about 'heroes' and 'villains'.[13] These cultural values are learned, and are transmitted from generation to generation through parents, teachers and other influential people in the community. Thus specific child-rearing practices play an important role in the formation of cognitive, affective and behavioral patterns.

These anthropological observations concur in affirming that cultural values color the modus operandi of a national culture, and life in Russia is no exception. Whether in Western Europe, the US, Africa, Australia or Russia, cultural values can be seen as the building blocks for behavior and action. As such, they have an influence on leadership practices and institutional arrangements. Comprehending the building blocks of culture in Russia will assist us to better understand the way Russians approach leadership style and run their organizations. Such an understanding may also help organizational leaders both within Russia and without to choose viable strategies for effectiveness on a global scale.

Existing conceptual frameworks for studying culture help in simplifying an extremely complex topic. Fortunately, there are quite a few of these frameworks to choose from. Among the better-known models are those of Talcott Parsons,[14] Clyde Kluckhohn and Fred Strodtbeck,[15] Edward Hall,[16] Geert Hofstede,[17] Edgar Schein,[18] André Laurent,[19] Fons Trompenaars,[20] Javidan and House,[21] and Fons Trompenaars and Charles Hampden-Turner.[22] All these models offer ways of simplifying culture's complexity. Many of them introduce a number of dimensions to highlight specific cultural patterns. These dimensions, frequently presented in the form of polarities, can be summarized in a simplified form as follows and (combined with the clinical formulations derived from the interviews) will be the red thread that runs through this chapter:

- **Environment.** One regularly applied dimension of polarity highlights the different ways individuals perceive both the world around them and their fellow human beings. Some of us enjoy a feeling of mastery over nature, while others feel controlled by our surroundings; some tolerate uncertainty well, while others avoid it; some view people as basically good, while others see them as basically evil.
- **Action Orientation.** Some people favor a *being* orientation, while others favor a *doing* orientation; some have an internal focus, possessing a sense of control over their lives, while others focus externally, feeling an absence of control.
- **Emotion.** Some people are emotionally expressive, while others exhibit great emotional control and inhibition.
- **Language.** In speaking and writing, some people use language that is high-context (that is, that uses circumvention and is difficult to interpret), while others generally use language that is low-context (that is relatively easy to understand).
- **Space.** Some people prefer to be in space that is private, while others prefer a public environment. This dimension also refers to the way individuals respect (or do not respect) another person's privacy.
- **Relationships.** In the course of personal and business relationships, some people tout individualism (and competition), while others rely on collectivism (and cooperation); some believe in the application of universalistic rules that apply to everyone, while others argue for particularistic rules that depend on the specifics of the case.
- **Power.** Some believe that status is achieved, while others value only ascribed status; some favor equality and advocate position based on

ability, while others stress the role of wealth, birthright, and other such factors.

- **Thinking.** Some people have a deductive approach to issues, while others take a more inductive approach; some analyse phenomena into parts, while others have a more holistic orientation, seeing patterns and relationships in a wider context.
- **Time.** Some people have a monochronic orientation (that is, they prefer doing one thing at a time), while others are polychronic (that is, they prefer doing many things at once); some are oriented toward the past, while others focus on the present or future.

Because all these dimensions have something to offer, we will refer to them occasionally in looking at Russian culture and analysing the Russian personality (see Figure 1.1 for an overview of the various dimensions).

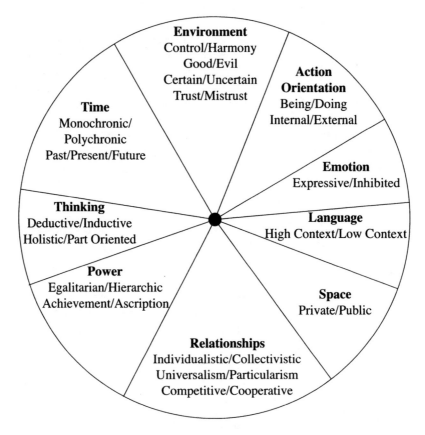

Figure 1.1   The wheel of national culture

A SNAPSHOT OF THE RUSSIAN CHARACTER

Romancing the Past

The film maker Mark Donskoy directed a popular trilogy on the life of the well-known Russian writer Maxim Gorky.[23] The first part of this film classic depicts the Bolshevik legend about his youth. In a very artistic way the director portrays some of the forces that make the Russians who they are. Moreover, the fairy-tale quality of the film facilitates audience identification with what Russians may view as essential characteristics of their native country and their own childhood. As a caveat, however, we can assume (given the era when the film was made) that the presented images represent a compromise between artistic insight and political correctness.

The film first introduces the empty plains and the Volga (to the accompaniment of balalaika music); the camera then shifts to a *mir,* one of myriad communal villages that were scattered in the vast land that is Russia, giving an intimate portrait of the behavior of the inhabitants. The film paints a stark contrast between the conduct of the men and that of the women. Women are portrayed as warm, caring, strong, generous and reliable (*babushka* types), but also as fatalistic and long-suffering. Men, on the other hand, are presented as having a self-destructive streak that is manifested through episodes of sudden violence and bouts of alcoholism.

The compelling *babushka* imagery is typically Russian. The mental picture of the generous, beneficent grandmother often serves as the mother-image of adulthood as well as childhood. Because of its staying power, this image has cognitive, affective and behavioral implications. It possesses a '*la vie en rose*' quality – that is, offering consolation in times of trouble. Taken further, it can become a longing for an earlier, simpler time – even a desire for some kind of symbiotic fusion. For someone ruled by this kind of mental imagery, adult reality is likely to be disappointing. The legacy of *babushka* imagery is often a lifelong yearning for 'Paradise lost', an undefined sense of pre-Oedipal, regressive nostalgia – a romantic sentimentality that is part of being Russian.[24]

It should be noted that during the period of Socialism, Russians 'institutionalized' *babushka* labor as a means of providing housekeepers and childcare. When grandparents retired, they often got involved in running their children's homes and overseeing the life of the grandchildren, continuing to exercise influence on their offsprings' families (very often there were several generations of Russians living under the same roof). Until perestroika, retired Russians often continued to support their children and grandchildren financially as well. *Babushkas* could be asked for loans, for favors, to take a child into their home while the child's parents pursued opportunities or sought a better life. In other terms, for a long period *babushkas* were a primary source of protection and help in troubled times.

Suffering and Violence

But this nostalgic yearning is not the only pattern explored in Donskoy's film. Viewers are subjected to sudden, unexpected eruptions of violence. Beating scenes fill the screen periodically, for example, and sadistic and masochistic behavior patterns intertwine. Accurately reflecting Russian life, the film identifies suffering, manifested in various forms, as another prevailing theme: suffering is needed to attain salvation for whatever 'crimes' – be they imagined or real – a person has committed. Sin, remorse and punishment have always been important themes in Russian history. The Russian Orthodox Church, with its imagery of torment, agony and martyrdom – its view of suffering as the way to seek and find God's grace and mercy – has played an important role in the formation of this aspect of the Russian psyche.

It can be argued that a sadomasochistic identification with authority – whether the authority figure is the Czar, a nobleman, a landowner, Lenin, Stalin, or a Communist Party commissar – has characterized the Russian people over the centuries.[25] We can add to this list more recent examples of authority figures with whom Russians often identify: governors of Russian regions, heads of companies and the country's president.

This attitude toward authority figures implies not only a readiness to be abused but also a willingness to assume the position of sadistic authority with others. This perspective on authority, described in clinical terminology as 'identification with the aggressor',[26] allows a person to rationalize an assault on the self by absolving the aggressor from responsibility; as a consequence, the person in ultimate authority is not blamed for unacceptable destructive deeds. Stalin was not fully aware of the atrocities enacted by his henchmen, this perspective would argue. If he had been, he would have done something about it; he would have protected his people. Another example of such behavior can be found in the 'Bloody Sunday' of 9 January, 1905, when a crowd of tens of thousands of people dressed in their best Sunday clothes marched towards the Czar's residence to 'inform' him of the misdeeds and crimes of his subordinates – they were sure he was unaware of this – and were gunned down at his order.

Through a process of mental gymnastics, the actions of the 'aggressor' are excused: 'He was unaware; he did it for the right reasons'. Slowly, the person being 'aggressed' begins to accept and then perpetuate the aggression, imitating the aggressor's abusive practices. Strange as this behavior may seem, there is a rationale behind it. Two purposes are accomplished by resorting to this defense mechanism: it creates an illusion of power (through the process of identification with the person in power and control), and it satisfies the victim's own repressed aggression; in other words, it turns into a form of aggression by proxy.

In the seminal book *Childhood and Society*, written by the psychoanalyst and human development scholar Erik Erikson, we find a chapter entitled 'The legend of Maxim Gorky's youth'.[27] In this chapter Erikson uses Donskoy's film about Gorky as a kind of projective test to explore what he saw as timeless, salient patterns in the Russian character – in particular, the sadomasochistic orientation. And he is in good company in emphasizing such behavior patterns. Indeed, they permeate Russian literature. The idea that suffering is a virtue is a recurring theme. Many of that tradition's most respected writers have painted shattering pictures of poverty and slavery, emphasizing distortions of the psyche caused by many centuries of serfdom, a practice that ended in 1861 but that has left an imprint on superior–subordinate relationships.

Donskoy's film also portrays paternal violence, a theme all too familiar in many cultures, including Russia. Problematic Oedipal relationships abound throughout that country's troubled history, with triangular relationships between parents and children offering the opportunity to act out high drama. People in positions of power and authority have set a dubious example in this regard. In what was then seen as a model of patriotism, Stalin refused to save his own son's life when Nazis took the latter as a prisoner of war during World War II, although Stalin was offered an opportunity to carry out an exchange operation. Czar Ivan the Terrible's impulsive murder of his oldest (favorite) son, and Czar Peter the Great's execution of his son Alexis, stand as key signifiers among many other dramatic episodes in Russian history, demonstrating unpredictable violence on the part of higher authority. Russian literature also offers ample examples of such violence. Fyodor Dostoyevsky's novel *The Brothers Karamazov,* for example, made famous the themes of patricide and suffering.

These examples from history and fiction portray the Russians as people possessed of a destructive passion, mercurial types who are prone to great mood swings, expressing extreme anger one moment and reverting to masochistic behavior the next. This great duality of passion and compassion is striking. The swinging of the emotional pendulum is exemplified in Czar Ivan the Terrible, who, after the murder of his son, was consumed by pangs of remorse and repentance. As a ruler who fell from one extreme mood state into another, he serves as an archetype of Russian leadership.

The Capacity to Endure

In spite of (or perhaps because of) the harsh circumstances under which the Russians have lived, predominately on vast, empty plains or on the Siberian taiga, Russians are a people of enormous endurance and stamina. Their history is illustrative. The creation of their nation, a process marked by hardship, was preceded by centuries of social unrest. People in what is now Russia had to deal with Viking raiders from the north, the Tatar–Mongol domination, the Polish invasion, and the Turks. Indeed, unrest has been Russia's constant companion. Not surprisingly, then, the 'Times of Troubles' (1598–1613) – a period of social and political upheaval during and after the reign of Boris Godunov, a period of great suffering caused by famine, epidemics and incursions by Polish adventurers – continue to resonate in the Russian collective memory. Nor have Napoleon's invasion or Hitler's military campaign been forgotten: we were shown the bullet holes in the city walls in St. Petersburg in a way that made it seem as if the siege of Leningrad had happened the previous week. But the Russians, with their indomitable stamina, have risen above the many evil forces around them – irrational authority, violent changes of regime, the civil wars, social disorder and foreign interventions.

This ability to endure, this capacity for survival, has prompted some observers to offer ice-fishing, an activity pursued by many Russians, as a metaphor for their character, for the hardiness and mysticism of the Russian soul. Sitting alone for hours in front of a hole on a frozen river or lake in Siberia under arctic conditions in the hope of catching a fish is an unattractive proposition to most people. It looks like an open invitation for frostbite or even death. While one might think that the activity's saving grace would be its opportunity for comradeship, in most cases it appears to be a solitary and rather isolating activity. But in spite of its predictable discomforts, a large number of Russians find pleasure in this pursuit. It is probably motivated by a need to escape overcrowded apartments and to forget the grimness of everyday life for a while. But whereas many of us would just sit on a park bench and feed the pigeons, Russians will go to great lengths, even traveling for hours by train, to sit on the ice in sub-zero weather. Their pleasure might be seen as an expression of their tolerance for suffering in the pursuit of a desire – in this case the desire for solitude. It may be the assertion of a kind of death wish, a risk-taking that makes them feel more alive, and having, in a sense, conquered nature, more powerful. This need for mystical unity with the forces of nature, and the courage it takes to confront them, are traits that exemplify the deep spiritual character of the Russians.

In 1993 one of the authors of this book, Manfred Kets de Vries, was a member of an expedition in the Pamir mountains in Tadjikistan (one of the former republics of the old USSR) on the border with China. He observed at first hand the incredible courage and endurance of the Russian people, and their putative love of suffering. He describes the experience:

> The purpose of the trip was to observe the rut of the mythical Marco Polo sheep – the largest wild sheep in the world. Unfortunately, we were not very lucky with the weather. Not only did we have to deal with extreme temperatures (more than 35 degrees below Celsius, even without factoring in the wind chill) and dramatic heights (more than 5500 meters), we also faced unusually deep and challenging snow

conditions. The lack of equipment for dealing with the deep snow, in combination with the oxygen-scarce air of extreme altitude, made climbing exceptionally difficult. To my inexperienced eye, it seemed as if it would be impossible to get close to the sheep. Other people would have given up – but not the Russians. They decided to press on, and to do so when the sheep could not see them so as to avoid scaring them away.

So I found myself, early one December morning (2 a.m. to be precise), trudging almost vertically through the snow and trying to minimize the extreme exertion by stepping in the footsteps of my guides – who, it should be noted, carried all the gear (tent, sleeping bag, cooking utensils, food, and so on) on their backs. I had been in many difficult situations, but this was the most grueling ever. Later the Russian participants named this night walk 'the battle of Pamirgrad', in reference to their most terrible battle of World War II.

During the night's walk we succeeded in getting closer to the sheep, but not for long. As soon as the sun rose above the horizon, 500 watchful sheep discovered us, and within minutes the herd disappeared over the next mountain top. But on we went, following them. That night, in spite of being covered by two sleeping bags, I had the coldest experience of my life. I still remember how the next morning, I had to heat my frozen shoes above a pitiful flame (starved of oxygen) to be able to put them on.

Character in Transition

Decades have passed since the making of Donskoy's film about Maxim Gorky's youth and the writing of Erikson's article. In the intervening years, dramatic changes have occurred in Russia. Russia has imploded into the Russian Federation; many of the countries that belonged to the old USSR have become independent; the glasnost and perestroika introduced by Mikhail Gorbachev, and the reforms attempted and implemented by Boris Yeltsin and Vladimir Putin, have resulted in a dramatic transformation of Russian society. The consequences of many of these changes have been mixed, however. Although certain segments of society have profited from the new situation, the chaotic transitional stage of the Russian economy has left many segments of the population feeling alienated and disenfranchised.

The fact that Russia is still in the middle of a radical transformation makes any attempt to decipher the Russian personality a challenging task. The great diversity of Russia, which has long been a melting pot of different races, religions, languages, regions and cultures, stretching in territory from Eastern Europe through Siberia to the Far East, makes the task even more difficult. In spite of the complexity of the culture issue, however, various themes touched on by the Donskoy movie can be seen as illustrative of Russian culture not only then but now. In other words, there is certain stability to the essential nature of Russian character; there are certain distinctive characteristics that have retained their significance regardless of place, time or regime. And these national characteristics – 'modalities of behavior and of view of the world and experience in it which are found or claimed to be characteristic of a specified national or ethnic population at a particular period in time'[28] – influence values, beliefs, attitudes and motivation, all of which are important factors in the context of leadership and organizational practices.

CONTEXTUAL FACTORS IN THE FORMATION OF THE RUSSIAN CHARACTER

The Impact of Nature

We are all affected by the physical world in which we live. Not surprisingly, then, seasonal changes and the weather affect human behavior. What's more, they do so in an enduring rather than a transient way: the states of mind evoked by the seasons and the weather become part of an area's cultural heritage.

The Russians have a widely held reputation for courage, endurance, hardiness and resilience. It could be argued that these virtues have their roots in the harsh climate of Russia – the cruel, long winters offset by short, hot summers – and the difficulties imposed by that climate. Born long years ago out of necessity, these virtues have been reinforced through stories of overcoming hardship that themselves have become part of the cultural heritage and will help shape future behavior. Chronicles that resonate in the cultural memory include the narrative (immortalized in literature) of the Russians wearing down and destroying the armies of first Napoleon and later Hitler during the winter.

Given the extremes of weather in Russia, a country that is half given over to permafrost, Russians experience a sense of constraint toward their environment; they are acutely aware of the degree to which they are subject to environmental whims. This outlook may help explain the patience, submission and caution that are typical of Russians. They do not experience the sense of control that characterizes people in many cultures not exposed to such extreme climate conditions. As they alternate bursts of activity with periods of weather-determined passivity, they oscillate between feeling that they are in control and feeling that they are being controlled. Adding to this swing of the pendulum is the fact that the willingness to endure, to submit to nature's consequences, represents a slightly masochistic dimension in the Russian character – the tolerance (or even desire) for suffering mentioned earlier.

The harsh climate has also given rise to the bear metaphor that is associated with Russia. That metaphor is symbolic of a low energy level in the winter and an elevated mood state in the summer, when food is abundant. Like bears, Russians can 'hibernate' for long periods of time, awaking to remarkable spurts of activity. In Russia, farmers can work only for limited periods of time, given the short planting and harvesting seasons, but they show their capacity for hard work and endurance during those short seasons. While the bear metaphor primarily illustrates the duality between *passivity* and *activity* among Russians, it also addresses the duality between *order* and *disorder* – a theme that will be developed later.

Parts of the Russian population still live and work in climatic conditions that can hardly be called livable. Oil, arguably the country's primary source of economic and social well-being, is extracted from fields located in northern parts of Russia. Nickel and other rare-earth metals are produced in the Arctic Circle region.

Furthermore, the short winter days and the long darkness make Russians prone to seasonal affective disorder (SAD), which is characterized by dramatic mood swings that alternate between depression and exhilaration, depending on the season. They aren't alone: seasonal changes in behavior are quite prevalent in Nordic countries.[29] The 'winter blues' may also explain the Russians' frequently bleak outlook on life – their pessimistic, gloom-and-doom perspective.

Whether the mood is down or up, Russians tend to be extremely *emotionally expressive*. They exhibit their feelings freely, embellishing them with a fine touch of drama.

The Legacy of the Mir

In spite of Russia's heavy industrialization, the country is still highly agricultural. In previous centuries, only the occasional agricultural village commune, or *mir*, broke the vastness of the land. The *mir* – a word that also means 'world' or 'peace', concepts that carry highly symbolic meanings – has had a great impact on the Russian *Weltanschauung*. While the *mir* was largely succeeded by the communal farm (one run by a Soviet, or 'community council') and in some regions supplanted by urbanization, the philosophy behind this self-contained community lives on.

Indeed, the *mir* mentality pervades all of Russia. It affects, for example, the Russians' outlook toward what we in the West tend to call 'personal space' – the extent to which one's immediate environment is private versus public. Because of the closeness of living conditions in the *mir* (and in overcrowded communal apartments), Russians tend to be rather intrusive; *they do not respect other people's private space* as much as people in other cultures do.

The *mir* mentality has also had an influence on the way Russians look at relationships. They favor, in all realms of human endeavor, the *collectivist orientation* that is at the heart of the *mir*, an orientation that subordinates individual interests to those of the group. In the agricultural village commune of yesterday, with people dependent on each other for survival, the communal good always took priority over individual needs and rights. Furthermore, each person had to make his or her contribution to the common good. And the *mir* did not hesitate to intervene as needed in the lives of its members to ensure both harmony and the common good. They did so through a board of village elders responsible for arriving at a group consensus, defining the common will, and making recommendations to the chief elder, who answered to the ultimate authority of the board. This way of operating continued under the Soviet system, with its Politburo at the top of the chain of command. An example which is sad and funny at the same time, is the way some families tried to resolve internal family dispute: a wife who caught her husband cheating on her (or suspected him of doing so) might address her husband's workplace-based Communist Party committee with a request to punish the unfaithful man for his misbehavior. The result of the Communist Party committee's intervention could be a delay in promotion, reduction of the bonus amount, and other punitive measures that, ironically, would eventually punish the whole family, including the disgruntled wife.

The *mir* mind-set in contemporary Russia shows itself in a certain 'we' consciousness that dominates the social system. The collective will is more important than the will of any individual. The legacy of the *mir* is also revealed in Russia's atmosphere of mutual dependence, in which the group provides emotional support and moral guidance for its individuals. Russians display a great need for affiliation. They like to belong, to be attached to a group, and they feel extremely uncomfortable when excluded. Many of their activities, social or otherwise, are conducted in a group setting. The *mir* legacy also makes for a clannish loyalty that expresses itself in chauvinism and passionate patriotism: the love for the motherland. A corollary to the *mir* mentality is an emphasis on the role of self-sacrifice out of a sense of duty. Russians are prepared, when the situation warrants it, to make extraordinary sacrifices for the sake of the community or the nation. Russia has seen incidents of mass heroism seldom paralleled in history.

The *mir* mentality has also contributed to the Russians' *preoccupation with egalitarianism* and their great need to equalize. Leveling has always been a popular pastime, and envy an important controlling device to remind people of their proper place. A well-known Russian proverb states that the tallest blade of grass is the first to be cut. And Russians savor the story about a peasant to whom God granted the fulfillment of any wish. There was, however, a catch. Whatever the peasant chose, God would do twice as much for his neighbor. The idea that his neighbor would be better off then he was, whatever he did, troubled him. After mulling over the offer, the peasant finally said, 'Take out one of my eyes'.

These examples illustrate the degree to which individualism and personal achievement as known in other societies are frowned upon in Russia. While in certain other cultures it is a sin to be a loser, in Russia – at least until the dissolution of the Communist regime – it was a sin to be a winner. The expression of individual desires was associated with selfishness. Anyone wanting to stand out was looked at with suspicion. As a consequence, many Russians are still very low-key about their individual accomplishments, boasting is frowned upon, and most people are careful not to be ostentatious in their habits. Succumbing to these perceived faults is a sure invitation to envy, spite and vindictiveness.

Under Communism, this well-intentioned *spirit of egalitarianism and collectivism* became perverted. Over time, ideological – even romantic – Communist fervor turned into stark disbelief for many, and disillusionment with and alienation from the system set in. These factors led to a rise in materialism and opportunism, an increase in corruption, and insidious moral decay. The privileges of the *nomenklatura* (the 'nomenclature' or 'secret roster' of people in positions of party leadership or in jobs within the party *apparat*), with their reserved shops and special hospitals, became all too common, and were in direct conflict with Russian cultural values.

The *mir* mind-set also implies the embracing of conservatism: a defense of traditional values and a fear of change. The *mir* has become a symbol of resistance to change – of not rocking the boat, of conforming.[30] In this era of increasingly free enterprise, this attitude is an important barrier to the transformation of Russian society.

The harsh climate and the *mir* legacy together created the context in which the character development of the Russians has taken place. The challenge now is to determine how we can weave these contextual factors into a consistent portrait of the emotional, cognitive and behavioral factors that distinguish the Russians. What is it about their character development that makes them different?

THE MAKING OF THE RUSSIAN CHARACTER

Swaddling in Infancy

Erikson, in his article on Gorky's childhood, hypothesizes that the ancient Russian childcare custom of swaddling is significant to the development of the Russian personality. Swaddling is a practice whereby newborn infants are bound from foot to neck in *pelenka* (a wrapping similar to that used in mummification) for the greater part of both day and night for three to five months (or, less typically, for as long as a year and a half).[31] This particular approach – making what they call a 'log' out of their babies – is still practiced today, particularly in rural areas, albeit to a much lesser extent. The usual argument given in favor of this custom is that it prevents the infant from hurting him- or herself. Some people also claim that it helps straighten out limbs long bent in the womb and lessens the danger of spinal curvature as the baby develops. A more practical justification may be that parents can accomplish household tasks with minimal distraction when a child is swaddled.

The swaddled infant experiences long periods of serious restraint alternating with short periods of freedom. He or she experiences the joy of locomotor liberation, along with the ability to discharge emotion physically (the only emotional outlet other than crying that newborns know), only in temporary bursts. The freedom of movement that babies in other societies enjoy is not permitted.

Oversimplified cause-and-effect inferences based on early childcare practices are always open to question, given the influence of other significant factors throughout the life cycle. But at the risk of oversimplification, we would argue that Erikson had a point in assigning some significance to swaddling. It may have a conditioning effect, influencing character formation and leaving a legacy, affecting younger generations, with respect to the management of emotion and action.

Schooling and 'Moral Upbringing'

Whereas the influence of swaddling may still be open to debate, there is no question that throughout their lives Russians are subjected to a kind of psychological swaddling beginning in early childhood. Because of their great rigidity, the school years prolong the *sense of externality* that Russian youngsters develop. Discipline and regimentation are the order of the day in the Russian classroom. Authoritarian methods prevail; a uniform and tightly controlled curriculum dominates; rote learning and unquestioning acceptance of authority are generally the rule.[32] Public shaming for misbehavior or poor performance is the method of choice for behavior modification at school (a method that also colors superior–subordinate relationships in the adult world). As a result, Russians tend to be very sensitive to public humiliation. Russian teachers engage in what we might call intrusive guidance: they are involved in every detail of a child's upbringing. They are not very respectful of the child's private space. From nursery school onward, teachers are extremely active in 'socializing' each child in the 'right' way of doing things. Few deviations from the rules are permitted.

In the Soviet past, 'moral upbringing', implying training in areas such as patriotism, atheism, collectivism, and other state-supported activities, was an important function of the schools.[33] The role of teachers was to bring children up in the spirit of Communist morality. In accordance with the centrality of collectivism, the well-being of the group superseded individual considerations; all conduct had to be aligned with the wishes and actions of the group.

In this educational atmosphere, children learned early (and repeatedly) the futility of arguing back with authority figures. And parents supported that model, toeing the line drawn by teachers. Under the Communist regime that line had clout: teachers often informed parents' supervisors of problems with specific children. In contrast to child-rearing practices in most Western societies, decision-making about the proper education for any given child was one-directional: the educators were the all-knowing givers, while the parents were the passive receivers. Suggestions about alternative ways of doing things were almost unheard of (and certainly unwelcome).

Such an educational approach cultivated the belief that, in public situations, one could *think* what one wanted but not *say* what one wanted (the kind of psychological swaddling pointed out earlier), fostering secret 'anarchistic' desires. While freethinking was not constrained by this approach, neither was it fostered. And where the asking of imaginative, probing questions is not encouraged, neither are creativity or innovation.

In this setting, children learned early the importance of conforming, of blending in. Conformity offered the least painful passage through their school years, and indeed through all of life. The cost of non-compliance was simply too high for most people. Bad enough in the classroom, that cost became increasingly unpleasant as life progressed, involving public denouncements at the local Party headquarters, workplace demotion, and the loss of privileges or even position.

The practice of institutionalized tattling, a popular pastime under the Communist regime, strengthened the urge to conform. A head boy or girl was responsible for reporting to the teacher on the conduct of the children under his or her supervision. In addition, each child was taught, at an early age, to look over his or her shoulder and observe others. As was noted earlier, children who deviated from the prescribed code of conduct were publicly criticized, shamed and humiliated.

How does this conditioning effect manifest itself? A major red thread running throughout Russia's history is the violent oscillation between order and chaos. Time and time again we have seen 'orderly' Russians create pandemonium when freed from control. They seem to share a hidden (and sometimes not so hidden) *desire for totally unrestrained behavior* – an anarchistic feeling that may have its origin in the literal and figurative swaddling period. At the same time, the forced restraint of swaddling and authoritarianism may leave as a legacy a feeling of impotence against immovable forces. This *sense of impotence* – this apathetic attitude toward environmental forces (described by social psychologists as *externality*) – is another prevalent theme throughout Russia's history.[34]

In visiting a number of Russian business organizations, we found this oscillation between order and chaos was quite noticeable (though more so in 'brown fields' – existing organizations – than in 'green fields' – new start-ups). Senior management, time after time, told stories of violent eruptions in the workforce. Strikes, destruction of equipment, and violent behavior vis-à-vis senior management were listed as some of the manifestations. Closer analysis showed that the eruptions often were the result of a systematic pattern of injustice within the organization that had finally come to a head. Those employees who resorted to verbal or physical violence often expressed the feeling of victimization, frequently noting specific wrongs that had been done to them. In some instances, alcohol abuse played a major role in initiating emotional explosiveness, rendering the brakes of propriety ineffective. To cope with such incidents, a number of senior executives we spoke to had instituted a policy of instant dismissal for consumption of alcohol on the job (this practice, in fact, is supported by the Russian labor legislation). Wiser executives, however, tried to go beyond mere symptom suppression and look at the underlying causes of the problems. Some of the following sections in this book will further highlight this anarchistic streak in Russian character.

INTERNAL CONFLICT

Enforced compliance with a code of conduct does not ensure internalization of the values underlying that code, nor does it create a positive identification with authority figures. And without a stable set of values and beliefs, only the continued imposition of external authority can prevent a reversion to disorderly behavior. Without those values, discipline problems germinate in the absence of authority or strong group pressures. This lack of truly internalized values – which manifests itself as a lack of self-discipline – may be a partial explanation for the oscillation in Russian society between repressive (even despotic) authority and anarchy. There is not much middle ground. Rulers in Russian society have always felt that they needed to put the lid on tightly to prevent unrest from boiling over.

While great discipline was stressed at school and in other public organizations (for example, in Communist youth organizations such as the Young Pioneers and later the Komsomol) in the Communist era, greater permissiveness ruled the home. Family life revolved around the children then (as it still does now). In this other world, children were pampered, spoiled and protected. To be sure, the cramped living conditions of communal apartments (with the expected intrusions into private space) sometimes sparked emotional and explosive disciplining. Yet children had a counterweight to such explosions: the conviction that their parents loved them. And because many parents had experienced serious hardships during their lives, they made a strong effort to create a better life for their children.

Integrating two such different worlds – one of harsh discipline, the other of warmth and carefree abandon – was a great challenge to Russian young people, as it would be to any individual. A certain amount of confusion is inevitable in such circumstances. The 'true self' evolves through the kind of care that supports the child's continuity of being – of spontaneity of self-expression. When a person's developmental processes are governed by compliance, however, especially when that person is subjected to unempathic authority figures, he or she is in danger of being seduced into a 'false life',[35] of presenting a 'false self' to the outside world. Such state of affairs contributes to a sense of futility, makes for pseudo-maturity, and will not foster the creative side of the person.

Although a certain split between the public self and the private self is inevitable, in Russia – at least until glasnost – the presentation of self was especially conflicted, contributing to the experience of a 'false self'. The warmth and permissiveness that children experienced at home simply did not agree with the conformity for conformity's sake that they experienced at school. Furthermore, the lack of sincerity and consistency in the public sphere during the Communist regime – idealism having increasingly deteriorated into cynical opportunism – would not have escaped their notice (since children always hear more than their parents tell them).

In the best of all worlds, children internalize an inner compass that is aligned to true north by the parents, establishing a direction that is later reinforced by other important authority figures giving similar signals. Such development makes for a sense of consistent direction and inner stability. The Russians have not had the luxury of consistent direction. How could parents, or teachers, for that matter, teach clear standards of right and wrong when they were unclear about those standards themselves?

The Communist system taught people not the distinction between right and wrong but the need for sensitive attunement to external, often contradictory signals of approval and disapproval. Rather than listening to their conscience in deciding the morality of an issue, people listened to the publicly expressed and officially approved patterns of behavior, or, in the worst case scenarios very common during Stalin's time, listened for the early-morning knock that would send them to a gulag for some fabricated transgression. In the long run, the inconsistency and insincerity of that form of authority eroded individual authenticity and created inner conflict and a feeling of unreality.

With the arrival of Gorbachev's glasnost, the Communist Party for the first time publicly acknowledged at its April 1986 Plenary Meeting the existence of what was then called 'double morality' in the society: on the one hand, people repeated the Party slogans at official workplace meetings, and constantly approved the Party's dictates. On the other hand, those same people sat in their kitchen at home and criticized the regime, expressing considerable disagreement with the status quo in society.

With glasnost, this incongruous situation began to change. The older generation still has to work through the after-effects of their 'moral upbringing', but they are adapting to greater freedom of thought and action. The younger generation has embraced the new freedom with less emotional baggage. They now reap the rewards of the glasnost-engendered concern among educators about respecting children's individuality. The words *freedom, liberation, independent problem solving* and *creativity enhancement* can now be heard in the context of child-rearing. There is, however, still considerable tension, especially in schools, between old and new approaches to dealing with children.[36] The question Russia faces, in the classroom and elsewhere, is how to balance the increased freedom with obedience and structure. How these changes in attitude will affect the newer generation is only just beginning to be seen. Preliminary hints suggest that the effects will be for the better.

Take, for example, the developments we observed in one industrial company that had been acquired by a Western owner. During the first months after the acquisition, the employees merely went through the motions, behaving passively and not showing any initiative. However, when they realized that new ideas were rewarded and mistakes did not create a major uproar – on the contrary, the new managing director had instituted a 'failure bonus' for people who had the guts to stick their neck out and introduce something new (but failed in doing so) – a stream of initiatives resulted. It was obvious that a large number of employees had many good ideas – ideas that they had previously kept to themselves. Only when a corporate culture of trust replaced the old one of distrust did they begin to spread their wings, express themselves, and initiate improvements to the work processes.

SEPARATING THE PRIVATE AND THE PUBLIC SELF

As indicated, because of the authoritarian upbringing that Russians during the Communist regime experienced at school and in other public places, they acquired an acute sense of what was accepted and what was not – what they could get away with and what they had better let be. With a chameleon-like ability to conform to their surroundings, they knew how to lie low. This behavior pattern was reinforced as a national trait by the climate of fear and terror that permeated Russia for so many years.

During that Communist period, with its relentless Party propaganda about the 'unsurpassed achievements of socialism', indifference became the behavior of choice. In spite of vigorous attempts at indoctrination, most people merely went through the motions; they participated in the 'show' of ideological conformity and compliance. The Brezhnev era of stagnation epitomized this survival strategy. People had to compromise within and without, everyone becoming a Comrade Kompromis Kompromisovich.

Along with conforming, passive resistance was a favored way of coping with the onslaught of propaganda. As time passed, however, the discrepancy between the idealized public code of conduct and the reality of Soviet life (with all its bureaucratic mendacity) became increasingly noticeable. Ideological dry-rot was everywhere. Russians tell an apocryphal tale about Potemkin, the governor general of the southern Ukraine, who, in trying to impress Catherine the Great during her tour through his territory, constructed lavish façades to hide the shabby conditions of the villages. This Potemkin mentality was again alive and well under Communism. As the split between official and personal relationships increased, the integration of individual conscience with political dishonesty became an increasingly daunting task. It was extremely difficult to believe in the propaganda that promised 'a socialist utopia consisting of a society of equals with opportunities for all people' when the reality of inequality was so different. The general population gradually shifted from idealism, to conformism, to cynical careerism characterized by narrow self-interest and material gain.[37]

In spite of the erosion of Communist ideology and the encroachment of materialism, very few people had the courage to declare that the emperor had no clothes. Anyone who did so – who was true to his or her feelings – was exposed to public humiliation and to the wrath of others, a wrath that grew naturally out of the guilt people felt at not having the courage to speak out themselves. As time went by, living with this double standard became increasingly draining. The pervasive pattern of dishonesty made for feelings of depersonalization and gave life an element of unreality. Disillusionment and the development of a 'false self' were almost inevitable.

Times have changed in Russia, to be sure. But the legacy of political pressure for conformity will take time to dissipate, even in this post-glasnost era. Although even the older generation is learning to live without fear, it is in the younger generation – the generation that never had to live *with* this kind of fear – that we can expect the most secure adjustment. Because young people face less of a discrepancy in the psychic domain between the 'false self' and the real person, they experience less conflict in the inner self and develop a greater sense of security and confidence.

This generational distinction is making itself felt in the workplace. In the earlier-cited company whose managing director instituted a failure bonus, the younger employees were more daring than their elders in suggesting alternative ways of organizing the work. Many of the older employees, when asked what they would change if they had the power to do so, were rather suspicious of the question. Instead of taking it as a challenge for improvement, they went on and on about how marvelous everything was, how well everything was going, completely ignoring an outsider's observations about the difficult circumstances (sanitation, temperature, and air quality) under which many of the front-line workers had to operate. The HR director in this company, when interviewed, talked about nothing substantial. He emphasized the recent success of the company's soccer team and the marvelous vacation facilities that the company owned, closing up in extreme discomfort when asked more probing questions.

THE SUPREMACY OF FRIENDSHIP

Because of a legacy of fear, Russians sometimes come across as cold and harsh in their dealings with outsiders, but when a person has been accepted into their private sphere, they are capable of great warmth. Russians make deep personal friendships. As a matter of fact, the Russian language has a variety of words for 'friend', depending on the closeness of the relationship.[38] Russians value close friendships highly, setting great store by those they honor as *druzya*, those friends who are the closest. Such relationships are a compensation for the cold impersonality and unpredictability of public life. They are a kind of social insurance, if you will, serving as part of a mutual support system and offering an outlet for frustrations. Because of the intense nature of their friendships, Russians will go to extraordinary lengths to help their friends, making great sacrifices for those in their trusted circle.

The importance of friendship also affects the business dealings of Russians. While American and northern European executives are more task- than relationship-oriented, Russians need to develop relationships in order to successfully accomplish tasks. For them, it is not the enterprise that counts, but the people in the enterprise. Whatever Russians do, friends come first. Because they see business and friendship as being closely intertwined, they like to create networks of friends in their business dealings. Not surprisingly, then, new business is most often the result of references given by friends and acquaintances. Furthermore, Russians believe in bending the rules to help a friend: social obligations take priority over everything else. They take a contingency approach to rules. In other words, how they apply rules depends on the situation; *their orientation is of a particularistic nature*. Personal loyalty is much more important than fair play.

It is largely because of the importance of friendship that Russians tend to unwind in the kitchen, and have done since rural days. In this safe meeting ground, this refuge from the sterility of public life, they can reveal their true self in interactions with friends; they can share their real warmth, and bask in the warmth of others. Thus most meaningful conversations occur in the kitchen.

One Swedish executive mentioned to one of the authors the initial difficulties he experienced in dealing with his Russian colleagues. Needing the collaboration of these colleagues to get a number of projects off the ground, he approached them with the same task-oriented tack that his company was accustomed to. His initial attempts were not very successful. He could not seem to get the Russians to buy into the projects; they countered his every proposal with reasons why his suggested ways of organizing would not work in Russia. The impasse was finally broken almost by accident. He invited two of his colleagues for a weekend at a dacha outside Moscow to go wild boar hunting, something he knew they enjoyed. During that weekend, the Russians suggested several activities that felt to the Westerner like tests he had to pass in order to gain their respect – duel-like vodka drinking sessions, for example, and 'semi-torture' in a sauna. After he had shown himself to be a good sport, things began to change. One of his colleagues reciprocated and invited him to *his* house. That was the beginning of a warm and deep friendship, the likes of which he had rarely experienced in Western Europe. Furthermore, it created the kind of alliances he needed to make his new organizational projects a success.

EMOTIONAL EXPRESSION

As suggested earlier, there exists a deep duality in the Russian soul – an outcome of geography, climate, history and personal development. That dichotomy pits coldness against warmth. As was noted in the discussion of seasonal affective disorder, Russians are characterized by *great emotional expressiveness*. Prone to extravagant mood swings, they can be extremely cold, controlled, and even rude in a public setting, but they exude great warmth among friends. They can be melancholic and apathetic at certain times, while at other times they exude tremendous vitality. They can shift abruptly from serious introspection, self-doubt and self-torment to total exuberance, abolishing all bounds and limitations. For Russians in unguarded moments, emotions are flagrantly on display. There is a cyclothymic quality to their management of emotions, a continuous oscillation between unbridled optimism and crushing pessimism.[39]

Russia is a nation of stoics, as we saw earlier, but Russians are also romantics; they can be – indeed, often are – extremely sentimental. (Perhaps sentimentality is the counterpoint to stoicism.) In their best moments, Russians are the warmest, most cheerful, most generous people one could hope to encounter. At those moments, there is a spiritual immoderation to their behavior. Their body language is very telling: they like to touch, to embrace. There is an intensity of physical contact, of closeness, that is foreign to many Western cultures.

Russians are also quite introspective. They have an intuitive understanding of the human heart and the tragic sense of human life. When the occasion warrants it, they can be extremely sensitive and compassionate. These characteristics show themselves in Russians' love for the music of Rachmaninov and for romantic ballet productions such as Tchaikovsky's *Swan Lake* and *Sleeping Beauty*.

Russians can have great moments of illumination, but they often give in to impulsiveness, even when it leads to self-destruction. Furthermore, they can be extremely self-indulgent emotionally and physically, devoting themselves to pleasures such as eating, drinking and bathing. Not great believers in moderation or frugality, Russians live more for the moment. Writers such as Ivan Goncharov, Nikolay Gogol and Saltykov-Schedrin wrote unsurpassed satirical portraits of idleness, uselessness and drunkenness. In particular, the novelist Goncharov, in his famous novel *Oblomov*, astutely painted the pattern of passivity and futility. Although they can be extremely stoical when necessary, they can also be very hedonistic. It is not really surprising that luxury goods retailers are finding modern Russia a new Klondike for their operations.

OBLOMOVISM

The novel *Oblomov*, written and set in the mid-nineteenth century, emanates doom and futility. Its 'hero' and namesake, Oblomov, is unable to comprehend adequately the realities of life. Estranged from the real world, he is engaged in a regressive search for Paradise lost. In this tale of passivity and apathy – a tale that epitomizes the backwardness, inertia and futility of nineteenth-century Russian society – daydreaming, fantasy and escapism are substitutes for action. From the story of Oblomov is derived the Russian word *oblomovshchina*, a term encompassing behavior patterns such as inertia and laziness.

Although this novel caricatures a bygone epoch, it speaks to contemporary Russia as well. Even today, an element of phlegmatic fatalism, a sense of impotence regarding the powers that be, colors the behavior of many Russians. Many take a reactive, not a proactive, stand toward life, giving personal drive, ambition and achievement a low priority. Years of serfdom and Communism did little to transform the Oblomovian outlook. Nor did Russia's history of great suffering, some self-inflicted, some imposed – its terrible losses in war, its grievous struggles with nature, its incredible suffering in the Gulag. The sad consequence of the lingering Oblomovian outlook is an absence of a national work ethic ('We pretend to work; they pretend to pay us').

In a number of the companies we visited, the Oblomovian outlook still prevailed. For the most part, the negativity of that outlook was grounded in reality: these companies were doing very poorly; in some, the workers had not been paid for long stretches at a time, getting by on the barter system. However, people at a number of these companies were making a heroic effort to sweep lingering Oblomovism aside, taking a more proactive attitude in an effort to create a meaningful work environment. As mentioned earlier, in general it was easier to co-opt the younger people in taking a more proactive stand. Many of the older workers found it difficult to overcome their disbelief in a better future.

'BUREAUPATHOLOGY'

Nikolay Gogol, in such nineteenth-century satirical novels as *Dead Souls* and *The Inspector General*, mercilessly lampooned the often corrupt, ineffective bureaucracy of Russia. He was a master at placing a mirror in front of the Russians, revealing Russia to itself. The bureaucracy, first consolidated around 1700 under the rule of Peter the Great (to help him implement his vision for a greater Russia), was thriving in Gogol's time. It did not stop then, however. On the contrary, the bureaucratic mind-set continued to prosper, reaching a summit in the last phase of Communism and propelling tension between the public presentation of self and private self-doubts to unsurpassed heights. The vast and venal bureaucracy was like a foreign invading force strangling the population. The State Planning Committee – an army of bureaucrats known by the acronym GOSPLAN – drafted plans in Moscow for every economic unit in the country, micromanaging behavior without a full realization of the various constraints placed on these economic units.

The excess of meaningless rules and regulations found under the Communist Party (and still largely in effect today) can be interpreted as 'social defenses', a way of dealing with persecutory and depressive anxiety.[40] (Social defenses are systems of relationships, reflected in the social structure, constructed to help people control and contain feelings of anxiety in difficult situations. They function like individual defenses, but they are sewn into the very fabric of a society.) In other words, the Russian people furthered an already excessive bureaucracy in an attempt to deal with the angst and unpredictability of life under the Communist regime, and with the glaring contradictions between espoused theory and theory in practice (particularly when Stalin was in power). Every new rule or regulation, every additional protocol (a written record of a transaction, meeting or statement of intent) created the illusion of certainty. Although at a subliminal level Russians were aware of the meaninglessness of the whole exercise, the dysfunctional bureaucracy served a purpose: bureaucratic routines and pseudo-rational behavior obscured personal and organizational realities, allowing people to detach from their inner experiences and thereby reducing anxiety. Control and impersonality substituted for compassion, empathy, awareness and meaning.

These social defenses are still very much present, albeit not as strong today as at the height of Communism. Each Russian takes for granted the Byzantine network of rules and regulations that frames his or her existence. Interactions with public servants are expected to be extremely tiresome exercises. This 'bureaupathological' element in Russian society contributes to the Russian perception that *people are subjected to forces over which they have very little or no control*. Russians seem inclined to view chance, luck, or even supernatural forces as the determining factors of human destiny. Because they do not feel in control,[41] they are highly attuned to signals, demands and trends in the outside world.[42] Their sense of helplessness also manifests itself in inertia, inaction and disorder, and it leads to a conservative outlook toward life and a resistance to change. This conjunction of symptoms reflects a distrust disorder. People who seek refuge in rules and regulations are not risk-takers. They will not stick their necks out; they will not rock the boat. Reactive rather than proactive, they prefer the tried and tested to the new and unknown.

Ironically, however, the very bureaucratic routines that offer comfort make it hard to get anything done. Managing an organization (whether it be a company or a country) 'by the rules' is well nigh impossible once the rules take on a life of their own. As a consequence, when rules proliferate, so do loopholes. Especially during the Soviet regime, Russians became expert at finding subtle ways to beat the system. Knowing that a frontal attack on authority was dangerous, they had no ambition to reform the system. They preferred instead to step back, endure, go around, and find another solution.

As we saw earlier, Russians have long combined outward civility with inward disobedience,[43] in accordance with the Russian proverb that asserts, 'At home do as you wish, but in public do as you are told'. They rebel against regimentation however and whenever they can get away with it. And therein lies one of the great paradoxes of Russia: the Russian people developed rigid programming of activities as an expression of great discomfort with uncertainty (their preference being for predictability and stability); but now, with the process perverted, they have a strong desire to overturn that programming. Theirs is the irrepressible unruliness of people governed by a system engorged with rules and regulations.

Unfortunately, there are still many organizations (particularly in the public sector) where petty bureaucrats – people who make life extremely difficult for others – seem to be in control. This problem needs to be dealt with if Russians hope to be players in the global market economy. Like it or not, to have a competitive advantage in this increasingly boundaryless world, to have a chance to be world-class, organizations will have to employ benchmarking with companies that are 'the best in class'. Also, to have a competitive advantage, companies need to be fast. An abundance of often contradictory regulations is not helpful.

A climate of over-control and fear makes for an odd kind of creative problem solving. Many of the interviews we conducted with Russian executives were filled with horror stories of being caught in Kafkaesque rules that could be avoided only by paying off the appropriate authorities. Because of the absence of consistent legislation concerning private ownership and an arcane tax system, many of these businesspeople had found themselves in Catch-22 situations. On the other hand, in the past Russian executives developed 'creative ways' to supplement their meager incomes. The motivation to beat the system in one way or another is very much alive in contemporary organizational life in Russia.

PARANOIA: LEGACY OF THE CZARS

Russia has had more than its share of tyrannical rulers, and the authoritarian domination of six centuries has had an impact. The Czar legacy had created a preference for strong leaders long before Lenin or Stalin came along. The tyranny of Stalin, a man described as 'the Kremlin mountain man with a cockroach whistler's leer' by murdered poet Osip Mandelstam, was foreshadowed by the terrifying rule of Ivan the Terrible in the sixteenth century, the authoritarian controls instituted by Peter the Great in the seventeenth and eighteenth centuries (and further refined by Catherine the Great), and the autocratic rule of Nicholas I in the nineteenth century. The Communists only strengthened a centralized authoritarian system started centuries ago.

Most Czars saw any form of criticism against their rule as *lèse-majesté* – a challenge to their sovereignty – and responded with banishment or even death. This coercive process created in Russians *a perception of humankind as basically evil*. Even today Russians tend to assume that people will exploit others for personal gain, and to view the social environment beyond their immediate circle of family members and close friends as dangerous. Disturbing as this paranoid worldview may be, it is understandable: it has had survival value for centuries.

Because of this outlook, especially in conjunction with what we know about Russian child rearing, Russians have always sustained a *deep ambivalence toward authority*. Anarchists have always found a place among them. Even under the Czars there was an enormous amount of revolutionary activity, with very bloody results.[44] Lacking a positive identification with authority figures, Russians comply not because of commitment to shared values but simply to conform, or in some cases (as we saw earlier) out of identification with the aggressor. The central role of informers in Russian life has contributed to this deep ambivalence toward authority. The various governments of Russia, from the Czars' repressive regimes through Communism, have used informers to control the population, backing their authority with terrifying institutions – the *Oprichnina* under Ivan the Terrible, the *CheKa* under Lenin, and the KGB under Stalin.

This paranoid *Weltanschauung* has been reinforced by the collectivist nature of Russian society. Collectivist cultures tend to be *more distrustful* than others of outsiders,[45] distinguishing clearly between in-groups and out-groups (and regarding the latter with suspicion). Such an outlook lays the groundwork for fully-fledged xenophobia.

The sense of being besieged by external forces has been a recurring theme throughout Russian history. And this sense has had a basis in reality. Adversaries have always surrounded Russia; in addition, it has been 'infiltrated' by informers and other native opponents. For much of its history, Russia has been simultaneously waging war externally and struggling to maintain order internally. No wonder that in the eyes of the Russians, the world is perceived as a dangerous place.

Institutions such as the Russian Orthodox Church and the Communist Party – organizations deeply suspicious of, and sometimes even hostile to, the outside world – have reinforced this mistrust of foreigners. Under the banner of Communist internationalism, the world was kept at bay until the coming of glasnost and perestroika in the late 1980s. This paranoid *Weltanschauung* also means that people have tended to resort to the primitive defense mechanism of splitting; that is, they have perceived people and situations in stark, Manichean terms – in black or white, if you will.

Many of the non-Russian executives working for Western companies with an operation in Russia (or working for Russian organizations) commented on their difficulties in overcoming this paranoid outlook. Many described at length the efforts they had made to change the suspicious mind-set of the people working for them. While the results of these efforts were mixed, there were quite a few success stories of corporate culture transformation.

Unfortunately, given the nature of the business environment in Russia, someone with a paranoid outlook can always find a reality that meets their expectations.

CULTURE AND ORGANIZATION

Avoidance of Reality

Russians have difficulty facing facts that are perceived as unpleasant. (Centuries ago, they discovered the hard way that 'killing the messenger' was a popular pastime among their rulers.) Unwilling to be messengers of bad tidings, they prefer the safety of 'fudging' facts, ignoring the negative, and colluding with others (often through white lies) to conceal unpleasantness. When the truth is evaded too often, however, reality and fantasy become blurred; thought and action become interchangeable; ideas and daydreams turn into substitutes for action.

This avoidance of reality reached incredible heights under the State Planning Committee (GOSPLAN). Because decision-making was imposed from above, people charged with the day-to-day operation of the enterprise, whether company or government agency, were relieved of the task of setting realistic plans and targets. The realities that the enterprise had to deal with were ignored; the laws of supply and demand were suspended. This approach led to an abdication of personal responsibility for the work to be done. The main actors in this process created a castle in the air, a marketplace completely devoid of reality.

This decision-making process made for extremely unrealistic production targets, which in turn resulted in considerable improvisation – fudging of the facts at best, blatant deception at worst. What developed was a finely tuned, deeply rooted practice of deceiving higher authority. Many executives spent all their energy trying to reduce targets (often excessive) set from above and to shift responsibility to others. They colluded with managers and local Party officials to cook the books and deceive the higher-ups about the real levels of output in the factory or on the farm. 'In principle it can be done' was a manager's favored response to authority. But that attitude led to what by Western standards were irrational, cost-ineffective behaviors, such as maintaining extremely high inventories of finished goods, hoarding materials and labor, and accepting unconnected goods that could be bartered to get badly needed supplies.

During GOSPLAN days, 'storming' – working in a mad frenzy to fulfill certain agreed upon quotas – was part of the routine. Crash programs became a national pastime. In everyday life, people knew that if possible it was better to avoid buying complicated products (such as refrigerators or TV sets) with a manufacturing date at the end of a quarter or at the end of a year, as well as close to the anniversaries of the October Revolution, Lenin and so on. The reason was that in the rush related to fulfilling the quota, quality was often sacrificed for the sake of quantity of production. This fire-fighting mode is still typical of many organizations in Russia. Setting goals for the future is not given a high priority. Long-term planning and strategic thinking are often taken with a grain of salt. In most organizations, short-term survival is what counts.[46]

The Fluidity of Time

Russians have a more *polychronic view of time* than do Westerners.[47] They do not see time as a finite resource, structured in a sequential and linear fashion. On the contrary, they see it as loose or even non-existent. This perspective is a legacy of their agricultural heritage: on the farm, time is multi-focused, expanding (of necessity) to accommodate a variety of activities. Thus Russians plan activities concurrently, making for considerable fragmentation. In Russian business dealings, constant interruption is the norm, punctuality is often lacking, deadlines are taken as suggestions only, and scheduling is difficult.

This polychronic view of time reflects the fact that Russia is a *being*, not a *doing*, culture.[48] Russians tend to be more contemplative than action- or task-oriented. Their activities are relationship-centered. The experience counts more than goal accomplishment or achievement does. The harsh climate of Russia has certainly contributed to this *being* orientation: when people feel that they have little control over nature, they are not as inclined to take action; instead, they tend to be reactive.

Moreover, Russians demonstrate a *greater preoccupation with the past* than is the case in other cultures. In contrast to Americans, for example, they are more concerned with seeing things in a historical context. Russians place a high value on the continuation of tradition. They readily acknowledge – in spite of the Communist Party's attempts at reconstructing history – that their present and future are very much influenced by their past. This orientation influences their attitudes toward change. Change is perceived with apprehension, because it threatens long-established traditions. The result is an 'If it ain't broke, don't fix it' mentality.

THE DESIRE FOR STRONG LEADERSHIP

The authoritarian mind-set is still alive and well in Russia. In spite of Stalin's bloody history of forced industrialization, collectivization, mass purges and the Gulag, Russians feel a certain amount of nostalgia for the kind of leadership he provided. He is perceived by many today as a leader who created a modern state, was victorious in World War II, and made Russia a world power to be reckoned with. He is also viewed as a symbol of power, serving as an antidote to the helplessness that, as we have seen, is part of the Russian character. The remarkable persistence of the Stalin cult indicates the extent to which Russians have respect for power, not law. Many people in Russia see the cure for every crisis as autocratic leadership: if an autocratic leader were in charge, they say, he would show everyone the meaning of discipline.

Power has always been concentrated at the center in Russia. As we have seen, strong central leadership has been perceived as necessary, to hold the dispersed Russian realm together. Because Russian leaders have always been at least subliminally aware of their people's latent desire for disorder, they have had a deeply ingrained fear of anarchy and the centrifugal forces that could rip their country apart. And that fear is valid. Consider the period of glasnost and perestroika: with strong centralized leadership lacking, the USSR started to break up.

The centralized despotism that has always been Russia's answer to the fear of chaos lacks checks and balances to power, and that lack has exacted a price. Plato's philosopher-king has never emerged in Russia. In general, Russians in positions of power have considered themselves to be above the rule of law and have often acted accordingly. This tradition is alive in many organizations where top managers often allow themselves to behave in ways that they publicly prohibit in their companies. With executive power ruling supreme, Russian leaders have disdained the judicial system. That the judiciary should be an independent body was always a concept alien to Russian rulers. They saw the law as existing to protect the state rather than the individual. Unfortunately, such a point of view can make for arbitrary rule. In addition, it makes people very distrustful of (and, when circumstances are disturbing enough, disobedient to) the law.

The *wish for a strong leader* is indicative of a prevailing anxiety about the human condition among the people in Russia. Like the collective system, this wish symptomizes a great dependency on strong leaders for protection, for 'containment' against the chaos around them. Russians want and expect their leaders to take care of them. (It is no accident that the Czars were called *Batiushka* – Little Father.) Russians hope that the paternalistic approach will bring security in a highly insecure world.

The Czars, the landowners, the Orthodox Church, and the Communist Party have encouraged this streak of dependency among the Russians through the years. Under Communism, state paternalism was the rule; life was planned by the state from cradle to grave. This paternalism contributed to learned helplessness – the tendency to wait for instructions to come from above. It did not teach people how to think, or encourage them to do so. It led instead to an orientation of passivity. With initiative and action left to people in the upper levels of the hierarchy, ordinary folks did not have to think about or be responsible for anything.

ATTITUDES TOWARD LEADERSHIP AND PATTERNS OF DECISION-MAKING

The wish for strong leadership has had a great influence on organizational life in Russia. Typically, power and control in any Russian organization come from the top.[49] Most of the more traditional organizations that we visited in the Russian Federation were centrally controlled, quite hierarchical, and very bureaucratic. Frequently, their rather authoritarian management was characterized by obedience to authority, a distrust of outsiders, the use of coercive power, and an emphasis on rank and status.

Because people in lower-level positions often feel helpless, they tend to project power onto those above them. And people at senior levels, pleased to be credited with both omniscience and omnipotence, act accordingly. Because Russians take comfort in this sort of relationship, they are more willing than many other cultures to accept unequal distribution of power in institutions and organizations.[50] Indeed, they place great value on power differences between individuals and groups. (The precision of the ranking of nobility instigated by Peter the Great can be seen as a forerunner of such an outlook.) Paradoxically – in spite of Russia's Communist heritage – elitist behavior is quite common. Even in organizations that profess egalitarianism, and many do, Russian executives place great importance on hierarchy and formal status: they distance themselves physically from the rank and file; they receive (and feel entitled to) privileges; they enjoy ceremony, pompous titles, and symbols of rank and accomplishment; and they see compromise in decision-making as a weakness.

The proposition can be made that decision-making in many Russian organizations is colored by the so-called *democratic centralism* that lay at the heart of Communism. With roots in the village democracy of the *mir*, this approach to decision-making linked democracy and centralism in dynamic tension. (One should not idealize the *mir* village as pure democracy, however, since abuse of the system was not unusual. For example, dictatorship by the village elder, or elders, was not uncommon.) Under democratic centralism, all party members participated in discussions of issues and policies, and all members cast a vote for leadership. After the leader was put in place, however, very little opposition to his ideas was permitted.[51] The leader was accorded the legitimacy to carry out his chosen policies in an extremely autocratic manner.

Democratic centralism is an interesting theoretical concept. With everyone given a voice, implying participation and delegation, this practice should (in theory) lead to empowerment. For many Party officials, however, democratic centralism was nothing more than a slogan used to suppress disagreement and genuinely free discussion. Because the subliminal message of democratic centralism (as exercised in Russia) was that lower levels in the hierarchy were not supposed to show much initiative, it acquired a *pseudo*-participatory quality. As form overcame substance, more and more decisions were referred to higher-ups, despite the label 'democratic'. In relatively short order, democratic centralism became a caricature of its ideal. Stifling true participation, it gave legitimacy to extremely autocratic behavior. The consequence was responsibility avoidance, a lack of empowerment, and the absence of delegation.

While the Russia of today is no longer the Russia of Communism, the mind-set of distorted democratic centralism is still alive and well, particularly among the older population. People lower in the hierarchy are generally reluctant to bring problems to their superiors. As mentioned earlier, confrontation about important issues tends to be avoided. Because fear still tinges all relationships with authority figures, subordinates shun difficult issues and suppress conflict. If a problem is so big that it cannot be ignored, subordinates raise the issue in a roundabout, indirect manner (using *highly contextual language*), favoring indirect communication as the decision-making pattern of choice. The Soviet-era view of independent thinkers as anti-social, troublemakers, hooligans – enemies of the people – still holds force and will need time to be changed.

The same authoritarian mind-set that encourages indirect communication fosters identification with the aggressor, a concept introduced earlier. As a result, Russian society, and the organizations that comprise it, is often ruled by mini-dictators at all levels. These people are extremely subservient toward those above them but act as dictators toward those at lower levels. Acting aggressively with the people below is a displacement activity – a way to get back at the system for all the hardships and frustrations it offers. Whatever meager authority people at lower levels have is generally used to make life hard on others. Small bureaucrats often use their power to harass others by imposing rules and regulations that serve very little purpose except making it clear who is in charge.

Russian organizations that constantly engage in fire-fighting and coping with crises are particularly fertile grounds for emergence of what is called charismatic leadership, whereby followers attribute leadership qualities to an individual who is capable of showing them the way out of a difficult situation. Cultivation of learned helplessness in individuals might, arguably, be one of the forces contributing to perception of charismatic leadership qualities in an individual at the top of the organization. Coupled with impression-management techniques used by organizational leaders, this propensity of many Russian followers to look for a messiah-type leader is often producing the same unquestionable acceptance of authority of people at the top. In large organizations, we can see a phenomenon of new bureaucratic layers being built between a leader who is perceived as charismatic and the followers, that is, rank and file employees. These bureaucratic layers, capitalizing on their closeness to the leader, survive and prosper by 'translating' the ideas of the leader for the 'masses', controlling access to the decision-maker and selectively deciding on the issues to be put on the agenda of the leader, and, not infrequently, filtering information that is coming to the leader from the bottom of the organization. Basking in the reflected glory of the charismatic leader, this entourage gets attention and creates enormous power for itself in the organization.[52] We have witnessed huge bureaucratic machines put in place in large and apparently successful Russian organizations where principles and mechanisms of work are copied from the Soviet bureaucracy analogues.

As noted earlier, this bureaupathology is indicative of a social defense run amok. Until it (and the authoritarian mind-set that engenders it) can be reined in, trust – a crucial precondition for effective leadership – cannot prevail. Only in a trust-based corporate culture where people have a feeling of community, enjoyment, self-determination, competence and contribution can leadership bring excellence out of its workforce.

The seeds of such excellence have been planted in Russia and must now be nurtured. The behavior of many of the younger executives we met contradicted much of what has been said here about the autocratic mind-set. Their behavior was more in tune with the original ideals of democratic centralism. Participating in discussions with these younger people (many of whom were involved in start-ups), we saw little evidence of the command–control–compartmentalization paradigm that characterizes so many of the more traditional Russian organizations. Instead, we discerned give-and-take, constructive conflict resolution (rather than conflict avoidance), a willingness to stand up for one's opinions, and the courage to challenge authority.

A LONG NIGHT'S JOURNEY INTO DAY

Given Russia's history of pendulum swings between excessive control and chaos, it comes as no surprise that the new freedoms of the past 15 years have not satisfied people's high expectations. The benefits of perestroika have arguably accrued to only a very small number of individuals. Privatization has led to untamed capitalism and unheard-of wealth for the limited *nomenklatura*, many of whom have become oligarchs and robber barons of their 'red' businesses (companies set up with siphoned-off state resources). 'Black' businesses (holdovers from the black market in the late Soviet era) have also done relatively well, while 'white' businesses (new firms emerging in the fledgling market economy) are struggling.

For a period in the early 1990s, Russia turned into the 'Wild East'. Bribery, as in the past, greased the wheels of commerce, and corruption was rampant. Much of what is considered corruption in other countries was standard practice in Russia, given the difficulties associated with GOSPLAN. In spite of this attempt at rationalization, however, it cannot be denied that the Russian business world became to a certain extent Mafia-ridden.[53] The Russian Mafia is a rather amorphous group of powerful, corrupt government officials, economic managers and criminal elements. There is little respect in their world for any rule of law other than that of the Kalashnikov submachine gun.

How did things get so out of control? The answer is both simple and complex. When the Communist ideology was discredited, it was not replaced by another set of values; no new ethical compass replaced the old. As a result, there was an absence of moral authority. Add to this the lack of political consensus necessary for reform, the inaction and inconsistency of Yeltsin as an ailing president, the activities of a group of politically inept economic reformers, and the presence of a number of venal, newborn capitalists and you had a recipe for disaster. In addition, the extremely rapid pace of privatization, of which we will say more later, encouraged an all-out grab on the part of a limited number of powerful people.

The 1998 financial crisis in Russia and the election of President Putin in 2000 are two significant events that seemed to have been a kind of shock treatment to Russian legislators, however. Although we cannot say that the Mafia no longer has any influence, we have noticed a trend towards more transparency in corporate governance. Many of the companies we visited now use International Accounting Standards, deal regularly with Western partners, and are even quoted on Western stock exchanges. With the tacit agreement of

Putin, major Russian corporations and most Russians seem to feel that in the interest of developing a stable economy, the past is a closed book, but the future will be a fairer, cleaner one.

FROM FEUDALISM, TO COMMUNISM, TO ATTEMPTS AT DEMOCRACY

When asked what he thought of Western civilization, the Indian leader Mahatma Gandhi replied that it sounded like a good idea and should be tried sometime. The same could be said of democracy and capitalism in Russia: they are worth pursuing.

Has Russia's leadership committed itself to a model of modern democracy and capitalism? The answer to this question is still unknown, but it is clear that Russia has not yet instituted either widely distributed leadership or a fully open and fair competitive market system with the necessary checks and balances. Good corporate governance is still a long way off. The oscillation between order and disorder is still there for all to see. Insufficient mechanisms have been put into place to control human avarice and the lust for power.

Democratic forms of leadership are certainly not a panacea, and they exact a price in the form of uncertainty and decision paralysis. But given the alternatives, many Russians may prefer to pay. History has shown the dangers of authoritarian leadership: possessing centralized power and authority tends to bring out the worst in people. Lord Acton's statement that 'power corrupts, and absolute power corrupts absolutely', has not lost its ring of truth. The lack of power contributes to a sense of alienation, impotence, disenfranchisement, passivity and inertia. Moreover, power – as Stalin's reign showed very clearly – can consume the best and the brightest of a generation.

Given the present state of flux, the question remains open whether Russia will be able to construct a stable democracy that will serve as the foundation for free enterprise. But what is the alternative? It is hard to find a better path to stability and prosperity than the one drawn up by Western democracy. Russians know all too well the downside of a totalitarian system. And quasi-democratic and quasi-capitalistic solutions, examples of which can be found in many Latin American countries, have a lesser success rate than fully-fledged democracy.

The change process will not be an easy ride given the existence of certain cultural patterns. There are many reasons for being optimistic, however. Given the country's history – the fact that it has never experienced real democracy or political pluralism – it has come a long way in a very short time. Although political and economic reforms have not moved in tandem – after all, mourning the loss of an empire takes time, as does coming to grips with the legacy of the vast, terrifying omnipresent network of the Gulag – many difficult hurdles have been overcome. Many of the building blocks needed to facilitate a social transition to political pluralism have been laid. The business climate in Russia is gradually improving. The rudiments of a market economy have appeared. Prices have been deregulated. Steps toward currency convertibility have been made. The notion of 'small is beautiful' is increasingly recognized in Russia; as a result, the enormous vertically integrated monopolies of the Soviet era are becoming things of the past. Privatization is proceeding in spurts. The first steps are been taken to protect property rights. With great difficulties, an overhaul of the legal and tax system is taking place. Great setbacks notwithstanding (the financial sector being a good example), the basis for a private sector, risk-based, entrepreneurial market economy is gradually emerging. Furthermore, the shock treatment the population received under Gorbachev, Yeltsin, and now Putin has encouraged many people to take dramatic personal action – to reinvent themselves, as it were. Many people have taken advantage of the new ways of doing things. They have embarked on new lifestyles, new careers. After centuries of isolation, Russians seem prepared to embrace the world outside.

Many characteristics of Russia and its people favor a successful transition toward a market economy. For example, Russia has an extremely high literacy rate. Many of its people are very well educated and highly skilled. And there is a positive kind of creativity to be found in Russian factory workers who manage to keep ancient, decrepit machinery running. For example, one French expatriate executive remarked that he was amazed by the Russians' ability to adapt. He said that no French factory workers would be able to manufacture a marketable product under similar conditions in France. We also found that Russian workers are quite eager to present their ideas for improvements if they get the right encouragement.

If the Russians' strengths are encouraged, re-education for success in a global economy will be much easier than would be the case in many other societies. Furthermore, most Russians, though present hardships engender a kind of nostalgia for the days when their empire was still intact, do not want to return to Communism or hard-line xenophobic nationalism.

A critical factor in the transition to a market economy is the fact that the younger generation carries less ballast from the past than their elders do. They are willing (and in many cases eager) to push the collectivist legacy aside, and they have a greater tendency than their elders to be entrepreneurial. Having tasted freedoms their parents never had, they cling to those freedoms tenaciously. They utilize their 'anarchistic' disposition to create more open organizations and strive for a better life. However, some students of Russian history have argued that democracy does not come naturally to Russians. For example, Figes suggests that the failure of democracy at the time of the Russian revolution was deeply rooted in Russian culture and social history.[54] Given the Czarist history, he says, what started as a people's revolution contained the seeds of its degeneration into violence and dictatorship. We can only hope that history does not repeat itself.

BACK TO THE FUTURE

In these pages, we have reviewed a number of salient themes pertaining to Russian character and leadership style, examining them through a clinical and cultural magnifying glass where possible. The objective in using this approach has been to unravel some of the mystery that surrounds Russian behavior patterns in the workplace.

Given the major transformations occurring in Russian society today, some of these themes are presently in a state of flux. More research is needed to explore their ongoing evolution. Many of these themes, however, given their developmental origin, have the kind of robustness that will endure, retaining their significance for those attempting to understand and deal with the Russian people.

In 1919, Lincoln Steffens made a trip to Russia as part of a mission on behalf of President Woodrow Wilson. When later asked about the experience, he said, 'I have seen the future and it works'.[55] For years this comment was taken as an indication of naïvety: Steffens did not foresee the terror that the Communist regime would bring. But maybe we should give Steffens a second chance. He may have recognized in the Russian character a constructive anarchistic quality – a creative, innovative core – that will enable the Russians to construct organizations that are attractive work environments, and create a society that gives meaning to all its members.

NOTES

1. Kets de Vries, M.F.R and E. Florent-Treacy (2002), 'Global leadership from A-Z', *Organizational Dynamics*, Spring, **30** (4), 295-309.
2. Kets de Vries, M.F.R. (2001), *Struggling with the Demon: Perspectives on individual and organizational irrationality*, Garden City, NJ: Psychosocial Press.
3. Mead, M. (1951), *Soviet Attitudes toward Authority: An Interdisciplinary Approach to Problems of Soviet Character*, New York: Schocken Books; Leites, N. C. (1953), *A Study of Bolshevism*, Illinois: Free Press; Kluckhohn, C. (1961), 'Studies of Russian national character', in A. Inkeles and R. A. Bauer (eds), *Soviet Society: A Book of Readings*, Boston: Houghton-Mifflin, pp. 607–18; Granick, D. (1962), *The Red Executive*, Garden City, NY: Doubleday Anchor; Smith, H. (1976), *The Russians*, New York: Quadrangle; Smith, H. (1991), *The New Russians*, New York: Avon; Hingley, R. (1977), *The Russian Mind*, New York: Charles Scribner's Sons; Hosking, G.A. (1985), *A History of the Soviet Union*, London: Fontana/Collins; Mikheyev, D. (1987), 'The Soviet mentality', *Political Psychology*, **8** (4), 491–523; Laqueur, W. (1989), *The Long Road to Freedom: Russia and Glasnost*, New York: Scribner's; Puffer, S. (ed.) (1992), *The Russian Management Revolution: Preparing Managers for the Market Economy*, Armonk: New York; Moynahan, B. (1994), *The Russian Century: A History of the Last*

Hundred Years, New York: Random House; Murray, D. (1995), *A Democracy of Despots*, Boulder, CO: Westview Press; Richmond, Y. (1996), *From Nyet to Da: Understanding the Russians*, Yarmouth, ME: Intercultural Press; Stephan, W.G. and M. Abalkina-Paap (1996), 'Russia and the West', in D. Landis and R.S. Bhagat (eds) *Handbook of Intercultural Training*, second edn, London: Sage, pp. 366–82; Brown, A. (1997), *The Gorbachev Factor*, Oxford: Oxford University Press; Freeze, G. L. (ed.) (1997), *Russia: A History*, New York: Oxford University Press; Figes, O. (1998), *A People's Tragedy: The Russian Revolution 1891–1924*, New York: Penguin.

4. Glaser, B.G. and A.L. Strauss (1967), *The Discovery of Grounded Theory*, Chicago: Aldine; Argyris, C. and D. Schon (1974), *Theory in Practice*, San Francisco: Jossey-Bass.
5. Devereux, G. (1978), *Ethnopsychoanalysis*, Berkeley: University of California Press; Van Maanen, J. (1988) *Tales of the Field*, Chicago: University of Chicago Press; Schein, E. H. (1987), *The Clinical Perspective in Fieldwork*, Beverly Hills, CA: Sage.
6. Geertz, C. (1973), *The Interpretation of Culture*, New York: Basic Books, p. 20.
7. Kets de Vries, M.F.R. and D. Miller (1987), 'Interpreting organizational texts', *Journal of Management Studies*, **24** (30), 233–47.
8. Kets de Vries, M.F.R. and S. Perzow (1991), *Handbook of Character Studies: Psychoanalytic Explorations*, New York: International Universities Press.
9. Schneider, S. and J.-L. Barsoux (1997), *Managing across Cultures*, New York: Prentice-Hall, p. 19.
10. Mead, M. and M. Wolfenstein (1954), *Childhood in Contemporary Cultures*, Chicago: University of Chicago Press, p. 10.
11. Geertz, C. (1973), *The Interpretation of Culture*, New York: Basic Books, p. 5.
12. Hofstede, G. (1991), *Culture's Consequences: Software of the Mind*, New York: McGraw-Hill, p. 5.
13. Hall, E.T. (1966), *The Hidden Dimension*, Garden City, NY: Doubleday; Hall, E. T. (1973), *The Silent Language*, Garden City, NY: Anchor Press; Deal, T.E. and A.A. Kennedy (1982), *Corporate Cultures: The Rites and Rituals of Corporate Life*, Reading, MA: Addison-Wesley; Schein, E. H. (1985), *Corporate Culture and Leadership*, San Francisco: Jossey-Bass.
14. Parsons, T. (1951), *The Social System*, New York: The Free Press.
15. Kluckhohn, C. and F.L. Strodtbeck (1961), *Variations in Value Orientations*, Connecticut: Greenwood Press.
16. Hall, E.T. (1966), *The Hidden Dimension*, Garden City, NY: Doubleday; Hall, E.T. (1973), *The Silent Language*, Garden City, NY: Anchor Press.
17. Hofstede, G. (1984), *Culture's Consequences: International Differences in Work Related Values*, Beverly Hills, CA: Sage; Hofstede, G. (1991), *Culture's Consequences: Software of the Mind*, New York: McGraw-Hill.
18. Schein, E.H. (1985), *Corporate Culture and Leadership*, San Francisco: Jossey-Bass.
19. Laurent, A. (1983), 'The cultural diversity of Western conceptions of management', *International Studies of Management and Organization*, **13** (1–2), 75–96.
20. Trompenaars, F. (1984), *The Organization of Meaning and the Meaning of Organization – A Comparative Study on the Conceptions and Organizational Structure in Different Cultures*, PhD. Thesis, University of Pennsylvania; Trompenaars, F. (1993), *Riding the Waves of Culture*, London: Nicholas Brealy.
21. Javidan, M. and R. House (2001), 'Cultural acumen for the global manager, lessons from Project Globe', *Organizational Dynamics*, **29**(4), 289–305.
22. Trompenaars, F. and C. Hampden-Turner (1993), *The Seven Cultures of Capitalism*, New York: Doubleday.
23. Donskoy, M. (1938), *The Childhood of Maxim Gorky*.
24. Chassequet-Smirgel, J. (1975), *L'Ideal du Moi*, Paris: Claude Tchou.
25. Murray, D. (1995), *A Democracy of Despots*, Boulder, CO: Westview Press.
26. Freud, A. (1946), *The Ego and the Mechanisms of Defense*, New York: International Universities Press.
27. Erikson, E.H. (1963), *Childhood and Society*, second edn, New York: W.W. Norton.
28. Kluckhohn, C. (1961), 'Studies of Russian national character', in A. Inkeles and R. A. Bauer (eds), *Soviet Society: A Book of Readings*, Boston: Houghton-Mifflin, p. 607–18.

29. Goodwin, F.K. and Jamison, K. R. (1990), *Manic-Depressive Illness*, New York: Oxford University Press; Rosenthal, N. E. (1993), *Winter Blues*, New York: The Guilford Press; Whybrow, P. C. (1997), *A Mood Apart*, New York: Basic Books; Kets de Vries, M.F.R. (2001), *Struggling with the Demon: Perspectives on individual and organizational irrationality*, Garden City, NJ: Psychosocial Press; Kets de Vries, M.F.R. (1999), 'Managing puzzling personalities: navigating between "live volcanoes" and "dead fish"', *European Management Journal*, 17, 8–19.
30. Obolonsky, A. (1995), 'Russian politics in the time of troubles: some basic antinomies', in A. Saikal and A. & W. Maley (eds), *Russia in Search of its Future*, Cambridge: Cambridge University Press, pp. 12–27.
31. Kluckhohn, C. (1961), 'Studies of Russian national character', in A. Inkeles and R.A. Bauer (eds), *Soviet Society: A Book of Readings*, Boston: Houghton-Mifflin, pp. 607–18.
32. Bronfenbrenner, U. (1970), *Two Worlds of Childhood: U.S and USSR*, New York: Sage; Pearson, L. (1990), *Children of Glasnost: Growing up Soviet*, Seattle: University of Washington Press; Eklof, B. and E. Dneprov (eds) (1993), *Democracy in the Russian School: The Reform Movement in Education since 1984*, Boulder, CO: Westview Press.
33. Ispa, J. (1994). *Child Care in Russia*, Westport, Conn.: Bergin & Garvey.
34. Rotter, J.B. (1975), 'Generalized expectancies for internal versus external control of reinforcement', *Psychological Monographs*, 80 (Whole No. 609).
35. Winnicott, D.W. (1975), *Through Paediatrics to Psychoanalysis*, New York: Basic Books.
36. Ispa, J. (1994), *Child Care in Russia*, Westport, Conn.: Bergin & Garvey.
37. Bauer, R. and A. Inkeles (1968), *The Soviet Citizen*, New York: Atheneum.
38. Dabars, Z. and L. Vokhmina (1995), *The Russian Way*, Lincolnwood, Ill.: Passport Books.
39. Whybrow, P.C. (1997), *A Mood Apart*, New York: Basic Books; Kets de Vries, M.F.R. (1999), 'Managing puzzling personalities: navigating between "live volcanoes" and "dead fish"', *European Management Journal*, 17, 8–19.
40. Jaques, E. (1955), 'Social systems as a defense against persecutory and depressive anxiety', in M. Klein, P. Heimann and R.E. Money-Kyrle (eds), *New Directions in Psychoanalysis*, London: Tavistock; Menzies, I. (1960), 'A case-study in the functioning of social systems as a defense against anxiety: a report on a study of the nursing service of a general hospital', *Human Relations*, 13, 95–121.
41. Riesman, D. (1950), *The Lonely Crowd*, New Haven: Yale University Press; Rotter, J.B. (1975), 'Generalized expectancies for internal versus external control of reinforcement', *Psychological Monographs*, 80 (Whole No. 609); Lefcourt, H.M. (1976), *Locus of Control*, New York: Wiley.
42. Trompenaars, F. (1993), *Riding the Waves of Culture*, London: Nicholas Brealy; Trompenaars, F. and Hampden-Turner, C. (1993), *The Seven Cultures of Capitalism*, New York: Doubleday.
43. Hamilton, V.L., J. Sanders and S.J. McKearney (1995), 'Orientations toward authority in an authoritarian state: Moscow in 1990', *Personality and Social Psychology Bulletin*, **21** (4), 356–65.
44. Figes, O. (1998), *A People's Tragedy: the Russian Revolution 1891–1924*, New York: Penguin.
45. Triandis, H.C. (1972), *The Analysis of Subjective Cultures*, New York: Wiley; Triandis, H.C., R. Bontempo, M.J. Villareal, M. Asai and N. Lucca (1988), 'Individualism and collectivism: cross-cultural perspectives on self-ingroup relationships', *Journal of Personality and Social Psychology*, **54** (2), 323–38.
46. Michailova, S. (1997), 'Interface between Western and Russian management attitudes: implications for organizational change', *CEES Working Paper Series*, No 8, Copenhagen: Center for East European Studies, Copenhagen Business School.
47. Hall, E.T. and M.R. Hall (1990), *Understanding Cultural Differences*, Yarmouth, ME: Intercultural Press.
48. Hall, E.T. (1966), *The Hidden Dimension*, Garden City, NY: Doubleday; Hall, E.T. (1973), *The Silent Language*, Garden City, NY: Anchor Press; Laurent, A. (1983), 'The cultural diversity of Western conceptions of management', *International Studies of Management and Organization*, **13**(1–2), 75–96.

49. Gurkov, I. and Y. Kuz'minov (1995), 'Organizational learning in Russian privatized enterprises', *International Studies of Management and Organization*, **25** (4), 91–117.
50. Hofstede, G. (1984), *Culture's Consequences: International Differences in Work Related Values*, Beverley Hills, CA: Sage; Bollinger, D. (1994), 'The four cornerstones and three pillars in the "House of Russia" management system', *Journal of Management Development*, **13** (2), 49–54.
51. Lawrence, P. and Viachoutsicos, C. (1990), *Behind the Walls: Decision-making in Soviet and U.S. Enterprise*, Cambridge, MA: Harvard Business School Press.
52. Kets de Vries, M.F.R. (1993), *Leaders, Fools and Impostors*, San Francisco: Jossey-Bass.
53. Handelman, S. (1995), *Comrade Criminal: Russia's New Mafia*, New Haven: Yale University Press.
54. Figes, O. (1998), *A People's Tragedy: The Russian Revolution 1891–1924*, New York: Penguin.
55. Steffens, L. (1931), *The Autobiography of Lincoln Steffens*, Vol. 2, New York: Harcourt Brace & Co., p. 799.

2.   An East–West dialogue

Russians know too little about Russia.

Alexander Pushkin

Wretched and abundant,
Oppressed and powerful,
Weak and mighty,
Mother Russia!

Nikolai Nekrasov

The discussion that follows can be seen as a snapshot of the kind of dialogue that took place between 'Western' contributors and Russian ones during the writing of this work. As a snapshot it represents an archetype, reflecting some of the biases Westerners have toward Russia. The original discussion on which this interchange is based took place in an obscure spa hotel outside Petropavlovsk, a city in the Russian Far East. Petropavlovsk is considered the largest and most important city on the Kamchatka Peninsula. Although located in a beautiful, mountainous environment, to Western eyes the city is quite decrepit with decaying houses and a dwindling population of people who were brought to the peninsula by force or worked for the military. The city offered a very different perspective, far removed in more ways than one from the impressive central districts of Moscow or St. Petersburg. Petropavlovsk can be viewed as part of what the French would call *La Russie profonde*, deep, basic Russia. The setting offered the opportunity to explore Western perceptions of Russia. There the following dialogue took place, between a Russian business leader and a Western academic.

The Russian executive (East): One hundred years after Peter the Great's death, Alexander Pushkin said that the first Russian emperor 'cut a window to Europe' for Russia, where the country now 'stands on a firm foot'. One century after that, another Russian poet, Alexander Block, called Russians 'Scythians and Asians with slanting and greedy eyes'. The question of Russia's cultural destiny is as old as the country itself. How does the West see Russia today? Is it a part of Europe, Asia, or a continent apart?

The Western professor (West): Whereas Americans still think of Russia as a land apart, most Europeans consider Russia as a part of Europe. Most Westerners have heard of, and may have even visited, Moscow or St Petersburg. They may know a little about other regions in Russia such as Siberia, but they don't really know anything about the Russian Far East or the South. They don't realize that certain regions of Russia are very close to countries such as Korea, China and Japan or to various Moslem countries. They may associate Russia with long winters, caviar and vodka. The more educated among them will have heard of classical Russian writers such as Turgenev, Chekhov, Tolstoy and Dostoevsky. The man in the street, however, doesn't realize the extent to which Russia, like the United States, has long been a melting pot of different ethnic groups. Most Russians – if they trace their background – will be surprised to see the extent to which they carry within their genetic make-up a pot-pourri of different ethnic groups. This has colored Russia's past and, we assume, will very much influence the future. What are your perceptions of the present situation in Russia?

(East): The Russian empire, formed during the 16–20th centuries, was a multiethnic place indeed, with more than hundred different languages spoken. Even before that, both ancient Kiev Rus and the micro-kingdoms of the 13–15th centuries experienced the strong influence of foreign cultures, especially Polish and Tartar. However, the Russian language, Orthodox Church, and 'Russian way' of life always dominated the country. National cultures and identities were, if not oppressed, then limited to the traditional regions controlled by smaller ethnic groups. Of course, Russian culture absorbed some of the other cultures, but by no means did those cultures melt together. Russians like food such as *shashlyk* and *plov,* and appreciate Georgian dances, but for a long while, that was as far as it went.

Seventy years of Communism did not change the fundamentals, even though societal transformation caused migration, dramatically increasing the number of Russians living in national republics and vice versa. Despite this proximity to other nationalities, Russians have always made an effort to preserve their language, culture and habits. People of other nationalities usually were encouraged to immerse themselves into Russian culture, often becoming 'more holy than the pope'. Lenin criticized his comrades in arms Stalin (Georgian) and Dzerdzinski (Polish) for becoming too Russian and oppressing national minorities too strongly.

After the Soviet Union collapsed, the national republics went their own way, and today 80 per cent of the Russian Federation's population is of Russian origin. The Russian nation and its culture are dominant, and business and organizational practices reflect this fact.

What are most influential now, however, are regional, economic and social, *not* cultural differences. There are several 'Russias' within the country. Moscow is a virtual country in itself, an absolute center of power, and a center of financial power as well. Some estimates show that Moscow has about 80 per cent of the country's wealth.

There are other developing regions with entrepreneurial traditions, infrastructure and a mild climate, such as Southern Russia and Southern Siberia. There are bright spots in Central Russia such as Novgorog and Nizhny Novgorod, but there are also many areas in the countryside in which villages are dying, populated by elderly people living on bread, potatoes and some milk, whose children and grandchildren have moved to the cities. There is fast growing oil-rich Western Siberia, but there are also areas like Kamchatka and Magadan, which were populated by force. These regions will continue to decline, since it's difficult for human beings to live there. To understand the situation in Russia today, one has to keep in mind those differences.

To summarize, the present outlook for Russia Inc. is quite unclear. But that is very typical of the country; it has always been difficult to predict its future. This nebulous situation, however, has implications for the rest of the world. The country's political history has often been violent, xenophobic, and extremely conservative. Some of these tendencies still linger. If we look at the situation today we still can see a lot of violence, brutality, and some signs of chaos. But there have been some massive improvements over the past years as well.

But an interesting question to me is, why should the rest of the world be interested in what is happening in Russia? If you look at the country's economy, it remains very small compared to other Western countries. It is also a country with an outdated infrastructure, arguably corrupt government, and a passive population. Could Russia's story be of any relevance for the developed world?

(West): The Chinese sign for change is 'risky opportunity' – therein lies a flippant answer to your question: that one could learn something from a country's transformation. The contradictions and paradoxes we see presently in Russia can teach other countries a number of important lessons about change. For many people, it is also interesting to see how Russia is dealing with the 'narcissistic injury' of having lost so much of its prominence in the world. It is a little bit like what happened to countries such as Austria, France and England. Each of them had to give up their empires.

To come back to your question, one of the reasons people are interested in Russia is a very pragmatic one. Consider the country's nuclear arsenal, which certainly warrants attention. As the gangster Al Capone used to say, 'You go much further with a gun and a smile than with a smile alone'. When a country has the capability to destroy the rest of the world many times over, you pay attention. Given Russia's military potential, many people are also worried what would happen if the country disintegrates. And many fear that weapons of mass destruction could fall into the hands of terrorists – a notion that is not so farfetched.

Furthermore, this military might – even if it is much less powerful now – is coupled with a highly educated population. Russia combines remarkable backwardness (which is very noticeable when you go to the backcountry) with some of the best brains in technology in the world.

We should also not forget the sheer size of the country. Russian territory covers one-seventh of the globe. It possesses an incredible amount of important natural resources such as oil, gas, and other minerals. Many entrepreneurial types in other countries covet these resources. For entrepreneurs, Russia looks like one of the most exciting places to 'play' in the 21st century. Actually, in a rather reductionist way, it can be said that fear and greed are the factors that drive much of this interest in Russia. But hopefully, apart from the fear and greed factor, there are also more idealistic people who, after years of cold war, would like to help create a new, democratic society. As Western Europe had a Marshall Plan after the Second World War, some see a similar opportunity to build a new society. But, whatever happens, Russia is not going to turn into a nice, conventional democracy overnight.

(**East**): In the context of building a new society, there are a number of facts or trends in very recent Russian history that are of interest. For example, the number of billionaires that emerged in Russia from 1993–2003 is probably greater than in the rest of the developing world combined. What is more important, however, is the second layer of the wealth pyramid: there are thousands of multimillionaires, and several hundred thousand people with a net worth over $1,000000 (in contrast, Russia's official income per capita stands at $2400 per annum). While oligarch-billionaires largely accumulated their wealth by acquiring state assets at often ridiculously low symbolic prices during the privatization period, and by exploiting natural resources, the absolute majority of the second group earned their wealth through ingenuity and hard work.

These people fostered much of the change in Russian economy and society, including the very impressive economic growth of the early 2000s. Unlike in China, foreign direct investment has not up to this point played an important role in the economic development of Russia. Paradoxically, one can even argue that the Russian financial crisis of 1998 was a godsend; isolation and a pariah status forced Russia to mobilize internal resources. During the perestroika years, everybody in the country was really excited about Western management techniques, and most Russian business people wanted to learn these practices. But when some of the new methods, and the Westerners who provided them, failed to deliver the golden pot at the end of the rainbow, Russians became gradually disillusioned. At the same time, they realized that many business practices that had existed in Russia in the past could still be used effectively

– in a somewhat adapted form. The result has been that Russians found unique ways of managing people and organizations, a way of doing business more in line with their own societal structures. Now we see this know-how continuing in many different forms, but still under the banner of creating a unique Russian way of doing things.

The role of the younger generation should also be acknowledged, as they are the major driving force of positive change. Young entrepreneurs have taken the initiative. They learned quickly and have picked up best practices from other countries. The multinational companies and other foreign firms that came to Russia gave these people some good ideas. But Russians have done a remarkable job of transforming and adapting their organizations themselves, in spite of a government that has not been very supportive, particularly not during the Yeltsin years. It is the business community that has been driving economic and social change under very unfavorable conditions.

Let's come back to some of your earlier comments about Westerners' associations concerning Russia. When foreigners are asked why they find Russia simultaneously mysterious and attractive, their most common response is: its size and its unpredictability.

(West): The unpredictability factor is certainly there. Thinking about such imagery in fantasy, consider the symbolism of the Russian bear. Bears can be surprisingly fast and violent. Power and unpredictability are certainly important factors in the context of Russia. It is a country that invites extremes. The activity–passivity polarity is very striking. Like the bear, people seem to be either operating at full speed or they are totally inert.

Continuing our discussion of symbolism and the role it plays in the formation of Russian national character, there are many myths, legends, fairy tales and folkloric facts that can give insight into what Russia is all about. Furthermore, in this 'textual' interpretation what is also important in the formation of national identity is the choice of heroes in a society.

(East): One of the best-known Russian heroes is a mighty man called Ylia Muromets, who lived during the 13th century, and who later became a central figure of many tales. According to the legend, he remained totally inert until he was 33 years old. At that age, he all of a sudden realized his enormous physical power, got up on his feet and started to fight the enemies of Russia and the Orthodox religion. We can find here an analogy with the bear symbolism; long periods of inertia alternated by outbursts of activity.

Another person is Ivan the Fool, found in many popular folk tales. One of his incarnations is Yemelia, a hero of one of the most popular Russian fairy tales. In this tale, Yemelia, the unmarried third son of a peasant, lived with his extended family, spending his days lying on top of a Russian stove and daydreaming. One day his sisters-in-law decided to force him to become more helpful. They asked him to fetch water at the river. While doing that, Yemelia caught a magic pike. The pike told him, 'If you turn me loose, I will fulfill any wish you have'. And what do you think his wish was? Ironically, Yemelia's wish was to continue lying on his favorite stove, to be left in peace.

The Russian historian Mikhail Pogodin, who lived in the 19th century, compared both the Russian people and their government to Ivan who 'sleeps on top of the stove while his brothers are working; he only realizes his strength and cleverness when there is a threat or a heroic opportunity. But as soon as his effort is over he prefers to climb back on top of the stove and fall into a deep, lazy sleep'.

A similar hero is Manilov from Gogol's *Dead Souls,* who dreamed of building a bridge between an obscure town where he was living to St Petersburg (which was a thousand miles away) so he could greet the Russian emperor. Like Ivan the Fool, he never took any action though, other than in his dreams. These heroes and tales illustrate some of the fundamental features of the Russian national character: the expectation that a magic force will change one's life for the better. This is a very different attitude from the Americans, who have a much more 'can do' outlook. With some Russians, on the other hand, there is a disconnection between happiness, wealth and hard work. The good life should come without working for it. I often notice this oscillation between passivity and enthusiasm, naïvety and cleverness, and brutality and sentimentality. Many of these tales also illustrate the dual nature of Russian character – the existence of incredible mood and behavior swings.

(**West**): Commenting on this kind of behavior from a clinical point of view – this dramatic active–passive mode – inferences can be made about the kind of child development taking place in Russia. To what extent do the parents provide 'containment', create a holding environment for their children? Infant development studies demonstrate that the precursors of adult mood swings are temper tantrums. What do the parents do to calm children when they are upset? How are emotions dealt with in the family? There may be a lack of consistency between parents, accentuated by a discontinuity between a person's presentation of self in private and public life. In commenting on this discontinuity, I am particularly referring to the period where the original idealism of the Communist system turned into an exercise in ritualism. Parents would say one thing at home, while telling the child to behave differently outside the home. They had to toe the line given the ideology of the Communist Party.

(**East**): Almost two hundred years ago, our Russian poet and philosopher Khomiakov said that 'Russian family routines…contain a secret of Russia's greatness'. I am not sure he was entirely right, but this says a lot about how

Russian society functioned. The traditional Russian family was an extended family, with three generations living under the same roof in a peasant's house. Even in 1917, just before the Revolution, 75 per cent of the population lived in the countryside. A strong patriarch was in charge of the family organization. It was either a still-working grandfather or his eldest son. Keeping in mind that hard work and often malnutrition took their toll (in pre-revolutionary Russia life expectancy was only 32 years) the latter situation was quite common. Men spent most of the time working out in the fields or in the city (in the winter).

Women took care of their numerous children and the house. The mother's position in the family hierarchy was always weaker compared to the father. Her primary task was to keep father happy, almost at any cost. There was a considerable amount of physical violence within the family. Dostoevsky's descriptions of the various characters in his novel *The Brothers Karamazov* are very telling. Beatings were the normal way of educating people. The father would beat not only the children but also the wife. The mother was close to the children but could do little to protect them. Furthermore, overwhelmed with household work and their husbands' violence, women also beat their children, alternating periods of love with those of hate. Later this maternal approach to child raising, favors alternating with brutal punishment, became almost universal for Russian families. This may be another factor contributing to a basic insecurity of the Russian people and their tendency to resort to extreme forms of behavior.

(**West**): The way power and authority are dealt with in the family very much determines a child's specific outlook later in life. After all, the first organization we get to know is the family organization. In the Russian family, the way you describe it, there seems to have been a great power difference between mother and father. The questions we can ask ourselves are, how did a child integrate into his later outlook toward life these feelings of helplessness, humiliation and anger at seeing his mother being beaten, since he was unable to protect her? How did a male child experience being beaten himself? There was also the inconsistency of the child's relationships with his father and mother. The father was often the more violent or drunken parent, while the mother was the more caring one. This makes for a lack of unity, leading to confusing imagery. It most likely contributed to the explosiveness – passively experienced humiliation needs an outlet – of the Russian national character. We could also hypothesize, however, that in spite of the existence of parental inconsistencies, the family would most likely show a united front to the outside world if threatened. And in spite of all the emotional turmoil in the family and beyond, children also experienced caretakers that loved them (although not necessarily in a systemic way). The family remained a safe haven compared to the dangers of the outside world.

(East): Russians have recognized in themselves this pattern of mood swings. In the 19th century the Russian historian Vassily Kluchevsky tried to give a scientific explanation for it. His theory was that the essentials of Russian national character were formed during the period of the creation of the nation in the 12th to 15th centuries in the area around Moscow and Upper Volga. Russians settled there as a consequence of being driven away by invaders. The conditions under which they lived were very severe however; they had to survive long winters with little light, and very short summers. People had to work very long days for a short period of time to harvest enough supplies for the winter, a time when they didn't have much to do. At the same time that environment was full of wild animals, nomads and bandits. Life was extremely unpredictable. People lived day-to-day. If you made it to the next day, that was happiness. Such conditions do not make for a great future orientation.

(West): This historian seemed to have resorted to a very climate-oriented explanation for national character. Taking climate as a point of departure, we could hypothesize a similar outcome for the Nordic countries of Europe. But they turned out differently. Perhaps an explanation for this difference is that the women played another role in the Scandinavian countries. While the Vikings were 'raping and plundering' on their expeditions, their women stayed at home, running the homesteads. It created a group of very strong, independent women. What I am trying to say is that apart from climatological explanations, there are also developmental processes that contribute to these types of resolutions.

(East): Kluchevsky referred to climate and geographical location to explain mood swings in Russian character, which we can also find in Norway or Finland, countries with similar conditions. The power distance in the family, according to him, was a result of the fact that men were by far the primary providers for the family – not only were women less skilled at hunting or capturing and selling domestic and wild animals, but it was also too hard for women to grow much on the infertile land. It's hard to overestimate the importance of geography in Russian life. As Peter Chaadaev, arguably the brightest Russian mind of the first half of the 19th century, said:

> All our history [is a] product of the nature of the immense land, which we received in our possession. It was [the land that] dispersed us in all directions and scattered us all over the place from the first days of our existence; it instilled in us blind obedience to external forces, to any power which would proclaim itself our master.

(West): Religion must also have played an important role in character formation. The Russian Orthodox religion does not seem to be very action oriented. It is also a rather hierarchical, structured religion. Furthermore, again coming back to the issue of women, in Russia women seem to have very little power within the system. The Protestant church provides much greater equality of the sexes. Also, in the Protestant religions, there is a greater emphasis on activity, on hard work as a way of proving that one will go to heaven. Again, the Russian Orthodox religion doesn't emphasize the value of hard work. But apart from religion, in the context of national character formation, we should not forget the long period of serfdom in Russia that lasted until the 19th century.

(East): The reason why serfdom lasted so long brings us again back to the issue of Russian inertia. When the serfdom was abolished in 1861, many liberated peasants did not want to leave their masters. Many never took the initiative to acquire some land or to start a business. Tragically, many of the peasants starved to death.

The old system gave them stability: landowners had a claim on their lives and time, but also an obligation to look after them. Too often we have one-sided pictures of serfdom as slavery and savagery on the part of the landowners. Terrible incidents did occur, but paternalism had also a positive side. The landowners made the peasants pay taxes and send recruits to the army, but they also looked after their health and education and ensured order. In years of poor harvest, landowners fed their peasants. As in most situations, people differ in the way they treat each other. Some landowners were more benign, others were horrible, but that was the way of life, a social contract between the two parties. For centuries, people lived in this relationship of mutual dependency. We can view this social contract as a model for future organizational relationships. Mutual dependency became a salient feature of Russian national character.

In the peasant–landowner relationship, there was also unpredictable explosiveness. Peasants and household slaves obeyed their masters for decades and, then all of a sudden, would rebel, burn their estates and engage in an orgy of killing. Resentment about specific actions taken by their masters would simmer, and then suddenly boil over. Pushkin's phrase 'Save us God from seeing Russians revolt, senseless and merciless' has been cited many times since he wrote it in 1828. Those revolts were always of a collective nature, with every new member of the gang adding oil to the fire. But as soon as they met any significant resistance most of the rebels would run…back to the master to seek protection, almost always in vain. One famous rebellion leader, Emelian Pugachev, who terrified Russian nobility and even Catherine the Great for two years, was turned in to the authorities by his closest collaborators after the rebels suffered a number of serious defeats. The traitors were executed along with their boss. Peasants' violence was always met with savage repression. As late as 1921 the Bolshevik government sent in its best generals, planes, artillery, tanks and tens of thousand of troops to halt a peasant rebellion in the Tambov region of Central Russia. Hundreds of thousands of people were killed by gas, hanged or sent to Siberia. It's important to remember that this pattern of obedience interrupted by periodic rebellions runs well into the 20th century.

On the other hand, even though landowners and serfs often lived close to each other and had mutual responsibilities, they did not really know and therefore did not understand each other. They represented almost different nations, so different were their ways of life. Nobility had access to the best European education and products of European civilization; they lived European lives; and they even communicated with each other in French. Serfs, to whom the landowners referred as 'Russian people' underlining the serfs' special status as a 'nation' to themselves, continued to live life the same way as their ancestors of the 16th century. As we all know, when you don't understand your followers you cannot effectively lead them, and when two people don't understand each other they begin to fear each other and cannot trust each other. That largely was the case in the serfs–landowners relationship, which later projected onto leader–followers interaction in Russian context.

Another negative consequence of serfdom was the crushing of the entrepreneurial spirit. Because of the master–serf relationship, and this social contract of mutual dependency, it was difficult, and often anti-social, to become an entrepreneur. People were rather passive; they wouldn't take initiative; and they wouldn't take risks. Of course, there were some important exceptions; entrepreneurship did exist in Russia, but as in many other societies its heroes did not come from the mainstream – landowners (nobility) and serfs – the two principle classes of Russian society. In large part, it was the free peasants from the Urals, Siberia, European North, and some Southern areas – territories with little or no serfdom – who engaged in trade, light industry, and later in larger enterprises such as steel mills, iron and coal mines, and oil exploration. As in many other societies, ethnic and religious minorities, such as Jews, Greeks, Tartars, Germans, old ceremony Russian Orthodox, and Protestants, in spite of being heavily repressed, also played a very important role in the development of the Russian economy, setting up and running various service businesses, textile factories, breweries and production plants.

(West): In highly structured situations, people try to find ways to escape structure. They will find paths of improvisation. There will always be a certain amount of entrepreneurship, even in the most structured societies. It may occur under a different name. In Communist society it was seen as a criminal activity.

(East): Yes, a minimal amount of entrepreneurship and improvisation has always been around. Such inventiveness may have influenced national character, as Russians frequently have to deal with unpredictable, seemingly impossible situations. The creativity and visionary skills have always been there, but the ability to produce on a long-term basis and organizational savvy were missing.

(West): In situations of heavy government intervention, the Communist system being a prime example, there will always be many entrepreneurial types looking for loopholes. Their activities are not necessarily visible, but they are present. Such people would keep a very low profile because it was dangerous to have a high profile under the Soviet system.

(East): The Soviet system produced some very talented entrepreneurs, and some of them prosper today in Russia or abroad. Others unfortunately were hampered in their activities or gave up, often with government 'help'. The system was very restrictive and oppressive and exploiting loopholes was life threatening. The possibility that life would end in a gulag was always there. Nevertheless, many people provided professional and other types of services. There was also big money to be made in hard currency trading rings, large scale profiteering in the food, clothing and car manufacturing industries, and even underground factories producing shoes, jewelry and textiles.

(West): But let's talk more about how the more recent past affected people's outlook on things. What was it like to live in the Communist system? For example, what was it like to grow up during the times of Brezhnev, a period that has been characterized as one of complete stagnation?

(East): Communism was a fairly recent phenomenon; the lives of ordinary citizens did not change much. The historical roots of Russia are in a thousand-year-old absolute monarchy in which slavery, serfdom and religious discrimination did not provide the best environment for free expression of the self. Russians have always looked at the environment as something dangerous. Russians are reserved; they don't show much of themselves, at least not to strangers. The assumption is: because you don't know the person, he or she might turn out to be dangerous. Building trust takes quite a long time. Among Russians there exists an attitude of 'shutting up and obeying' to avoid potential trouble. There are good historical reasons for that. Russian czars always had their spies wandering around within different strata of population from the very top to the very bottom. Being referred by them to the authorities for any reason almost automatically meant torture, exile and death. Under Stalin the reporting phenomenon reached its apogee with secret services counting about a quarter of the adult population among their informers.

(West): Coming back to trust, basic trust is the foundation of personal development. It is also the building block for great institutions. Trust makes for constructive dialogue, commitment and accountability. The ability to trust starts with behavior patterns in the family. When there is no basic trust in a child's family, there will be serious impacts on his or her adult behavior. I suspect that in most Russian families, there would be basic trust in the nuclear family, but parents would also caution their children to be careful of a very dangerous external world. These kinds of cautionary remarks must have left their mark. I wonder what years of this kind of exposure does to the mind – having a foreign body in the form of the Communist system superimposed on character development, having 60 or 70 years of such 'brainwashing'.

(**East**): Actually, trust was not only an issue under Communist rule; the Czarist system had very similar problems. Look at the leaders in Russia. Ivan the Terrible killed or forced into exile most of his closest collaborators. Peter the Great complained about having 'only thieves and cowards, who one cannot trust' around him. Stalin eventually became paranoid, making Politburo members spy on each other and from time to time killing some of them.

At the same time every leader searched for trustworthy advisers, people they could rely on. Early Moscow Czars had a so-called Boyarskaya Duma (Chamber of Old Nobility), a powerful body of people from old families exercising significant advisory power. The young Ivan the Terrible and his handful of close confidants ignored that body. Later the Czar outmaneuvered the Duma, making it a living anachronism without any influence. He also got rid of all members of his first inner circle, replacing them with people from less famous families. Peter the Great built his advisory group from his youthful acquaintances, such as Swiss–French Leforte, Scotsman Patrick Gordon, and royal stableman's son Alexander Menshikov. Peter later selected a few Western-educated people as his close advisers. However, he ended up with his second wife Catherine being the only person he trusted. Even handpicked members of the inner circle could hardly be trusted, as the history of 18th century's royal coups d'état demonstrated.

(**West**): This lack of trust must have lingering implications for leadership style and organizational structure. How can you create high performance organizations when trust is such a rare commodity? How can teams function at creative capacity when trust is such an issue? How can leaders really delegate when there is a lack of trust? The first organization we become acquainted with is the family. If the family tells you 'be careful, don't open up too much to the outside', this will have an implication later when you are working in an organization. In the same vein, when talented individuals join organizations in Russia, they do not necessarily develop a deep level of organizational identification, because they do not necessarily trust the course of actions of their leaders and, by extension, their own future in the organization. We'll see an example in one of the case studies in this book, when a leader who invested a lot in an individual employee is terribly upset by the fact that the individual decides to move to a different organization. The leader sees the employee's resignation as a personal treason. In another case study, we'll see how an entrepreneur is reluctant to admit that the friends who helped him start his business have outgrown their usefulness. He has a hard time accepting that he should replace them with professional executives.

THE PSYCHOLOGY OF LEADERSHIP

(East): Given some of the observations we have made about Russian national character, what do you think are effective ways of leading the Russian people?

(West): We can make a comparison between different leadership styles, contrasting the French, the Germans, Anglo Saxons, the people from Nordic countries, and so on. I have found similarities between the Russian leadership style and the kind of leadership found in France, in some African countries and in the Bedouin societies of the Middle East. In Africa people often refer to the leader as the 'Big Man'. Russia can be described as 'democratic centralism'. The original intentions behind this style of leadership are commendable. A leader is a *primus inter pares* among a group of counselors. He considers their advice carefully and then makes decisions. In its pure form, democratic centralism gives a leader, like anybody else, just one vote. Unfortunately, all too quickly, the countervailing power role of the counselors will be undermined as narcissism raises its ugly head, and the leader begins to monopolize power. Power soon becomes perverted. Power is addictive. The more you have, the more you want. What was once democratic centralism – with leaders welcoming input by others – turns into a leadership style with very few checks and balances. On the positive side, it needs to be said that the leader often feels quite responsible for his or her people, as in the case of the master–serf relationship.

Narcissism lies at the heart of leadership. Clinical research on leadership has shown that many leaders possess a strong narcissistic streak. The presence of a solid dose of narcissism is a prerequisite for the attainment of a leadership position. It is a predictor of who will rise to the top of an organization. Narcissism contributes to creativity, assertiveness and the conviction of the righteousness of a person's cause, whatever that cause may be. The narcissistic leader's 'magnificent obsession', or strong conviction that his or her group, organization or country has a special mission, inspires loyalty and group identification. Narcissism, however, can also be seen as a very toxic drug. It is a key ingredient for success, but too much becomes a dangerous overdose.

In referring to narcissism, conceptually we can make a distinction between two forms: constructive and reactive narcissism.[1] Leaders with a more constructive form of narcissistic development were very fortunate when growing up. Age-appropriate frustration (which can be described as well-timed, delayed gratification) by loving caretakers molded them into people with a secure sense of self-esteem, and feelings of inner security. Such people do not experience the need to distort reality as a way of dealing with life's frustrations, nor are they prone to anxiety attacks. These people generate a sense of positive vitality and self-worth. Because leaders with this kind of personal background are characterized by a greater sense of balance, the enterprise is less vital to them for maintaining their mental equilibrium and therefore less susceptible to their whims.

More common, however, is the other sub-group of leaders – the reactive type – individuals who had (for various reasons) a much harder time in dealing with the vicissitudes of growing up. Age-appropriate frustration (influenced by the quality of the interface between infant and caretakers) did not take place smoothly. Given their experiences, their sense of self-esteem is less stable than that of the more constructive narcissistic types, contributing to feelings of insecurity. Such people experience a strong desire to prove to the world that they are worth something. They want to be noticed; they want to build something; they want to leave a legacy. Given their more shaky foundation, many of them never feel truly confident about their self-worth. Fear of failure and fear of success follow them like inseparable shadows: success is frequently accompanied by the fear that it will not last. Although these people may come across as confident and self-assured, appearances can be deceptive. Quite a few of them use excessive control and activity as a way to counteract feelings of low self-esteem and helplessness. By turning the passive into the active, they make an effort to control seemingly uncontrollable events.

In thinking about leadership we need to consider transferential processes. 'Transference' means that no relationship is a new relationship. All relationships are colored by previous relationships. People are inclined to behave toward individuals in the present as they have behaved to other individuals in the past. Often in relationships – as mentioned before – there is confusion regarding time and place. Significantly, because leaders are authority figures they are prime outlets for transferential processes. People have a tendency to idealize their leaders because this makes the people themselves feel more powerful. And in general, leaders encourage this. They like to 'mirror' themselves in the admiration of their followers.

There is a complementarity between the idealizing and mirroring transference. We can explain this by using the analogy of the leader in a hall of mirrors, seeing only what he or she wants to see. Eventually, the leader is surrounded by sycophants and 'liars', people who tell the leader what he or she wants to hear.

This process accentuates the leader's already formidable narcissistic disposition. It also reinforces the attitude that rules are for others, not for the leader. These psychological processes impair healthy decision-making, putting the success of the organization at risk. Personality cults, like those that developed around Lenin and Stalin (and even continue with Putin) are clear indications of these processes.

(East): We can apply this to some of the role models of effective leadership for Russians, for example Alexander Nevsky, Duke of Novgorod in the 13th century. He slaughtered Swedish, Livonian and Lithuanian knights; protected and expanded Novgorod's territory; ensured his personal power by putting down a rebellion of his own family members; and he refused to yield to Catholicism. The fact that he managed to pacify the mighty Tartars by spending long months at the Khan's headquarters and becoming the latter's vassal is of less interest to people listening to his story. Peter the Great remains in Russian collective memory as the most effective leader the country ever had – visionary, assertive, decisive and combative, and at the same protective and sensitive to rank-and-file people. He is remembered as the man who created the most modern army and navy of his era; who conquered important Baltic shores; humiliated Swedish king Carl XII; and destroyed the old ruling class of Boyars; and who put some commoners into important government jobs. Peter's brutality and the enormous human cost of his reforms are accepted as the ransom of glory. And whether you like it or not, Josef Stalin is still admired by a large part of the population. He is seen as somebody who did get a lot of things done. Clearly, there is a trend here. The Russian 20th century poet Maximilian Voloshin called Peter the Great 'the first Russian Bolshevik'. I think calling Stalin a guardian of a centuries-old leadership tradition is, ironically, more appropriate.

This explains why true democratic centralism has never really existed in Russia. For example, Alexander Nevsky had a number of senior counselors. He selected them himself, and fired them when he felt they became too powerful. (Ivan the Terrible preferred killing to firing). He never gave anybody a chance to question his leadership. Peter the Great was never an advocate for true democratic centralism. He also preferred the more perverted form. Any questioning of his regime was put down with extreme brutality. In the aftermath of the second Streltsy revolt (the Streltsy were Royal guards), Peter personally cut off a few dozen heads, quite a remarkable feat for a 27-year-old. He also imprisoned and tortured his only son Alexey, who had tried to run away from his dominating father, and then Peter gave the order to kill him. Peter was known to repeat, 'His Majesty [referring to himself] is a sovereign ruler, who is not responsible to anybody in the world'.

Democratic centralism was, of course, the official organizational model of the Bolshevik and later the Communist Party. Supposedly, it did work in the early days; there are records of both Lenin and Stalin becoming quite disturbed a number of times, when decisions they advocated were voted down. Clearly, this form of leadership didn't last. Stalin refined the darker side of democratic centralism. When he was officially accepted as the head of the Party, he switched to more traditional Russian politics – blackmail, power games and even murder. Under him, democratic centralism became pure tokenism, form without any substance. He ruled as an absolute dictator.

After Stalin's death, however, members of the Politburo tried to return to collective decision making at their level to make sure they wouldn't end up with another dictator. When Khruschev became too authoritarian he was peacefully voted down according to democratic procedures. This tendency, however, brought about the Brezhnev phenomenon – a passive leader without vision or passion, absolutely sterile and therefore relatively harmless to his aging entourage. Collective Politburo eldership degenerated into an authoritarian miasma. Democratic centralism failed to produce anything but decay.

(West): Continuing with the history of Russian leaders, it seems that the Yeltsin period will not be considered by history as a time the country progressed very much, except maybe in its last year. Gorbachev was arguably very important to the country because he had the courage to look at the Communist system and admit something was not right (although many Russians did not agree). He made an attempt to reform the Communist system from the inside. However, as he discovered, the dry rot had gone too far. The Russians blamed him for letting a great country fall apart, although many believe this was inevitable, given the distressing state of Russian society.

Change agents are frequently labeled as scapegoats. In many instances, if you want to engage in a dramatic change process, a scapegoat can be quite useful. He or she is like the whistleblower, signaling danger. As we all know, these doomsday forecasters do not win popularity contests. Such proposals for change raise the hackles of the people in entrenched power positions. And they 'kill' the change agent by removing him or her from power. Surprisingly enough, after this ritual 'sacrifice', people seem to be more prepared to consider whatever changes are needed.

(East): We can also look at Gorbachev's story a different way. When he took the top job, he still had a relatively fresh mind, and could recognize some underlying trends with the help of people who understood the numbers. He acknowledged that the economy was in awful shape. Having assessed the state of affairs, he came up with the idea of *uskorenie* or acceleration, to boost the Soviet economy. He also realized that something needed to be done about the Soviet Union's image in the world and its relationship with other countries. That's how the idea of *glasnost* or openness was born. To change the system, however, was not something he intended. He wanted only to tinker with the system that he had inherited. He tried to reform the Communist system from within. He wanted to make it more honorable. But did he get a surprise!

Looking back, it could be argued that his major problem as a leader was that he didn't have an overall vision. He had no idea where he wanted to go. And to quote a well-known saying, 'If you don't know where you are going, you may end up somewhere else'. This kind of outlook is very typical – you try to keep all good things of the existing system and you try to get rid of all the bad things. You want to improve the system without changing its fundamentals. It didn't work that way for Russia, however.

(West): Despite what Russians may think of him, Gorbachev is still somewhat of a culture hero in the West. To us, he seemed to have the vision of trying to reform a totally stagnant system. He lowered the risk of nuclear war. He transformed what Ronald Reagan called the 'evil empire'. The surprise was that when the genie was taken out of the bottle, the process spun out of control, and he found himself without a country.

(East): A caveat is required here. He was not as selfless as some people perceive him. I heard that in his last, six-hour meeting with Yeltsin, when the Soviet Union was collapsing around him, they talked about the country for ten minutes. The rest of the time was devoted to Gorbachev's retirement package.

But he never abused power the way other Russian leaders did, he always sought advice, and often waited for consensus to be built before moving on. He clearly did not have the courage of Peter the Great or Yeltsin, which would have allowed him to turn the helm 180 degrees in one instant. Other Russian change leaders undertaking huge change programs didn't want to waste their time being subjected to any participative form of government.

(West): True enough, in situations of creating a turnaround situation, absolute power helps. Things may get done much more quickly. It is either lead, follow or get out of the way, otherwise you will be run over. But, given human nature, the risk is quite high that power becomes perverted. To prevent excess, we usually need some form of checks and balances.

(East): In Russia, these checks and balances have rarely been in place. Even today Russian society remains very much an authoritarian society.

(West): Russian society is not just of an authoritarian nature. Isn't it better to describe it as a combination of authoritarian and patriarchal?

(East): That brings us to another point: If you look at the people considered to be great leaders in Russia, you see that they all looked after their followers (at least that is the perception), each in their own way. They were 'fathers' of the nation, making people proud to live in a great country. The people were prepared to make huge sacrifices for their leaders and that country. Rank-and-file people always wanted to associate with somebody who was strong. Even intellectuals who were skeptical about any political system were usually sympathetic towards the person at the top. The person in charge was considered as a near saint – even if he stole the throne or the General Secretary's job. People around him might be incapable and corrupt, but Number One could do no wrong. Both the conservative Lomonosov and the progressive Pushkin compared Peter the Great to God, and Stalin was routinely referred to as 'Father of the people'.

(West): It is interesting to note this 'splitting' phenomenon, humankind's tendency to divide the world into saints and sinners. One person will be deified; the other will be viewed as the devil. For the reason of group cohesion, we need scapegoats. Leaders may claim that they had nothing to do with whatever vicious action is undertaken; therefore others are to blame. Of course the leader was the designer of the process. But he was smart enough to have someone else do the dirty work, and he avoids the wrath of the people.

When leaders resort to 'splitting', dividing the world into enemies and friends, the world becomes quite dangerous. A continuous search for enemies is needed to neutralize discontent with the leader himself. And when enemies cannot be found outside their borders, despots will begin to eat their own. It is their way of keeping the momentum going. They will do anything to stay in power. Any form of questioning of their rule will be met with great brutality. They will terrorize their own people. New victims have to be found to subdue the population.

(East): The last point you made concerning leadership is important for Russia. The brutality of Russian leaders, the callousness with which they treated their people is remarkable. Respect for human life has never been high in Russia. Unfortunately, you don't need to go far to find examples. The Chechen war provides plenty of them, including the way the dramatic Moscow theater hostage crisis of October 2002 was resolved. In war, Russian commanders were rarely concerned with their soldiers' lives; just compare the Russian casualties with the Nazis' during World War II, or to the French casualties during Napoleon's Russian campaign of 1812. Or take peacetime examples: the construction of the St Petersburg to Moscow railroad in the mid-19th century cost 100000 lives; the Moscow–White Sea channel took 500000 lives in 1932–1935. The result has always been much more important than the process. The individuals did not count; they were disposable. In stark contrast, leaders were put on a pedestal.

We have always had our personality cults; Stalin did not invent this. He was only one person in a long line of terrifying predecessors.

(West): Speaking of personality cults, we don't see statues of Stalin, but Lenin is still very much present.

(East): They demolished all Stalin's statues after the Twentieth Congress of the Communist Party, where Khrushchev called him a man who established a personality cult. Lenin escaped such an accusation. He was always portrayed not only as an organizational genius, founder of the Communist Party, but also as great theorist at the level of Marx. We know better now. He certainly had a darker side. Now nobody talks about Lenin any longer, his writings are forgotten; his deeds are no longer known. Ironically, the ghost of Stalin is still very much alive. He is seen as somebody who could get things done. He is still a hero and role model for a segment of the population.

Looking at the country's history, Stalin's style of leadership worked quite well for some time. From the 1920s through the 1940s there was a period of great transformation and some remarkable achievements: the creation of a universal education and health-care system, industrialization, fast growth of urban population, and a dramatic increase in life expectancy. It was a period of great projects and great excitement. People were proud of what they were doing and proud of their own contributions. They were part of a great transformation. They did not know the real cost, nor did they want to know it. Then came a period when the population began to realize that whatever they did, it wouldn't make any difference. Individuals were totally insignificant in the greater scheme of things. Whether you were productive or lazy, it didn't really matter because the outcome for you would still be the same. People began to lose their idealism. (And the gulag system didn't help as a morale builder.) You can't run full-steam for 30 years on excitement only. But by the time that the Russians figured this out, Stalin was dead.

(West): This continuing personality cult, this persistent admiration of Stalin, is quite ironic. Most Russians must have lost family members in a gulag somewhere. I don't think many people in Germany would consider Hitler as an ideal type. So why does this idealization of Stalin persist? Why hasn't there been more discussion about the gulag system? Why hasn't there been more soul-searching about what happened? If people don't acknowledge and mourn past tragedies, the atrocities that took place could happen again. To make the gulag system work, there must have been numerous collaborators. In spite of all the atrocities committed by Stalin and his henchmen, he is still idealized by some people. Perhaps this is a response to a basic need for a symbolic, strong father/mother figure, a person who will make everything right, who will provide 'containment' to deal with the enormous amount of persecutory and depressive anxiety among the population during these very difficult years. It must have to do with a common human characteristic to repress the bad news and only remember the good news, to look at life as '*la vie en rose*', seeing it through rose-colored glasses.

(East): Stalin's continuing popularity is due to the fact that he epitomizes some of the features of an ideal Russian leader: he was decisive; he always seemed to know what he was talking about and what he was doing; he was authoritarian, but he was portrayed as somebody who cared for his people. Furthermore, he got things done; he changed the country; he brought Russia back from the ruins to the position of world superpower. That's what counts. The means never were important.

Stalin offered a very simple psychological contract to the people: 'I tell you where to go and I tell you how to go there. I will take care of you. You don't have to do any thinking. Just follow the rules. If you take one step off the road I spell out for you, however, you will be removed.' I hate to say it but it was an effective leadership style at that time. In the early 20th century, the Soviet Union had a very uneducated population, and masses of people were moving from the countryside to the cities, from the national republics to the industrial center. The country was in the middle of gigantic developmental projects. The situation required a concentrated and well-orchestrated effort, and firm direction.

Stalin's fans tend to be older people and those, to put it kindly, with a limited capacity for intellectual analysis, since his brutality, cowardice and paranoia are obvious. But in spite of all his deficiencies, there are a large number of people in Russia (apart from the previously mentioned group) who would argue that Stalin had many of the attributes of effective leadership.

One of the most admired leaders in Russia is Marshal Georgy Zhukov. He was the number one strategist for Stalin during World War II. His subsequent political career was less brilliant. After the war, his extraordinary popularity apparently caused him to be regarded as a potential threat by Stalin, who assigned him to a series of relatively obscure regional commands. (He was too popular to be executed.) Exiled by Stalin to head the Urals military region, he later became Soviet Minister of Defense under Khrushchev.

Zhukov is best remembered for producing many victories for the Soviet army in the Second World War, and for his iron will to win. He organized the defense of Moscow, in late 1941 through early 1942, when German armies were rolling over Russian territory. Soviet troops managed to stop the enemy troops just at the gates of the city, then later to drive them back 250–300 kilometers. Zhukov won that battle by ordering soldiers to die rather than retreat one step. He made sure his orders were filled by executing those who retreated, and bringing fresh troops to the front every day. There was enormous heroism on the part of the soldiers, but the cost of that victory was 2.2 million lives on the Soviet side and 700 000 dead on the German side, even though the Germans were on the offensive for most of the time.

Zhukov had first come to Russians' notice in 1938 when he defeated a Japanese infantry division with a frontal tank attack. The Soviets lost half of their men and two thirds of their equipment. Zhukov is credited with a number of similar victories, including the recapturing of Kiev in the autumn of 1943, under orders from Stalin who wanted the city to be in Russian hands by November 7th, the anniversary of the Bolshevik Revolution. Zhukov's frontal assault across the icy Dnepr cost the lives of half a million Soviet troops. A very similar situation can be seen in the invasion of Germany at the end of the war in 1945. Stalin and Zhukov wanted to capture Berlin before the Allies could do so, and many Russian soldiers died there as well. The legend says that Zhukov liked the Russian proverb equivalent of 'You cannot make an omelet without breaking eggs'. He was certainly in the business of breaking eggs!

(West): We've met quite a few Russian business leaders with the same attitude; the Zhukov leadership style seems to be alive and well in Russia. Some Russian leaders have told me that they pay a few of their people to think, and the rest had better execute orders. Given, however, what we know about best practices in Western organizations, we can argue that such a leadership style doesn't get the best out of people. It is not the way to use their people's creative potential. People will not make an extra effort, but behave more mechanically. It is the ghost of Frederick Taylor, with his Scientific Management, revived. But in a knowledge society that favors organizations with a highly trained workforce, it is essential to tap people's creative potential.

(East): You have a good point there. In Russia we still have to discover what kind of leadership style will be most suitable for us, given all the changes taking place in society.

LEADERSHIP DEVELOPMENT

(West): Now let me change the topic somewhat. Let's steer our conversation to leadership development. In a more behavioral sense, psychologists sometimes make a distinction between two kinds of people: people who are more internally directed, and the ones who are more externally directed. The first group of people believes that they can make a difference – they can control their environment with their actions. The second group doesn't share this feeling. They believe that there are many forces over which they have no control. They see themselves only as peons in a greater scheme of things. They feel they have very little influence on the environment. Such differences in attitude color the way these two groups function in organizations.

This kind of *Weltanschauung* starts early. Parents, and later teachers, are the ones who cultivate such outlooks. In America you find children's books like *The Little Engine that Could*, promoting a strong belief in self-efficacy. The books of Dr Seuss are also good examples. From my experience studying people in organizations, 'internals' tend to be more proactive, innovative and entrepreneurial. In addition, cultures can be more internally or externally oriented. For example, America has a Horatio Alger attitude to life. There is admiration for the successful businessperson, for the self-made man. There is a continuous search for the businessperson, the person who gets things done, to set up as a culture hero. There is the belief that, if a person set his or her mind to it, everything is possible.

In contrast, it appears that in Russia there is much more of an external outlook. People tend to be much more fatalistic (particularly in comparison to the Americans) about what they can do. There exists less of a feeling of self-efficacy. Moreover, the businessperson is everything but a culture hero. In the Soviet days he was considered almost a criminal. Many still see him or her as somewhat of a crook. To change that outlook, new role models have to be introduced. In Russia, until recently, a truly entrepreneurial environment has been non-existent. People have not been very adventurous; they have been risk averse. In organizations, there has been too much of a blame culture. People are often afraid of making mistakes. And as we all know, people who don't make any mistakes are not doing anything. We should not overlook, however, the experiments with capitalism undertaken by some of the Communist youth organizations in the early 1990s. They apparently played an important role as 'venture capital' and incubator organizations.

(East): You are correct in saying that the organizational environment in Russia until very recently has not promoted entrepreneurial attitudes, and has not encouraged the development of independent thought or action. The structure of most organizations was completely hierarchical. There were too many constraints: all the decisions were taken at the top; people had very little autonomy even when it came to implementing leaders' decisions. Everybody was supposed to obey orders. There were very few developmental opportunities, the possible exception being a career within the Communist Party.

The Party had its own approach to development of future leaders. It was based on the assumption that any system needs a few very capable people at the top and armies of followers, each trained in a specific skill, at the bottom. For example, Lenin was a fan of Frederick Taylor's Scientific Management. Therefore the Party selected and developed leaders of different 'sizes' – creating super-loyal and hard-working 'robots' for lower-skilled jobs; Marxist intellectual apparatchiks with multidisciplinary work experience for district and regional level jobs; and very capable bureaucrats with a broad knowledge and experience base for key political and industrial positions. The problem with this well-designed, large-scale centrally managed system was that succession planning and development was a very difficult exercise.

Also, we have to come back to the question of trust. Relationships take time to develop. In establishing work relationships, loyalty becomes the overriding factor, not competence. Soviet and post-Soviet leaders are known for keeping a group of close associates for decades, moving them from one job to another; Khrushchev had his 'Komsomol' group, Brezhnev his 'Dnepropetrovsk' group, Putin the 'Leningrad' and 'KGB' group. And in fact we see similar loyalty to some of the business leaders described in our book.

In the Soviet era, leadership development and selection of potential leaders started at the level of the Communist youth organizations. These organizations, which had 60 million members, had two functions: to control the younger population and to spot talent. The Young Pioneers organization took care of children from 10 to 14. Komsomol (Young Communists' League) enrolled people from age 14 to 28. Many of today's business leaders came from these organizations.

These organizations, particularly Komsomol, offered young people early leadership responsibility. Some of the tasks could be quite challenging for leaders without formal power – to get the other members to provide free labor on a Saturday; organize aid to elderly people; or improve the success rate at university exams. Komsomol was also in charge of so-called student construction detachments (or SSO in Russian), which served as a real training ground for sharpening leadership skills. SSO provided students with summer jobs, primarily in construction, and their commanders were responsible for everything from business results (which determined participants' pay) to safety and food for the group.

These young leaders were really stretched in the best management development tradition. When they were first tapped for leadership positions, they were scared; they didn't really know how to make things happen. It was the best learning experience they could ask for. It should be noted that the most successful leaders of such student groups managed not only to motivate people to work, but also achieved pretty remarkable personal financial results, although this side of the summer student construction 'detachments' remained low profile.

If you look at today's Russian business leaders, many of them have had leadership experience in these youth organizations. They were undoubtedly an important incubator for many of our present leaders.

(West): How were these young leaders selected?

(East): The exact selection criteria are still something of a secret. But the people in charge were basically looking for three things: loyalty to the Communist Party, since it was the cornerstone of the regime; intelligence; and the ability to work hard and get things done. I don't think they looked for visionary or charismatic leaders. After all, the vision was already there, developed by Lenin and adjusted by later leaders.

(West): Was selection completely based on merit or were there other practices involved?

(East): From the start in the 1920s, the idea was to select and promote the best and brightest, but *only* people from specific social strata. For a person with a so-called proletarian background (from an industrial worker's family, for example) all doors would open. Children of poor peasants had the second-best opportunities. People from noble families didn't have a chance. Subsequently, all formal distinctions disappeared, and selection became more merit-based. As the Communist system was maturing, especially during the decay of Brezhnev's era, family background became important again. This time it was the other way around: if you were from the family of the nomenclature then you had much better chances. The nomenclature was a sort of pool of high-ranking officials and people of high potential from which all the top positions were filled.

There were a number of prestigious institutions of higher education, similar to the French system of *Grandes Écoles*. The quality of education was much higher at those prestigious institutions, since they had the best faculties and best equipment available and took only the brightest students. That was in theory, however, in practice, to get in you not only needed an exam certificate, you also needed to have connections. Theoretically, of course, every candidate was equal, but there were so-called 'lists' of preferred candidates determined by their parents' connections.

(West): What was the career trajectory for a young person with the right contacts?

(East): A young university graduate could start as an 'instructor', the lowest level managerial job, at the district Komsomol organization. He (or she) would stay there for two to three years. Then he might be moved to the Communist Party district organization for a relatively low position, or to a city Komsomol organization for another three to five years. From then on, there were a number of career paths. One possible career trajectory would be to go to into industry. Another possibility would be to go back to the Communist Party school for two to three years of ideological training, orientation in world politics, and soft skills development. Subsequently, he might return to his original organization, and continue to climb the ladder there. Individuals could also be asked to move geographically. After graduation, they could be sent to a remote location to prove themselves as a Communist leader.

(West): To be sent to 'Siberia' is probably the wrong term in Russia, but what could go wrong in their careers to derail their progress?

(East): Primarily, being exposed to scandal, which meant not showing enough loyalty to the party, getting publicly drunk, or having some serious problems in the area of one's responsibility. An example would be a big fire where a large number of people got killed, or similar large-scale work-related accidents. Another career killer would be having a dissident among the people under your responsibility who gave an interview to Radio Liberty. Another reason could be not fulfilling the Plan (GOSPLAN quotas) or not completing an important project on time.

(West): It seems that in many instances the five-year plan was a very 'academic' exercise in manipulating data. The plan was not really 'lived'.

(East): You know the line: we pretend to work and they pretend to pay us. Some parts of the five-year plan could have great impact, however. Let's say a new manufacturing plant was to be built in the region you were in charge of. If the plant was not completed on time, your head would be on the line, because it was a highly visible project. But if the whole region did not fulfill its quota of delivering 10000 liters of milk, nobody cared. So being in charge of a high visibility project within the framework of the five-year plan or the one-year plan could have an impact on a person's career.

One's personal moral stand could also be important. If your wife told members of the Central Committee that you had a mistress on the side, it was very likely that you would end up in a new job, often in remote location. With the old wife, by the way. There existed a number of unwritten but well-known rules.

In general, the culture of the Soviet society as a whole and its specific organizational environment were not particularly supportive and encouraging for leadership development. The Communist Party was sort of an exception, but even the development of leaders within the party had more to do with loyalty, technical skills, and connections than with leadership competencies. As time passed, the Communist Party became increasingly bureaucratic. Selection and promotion were increasingly based on personal connections and personal background.

(West): In many global companies, remuneration of executives is based not only on financial returns, but also on the number of new leaders they have delivered to the organization. What can you say about present-day leadership development in Russian business organizations? Is there a serious effort made for succession planning? Or is it more a system *à la Louis XV*, 'Après nous, le déluge!' As you know quite well, organizations that make a serious effort at succession planning do much better than organizations that don't. Great companies have leadership development as a core competency. They are also more likely to survive in turbulent times.

(East): Let's look at the history of succession at the top of Russian society – one can hardly find happy cases. The absolute majority of incoming leaders were not trained or prepared for the job; they even did not know they would get a job. Leaders such as Nevsky, Ivan the Terrible, Peter the Great and Stalin left a mess after their death. The only Russian monarch who devoted a significant amount of time to developing a successor was Catherine the Great, a former German princess without a drop of Russian blood. Skeptical about her son's ability to rule the country, she made a great effort to develop her grandson, the future emperor Alexander I, for the top job.

The situation is not very different these days. To illustrate, I know a successful entrepreneur from the Urals who is 50-plus and who laughed when I asked him about succession planning. He thinks he is going to be around for the next 20 years. He is not interested in developing a capable successor for himself. Of course, we can provide some cultural explanations. As we have discussed earlier, the Russian culture is hierarchical. People who like power don't like to have crown princes around. It can be risky. There are too many historical examples of betrayal. Alexander Nevsky had a bad experience. The same is true for Ivan the Terrible and Peter the Great.

Furthermore, people in Russia are very past and present oriented. They don't think much about what is going to happen after they are no longer running their organization. Actually, some of them openly say that it's irrelevant for them. In addition, most Russian business leaders are very young; not only in terms of their actual age, but in terms of the amount of time they've been in the driver's seat. As is also the case with Western entrepreneurs, in this early phase of their careers, they don't recognize the importance of leadership development yet.

In a few of the larger Russian companies, one can find some elements of leadership development programs – human resource managers, assessment centers and training programs. All too often, however, they may be doing certain things because it looks good. Consultants from the West tell them that these actions will improve their image; possibly raising their market capitalization. But it is not something the leader really believes in yet. However, the day will soon come, I believe, when the top guys start thinking about bringing in younger people to give them a hand.

THE ROLE OF THE LEADER

(West): Effective leaders play two roles – a charismatic role and an architectural role. In the charismatic role, leaders envision a future for their organization and empower and energize their subordinates. By taking on the charismatic role, they try to get the best out of their people. These leaders have an action orientation, and are able to drive the process. After all, vision without action is merely an hallucination. In the architectural role, leaders address issues pertaining to organizational design, and control and reward systems. Here we need to keep in mind that the architectural role refers to the implementation by the leader of structures and policies that allow him or her to carry out the envisioning, empowering, and energizing responsibilities of leadership. I have suggested that effective leadership cannot exist unless both roles are present. Neither role, in the absence of the other, is sufficient (though one role is often less dominant than the other, depending on the situation). These two roles have to be aligned.

Leaders need to take on different responsibilities. Apart from providing strategic direction, allocating financial resources, and monitoring the key indicators that provide information about the performance of their organization, they also need to provide containment for their people. They need to speak to their followers' collective imagination, to create a group identity. Leaders need to take on much more of a coaching role, a cheerleader role, and a storyteller role, particularly with knowledge workers. Leaders need to be visible; they need to walk around. They also have to encourage strategic innovation, to stimulate the creative process in their organizations. Furthermore, they need to be concerned about the transfer of knowledge to various parts of the organization, to make the company boundaryless.

Moreover, I have seen that many effective leaders possess specific personality traits and competencies such as assertiveness, action orientation, conscientiousness, emotional intelligence, adventurousness and extroversion. Their upbringing, as we discussed before, will have an influence on the development of these traits and competencies. Leaders need to figure out what they are good at. They also need to identify their weaknesses. They need to build on their strengths and compensate for their weaknesses. Here the concept of the executive role constellation becomes relevant. The challenge for leaders is to surround themselves with people who can serve a complementary role.

Now, how do Russian executives fulfill these various roles, functions and competencies?

(East): We have already spoken about another very important leadership role: the developmental responsibility. Spectacular evolution in business leaders' mental models has taken place over the last ten years. Let's look at one prominent Russian business leader, now in his late thirties, and follow the evolution of his business model. His vision of creating wealth for himself remained unchanged; however in the late 1980s he knew that to achieve his goal he needed to buy and sell goods with a mark-up, pocketing a profit after every deal. In the early 1990s he realized that controlling (not necessarily owning) an enterprise was a much better proposition – one can take cash from it and later move on to another one. In the mid-1990s, he sought privatized assets with export potential to create stable cash flows. By the beginning of the new century he realized that long-term wealth creation is based on sustainable performance and business transparency for investors. He then started to build a highly professional management team, launched a 'transparency improvement campaign', recruited foreign experts to his board and made himself a public figure.

At the first stage, leaders paid very little attention to processes such as energizing or empowering subordinates. The assumption was that since everybody was hungry, everyone was happy just to make a living. To single people out, to give some individuals special attention, to be concerned about motivation, would be a waste of time. The assumption was that everyone was motivated as there were very few better paying jobs to go around.

As the scale of their businesses increased, smart entrepreneurs began to realize that they could not do it all by themselves, that they needed the help of others. They needed an organization to get things done. At that stage it was usually a small organization, made up of a group of trusted people. With regard to this small organization and its members, entrepreneurs would take on a charismatic role. Entrepreneurs did empower their followers by giving some areas of responsibility, and energized them by gain sharing as well as praise of common cause. As far as the architectural role is concerned, until a few years ago Russian businessmen did not put much thought into the process of designing and creating organizations and they didn't pay much attention to systems. They love to draw organigrams and shove people from one box into another, but they didn't see this as a very important leadership function. Times have changed, however, and now we see very serious efforts to create effective organizations.

(West): Many entrepreneurial organizations got their start with a leader and his or her 'band of brothers' – the inner circle – making it happen. But people grow at different speeds. At a later point in time, some members of the inner circle can become a hindrance. They are unable to grow with the organization. They were able to function in a small entrepreneurial organization but are unable to help bring it to the next stage. This inability makes it difficult for a company to grow. The problem, particularly for Russians, is finding a way to develop, or separate from, these people.

(East): As a matter of fact, some of these people didn't really even have the talents required for a very small entrepreneurial organization. They just became members of this inner circle because the entrepreneur was desperate for help. The entrepreneur was looking for support from people he could trust. Take for example, the Russian founder of VimpelCom, a cellular communication company (one of the case studies in this book). When he started, he brought people from his old research institute along with him, people from his inner circle. Later many of these people became a huge burden for him and the organization. But he was reluctant to get rid of them. He knew they were incompetent, but still he would not do anything about it. At the time, I even suggested creating a special organization for them and placing them all there. In the West that would be called a 'turkey farm'. But that idea didn't fly. He was unwilling to take that step. Also, it was doubtful those people would fall for it. The prestige of the job and being close to the boss was too important to them. In fact, as we'll see in the cases later on in this book, some leaders have decided to follow the path of a 'turkey farm' creation: they set up 'special projects' units or give their inner-circle members some meaningless jobs with important titles. The real issue is to make sure that people in the 'special projects' groups cannot interfere with the key processes in the organization. The evil of paying these people for doing nothing may be smaller than that of allowing them to have any influence on organizational life.

Managing the Organizational Culture

(West): The CEO can be considered the 'high priest' of the organization. An important role of this high priest is to manage the corporate culture, to ensure the corporate identity and values. In the West, people have understood the importance of corporate culture, particularly in the context of mergers and acquisitions (M & As). They discovered that financial and strategic synergies are not enough to create a high performance organization. Over time, people came to realize that if no attention were paid to corporate culture, many, if not most, of these M & As would go sour. What added to this interest in corporate culture was that people found out that companies with strong corporate cultures tended to perform better and would last longer. So here is another challenge for leaders. They need to ask, 'Do we have the right organizational culture to create a great corporation? What makes our corporate culture so special?'

Let me tell you an anecdote. A few months ago I had dinner with the president of a large Finnish organization who had been buying companies in many countries. He now wanted to find out the best way of integrating these various companies – how to create a common culture. What values should the people in his organization adhere to? Surprisingly, one of the values he found important was humility – a rare value in many organizations. Rightly so, he viewed this value as an antidote to organizational arrogance, a factor that often plays a role in the decline of organizations. His plan was to be very systematic about the way he was going to manage corporate culture.

The point is, because *how* things are done says as much about meaning as *what* things are done, leaders need to develop a strong sense of shared values. Leaders need to institute collective systems of meaning. They need to create a sense of purpose for their people. They need to create a sense of self-determination among their employees. For the sake of organizational mental health, it's essential that employees have a feeling that they have some control over their lives. They need to see themselves not as mere peons in a larger scheme of things, but as actors who can make choices. Leaders need to create the perception among their employees that each person can make a difference. That is what empowerment is all about. They need to foster also a sense of competence among all employees, so that organizational participants have a feeling of personal growth and development. Continuous learning is essential: only when a person's exploratory desire finds an outlet can their creativity blossom. Given these observations, I wonder to what extent Russian business leaders pay attention to these elements of corporate culture?

(**East**): We can see three stages in Russia's business history with respect to corporate culture. Stage one: people are not really aware of such a thing. Of course, a corporate culture exists, but they do not pay attention to it. Stage two: they have heard of the importance of corporate culture, but they pay only lip service to it. A business leader may appoint some people in human resources to develop a list of internal values, but they never really pay attention to it. It is not being lived. At the third stage, leaders begin to understand corporate culture as something that can make or break the business. But that realization may only come when they have been involved in the mergers and acquisitions game.

Designing Organizations

(**West**): In Western societies we have gone from the three Cs: the command, control, compartmentalization paradigm (3Cs) to the three Ps paradigm: people, purpose, processes (3Ps), or the three Is: ideas, information and interaction (3Is). The world is changing, particularly due to the impact of technology. The impact of technology on the world of work is very noticeable. Organizations have become much more dependent on networks. The traditional hierarchical model is increasingly becoming a thing of the past. New organizational forms are emerging. Some can be described as the amoeba-form organizations, where parts continually split off. Another form would be the 'chemical soup' form of organization where new permutations and combinations occur on a constant basis. What can you say about organizational forms in Russia?

(East): Both of your metaphors could describe Russian organizations created by new business leaders, who have no pietism for 'organization' itself, considering it to be just one among many tools to manage their business. They easily buy and sell assets and companies, transform them from one legal entity into another, and move people between functions and locations. However, these types of organizations have a strong Russian flavor – to expand on your description we could say that the leader-chef stirs the 'soup' him/herself, or that the 'amoeba' receives commands from the leader's nervous system. Whether in behemoths like LukOil and Gazprom, or flat and fast-moving companies like MDM and Troika Dialog (a company we will describe in depth later), the leaders stand out. Without them, nothing will happen.

The number of organizations (or parts of organizations) built using the 3Cs paradigm is quite high and probably growing. There are some good reasons for that, primarily cultural and historical. For example, when IKEA put into operation its plant in Tikhvin, in the north-west of Russia, they set the conveyor belt at a speed that was about 50 per cent slower than a similar facility in Poland. Their intention was to bring the Russian factory's speed, and production, up to the same level as the Polish factory over time. Three days after the factory opened, the Russian workers' delegation approached management asking them to slow down the belt in exchange for lower wages, which are at around $100 per month. This anecdote illustrates that the Russian labor force needs strict procedures, thorough controls and discipline to improve its productivity, and must develop different work ethics to be able to go to the next step and work in 3Is-type organizations.

Another reason for the continuing proliferation of the 3Cs system is more worrisome – the unwillingness or inability of middle and even many senior management to embrace newer paradigms. When we ask Russian managers to draw the image that comes to mind when they hear the word 'organization', more than two thirds of them draw a pyramid. For them organization is still a power hierarchy, dominating its members. They know how to command and control; they feel a need to receive commands and to be controlled, and that is the essence of management for them. They are incapable of turning the pyramid on its head, making it start with the customer, with the CEO at the bottom.

Another way to illustrate different organizational forms in today's Russia is by drawing a very simple matrix. One axis on the matrix would represent a leader's social orientation toward the importance of followers and the other one toward the importance of results. Taking this matrix as a point of departure, the low results, low people orientation would be the typical Russian organization before perestroika. The Soviet ministries of the last days of the USSR can be taken as prime examples. They could be called 'oppressive sadomasochistic organizations'. At the other side of the matrix we can find organizations where people have some freedom and opportunities to make decisions, and organizations that are also result driven.

And we have two more quadrants. Troika Dialog (described later in the book) is an example. Results are a top priority, but are not all-important. The primary focus in that organization is to look after its staff. The implicit message is 'we are members of a family'. There is also another result/people oriented-type organization, but focused on results of a more short-term nature. Leaders who I call *pakhan* (Russian slang for the criminal leader or head of a gang) run these organizations. They are concerned about the other 'gang members', but this concern is secondary, because short-term results dominate their leadership agenda. They have no long-term vision for the company nor long-term commitment to people. Companies that represent intermediate forms take the other positions in the matrix.

(West): A striking feature is the 'family' nature of these different types of organizations. What you point out is the strong psychological contract between leaders and their people. As a matter of fact, the better companies to work for in the West have similar features. In these companies there is a sense of direction. These companies are entrepreneurial. To stimulate entrepreneurship, small units characterize their organizational design. Such organizations are 'flat'. People feel that they have 'voice', meaning that they can make a difference. People are held accountable. These companies are fast. They provide a certain amount of security. Fair process characterizes these companies, making for feelings of trust. They are very transparent, minimizing secrecy. By designing companies in such a way, their leadership hopes to get the best out of their people.

(East): The problem is that to create this type of organization you need a special type of workforce. If you took the Russian proletariat of the beginning of the 20th century and you put them in this kind of organization, they would be lost in its more fluid environments. They need to be told what to do. They need structure; they need direction, otherwise, they will become too anxious. Unfortunately, a significant portion of the present Russian labor force has similar traits, and that is why the 3Cs approach still has legitimacy.

You need a fairly sophisticated workforce in organizations you described. The leadership necessary to develop such employees does exist in Russia, but usually it is limited to professional service organizations, or start-ups employing younger people with advanced professional skills and no burden of large company experience.

(West): All companies have a set of values that employees are expected to adhere to. The best companies to work for have a number of meta-values which can be summarized as *enjoyment*, meaning people have a sense of pleasure in what they are doing; *community*, being part of a group; and finally, *meaning*, the feeling that the work they are doing makes sense. People work for money but they will die for a cause. Of course, meaning can be easier to define if you work for the Red Cross than if you are the employee of a tobacco company.

(East): Little thought is given to these questions in Russia at the present time. Russian leaders, with some exceptions, don't think much about 'meaning' for their people. They have more of an industrial engineering outlook to managing people. Working in an organization is seen rather as a simple exchange relationship: you give me your labor, and I give you a salary. I may create some limited career development opportunities for you. It is a little bit like the first Henry Ford with his $5 day. As has been said, the ghost of Fredrick Taylor, the father of scientific management with his mechanistic way of looking at human behavior, is still haunting most Russian organizations. Nevertheless, there are new types of organizations where sense-making seems to be the major driving force for both owners and employees. Thus, one of the organizations described later in the book is trying to make a breakthrough in the perception of the quality of Russian-made goods, both in Russia and abroad, while another organization is offering its employees a vision related to helping Russian industry become more competitive in the world market.

Some new leaders are beginning to realize that people *show up* at the factory or office to earn money, but they actually *work* for other reasons. Two 33-year-old founders of a number-one Russian parquet company have realized after ten years of hard work and struggle for survival that they need to provide something more to their employees than competitive pay and hot food at the cafeteria. They are trying to fire them up with an image of a winning team that shares gains with its members, their families, and those in need. These young entrepreneurs redesigned their organization: delegating significant powers to the senior management; hiring a communication consultant to send the message down the ranks; and sponsoring Russian museums and orphanages. Whether this approach will be more productive than the *pakhans'* leadership style remains to be seen.

CREATING EFFECTIVE ENTREPRENEURIAL ORGANIZATIONS

(West): What about the future of entrepreneurship in Russia? After all, the prevalence of entrepreneurship is the lifeblood of any society. For the good of the development of a country, entrepreneurs need to become the new role models. Is the government taking any measures to foster entrepreneurship? Is venture capital easily available? Are there ways of helping new entrepreneurs by means of tax breaks? Are incubator areas created? In many of the more entrepreneurial countries we can also observe an enormous interchange between the universities and business. Is something like that taking place in Russia?

(East): Some people have doubts about the extent to which the Russian government really understands the importance of entrepreneurship. President Putin rarely praises entrepreneurs or encourages small business development. Perhaps we should see it as a good sign that the present government is only ignoring it, not stifling it, given low government efficiency in general, and in Russia especially.

A powerful organization that to some extent promotes entrepreneurship in the country is the Russian Union of Entrepreneurs and Industrialists, controlled today by the oligarchs. They have very strong lobbying power and have been of some help in steering the government in a more positive direction: income tax has been slashed to a flat rate of 13 per cent, the number of corporate taxes reduced, and the registration of small businesses simplified. However, the centuries-old bureaucratic machine is still in place and makes every entrepreneur's life very difficult.

And, of course, there is a cultural issue of the slow change in the generally negative attitude toward private business and wealth creation – the ultimate objective of every entrepreneur. One can hardly overestimate the importance of new role models for this process of cultural change.

(West): Education can change attitudes. Unfortunately, there is often a total disconnection between what is taught at universities and what business requires. Some countries, like India, in an effort to deal with this problem, have even created elite institutions to educate people who will take a business leadership position. In creating greater awareness for entrepreneurship, however, business schools can play an important role.

(East): In the late 1980s, business schools mushroomed in Russia. Unfortunately, most of them are not yet well developed, having no, or very limited, links with real business. Low salaries discourage talented young people from becoming business school professors, therefore making by default a core faculty of academics with no experience of the market economy. Russian business schools have a long way to go to become institutions capable of developing entrepreneurs or independently-minded managers.

Times are changing, however. Some of the better schools in Moscow have created entrepreneurship departments. Big business leaders who until very recently were small entrepreneurs encourage this development, and some of them even teach classes there. Recently we've witnessed the case of an oil magnate attempting to become the rector (head) of a university. Clearly the business schools need this ideological support, as well as financial resources, to become more effective in training future business people.

Fortunately, coming back to your comment about the significance of role models, entrepreneurs in Russia have become more visible, something that was not the case a few years ago. Many young people want to set up their own businesses. They also recognize the importance of acquiring the skills for doing so.

Of course, what businesses can also do is to create consortiums where companies pool their resources to build programs to develop the entrepreneurial disposition of the people in large organizations – to be *intra*preneurial. It is essential to get away from the hierarchical structures. What are needed are flatter, more organic structures.

To create intrapreneurship it is necessary to have an organizational climate where there is a 'healthy disrespect' for the boss. People should develop the attitude that it is better to ask forgiveness than to ask permission. True empowerment implies having a real dialogue between superiors and subordinates. The challenge is to tell people *what* needs to be done, and then give them the opportunity to figure out *how* to do it. They need to be less risk averse while still remaining accountable. At the same time, they need to be team players. Of course, in a country that is still quite xenophobic and rather secretive, to create this kind of transparency and openness is going to be a tough challenge.

(West): Furthermore, to stimulate entrepreneurship in Russia, we should also not forget the many talented Russians who went abroad to study and are returning. They could become agents of change. They could help create different kinds of organizations.

(East): Repatriation of these kinds of people is not always easy. These returning Russians are, however, beginning to play an important role. Russian organizations have to compete for this returning talent. Those Russians who were educated abroad are coming back with high expectations, not only in terms of compensation packages, but also with respect to opportunities to carry out meaningful work that will constantly contribute to the development of their skills and knowledge, as well as their personal value in the labor market. Since international borders are more open nowadays, including for Russians, these individuals are in a position to select among various employers, and various countries for their residence.

Initially, Russians with Western education and experience were looking for positions in multinational companies operating in the Russian market. What became a good niche for them was the replacement of costly expatriates, a trend clearly noticeable in the Russian labor market after the 1998 financial crisis. Gradually, Russian organizations started to realize the need for Russian executives in their managerial ranks with a very different mind-set. Naturally, with their arrival, lots of things are beginning to change in the way businesses operate in Russia.

Another point to mention here is that certain xenophobic elements are still sometimes noticeable in the attitude of Russian organizations in terms of employing Russians returning from the West. Not long ago, *Vedomosti*, an influential business daily, published an article about foreigners of Russian descent coming to work in Russia. In an interview the head of the Russian operations of a large international business software company openly said that when hiring new managers, he sends to the dustbin all résumés of foreigners of Russian descent, and very reluctantly looks at the résumés of Russians working in the non-Russian offices of his own company! Still, most other companies consider international experience and education to be a helpful, if not obligatory, element in the development of leaders.

As mentioned before, we should, however, not underestimate the cultural dependency of the Russian population. Dependency and the concept of avoiding responsibility remain lingering patterns that can act as blockages. Such attitudes need to be reversed. Leaders can be helpful by rewarding people who demonstrate independence of action, people who show initiative. These people need to be singled out and made known to the rest of organization. Russian organizations need to create new role models by promoting employees who have the courage to take responsibility. To create such a mind-set also necessitates a considerable measure of self-restraint on the part of leaders, who must avoid putting their people in dependency situations.

(West): That brings us to a topic that is presently quite popular in the West: the idea of mentoring and coaching. Both superiors and subordinates need to be encouraged to find new ways of doing things. They have to recognize their strengths and weaknesses. They need to be made aware of their blind spots. In Western Europe and North America we spend a lot of time on these issues, having developed 360-degree feedback instruments to help executives discover which leadership competencies need further development. Working with a coach has become very popular; some people even suggest that it even has become a status symbol. Also, in the context of coaching for change, I think it is important that the new Russian business elite make an effort to develop much more of a future orientation.

(East): It's possible that many Russian top executives today have a latent sense of insecurity. They may feel that they don't have the right education, specifically an MBA from a respected university. On the other hand, they're in a hurry, ever conscious of the opportunity costs of time away from the office, so they are reluctant to take even short-term executive courses. However, there is a growing awareness that the 'all-powerful CEO' does not exist. Their own 'rough edges' need to be modified if they are to be successful. The compromise now is that some Russian CEOs work with Western consultants, for example, McKinsey, and more recently, with Russian consultants, who indirectly serve as mentors and executive coaches. Some are taking executive programs that include a section on coaching. In any case, Russian executives are increasingly aware of their need to educate themselves, and as younger, more Western-oriented executives move up through the ranks, we will see significant change in this area.

To answer your second observation about future orientation, the notion of stock market presence and capital gains is helping to encourage this. Many Russian business leaders have realized that merely going for quick gains is not good enough. They would get much more value out of the business if they looked at it on a longer-term basis. Here the concept of shareholder value has come into the picture. People who couldn't change their business models and couldn't learn new things have just disappeared. People whose mental models and business models evolved have become very successful.

CORPORATE GOVERNANCE

(West): We haven't talked about corporate governance. In each company there are issues of selecting, supervising and monitoring the top executive team. This topic may also be very appropriate in Russia, given the tendency towards autocratic leadership and the habit of many leaders to surround themselves with yea-sayers.

(East): Presently, there is a growing interest in corporate governance in Russia, partially fueled by the recent accounting scandals in the United States. There is a growing conviction among Russian businesspeople that transparent corporate governance is the factor that will make companies more valuable and sustainable.

(West): Corporate governance is so important because human behavior often has a darker side. The danger of democratic centralism as a leadership style is that the leader is surrounded by sycophants. This can very quickly lead to a self-destructive spiral. It can turn into caricature-like entrepreneurial situation in which the entrepreneur wants to have total control and becomes a micro-manager. As a result the person loses the sense of the big picture of the enterprise. The enterprise cannot grow because of such behavior. This type of entrepreneur is the opposite of someone like Richard Branson of Virgin, who could be called a 'Renaissance' entrepreneur because he possesses the ability to delegate.

(East): There is a story about two hunters in Russia who hire a small bush plane to go hunting bear. The pilot reminds them that the plane can carry only two passengers and one bear. After a week the pilot returns to pick them up and finds the hunters not with one but with two bears. The pilot protests, saying that he cannot put the second bear carcass on board. It will overload the plane. The plane will not be able to take off. The hunters protest, 'That's the same story you told us last year. But after giving you a hundred dollars, you let us take the extra bear aboard. Here are a hundred dollars'. After take-off the plane crashes. Although somewhat bruised, the pilot and hunters survive the crash. After the hunters pull themselves together, they ask the pilot, 'Where are we?' He replies, 'The same place we crashed last year'. This is a pessimistic story. But sometimes working in Russian organizations is like going one step forward to go two steps backward. Fortunately we are seeing signs of change.

(West): Many people in the West think business in Russia has a darker side, the Mafia and corruption. The added costs of doing business in countries of high corruption can be enormous. And when it has become ingrained, it is very difficult to get rid of it. What has been happening recently in the West – creative accounting scandals as represented by Tyco, Enron and WorldCom – is indicative.

(East): A real concern is that people may take a corrupt government official as a role model. For a well-functioning society, you need clean government. Granted, some form of corruption is always going to be there. The challenge, however, is to minimize it. Count Bobrinsky, a Russian sugar baron of the 19th century, once called a bribe 'our [Russian] Magna Carta'. The situation has not improved since those times. According to an independent survey in 2001, bribes in Russia totaled $62 billion, which is an enormous amount of money for a country with an official GDP of $260 billion. In Russia even some federal ministers own businesses that present a complete conflict of interest. It will be difficult to wean many of them away from their side income, however. What is worrisome is that some businessmen view corruption as a normal practice. They even budget for it, instead of fighting it.

(West): Perhaps, like in America in the times of the robber barons at the end of the 19th century, we see similar patterns in a Russia that is only now experimenting with the capitalist system. Hopefully, it is just a transitional stage. Hopefully, Russia will not make similar mistakes as in the West but learn from experience. Furthermore, the resilience of the Russian people is impressive. Obviously, certain regions have been in the forefront, particularly the Moscow area. But the 'small wins' that we can see in the form of healthy, successful business ventures are very encouraging. These small wins will be the examples that many entrepreneurial individuals will try to emulate. And these entrepreneurs will be the ones to build a new society. To quote Peter Drucker, 'Elephants have a hard time adapting. Cockroaches outlive everything'. Entrepreneurs are the ones who find new ways of doing things; they know what creative adaptation is all about. After all, we should not march backwards into the future. To the best of my knowledge, there are very few rich pessimists!

NOTE

1. Kets de Vries, M.F.R., (2003), *Leaders, Fools and Impostors*, New York: iUniverse; Kets de Vries, M.F.R., (2001), *The Leadership Mystique*, London: Financial Times Prentice Hall.

PART TWO

Case studies and commentaries

3. The Bolshevik evolution

In designing our research strategy for this book, we decided that the best way to show the incredibly rapid pace and scope of the transformation in Russian business leadership would be to write a series of case studies. The massive and unprecedented transfer of equity from the Soviet State to private owners in 1992–1996 was lauded by some and bitterly criticized by others. What cannot be disputed is that this was the ground zero for the development of Russian capitalism. Therefore, with this case we begin at the beginning, by following and analysing the implications of this privatization process first hand, within one company.

In 1999, we contacted Jacques Ioffé, the General Director of the Bolshevik Biscuit Factory, who agreed to let us interview him and visit his factory several times. Bolshevik was one of the first ex-Soviet factories to be privatized, and one of the first to be acquired by a Western corporation. When we met him, Ioffé had been at the head of Bolshevik for two years. Over the four years that we studied Bolshevik, we saw an archetypical Soviet factory, formerly run by a 'Red' director according to the dictates of a planned central economy, transformed into a subsidiary of a global organization, although it should be noted, not a fully integrated subsidiary.

We have tried to identify the factors that led to the success of this transformation. Was it due to the relative benevolence and long-term strategy of the acquiring French corporation? Could it be the bi-cultural affinities of the General Director, who is Russian but lived for many years in France, working for French corporations, before returning to Russia? Could it have something to do with the way he was able to dismantle the old paternalistic Soviet organizational system? Should we credit the ingenuity of the employees themselves, who were able to produce top quality products with little money and ancient equipment? We think that it is undoubtedly all of the above.

ROSTROPOVICH AND THE BISCUIT FACTORY

The world-famous cello virtuoso Mstislav Rostropovich, who emigrated from Russia many years ago, has always remained deeply passionate about the political and economic fate of his homeland. As dramatic changes began to take place early in the 1990s, Rostropovich saw opportunities to play a part in the reconstruction of Russia. With many of the world's most powerful people among his friends, Rostropovich did what he could to encourage foreign investments in his country. Finding himself at an event with Antoine Riboud, the French Chairman and CEO of Danone, Rostropovich sensed that he had found a sympathetic listener.

Several years before that conversation, as the collapse of the Soviet empire in 1989 opened up a whole new market in Eastern Europe, Danone had sent teams to the former Communist bloc countries to explore the possibility of moving into the area. Danone first focused on selling in Eastern Europe the goods (produced in Western Europe) with which the Danone name was most strongly associated: dairy products, sweet biscuits (cookies) and mineral waters. In 1990 Danone increased its expansion into Eastern European markets by signing joint venture deals with dairies in Poland, the Czech Republic and East Germany, so that at least a few Danone items would be produced locally. In 1993, Danone extended its activity in the region through deals with dairies in Hungary, Russia and Bulgaria.

During his chance meeting with Rostropovich in 1994, Riboud was swayed by the musician's conviction that Russian markets were ready for more serious Western investment. Riboud was already aware that the time had come for Danone to move more aggressively into former Communist bloc countries. He hesitated, however, arguing that he did not know enough about Russian investment opportunities and targets to commit Danone any further in a region whose political climate was still uncertain. Furthermore, there was not much foreign presence in Russia at that time. Even many of the multinationals that had chosen to do business there restricted their involvement to a wait-and-see position. While a few multinationals had formed joint ventures with factories in Russia (Nestlé, PepsiCo, Procter & Gamble), many preferred greenfield start-ups (Coca-Cola, Mars, Cadbury/Schweppes, Wrigley) as a way to avoid the excessive complexities associated with brownfield investments. In general, foreign *investment* was welcomed in Russia, but foreign *control* was not, because the wary attitude towards outsiders that had been cultivated in the former USSR was still strong.

Addressing Riboud's concerns in his typically straightforward way, Rostropovich sent a short letter to another of his friends, Anatoly Chubais, head of the State Property Committee. Rostropovich told Chubais, who had masterminded Russia's mass privatization program, that Danone was looking for an appropriate investment target. The response soon came: Chubais proposed that Danone acquire Bolshevik, a large and well-established Moscow producer of sweet biscuits and cakes. Bolshevik had first been privatized in 1992, as a part of an early wave of privatization in Russia. In September 1994, Danone took control of Bolshevik.

Riboud was pleased with this decision. Though he was realistic about the situation in Russia, Bolshevik had definite synergies with Danone, and he felt that it could become a solid partner in Danone's ongoing process of globalization.

THE DANONE GROUP

The Danone Group is itself the result of the merging of several European companies. The first, Boussois-Souchon-Neuvesel (BSN), was founded in Lyon (France) in 1967 and produced glass bottles. In the early 1970s, BSN foresaw that glass bottles would eventually lose their monopoly in the beverage industry to plastic, cardboard and metal containers. Anticipating this market change, BSN decided to make the *contents* for their containers as well. This strategy eventually led BSN to take a closer look at Gervais-Danone. Charles Gervais, inventor of Petit Suisse soft cheese, founded Gervais in the mid-19th century. Later, a man named Isaac Carasso started a company near Barcelona in 1919 to produce yogurt. He was so proud of his product that he named it Danone, after his son Daniel. The two companies joined forces in 1967 to form Gervais-Danone. BSN and Gervais-Danone merged in 1973. The company that was formed by these mergers was renamed the Danone Group in 1994.

Though in the early 1970s Danone had focused on the French and European markets, today it is a truly global organization with established presence in 150 countries. Danone is the world's number-one producer of dairy products and sweet biscuits, and the second-largest producer of bottled water.

Danone had three strategic priorities in the mid-1990s: to refocus on the three core businesses in which it was already the leader in world markets, to expand international presence and to enhance profitability and shareholder value. Putting these priorities into action, at the beginning of the 1990s Danone decided to capitalize on its experience and expertise in France and other Western European markets by moving into rapidly emerging markets in Asia, Eastern Europe and Latin America. Implantation in these areas would give Danone a more broadly based international presence and a strong foundation for the Group's continued growth.

Concerning the pace and extent of Danone's international expansion, Franck Riboud (the CEO of Danone and the son of Antoine Riboud) stated in 1998: 'We will be [moving into new countries and making the most of market potential] without losing sight of our fundamental values, which stress the quality and nutritional value of our products, attentiveness to consumers and Danone's longstanding dual commitment to business success and social progress.'[1]

THE BOLSHEVIK BISCUIT FACTORY

Although two French entrepreneurs had founded the Bolshevik biscuit factory in 1855, at the time it was acquired in 1994 its similarity to Danone ended there. A true product of its era, it had been deeply marked by the social context in which it had long operated, beginning with the name Bolshevik, of which employees were very proud.

In 1903, the Russian Communist Party Congress held a principle vote on the course of its future. The majority supported Lenin's plan, which among other measures proclaimed armed revolt and the seizing of power through revolution. One outcome of this vote was that the Communist Party broke into factions, with Lenin's followers labeled *Bolsheviks*, from the Russian word *bol'shinstvo*, which means 'majority'. Russians had a tradition of naming enterprises after party leaders, political events, or revolutionary heroes. The large Moscow biscuit factory was given the name Bolshevik by Lenin himself, a name that it has retained despite changes in prevailing political winds. Although at the time of the acquisition Danone management felt 'uncomfortable' having such an anti-capitalistic brand name, market research showed that Bolshevik brand awareness was about 99 per cent in Moscow. Marketing considerations won over ideological 'inconvenience', and the Bolshevik name was kept.

Bolshevik was the largest biscuit producer in Russia. The factory was owned by the founding French entrepreneurs until the Revolution of 1917, when it was nationalized. During the following decades it became the leading Soviet producer of sweet biscuits, wafers and cakes, and was awarded the Order of Lenin in the 1980s – the highest award for an enterprise granted by the Soviet State – as a sign of recognition of an enterprise's superior performance and its contribution to the development of the Socialist economy.

When Bolshevik was privatized as part of the program launched by the pro-reform Russian government in the early 1990s, the majority of the stock went to the factory employees and management. Later, a controlling block of shares was acquired by a large Moscow bank for eventual sale to a strategic partner.

Located on six hectares in the center of Moscow, just a 15-minute drive from the Kremlin, Bolshevik was scrutinized by many watchdogs (party authorities, sanitary-epidemic commissioners, city administrators, and so on). The ability to 'please' the various controlling organizations was vital to Bolshevik's prosperity, and the continued provision of various social benefits distributed by these powerful entities. As a result, networking and currying favor were an important part of top managers' professional responsibilities, and managers' credibility depended to a large extent on these connections. In spite of the dubious ethics of influence peddling, *blat* – meaning influence, connections, the ability to pull strings – was the only way to get things done, given Russia's bureaupathology.

Production facilities were divided between a number of small, poorly designed buildings. Improvement of the production process, including modernization, was hampered by the awkward layout of the buildings. However, given its location in the center of Moscow, there was no way to expand the existing site, meaning that reorganizing the production line would have been difficult, and constructing additional facilities impossible. Therefore, not only was production capacity not maximized, but Bolshevik also had trouble stocking finished products. One major question hanging over employees and managers alike was whether or not the production site should be, or would be, moved to another location outside of Moscow.

Given the climate of paranoia and control in the USSR, Bolshevik's former general directors had always tried to concentrate as much power as possible in their own hands. Even in 1994, while the formal organizational chart showed a second-level management layer, in reality about 45 managers reported straight to the general director.

The general director at the time Danone acquired Bolshevik was a self-made boss, a typical 'red' director. He had spent most of his life at the factory and started his career from the position of a mechanic at one of the factory workshops. His physical appearance and behavior were intimidating: he was a noisy, corpulent man with a large tattoo on his wrist and a thick gold chain around his neck. While his manners left much to be desired, he knew the business and was a master at controlling relationships with subordinates. Although he was not required to run Bolshevik according to Soviet-era quotas – the 1992 privatization had freed him from that constraint – his typically Soviet distrust of his subordinates influenced his management style of vigilant supervision, intimidation and power hoarding.

Problems at Bolshevik were discussed at lengthy meetings with broad and often unspecified agendas, attended by all top and middle managers. Discussions frequently became overly emotional and often broke down into quarrels. Outcomes and decisions never had much weight or permanence in any case, because the director was almost solely responsible for critical decisions and could intervene directly in any area of the enterprise's activities, bypassing responsible managers. Any minor decision by subordinates, on the other hand, required his approval, whether purchasing raw materials, dispatching finished products, vacations or hiring and firing; even permission to open the factory gates. The general director had two close allies, and this 'trinity' represented the informal center of power in full control of all of Bolshevik's activities (unofficial as well as official).

Most of the managers working under the director had spent their entire career at Bolshevik, and their average age was around fifty. As at most Soviet enterprises, the management team consisted of people with very different levels of talents and capabilities. There were some technically knowledgeable specialists and some natural-born wheeler-dealers whose talents lay in maintaining relationships with the company's business partners. There were some honest and hard-working people, but also a significant number of corrupt freeloaders. There were also many mediocre managers who seemed to be there by default.

Despite this fossilized and anachronistic organizational structure, the factory stayed out of the red in the early 1990s. Bolshevik had good production volumes and whatever was produced was immediately sold. Production management was a nightmare, however, as there was an acute deficit of raw materials. Nevertheless, the company stayed fully operational even during the most severe economic periods in the early 1990s, by calling in favors from powerful connections and by making the most of the purchasing department's 'creative' tackling of the materials shortage problem. As economic reforms continued and prices were deregulated in 1992–93, however, demand slowed, competition intensified and imported products flooded the market. Sales plunged as a result. Bolshevik's managers were confronted with a crisis they certainly were not prepared for. For almost a century, Bolshevik's only concern had been to produce a required number of biscuits; no one had given a thought to sales. Now their world was turned upside down.

It was at this point that two events so significant that many people saw them as a stroke of destiny occurred simultaneously: the Moscow bank that owned Bolshevik's controlling block of shares demanded that management find a strategic partner within six months, and cellist Rostropovich sent his inquiry to the Russian government about investment opportunities for Danone. Before long, the acquisition was completed, and new masters arrived at Bolshevik.

DANONE IN LENINLAND

The first two years following Danone's acquisition of Bolshevik were difficult. The incumbent Russian managers, most of whom had been at Bolshevik since the 1960s, had little idea of how to operate in a market environment and clung to outdated practices: a ponderous organizational structure, inadequate reporting, ineffective decision-making procedures, poor discipline and serious overstaffing. The French expatriate managers sent by Danone made early attempts to gain the Russians' cooperation, but the new initiatives they introduced were met with fierce resistance. The French team realized that they had to tread carefully. The situation was delicate and extremely complex; furthermore, their power to intervene decisively was formally limited by the acquisition contract for the first five years. The French managers had consultant status only, with no right to implement their own recommendations. In any case, the Russian managers were not interested in the French managers' recommendations; they were more comfortable with the devil they knew. In short, although the Russians could see that the situation was becoming critical, they were not only unable, but also unwilling, to implement new business practices.

In 1996, Danone sent French consultants to carry out an official 'diagnosis' of Bolshevik to find ways of dealing with what was proving to be a difficult transformation process. The first step in the process was to clarify the reason Danone had acquired Bolshevik:

> Danone chose to produce cookies, cakes and biscuits in Russia, rather than simply sell Danone products made in other countries. Danone intends to develop new products that are suited to the Russian culture and market, to modernize the production process and to transform the organization and its management. Danone recognizes that this is a long-term investment, driven by the desire to be present in a newly emerging market of over 200 million people. Danone is committed to supporting the transformation of Bolshevik.[2]

The resulting report characterized Bolshevik as a company with 'tension at the top layers, and worry at the bottom'. It was essential to identify and understand the reasons for these tensions and worries if the transformation process was to proceed successfully. Employees, in particular, the workers, didn't seem to be fully engaged in the change process. They were still concerned about how Danone's takeover would affect their lives. They were worried by many problems that the Russian top management had not dealt with. Employees' salaries were low considering the cost of living in Moscow. They were extremely preoccupied by the idea that diminishing sales in a weak economy could result in layoffs, something that had been unheard of for several generations in Russia. They were disturbed by the fact that, although some changes had been made, working conditions had not significantly improved thus far under Danone's management. The Russian managers, in particular, were fairly critical of the Danone Group. Some felt that Danone appeared to have bought Bolshevik only to ignore it.

It was clear from Danone's diagnostic report that both Russian management and Russian workers had counted on Danone to solve Bolshevik's problems quickly. Just how helpful Danone had been, when it came to the bottom line, was not so clear: the turnover for 1995 was either a profit of 42 million French francs, as calculated by the Russians, or a loss of 15 million French francs, according to Danone's accountants.

The Danone team who studied Bolshevik were favorably impressed by one thing, though: despite the fact that it was unusual in Russia for top management to ask for employees' opinions and suggestions, employees did seem willing to cooperate. The hostility of the top Russian managers didn't seem to have affected the workers at the bottom level of the company. They saw the Westernization process as being in their best interest and they seemed more willing to trust the consultants and expatriate managers and less inclined to hide data and practices from them than their managers.

Over the course of the next few weeks of the diagnosis process, it became clear that the structure of the old Soviet system of planned economy still influenced the way Bolshevik operated. The French consultants aptly identified this as '*la permanence du passé*' (the permanence of the past) and saw it as a force to be reckoned with. The economy had tightened and sales had decreased, but the process at Bolshevik still focused on production capacity rather than on market factors such as customers' demands and tastes. In fact, Bolshevik considered its 'clients' to be the wholesalers; 90 per cent of biscuits were sold directly to wholesalers who came to buy them at the factory. Thus Bolshevik had no way of measuring customer satisfaction. The situation was summarized in the words '*Le client arrive avec ses idées et repart avec nos produits*' (The client arrives with his ideas and leaves with our products).

Another factor at work in the Moscow Danone plant was also deeply rooted in Russian, and later Soviet, tradition: a paternalistic and authoritarian management style. Similar to the French system (from which it was partially derived before the Revolution), the management structure was tightly hierarchical, with a closely controlled flow of information. The leader was seen to be, by virtue of his position, all-powerful and always right. This was true at Bolshevik, certainly; only a few people had a global view of the company and the way it functioned, and power was concentrated in their hands. The managers of the various departments were there only to carry out orders. Information systems were not always able to measure and report performance accurately; there were few computers. In addition, there was very little official communication or cooperation between departments or divisions. It was a typically bureaucratic system of decision/execution/control, dominated by authoritarian leadership, with employees managed by a system of rewards and sanctions.

On the other hand, this structure also favored the development of covert coalitions or agreements between managers of different departments. The company (as a hangover from its days as an extension of the state) also functioned as a social network and safety net, with close ties among members of the same hierarchical layer.

As a result of the lessons of its history, Bolshevik management had little concern for, or awareness of, strategies that were central to Danone: increased knowledge of the market and customers; evaluation and improvement of the company's relationship with wholesalers; modernization of the production lines; high-quality products; more efficient production; and last, but certainly not least, engagement of the employees in the change process.

This last point was in fact a critical one in Danone's evaluation of Bolshevik in 1996. It was clear that innovations were essential in production, products, marketing and diversification. But it was equally clear that these innovations would not occur if employees were not behind them. It was important to understand, then, how anticipated changes would affect working conditions. That question led to an even more important one posed by the report: '*A quelles conditions les salariés de l'entreprise Bolshevik peuvent-ils être moteurs dans l'evolution de leur entreprise?*' (What are the conditions under which Bolshevik employees can become a driving force in the transformation of their company?).

The Danone team had been impressed by several factors that they felt would influence the transformation process positively. The first was the strong capability of Bolshevik's workers to keep outdated and decrepit machinery running, and to make a fairly standard product despite fluctuations in the quality of the raw materials. One French expatriate remarked that workers in France would not be able to make biscuits or cakes under such conditions. They were also able to start up new production lines very quickly. Second, despite the official rigidity of the hierarchy, employees seemed to establish creative networks where necessary to meet quotas and ensure production. Third, hidden behind the excessive 'Taylorization' of the factory was a great deal of underexploited potential. (Ideas for new projects – for example, a better carton for certain biscuits – had been proposed and then dropped without follow-through. Some of the Russian workers remarked that, although they were capable of realizing these projects, the French expatriate managers seemed to be unable to let the Russians take the lead.) Finally, though many of the workers and management at Bolshevik had strong criticisms of Danone and the existing organization at Bolshevik, others had a more positive attitude, and voiced great expectations for future investments, organization and working conditions.

Antoine Riboud decided that the time had come to put a new director at the head of Bolshevik. The challenge that faced the new director was laid out in the report: transformation from a strategy dictated by a central planned economy to one that was demand driven and market oriented would require not only a reorganization of Bolshevik's production lines and systems, but also an important corporate cultural transformation. The result would be a radically different vision of Bolshevik's customers, improved relations between services and suppliers and a new understanding of the company's responsibilities for its employees' welfare.

This transformation process would have to be specifically designed to work in the cultural and economic context at Bolshevik. Riboud knew that Danone could not proceed as if this were a factory in France, despite the fact that, as the report pointed out, Bolshevik was similar in many ways to Danone biscuit factories around the world as far as infrastructure and production techniques were concerned. (A biscuit by any other name is still a biscuit, after all). Yet, due to cultural and historical differences between the French expatriates and the Russians, cultural stereotypes prevailed and assumptions were made by both parties that made the transformation attempt difficult. One of the Danone team members said:

> The reorganization of Bolshevik will result in a redistribution of power, a new definition of role, and a change in the system of management which Bolshevik employees were accustomed to. The transformation process will have to concurrently, on the one hand, quickly implement necessary changes and, on the other, preserve certain aspects of corporate culture that serve as a foundation for Bolshevik's identity and dynamism.

Though modernizing the factory was a top priority, the transformation process would be considered a longer-term project, adapting the pace of the evolution as much as possible to the capacity of employees to change their culturally-derived habits, expectations and mentality. Because employees' adaptability and motivation would be key to the evolution of Bolshevik, the challenge for management was twofold: all employees would have to understand and accept the objectives for Bolshevik's transformation, and there would have to be a mutual 'learning process' between the Russian managers and the expatriate French managers from Danone. Part of the learning process would clearly need to be a mutual comprehension of the historical and national cultural influences on behavior and management practices, in order that these differences should not result in misunderstandings that would slow progress. The situation was described by one person in even more dramatic terms: if Danone succeeded in turning the factory around, it would be seen as a victory for the West; if not, it would be seen as a victory for Russian conservatives.

Riboud wanted to see Bolshevik evolve and align its management to Danone's international standards, but he knew that it would be a process unlike any other in which Danone had previously been involved. Given the challenges and concerns pointed out in the diagnosis of Bolshevik, Danone's corporate values would be put to the test. How literally should the vision statement 'The success of our [Danone Group's] strategy will largely depend on the expertise, enthusiasm and personal commitment of our staff members' be applied to Bolshevik? If those words were to have any relevance at all to the Russian firm, the new director, before seriously implementing structural and organizational changes in the different departments, would have to bring about a sea-change in employees' attitudes and habits.

Easier said than done, of course. A multitude of questions loomed for Danone: how should the new director develop management resources, encourage employee involvement and debate, enforce commitment to Danone's professional standards and promote good citizenship (the four key Danone priorities)? Should Bolshevik be transformed with a GE's Jack Welch-style short, sharp shock, or would it be better to proceed slowly? And, finally, the most important question of all: what was the right profile of the new leader for Bolshevik? An insider or someone new? A Russian or a French expatriate? The choice was critical, but it would have to be made quickly.

JACQUES IOFFÉ

The name of the new general director was soon announced. The man selected looked good to all the constituents involved. He was Russian, and he had lived and worked for many years in France. It was also exactly the right career move for the man himself.

For Jakov Evgenievich Ioffé, a Russian émigré who had lived in France since 1977, Danone's offer to become the new General Director of the Bolshevik biscuit factory came at the right time. Ioffé was General Director of Hatier, a large French publishing house, where he had been responsible for a large-scale restructuring project. The success of the project, which resulted in healthy profits, had allowed the family owners to sell the company at a good price. At that point, Ioffé had decided that he was ready for a new challenge. Moving back to Russia to lead the transformation of a French-owned company had not been a part of his original plan, but after thinking it over he realized that he was uniquely qualified for the job. In the 20 years that he had lived in France, Ioffé had accumulated extensive managerial experience working at the top position in several large French companies. He was 49 years old and had reached the peak of his career.

Jakov Ioffé was born and raised in Leningrad (St Petersburg). His parents were workers at one of the Leningrad factories and he was an only child. Jakov's upbringing was typical of a good Soviet family. The boy attended public school, and he wore the red tie and sang the patriotic songs of the Pioneer Youth organization, of which he was a proud member.[3]

Ioffé's belief in the ultimate superiority and fairness of the Soviet system and his enthusiasm for Communist anthems were seriously challenged early on, however. In 1956, at the historic 20th Communist Party Congress, Khrushchev delivered a speech unmasking the many crimes that the Bolsheviks, led by Stalin, had committed. For young Jakov, the Communist Party and Comrade Stalin were sacred and this denunciation of holy symbols was a shock that made it harder to believe Khrushchev's assurances that, despite the terror and repression of the previous years, Communism was still the path to ultimate happiness. By the time the Soviet Union moved tanks into Prague in 1968, Jakov Ioffé had very few illusions about the true nature of the Communist regime.

By the end of the 1970s, under pressure from international human rights organizations, the Jewish community and forward-thinking dissidents from the Russian intelligentsia, Brezhnev's regime began to allow some emigration. Ioffé, who was 30 at this time, was eager to leave. He had been under surveillance for some time and knew what this portended. When the KGB let it be known that if he wanted to complete his doctoral studies, he would have to commit himself to future 'cooperation' with them, he realized that his options in the Soviet Union were narrowing still further. (He had already earned an engineering degree from one of Russia's best technical institutes.) For Ioffé, the only solution was to leave the Soviet Union. He explained: 'I was not a political opponent of the regime; I just could not stand it. If I had had stronger emotional ties to this country, I would have protested, but as it was, I was rather internationally minded.'

Emigration at that time was a definitive step. Communist authorities considered emigration high treason and treated emigrants accordingly. Those who left, left forever, with little hope of coming back to visit friends or even parents. (Soviet authorities did not allow Ioffé to return when his mother died, though in the late 1980s he got permission to visit his sick father, who died several days after his son's arrival.)

In 1977 Ioffé emigrated and settled down in France. Soon, though, he found that he could not get a decent job, because his new country did not recognize his diploma and qualifications. He took an exam to earn the French equivalent, but a professor who examined him advised him to change course and apply to a postgraduate degree program. Ioffé said: 'He knew some of my professors in the Soviet Union by name; they were world-famous. He assured me that my problem was not a lack of knowledge; my problem was that I didn't have the right piece of paper.'

His decision to enter INSEAD – one of the world's leading MBA schools, located in Fontainebleau, France (and now with a campus in Singapore) – came not because he wanted to study business administration but because it offered a postgraduate degree requiring just one year of study. And so, having lived in a capitalist country for only a year, barely able to speak English or French, he soon found himself, as the first Russian student at INSEAD, studying with members of the Rothschild and Swedish royal families, working on subjects that had little in common with the precise scientific approach he was used to. Ioffé had only a very vague idea of how an open market economy worked at that time. He said:

> I found it strange....After each marketing class I felt bewildered from asking 'Why?' over and over without getting a clear answer. We were talking about different companies competing for market share for their trademarks, but coming from the USSR I didn't know what a trademark was. Once when we were discussing a toothpaste case study, my classmates had to take me to the supermarket to show me all the different brands struggling for shelf space.

To survive in this new foreign environment, Ioffé had to work twice as hard as other students. His efforts were rewarded in the end, however: he was the only one from his class to whom McKinsey made an offer to join their Paris office upon graduation. He was the first Russian to work for McKinsey. Since they had little experience working with Russians, they asked the CIA to vet Ioffé before they hired him.

In the course of the following years, Jacques (as he now called himself) Ioffé's career progressed steadily. After three years with McKinsey he joined Renault, where he spent some time as assistant to the president and then headed a project to set up a new division responsible for the development of industrial production robots. Ioffé recalled: 'It was one of the most exciting jobs I did. To build a team in the high-tech field and to develop all the main functions from scratch was really exciting and challenging'. Unfortunately, the president of Renault was forced to resign. Ioffé himself left Renault about one year later. About his next (short) stint with the French bank Société Générale, Ioffé commented: 'It is definitely the most socialist-style company I have ever met in the West ... an administrative monster'. In 1990, Ioffé received the *Prix du Succès* awarded by the French business press to the most successful leader of the year.

When Danone's offer came in 1996, Ioffé was in a position to accept it. He commented: 'I was not looking for difficulties, but I thought my qualifications and background corresponded perfectly with Bolshevik's requirements'.

REINVENTING BOLSHEVIK

Ioffé had received a warning from his contacts at Danone headquarters: 'We don't understand what's going on at Bolshevik. Maybe it's because of the interpreters, but we don't understand what the people over there mean when they talk'. Despite that uncertainty, Danone's tacit agreement with Ioffé was that he would have a relatively free hand to act as he saw fit. As long as Bolshevik did not incur tremendous losses, Danone headquarters would be patient and allow Bolshevik a rather long leash.

When Jacques Ioffé arrived at Bolshevik in April of 1996, he found an organization nearly paralyzed by uncertainty. Managers and workers alike were wary of a capitalist future and, as a result, clung to the rigid structure they had known in the past. At the same time, they saw Danone as holding the key to salvation, but were not sure they could trust the French expatriate managers who had been timidly trying to run things from the sidelines. As noted earlier, the team of French specialists who had been representing Danone had the status of consultants, which meant nobody took them seriously: 'We could be told to shut up or even kicked out of the general director's office right in the middle of the meeting'. All the foreigners' offices were in a separate, recently renovated building, nicknamed 'the French building'. When Ioffé's predecessor first showed the French team their office, he handed them a key and said: 'Guys, don't forget to lock the door when you leave', implying that they would soon be leaving for good. To limit their power even further, every time the French managers wanted to visit a workshop, they had to ask for the permission of the chief production manager – permission that was not always granted. Even Ioffé was hemmed in when he first arrived. The former general director, who became the honorary president with Ioffé's arrival, arranged a nice office for his new colleague right next to his own. The man did not want anything to escape his notice.

Ioffé realized that his first task was to identify and understand the undercurrents at Bolshevik. He recalled: 'When I arrived first I did nothing, I just watched. When I started I had no plan; everything I did was by pure intuition'. After getting a feel for the place, he formulated his vision for the transformation process. His goal was to progress in three areas:

- Design a hierarchy that would function as a transition point between the steep pyramid of the old Bolshevik, and a new, flatter hierarchy that would be phased in when the organization was ready – that is, when people had become more accustomed to sharing and accepting responsibility.
- Establish a more coherent organizational structure.
- Accelerate and improve the flow of information.

There were no dramatic changes in the first few months. Ioffé spent a good part of his time going over the company's financial reports, first to gather some sense of the bizarre Russian accounting practices, and then to clarify Bolshevik's true financial position and introduce Western reporting and accounting systems.

Once this had been accomplished, he gradually began to involve himself more in the day-to-day management of the company. Ioffé's appearance and manner were very different from his predecessors', and his leadership style was a complete change from what most of the factory workers were used to. One of the Russian managers recalled an incident with the old director:

> Just after I started working at Bolshevik I got into an argument with a cleaning lady late at night. A man entered the room we were in, and shouted at us to stop fighting. At first I thought it was a gangster; his behavior was really scary. Later I found out it was the general director.

The general director depended on coercive power, and built relationships on the basis of intimidation bordering on physical abuse. His decisions were spontaneous and unpredictable. He was extremely distrustful, afraid to lose control or delegate, leading him to limit communication strictly within the organization. He had few close allies; most of his friendships were partnerships developed to advance his involvement in semi-legal activities.

Ioffé soon noticed that subordinates visited his office much more often than the office of the former general director himself. Ioffé said, 'I don't know why it happened, but I think the trick is very simple: I never shout'. A secretary who worked for the former director, and later for Ioffé, said, 'The whole atmosphere at Bolshevik has changed. Relationships between people have changed. It is quieter; nobody raises his voice; people have become more attentive. It's a more pleasant place to work now'.

Ioffé can be extremely stern, demanding and insistent. Although he rarely raises his voice, he does not hesitate to use coercive power when required, thus projecting the image of a strong leader with strict control over each and every issue. He has been called 'appropriately Machiavellian', meaning that the situation and the subordinates at Bolshevik required strong leadership. He described himself at that time as a 'contractual' leader, meaning that he was open to discussing subordinates' responsibilities to a certain extent, but once a decision had been made, he expected it to be fulfilled to the letter. He did not tolerate any violations of the 'contract's' terms later on. He said that this kind of authoritarian leadership style was dictated by the environment rather than being a reflection of his character.

Ioffé's broad business experience and technical background earned him a good deal of respect – and some apprehension – from the Russian managers, who saw him as a *khozjain*, an 'owner', which in Russia means somebody fully credible, capable of commanding order and accountability and possessing the power to punish, defend and reward.

In the next phase of the process Ioffé became more proactive. One of his first and most significant moves was to pressure the former general director to negate the clause that forbade expatriates to participate actively in the management of Bolshevik. Ioffé was then free to establish an executive committee. The heads of seven departments were made responsible for their areas, reporting directly to Ioffé. This brought Bolshevik into line with standard Danone operating procedures. All the members of the executive committee were new to Bolshevik, among them both French expatriates and new local people. Most of them had extensive experience in the area for which they would be responsible, though few had ever held a top managerial position. The Russian managers were slightly younger than their foreign counterparts, and all of them were younger than Ioffé. Ioffé believed it was very important to phase out older Russian managers and replace them with younger ones whenever possible. He said that many Russians over 40 belong to a 'lost generation' as far as their attitude is concerned; they will never be able to adapt to a market economy. Ioffé looked for and hired young managers with good potential who were not quite qualified enough to be snapped up by the big Western firms (like Coca-Cola or Mars). These managers were less expensive to hire, and Bolshevik could therefore invest more in their training. In fact, two of the seven executives who reported directly to Ioffé were only in their early thirties.

Though the new executive committee was now operational, Ioffé did not immediately dismantle the old management structure. Instead, as people got used to the way the new executive committee functioned and began to see results, power decisively and irrevocably shifted from the old to the new. With Ioffé's assistance and involvement, more and more questions and issues were directed to the newly assigned managers, leaving fewer and fewer points to be raised at the lengthy meetings still being called by the company president. Though gradual, this redistribution of power inevitably led to conflicts of interests, confusion, and clashes between the old and new managers, but Ioffé insisted that problems be handled with patience and self-control. In most cases, conflicts and quarrels were resolved before they could grow into destructive confrontation.

Eventually, it became obvious that despite the calming of surface tensions, the atavistic nature of the old top-management team was hindering progress. The streamlining of the organizational structure and the clear definition of newly assigned managers' responsibilities had quickly created a sense of accountability and control at the managerial level. As professional standards were raised and more effective practices introduced, some managers whose capabilities were inadequate could not adapt. In order to make further company restructuring possible, these managers would have to leave.

Some of these managers still held shares in Bolshevik that they had obtained in the original privatization of the company. (Danone obtained 87 per cent of Bolshevik shares at the time of the acquisition.) Danone offered the old management fair compensation for their agreement to give up their shares as they left the company. This proposal accidentally brought to light a quirky arrangement designed to line the pockets of some of these managers. It was discovered that some of the Bolshevik trademarks were registered in the names of top Russian executives, who received royalties from each unit sold. Although this was not strictly illegal, it was ethically dubious at best. Finally the former director agreed to sell his shares and royalties and leave Bolshevik entirely, and most of the old top managers followed his example. All the middle managers also sold their stock back to Danone, though most of them stayed at Bolshevik.

In the areas where the technical competence, experience and connections of the old managers were especially critical – namely, in production, quality control and purchasing – agreements were reached that the incoming team would work closely with their outgoing counterparts for some time. Though the process was not flawless, in general the continuity of the business was ensured.

All the reshuffling at the top had little impact on the people on the shop floor, however. Most Russian enterprises do not allow any participation of the workforce in the company's management, and Bolshevik was no exception. The workers' main concern in any case was the stability of their salary payments. Morale was so low that workers had no interest in product or process improvements. In addition, delinquency was rampant and theft a serious problem. For example, soon after Ioffé's arrival some employees were caught trying to embezzle part of a payment for several tons of butter using forged documents.

Establishing order and control in the workshops was therefore the first essential task once management issues had been addressed. A new security service was employed to wage war on theft, drunkenness and delinquency – the three most common and serious infractions – with the penalty being immediate dismissal. Most managers admitted that discipline improved after these measures were taken. The fear of losing a small but stable income proved to be an effective stick.

Although the number of dismissals was significant, Bolshevik was still overstaffed at shop-floor level. Overstaffing, combined with low productivity and low wages, was a chronic post-perestroika problem carried over from the Soviet era. It had been aggravated in the early 1990s by the dramatic related reductions in demand and production volumes. The old Bolshevik management had never addressed the problem, so there had been few layoffs prior to 1996.

The new managers were more decisive. Between 1996 and 1999, the number of employees in the company dropped from 2400 to 1200, a reduction that the executive committee tried to make as painless as possible. The firm outsourced some minor functions, such as cleaning and equipment technical support (Bolshevik managed to convince some of its subcontractors to hire Bolshevik factory employees who had been laid off). Some people took early retirement. Middle managers who failed to adapt to the new management practices and requirements were asked to leave. Bolshevik's human resource personnel helped departing workers with job searches, working extensively with employment options. This was unusual for a Russian company and the workers appreciated it.

When negotiating layoffs with unions, the new management proposed to reduce the workforce even further in order to increase salaries for the remaining personnel. The unions decided, however, to accept lower pay as a tradeoff for job security for a greater number of workers, demonstrating a typical Soviet-style proletarian solidarity. (Though unions were involved in the staff-reduction negotiations, in most cases their role was rather symbolic.) Job security remained one of the main issues still raised at the semi-annual meetings of the top management with company workers' representatives.

Being fully aware of people's mixed feelings toward the old Communist regime, Ioffé had symbolic reminders removed from prominent positions but not thrown away altogether. Items such as flags from Soviet days and portraits and busts of Lenin were placed in the factory museum. Lenin's monument in the yard, a typical attribute of a Soviet factory, was left intact. Social benefits, another intangible but appreciated 'symbol' of Communism – such as saunas, kindergarten, summer camp for children and medical treatment – were still provided by Bolshevik, though on an outsourced basis. (The buildings formerly owned by Bolshevik in which these activities had been housed were sold, which reduced the company's expenses considerably.) At the same time, a few new 'symbols' were introduced, including the Danone corporate logo. Posters with Danone advertisements in French – with a Russian translation carefully positioned next to the French text – were hung in some of the administrative buildings.

Investments in infrastructure were also gradual. The workers' locker rooms and showers were renovated once Ioffé took the helm. The infrastructure in the workshops, however, still left much to be desired. Ventilation was poor and most of the machinery, some of which had 19th-century parts, needed to be replaced. Some investments, none substantial, were made in this area. Ioffé authorized no showy or expensive renovation of the administrative infrastructure either. All managers moved to offices closer to the areas of their responsibilities, including the expatriates, who were no longer cloistered in the 'French building'. Some of the French moved into old managers' offices; others moved into new but modest quarters.

Even as ambitious plans were outlined for the future, many old procedures and habitual practices were retained for the time being, partly because of resistance to change. For example, the tradition of holding weekly planning meetings with the general director, attended by workshop managers and all members of the management team, was sustained for some time. Later, as production managers began to assume responsibility for production scheduling, these meetings were phased out. This frustrated workshop managers, who were used to dealing with the director himself and had been frequent visitors to his office. The hierarchical increase in the distance between workshop and top management gave the former the impression of helplessness and inferiority. This nostalgia for the days of direct interaction with top management lingered on; one workshop manager insisted that, although overall production management had become more professional and effective, it would be even better were the general director more involved.

Another continuing cause for frustration for older managers was the difference in compensation between old-timers and newcomers. The salaries of new bilingual managers, who were hired through professional recruiters in the highly competitive Moscow labor market, were much higher than those of the middle managers who have been with Bolshevik for some time. Their salaries were increased at the time of Danone's acquisition, but were still close to what they were in the past, when official compensation was fixed at a lower level. In addition, as control and accountability increased, many moonlighting opportunities for middle management were eliminated, leaving them rather worse off than they were before Danone came. Russian culture is a culture of envy, so the compensation differential festers. Not surprisingly, then, inequalities in compensation have a decidedly adverse impact on company morale in Russia. This issue was one of the undercurrents at Bolshevik that had yet to be dealt with. For the time being, however, there was little open complaint, because the fear of losing one's job income in the midst of Russia's economic crisis kept people quiet.

As we ended the first phase of our study of Bolshevik in 1999, there was still little official communication between the workers and top management. Ioffé saw excessive openness as a sign of weakness that could undermine managers' credibility. He retained both the power of the general director's position and a highly centralized chain of command. Some of the new young managers seemed reluctant to challenge him too forcefully, perhaps feeling that, having joined the company with limited managerial experience, they owed him some kind of debt. He remained at the center of all activities and maintained tight control over all major and many minor issues of the factory's functioning. Any spending, either within the approved budget or beyond it, required his personal approval. He had disengaged himself from some minor issues and questions, however, and his team effectively participated in decision-making (although he still had the final word). As Ioffé said himself, he quickly got bored with useless details and prefered to focus on the 'big picture'.

Although the transformation process at Bolshevik was going well, the situation in Russia was very unstable at that time. In August of 1998 with the economic crisis that hit the country, demand for most of Bolshevik's products slumped. The Danone Group had been prepared to write off losses. Despite this rather pessimistic forecast, Bolshevik made a profit in 1998, thanks to intensive cost management and sales efforts. However, overcapacity of production was becoming a serious problem. This uncertain financial situation was a basis for ongoing discussion between Danone and Bolshevik over strategy. The Bolshevik executive committee wanted to capitalize on and continue to develop Bolshevik's reputation as a manufacturer with a unique, top-quality product. They wanted to position Bolshevik products as something synonymous with indulgence, an affordable luxury. Danone Group policy was to reinvest 3.5 per cent of turnover back into its subsidiaries, which was adequate for a well-maintained factory in France but insufficient for the necessary infrastructure expenditures at Bolshevik, as a Bolshevik executive pointed out.

There was still a great deal to be done at the organizational level. The company's sales and marketing, distribution and purchasing strategies, for example, would require significant restructuring. Production planning and many of the quality control and product development procedures would also have to be revised. Bolshevik's financial reporting practices were being brought up to Danone's international standards, and a corporate IT system would have to be installed.

In spite of the uncertainties they faced, Bolshevik employees were on the whole positive about being a part of Danone. One of them said, 'Danone is serious about Russia, and is courageous'. They also appreciated the way Danone had respected the Soviet tradition of social benefits for employees. On the other hand, they were very worried about the decline in sales, as they believed that if a company that was part of a Western organization did not make a profit every year, it would be closed. They also said that, as far as they could tell, there was no strategy for the future. One said, 'The future is very unclear to us. Either there is a plan and it's being kept secret, or there's no plan at all'. They were optimistic, and yet still wary.

THE BOLSHEVIK EVOLUTION

Almost four years passed from the time we ended our visits to Bolshevik in 1999 to the time when we returned in 2003 to see what changes had occurred. Our first impression in 2003 was that the *Bolsheviks* are gone. The company might not look exactly like a Western organization, but it is definitely not what it used to be – a clunky, run-down production facility, churning out biscuit after biscuit in a mad race to meet planned quotas. There has been no sweeping replacement of equipment, and the factory still operates from the run-down 19th century building with the Lenin monument in front of it. However, the days are long gone when workers produced thousands of tons of biscuits 'with a cheap margarine taste' in grim packaging which looked as if it had already been used once. Bolshevik's main brand, recipes and some elements of the packaging design remain the same. However, the Bolshevik evolution has definitely continued, and the overall approach to factory management has changed.

By 2003, Bolshevik's general director Jacque Ioffé had been at the helm of the company for seven years. He had come to manage the biscuit factory at a time when the factory really had nothing but 'crumbs'; all the systems and processes he inherited were further from requirements dictated by a market economy than Kamchatka is from Moscow. After seven years of his stewardship, the company had been transformed from its financial and organizational structures, to its ability to respond to and capture market demands.

Bolshevik looks set to continue its development into the future. However, two questions remain unanswered. First, the company's long-term strategy – and its key element, a new production facility – is still undefined. Second, in 2003 Jacques Ioffé announced he would soon give up his operational responsibilities at Bolshevik. The destiny of his team and consistency of the change process were still as topical as they had been when Ioffé first arrived at Bolshevik.

FOUR YEARS OF BUILDING A FRAMEWORK

In 1999, we left Bolshevik with the last observation that whereas Jacques Ioffé had made a change in workers' mindset his first priority, quite rightly we felt, it was becoming increasingly urgent for him to focus on his architectural role as a leader. Bolshevik needed the organizational structures that would permit it to function as a part of a global group. Ioffé seemed to relish the challenge. Reflecting on his time at Bolshevik, Ioffé said he valued the periods of crisis most:

> Vive la crise! (Long live the crisis!) The crisis [Russia's 1998 default] actually helped us to leap towards much higher efficiency and solve quite a few problems. [In response,] I cut fixed costs almost by third and closed two workshops, which gave us significant savings and improved efficiency.

Some change was evident in all areas, including marketing, production, distribution, finance and purchasing. A new supply chain function had been created, ensuring smooth coordination across the departments. A number of initiatives were still under way within each area, most notably TPM (Total Productive Maintenance), a Japanese concept designed to revolutionize the traditional approach to equipment maintenance management.

These changes were accomplished in an economic climate that continued to be difficult to predict. In 1999 Bolshevik's sales volume hit a historic low of just 24 000 tons of biscuits, but as the Russian economy showed steady recovery after the 1998 financial crises and demand for most categories of goods grew at a healthy rate, Bolshevik managed to boost its production significantly. In 2001 the output reached 35 000 tons, which in terms of percentage growth set a record for the whole Danone Group. In 2002, however, traditional market segments saw some upheaval as consumers' tastes shifted into new product categories, and with the wave of the economic recovery, competition intensified. Bolshevik was not able to react quickly, and as a result there was a decrease in sales that year, with Bolshevik baking only 28 000 tons of biscuits. Ioffé felt this was partly due to a hiring freeze and a weak marketing strategy. In 2003 the situation changed again, with production volume increasing that year, but not as high as the record 2001 level.

Given this situation, stabilizing production and income remained a challenge, although much had been accomplished already. Bolshevik set regional expansion as the top priority and within four years built a national distribution network covering most of the large cities in the country. It also signed on sub-distributors to work in the regions that Bolshevik does not cover directly. Within main regions the company gained comparatively high distribution channel penetration, and captured significant shelf space in most of the channels. Although distribution had already expanded remarkably, it was an area that needed further development.

Ioffé and his executive team also focused on developing their marketing strategy. Sponge biscuits, waffle and waffle desserts and snacks, as well as other types of traditional biscuits were all new in the product portfolio and their emergence also strengthened margins and appealed to customers' craving for diversity. Bolshevik chose to stick to its traditional market for quality confectionery ('an affordable luxury') in the upper middle price segment for medium to low income consumers.

Production strategy was also overhauled. Bolshevik stopped producing unbranded biscuits sold in bulk, the major share of production volume in the past. This helped to boost margins and contributed to long-term brand equity development – although this came at a cost, as it is believed that the market share of the unbranded biscuits grew at a higher rate and retained a large share of the market, especially in the regions. This is not as dramatic as it may sound, given that 'Bolshevik' is the only brand name on the Russian market recognized throughout the country. Ioffé said, 'We have really renewed our product line. Before 2002, 40 per cent of our sales were for bulk biscuits and now it is zero. In 2002, one third of our sales came from the products that did not exist in 2001'. There are definitely more niches in a market characterized by very fast shifts of tastes of consumers who perpetually look for novelty, so Bolshevik may have even larger sales from new products in the future – on the condition that its marketing and production departments are sufficiently flexible and swift.

THE EXECUTIVE TEAM

Although Jacques Ioffé sees himself as the main driving force behind the Bolshevik reorganization process, and his role in maintaining good relationships with the Groupe Danone and ensuring mutual understanding was vital, no progress would have been possible without the hard work of Bolshevik's top executives. A highly professional team of young Russian managers, whose contribution to the restructuring process was essential for Bolshevik development as a whole, now runs the company. The executive group's accomplishments are all the more remarkable given that Bolshevik relied mainly on its own financial resources throughout the modernization and development process, and had no access to external funds from Danone or other investors (except for funds from the European Bank for Reconstruction and Development (EBRD) at the time of the acquisition).

Ioffé said, 'We have the youngest chief financial officer in the Danone Group and probably one of the youngest executive teams in Russia. There is not a single expatriate; the executives are all Russians, and most of them have been with us for at least four years'.

For many years, even after Ioffé's arrival, Bolshevik executives had felt that there was a lack of good communication and coordination of activities towards common objectives. Although they had a free rein in their respective areas, executives had difficulties aligning their efforts and coordinating their steps with each other. Two things helped to change this.

The first came in 2001 with the establishment of Bolshevik University to provide a forum for information exchange. The concept behind the creation of the University was to take all Bolshevik executives to a retreat where on the first day each of them would lecture his colleagues on the basic business theories or principles of his field (marketing, finance, sales, production) and then current issues at Bolshevik would be discussed. The second day was dedicated to team building. There were quite a few such seminars, and at the first one Ioffé gave all participants the opportunity to buy a virtual share in Bolshevik for a symbolic 100 roubles. Several years later the shares were bought back at the market price. 'Interestingly enough, we beat inflation', Ioffé said.

The value of the University can be questioned but the practice encouraged a better understanding of executives' goals, and allowed more coordination between individual functions. The result was a better consistency and coherency of initiatives in different areas. Informal relationships also emerged or improved, and some early tensions between managers eased.

The second influential action was the establishment of the supply chain function with its intrinsic task of cross-functional coordination. The independent supply chain function, raised in the hierarchy to the level of the production and sales, is a new Danone organizational practice which was successfully adopted in Russia and helped to solve the problem of inefficient coordination from the technical side and also ensured emergence of more professional planning. The supply chain function's top executive, Ekaterina Eliseeva, was an ex-Unilever logistics professional. She has put a significant effort into establishment of the formal as well as informal links between people, functions and processes, with measurable success.

In all other individual areas under supervision of the acting executives changes also continued. Another production line was added in 2001, although it was second-hand European equipment, which did little to reduce the astonishing average age of the factory machinery. The approach to production management has changed dramatically, and given the factory's original layout and Soviet legacy of overstaffing, the result is remarkable.

For six years, Andrei Makarenko headed production. In 2002, he launched TPM (Total Productive Maintenance), one of the most intriguing endeavors ever at the factory. TPM is a Japanese concept of equipment maintenance management, which in its final form embraces several frameworks including 'Kobetsu-Keizen' (individual improvement) and 'Jishu-Hozen' (autonomous maintenance). It assumes the creation of a pervasive system of equipment maintenance management that builds on assigning a significant share of the maintenance functions to stations operators. They assume more control and responsibility for equipment condition and performance. Andrei had high hopes for the system as a remedy to old Soviet shop floor plagues such as workers' apathy, lack of responsibility and uninvolvement. What will come out of the brave experiment, unique in Russia as well as within the Danone Group, everybody is curious to see. People within Bolshevik agree that the first test the program has to pass is Ioffé's departure – if that does not kill off TPM, the system may well modify the way people work on the shop floor, something that few people in Russia believe could ever be changed.

Regional expansion and growth in new regions has been and still is the key element of the Bolshevik strategy. Dmitry Bobkov became the commercial director in 1999 after a number of years at L'Oreal, where his last position was the head of the Eastern Europe export department at the company headquarters in Paris. Under Bobkov, Bolshevik shifted its distribution focus from retailers and small clients to large distributors and established its own sales force supporting regional distributors in 20 large cities. For smaller cities the products were distributed through local subcontractor distributors, thus increasing Bolshevik's market and also improving the efficiency of distribution channels. When Bobkov came, 70 per cent of Bolshevik's sales were in Moscow. 'We brought this figure down to 50 per cent', Bobkov explained, 'not because sales fell but because we increased our deliveries to other regions significantly'.

The marketing department organizational structure was changed and the total number of sales force increased. A new compensation system was also put in place. Other small changes also paid off. A huge accounts receivable deficit was a Bolshevik curse during the crisis period in the late 1990s, so Bobkov implemented new trade policies and procedures and strict control of the clients' payments.

Bolshevik employees had complained that the marketing function was somewhat isolated in its own endeavors and communications were not excellent. In 2003 a new marketing director, Dmitry Konstantinov, joined the company, replacing the last remaining expatriate manager. Konstantinov returned to Russia from Canada where he worked for several years as a marketing manager at Reckitt Benckiser. With Konstantinov's arrival the marketing function activities were soon better aligned with sales objectives and tuned to the needs of the sales organization. New merchandising and trade marketing initiatives were introduced to support Bolshevik sales in shops and undermine smaller unbranded competitors. The function was reorganized and more staff brought in, with processes and procedures improved.

The finance department saw more efficiencies (staff reduction) as Irina Olesova came to lead it in 2001 to replace a French financier whose early contribution to turning a traditional, General Ledger-focused accounting department and lunatic economists into a real finance function was essential. Bolshevik now has a standard budgeting process and reports under Russian as well as US GAAP accounting standards on a regular basis.

As executives worked on their own areas – be they production, finance, sales or marketing – technical links between the functions were also developed. Also, as a result, informal relationships emerged or were strengthened. Now, although Bolshevik top management are not trying to create a 'one big happy family' atmosphere, the executive suite seems more like a friendly neighborhood where nobody is embarrassed to lean over the backyard fence and borrow something (a grill) from a neighbor – although they wouldn't necessarily invite him or her over for a barbeque.

ON THE WORKSHOP FLOOR

Bolshevik employees, it seems, have accepted, apparently without too much difficulty, the fact that they now work for a global organization – perhaps because the transformation of Bolshevik from their perspective has been rather limited.

Their biggest concern is, quite understandably, their salaries. Salary levels still remain low for workers (beginning at \$150–270 a month) given the cost of living in Moscow, one of the most expensive cities in the world. Bolshevik's workers' salaries are in line with the general job market situation, however, which remains somewhat depressed. But as the economy grows, other Moscow-based companies are offering more attractive salaries, and some Bolshevik workers have been lured away. But it is not only the low pay at Bolshevik that irritates workers; there is still a lingering sense of unfairness about the difference in compensation between those who worked at Bolshevik before Danone took over, and those who were hired later. In particular the young, bilingual professionals hired on the competitive Moscow white-collar job market or recruited internationally have competitive compensation, often approaching French levels. As previously mentioned, such a difference in the country where envy is almost a cultural tradition is still a smoldering reason for conflict within Bolshevik.

However, there was not a single open confrontation between the workers and the management from 1996 to 2003. Even the workforce reduction, which was done gradually and often on rather beneficial terms for former employees (additional pension stimulus and extra welfare), did not meet fierce resistance and the remaining employees do not seem worried about job security. Marina Makarova, head of one of the production workshops, commented, 'We have got used to [layoffs]; I am not too concerned. We never had any lawsuits [from fired employees] or anything. Actually there were very few really painful dismissals in my workshop'.

Work conditions are the other major concern of Bolshevik workers, and another reason for dissatisfaction. Since Danone took over, work conditions have been improved to some extent. Bolshevik productions lines still occupy facilities with a cramped, outdated layout in a tall, multi-floor building. This means that Bolshevik is crippled from an operational, and to some extent organizational, point of view. Nobody has any illusions about the condition of the factory's infrastructure, as they still face on a daily basis the reality of working with machines with some 19th century parts. Some buildings or parts of buildings in the factory complex are in a shambles. Minor fires break out occasionally; leaking pipes are a norm; and electrical wiring is substandard in some areas, threatening security. In addition, it still gets very hot in the workshops, as the air conditioning system is inadequate.

Throughout the seven years of Ioffé's tenure, no external financial resources were available to the company. Thus modernization and development were financed through Bolshevik's own income, which was neither dependable or abundant given the 1998 crisis and 2002 setback in sales. But even if large investments were to be made, few things can be changed in the existing facilities due to limited space. Unless the company moves somewhere else, work conditions will remain well below international standards.

Despite lasting technical problems and poor work conditions workshop managers say discipline has improved and order has been established on the workshop floors. In addition, basic sanitary requirements have been brought back up to normal standards. The progress is especially apparent when compared with the wild, post-privatization years of the mid-1990s, when absenteeism, plundering, drunkenness and misdemeanors reached an apogee and became threatening. During and just after the Soviet era, dismissal was not a part of the contract between a worker and the factory at all. Now for any major misconduct the measure is applied consistently, and this threat has been a most effective tool in establishing good order.

In general the transformation at Bolshevik that was brought in by Danone was not seen as a real upheaval by most of the Russian employees. Their everyday work routine has not changed much, and their jobs are still fairly secure. However, the uncertainty they expressed to us four years before about Bolshevik's future, and their continuing fear of the factory's closure or sale by Danone, can still be sensed in the air, mingling with the sweet scent of baking biscuits and cakes.

AFTER IOFFÉ

The workers are not the only ones who look to the future with some apprehension. In late 2003, Bolshevik prepared for the departure of Jacques Ioffé and the arrival of a new General Director. Within the executive team, there were rumors that because regional sales are the top priority, the new CEO, who was previous head of sales and distribution for PepsiCo Russia, would bring in his own sales team. There were also fears, again based on rumors, that more executives from Danone headquarters would be brought in to tighten control over Danone's 'maverick' factory.

Jacques Ioffé was the key link between the Group headquarters and the Bolshevik local team. However, his direct involvement, which was high in the beginning, fell at a remarkable rate as standard procedures and processes emerged and new managers assumed their responsibilities. 'I was surprised', said CFO Irina Olesova, 'by how quickly Ioffé handed me responsibility for all finances. I did not expect that'. Bolshevik executives were definitely more autonomous than they had been at the time of Ioffé's arrival.

Communications with the Group, on the other hand, remained an area in which Ioffé retained his control and continued to spend significant time and effort. Probably because of the peculiar circumstances under which Bolshevik was bought, its technical backwardness and weak systems and structure, Danone apparently viewed the company as a black sheep in their family of modern production units. That's probably why Bolshevik's strategy, as well as operational issues and budgets, have always been subject to the Group's tight control and scrutiny. However, from Bolshevik's perspective, Danone's strategy often did not seem to reflect a thorough understanding of the local specifics – thus every decision required extensive communication. 'General rules can not be applied to Bolshevik', Ioffé said. 'There are particularities here that are strong and should not be underestimated.'

Therefore Ioffé, with his dual cultural background, remained the vital link between the local realities and French headquarters' visions. To some extent he played even a preventive role, serving as a buffer of volatile incursions from the headquarters. Bolshevik's CFO remarked, 'There are leaders who conduct stress from the top down to subordinates just like transistors; there are some who amplify it; and some who remove it. I think Ioffé is one of the latter'.

Jacques Ioffé was also recognized by the French government in 2003, when he was awarded the French Légion d'Honneur (Legion of Honor), an elite military and civilian medal that recognizes outstanding achievement in a selected field. This was awarded for his contribution to the development of the French–Russian economic partnership as the President of the Economic Council of the French Embassy in Moscow (a consultative body within all French Embassies that provides advice on regional economic matters to the French Government and promotes the interests of the local French business community). It should be noted that the award had nothing to do with his work at Bolshevik.

The biggest shortcoming of Ioffé's work at Bolshevik, it seems, was his inability to get Danone headquarters to agree on the keystone element to

Bolshevik's long-term strategy, a new greenfield production facility. This project remained undefined in 2003 just as it was four years before.

> I do not like repetitive plots. I had one top priority project, which I have already presented three times to the Group: the construction of the new plant and closure (sales) of the existing facilities. They are old; this is a 19th century factory after all, standing in the center of the busy metropolis. There could be a better use of the property, and better place for us elsewhere with a new facility. But I failed to get a green light for the new factory, despite the fact that our calculations clearly show the project would have a short payback period.

Ioffé's departure added to the uncertainty; Bolshevik's future would depend on his successor's priorities, and ability to establish good relations with the Group. The new general director was selected from three final candidates, two of whom were high caliber specialists with good experience of working in Russia – but were not Russian. The man who was finally chosen, Aleksei Mechanik, was responsible for regional distribution in his former post at PepsiCo. For Ioffé, Mechanik's experience in distribution was essential, as further development of Bolshevik's distribution system, Ioffé felt, was still the company's top priority. Ioffé commented on the new general director's chances of success,

> I think there will always be some cultural misfit between the local reality and the biases of any Western professional working in Russia, no matter how smart and experienced the person is. I wanted a Russian to take over from me. Even so, because Mechanik comes from PepsiCo, he may have a few surprises working in the Danone Group as we are not an American company.

Whether Mechanik's priorities would continue to reflect Ioffé's legacy remained to be seen, but Mechanik's arrival would very likely lead to changes in the team. Danone could also intervene with a more hands-on approach to Bolshevik's internal affairs. Whether this would lead to a dismantling of Ioffé's management team and a change in strategy was hard to predict. When we last spoke to him, Ioffé was optimistic: 'It is normal for a new leader to criticize everything that was done before he arrived. He will want to start from scratch, but it's always like that'. Jacques Ioffé smiled. 'I think everything will be OK.'

NOTES

1. Franck Riboud, Danone Group Annual Report, 1998.
2. Charpentier, P., F. Guérin, V., Laulhère and H. Rouilleault (1996), *Diagnostic sur l'organisation et les conditions de travail Bolshevik, Moscow, rapport provisoire* (Study of the organization and working conditions at Bolshevik, Moscow, working paper), p. 6.
3. The Pioneer organization was one of the three Communist youth (ages 10–16) organizations. The distinctive dress feature was a red tie worn at school.

Commentary: Jacques Ioffé's Bolshevik evolution

Though Bolshevik had been privatized two years before Danone acquired it, its management team had made few changes. It remained typical of a Soviet enterprise operating under the command-planned economy.

Under this system, all of an organization's activities and systems were designed to meet one goal – The *Plan*. The Plan, developed and controlled by a special government body known as GOSPLAN, dictated the kind of product, production volumes, raw materials, suppliers, distribution channels and even the consequence and size of capital investments. Under this system, the top management of individual businesses functioned as a controlling body responsible for Plan fulfillment, rather than value creation, profitability or sales volume. Not surprisingly, this type of organization was characterized by a gargantuan production over-capacity, ironically coinciding with technical backwardness, deep vertical integration and a technocratic culture. In order to advance up the career ladder, a person had to be either a Communist Party stalwart, or have superior technical skills.

As the Soviet Socialist political and economical systems began to unravel in the serious crises of the 1970s and the cynicism of the top Communist authorities became very obvious, the system became increasingly difficult to control. Low salaries and a perpetual shortage of daily essentials contributed to a rise in embezzlement and the growth of a flourishing black market. The government reacted by toughening the criminal code[1] and by reinforcing bureaucracy through the introduction of numerous parallel and redundant procedures aimed at strengthening control. This increase in bureaucracy naturally infiltrated the functions and practices of business organizations, where ironically the surfeit of controlling mechanisms often led to the opposite result: an avoidance of responsibilities and accountability.

The top managers in Soviet businesses ran their monstrous organizations in constant fear of missing Plan quotas, losing control of workers and overlooking any potentially criminal violations of rules or procedures. As a result, control and decision-making were concentrated at the highest levels of the management hierarchy, and there was an inherent lack of trust in employees. 'Red' directors relied on belligerence to get their message across; shouting and slamming fists on the table was common. (Even Khrushchev once resorted to banging his shoe on his desk at a United Nations assembly.) Top managers were involved in and responsible for every minor issue of the enterprise's functions, leaving only limited responsibilities and purely operational tasks to middle management. Middle managers lost their ability to carry out analytical work and make independent decisions.

Not surprisingly, when we began the interviews and visits to Bolshevik for this case study in 1999, direct foreign investment in Russia was only 1 per cent of GDP, and Russian industry was only half as productive in that year as in 1992. The prevailing opinion at the time was that privatization had only aggravated Russia's economic problems, and that foreign firms should avoid investing in Russia. The point of this case study is to show that, despite the Soviet legacy, Russian companies can be successfully modernized and integrated within a multinational organization.

But first we repeat the caveat emptor we stated earlier in this book: to create effective collaborative efforts a deep understanding is needed of differences in leadership and organizational practices between Russians and people from other cultures. Russian national character traits have had such a profound influence on organization culture and management style that no change process could be successful if these cultural factors are not dealt with. With this insight, it becomes possible to design integration and change processes that fit the cultural context. Observing the transformation of Bolshevik led us to conclude that an *Anglo-Saxon-style* revolutionary change process is not always the best way to proceed in Russian organizations; that the commonly accepted post-industrial goals of rapid change, employee empowerment, a flatter hierarchy, and networking structures are not necessarily appropriate in these organizations in the short term; and that even the definitions of trust, leadership, and patterns of decision-making can differ according to cultural context. The challenge lies in understanding the complexities – the lingering influence of the Soviet planned central economy, as well as the Russian culture and management systems. Bolshevik at the time of Jacques Ioffé's arrival was a 3Cs-type organization (as described in the East-West dialog in Chapter 2). It would have been a mistake to push Bolshevik's workers and managers too hard in the early days; they were not ready for any other organizational paradigm. However, Ioffé's leadership style and vision have inspired some polemic. At what point should the change process be speeded up? How long is a strong, authoritarian leader an appropriate choice for the transformation process? These are the types of questions that both Western investors and Russian business leaders have yet to answer.

CULTURE IS KEY

Bolshevik in 1994 was anachronistic, but the factory had reassuringly (to workers) predictable technology and rules. This dependence on regulations and order fostered a strong emotional resistance to change. Stability meant that at least next month's paycheck would probably arrive, and employees were loyal to their company and managers, autocratic though they were, because they provided stability. Promotions were made according to seniority – better the devil you know than the devil you don't. For the same reason, any kind of risk-taking or responsibility was avoided both on a personal and organizational level. There was little conflict and competition between employees, as there was a sort of herd mentality, and a feeling of safety in numbers.

As we observed events at Bolshevik, it became apparent to us that there were in fact many similarities between the Russians in the company and the French executives who came from Danone. The type of culturally influenced organizational behavior prevalent in Russia that we described earlier – authoritarian leadership, avoidance of uncertainty, power games and information-hoarding – also exists in France, albeit to a considerably lesser degree. France was, and still is, a very stratified society, and this heritage strongly affects business organizations. The delineation between *cadres* (top managers), *assimilé cadres* (supervisors) and *ouvriers* (workers) has always been crystal clear. The relationships between these groups are characterized by mistrust: 'Cadres think in terms of efficiency; non-cadres in terms of protest'.[2]

Another cultural similarity is found in the French and Russian perspective on the dimension of time. One element of this cultural dimension was described by the French consultants at Bolshevik as *la permanence du passé*, the permanence of the past. The other element is a shared preference for long-term strategy. For synchronous cultures, like the French and Russian, the past, present and future overlap in such a way that the past co-exists with the present, and both influence the future. There is an established final goal, but it can be reached in various ways. For these cultures the progression toward a goal is more long-term, and dependent on factors beyond individual control. Therefore, building durable, dependable networks and relationships is considered to be far more important than defining a sequential strategy.[3]

In fact, we argue that sequential planning processes work less well in unsettled markets like Russia. These processes are too dependent on a logical progression of predictable events and results. Their short-term strategic design lacks flexibility or built-in margins for change in circumstances. Synchronic progression towards goals, on the other hand, can assimilate trends and setbacks that sequential planning does not take into consideration.

We quickly realized that the similarity in the two cultures was a highly significant element in the success of the Bolshevik acquisition. Indeed, the Russians and French have a long history of cooperation. Catherine the Great was a friend and admirer of Voltaire. The French bureaucratic management style, with leaders selected among the graduates of a few elite engineering schools, served as a model for administration in pre-Revolutionary Russia.

It is known that followers who are managed in accordance with their cultural expectations will perform better.[4] Clearly, the similarities between the Russian and French management systems meant that for Jacques Ioffé, 'Danonizing' Bolshevik was more of an evolution than a revolution. The major mind-set transformation required of the Russians was made easier by vaguely familiar, and therefore reassuring, context.

TRUST IN LEADERSHIP

Often lacking in traditional Russian organizations, not surprisingly, is trust in the leader's ability to move beyond a phase of stability and into a risky future. Where trust is not established, people are paranoid and try to hoard any scrap of power that comes their way. They also strongly resist any change. The fact that Jacques Ioffé understood Danone executives as well as Bolshevik workers was a key success factor in the transformation of the Russian organization.

Ioffé's predecessor, as described in the case study, led by intimidation. His chief leadership attributes were his connections with powerful allies and his loud voice. He neither trusted his subordinates, nor did they trust him. Ioffé also projected the image of a rather autocratic and decisive leader. Many of his employees thought he was very egotistical, with a tendency to vaunt 'my' accomplishments and not 'our' accomplishments. Ioffé said that his authoritarian leadership style was necessary but not a reflection of his character; some would agree, but others say that he is in reality quite self-centred. His critics say he was just an 'average' leader, partly because they felt his transformation process was too slow, too cautious and too limited. Some saw him as more of a politician type of leader than a real business leader, someone who was good at burnishing his own image. Other employees we spoke to, however, seemed to appreciate having an authoritarian leader who protected them and did not rock the boat too much. They told us that Ioffé was fair and receptive to their ideas, although all final decisions were his. To sum up these conflicting perspectives, we would say that he did establish a sense of control, order and accountability that was reassuring, particularly to some of the older workers. The vision that he used to guide Bolshevik was probably an appropriate interim one: cautious progress. But some of the younger Bolshevik executives think that the time has now come for a different kind of leadership.

THE VIRTUE OF PATIENCE

Ioffé's approach to change management was rather spontaneous and intuitive. His gradual, as opposed to revolutionary, technique proved to be appropriate at the beginning, ensuring continuity of most of the activities and avoidance of otherwise inevitable resistance and conflict. It is also important to note that Danone agreed to tolerate this somewhat black sheep in their international group, and gave Bolshevik management enough time to raise product quality, production, customer services and management practices to Danone standards. Haste, at least in the early days of Ioffé's tenure, might have been counterproductive and could have led to serious problems and confrontation within Bolshevik and also with Danone.

However, as mentioned above, some people felt that the process should have been speeded up in the years that followed Ioffé's arrival. Ioffé could have pushed for a breakthrough after an initial gradual change process, but instead, in the eyes of some observers, he never galvanized the company to take it to new levels. He admitted himself that he enjoys the challenge of dealing with crisis; he does not like 'repetitive plots', and was discouraged by Danone's apparent reluctance to modernize the factory. Ioffé was an important link between the French headquarters and Bolshevik, a bridge between foreign aspirations and local reality. But when it comes to the most important issue of investment in new development, he was unsuccessful. He failed to gain support from headquarters; the question we cannot answer is: how hard was he really trying? We know, however, that Ioffé's main goal – drastic modernization of the factory – was not achieved, and no major investments were made in Bolshevik after the acquisition. Danone took the risk of buying the factory at a difficult time, but did not risk investing much money in it during Ioffé's tenure. Could it be that Ioffé's vision for Bolshevik was a reflection of Danone corporate policy – in other words, laissez-faire, but take no risks? In any case, we were left with a lingering feeling that achievements could have been much more impressive.

Perhaps as a result, the transformation of Bolshevik simply became less interesting for Ioffé as time went on. He has sounded slightly cynical about the company's accomplishments at times, as when he said that 'surprisingly', the appreciation of Bolshevik shares beat inflation – in reality, not such a great achievement.

Today Bolshevik is still far from an ideal Western company in terms of its capabilities, efficiency of its systems and processes, as well as its product mix and market position, and especially from a technical perspective. If Danone had wanted to leapfrog into the future right from the start, they probably should have constructed a greenfield plant and focused on one brand. This approach would have led to a break with history (for good or bad) and would have required huge upfront investments. Whether this approach would have proven to be more efficient and economically viable in the end is an open question. Justifying this kind of upheaval from a social standpoint is also up to discussion. In any case, acquiring new production facilities where a more advanced management approach could be implemented, and even higher efficiency could be achieved, is the most important issue on Bolshevik's agenda today. It is still up to Danone to decide how to go about it.

Another important question is how much of the achievements gained by the outgoing general director and his team will be retained, used and built upon by the new management and Danone. Will most of Ioffé's legacy crumble, with Mechanik changing what has already been changed? Ioffé said that Mechanik would undoubtedly be critical of his, Ioffé's, actions – could this have been a reflection of Danone's relationship with Ioffé? Mutual understanding and alignment of objectives and strategies between the Danone Group and Bolshevik are essential today as never before, and if the good relationship between the two were to fail, the consequences would be onerous. What is the future of Bolshevik? The brand name no longer sums up an image of boring biscuits in tacky boxes, but no one can say for sure if the future will have a residual 'cheap margarine taste' (as Bolshevik's biscuits were once described) or a rather a hint of '*la vie en rose*' to rival the pleasures of Danone's French delicacies.

NOTES

1. Business executives found guilty of theft could be sentenced to 10 to 15 years in jail; in extreme cases, they could even receive the death penalty. The early 1970s were marked by a series of major trials of this type of crime.
2. Hofstede, G. (1999), 'The Universal and the Specific in 21st-Century Global Management', *Organizational Dynamics*, Winter, 38.
3. Trompenaars, F. (1993), *Riding the Waves of Culture*, London: Nicholas Brealy.
4. Newman, K.L. and S.D. Nollen (1996), 'Culture and congruence: The fit between management practices and national culture', *Journal of International Business Studies, Fourth Quarter*.

4. Russian Standard

Emanuela Carboncini was, as she recalled, 'pretty desperate'. She had many clients who wanted to come to Moscow, but she could not find anywhere for them to stay. It was late 1988, when the developments of perestroika and glasnost were opening Russia to Westerners. Her company, Business Tour, specialized in booking hotel rooms in Moscow for Italian businesspeople. However, there were only four hotels in Moscow that were allowed to have foreign guests, and Emanuela was having great difficulty working with the slow, bureaucratic, corrupt and unresponsive official Intourist booking agency. She met and discussed her problem with many Russian representatives of the newly emerging travel cooperatives. They all proposed to show her clients 'the beautiful sights in Russia', but none of them were willing to take on the challenge of finding them rooms.

One day a young man, Roustam Tariko, came into her office. He worked for a small cooperative that provided transportation services to foreigners. Emanuela recalled,

> Right from the first, I saw something very intelligent in his face. I said to him, 'If you want to make money, help me with one simple thing. Get me access to decent hotel rooms in Moscow. If you can do this, you will be very rich. Go to the Rossia Hotel, for example. They have 4000 rooms; I can't believe that there aren't at least two or three for me!'

Tariko agreed to help Emanuela find a way to circumvent the laborious Intourist process.

The imposing and prestigious Rossia Hotel, overlooking Red Square, was one of the four hotels officially sanctioned by Intourist – not an easy target for Roustam Tariko. The director of the hotel was accustomed to dealing with dignitaries; when told that there was a young man with no appointment waiting in the lobby with a business proposition to discuss with her, she commanded that he be sent away.

As she left work later that evening, she saw the young man still waiting in the lobby. The director became intrigued by such endurance: he had been sitting there for five or six hours. Though he looked very young, perhaps he had something interesting to say. She decided that there would be no harm in hearing him out.

Tariko told her that he represented Western clients who were not able to come to Moscow because they could not find hotel rooms. However, he explained, this situation could be turned to his company's benefit as well as that of the Rossia Hotel.

> You have the connections with officials to get permission for foreigners to enter the Soviet Union, but the Rossia is paid only US$3 per room, while Intourist charges US$70. On the other hand, I have a list of hundreds of businesspeople wanting to come to Moscow who can't get permission or rooms. If we worked together, it would solve problems for both of us.

The director agreed that the idea was an interesting one and asked Tariko to come back the next day.

As soon as Tariko entered the director's office for their next meeting, she told him that she had permission for the Rossia Hotel to deal directly with foreigners. The paperwork was drawn up in due course and they signed a contract. As one of the first people in the Soviet Union to find a way to turn Intourist's stonewalling into an advantage, Tariko earned enormous commissions over the next nine months – the time that he worked with Emanuela – proving that her prediction about him had been accurate.

During his very successful partnership with Emanuela Carboncini, Tariko had already begun to ask himself, 'What next?' Emanuela had introduced him to many Italian businesspeople, and after rubbing shoulders with the best of them, he realized that what he really wanted to do was to go into business himself. Because of his commissions, he had generated a great deal of start-up capital very quickly; at 27 he was well on his way to becoming a successful entrepreneur by Russian standards. But for Tariko, this was only the beginning. He decided to risk the capital that he had already earned to start his own import and distribution business.

Assuming that, like himself, most Russians were tired of the monotony and scarcity of food products, he approached representatives of Ferrero, the Italian chocolate manufacturer, whom he had met through Emanuela. He convinced Ferrero that they should offer for rubles goods that had previously been available only in Russia in hard-currency stores; by factoring inflation into the ruble price, they would make more money than they did selling for hard currency, and they would reach a much larger market. Agreeing to test Tariko's theory, Ferrero provided him with a consignment of chocolates. Tariko remembers the first time that Kinder Surprise chocolate eggs went on sale in a Moscow shop; in the poorly-stocked, not very clean surroundings, the Ferrero display stand stood out like an apparition from another world. Everyone who came into the shop, from babies to *babushkas*, went straight to the stand, and when Tariko explained that there was even a toy inside each egg, they were eager to buy. Despite the very high price to Russians, the chocolates sold out immediately.

Tariko followed this success with a presentation of a business plan for importing Ferrero chocolates on a larger scale. Impressed by the plan, the firm hired him as their consultant for the Russian market.

News of this young Russian traveled fast in the Turin area of Italy where the Ferrero headquarters were located. Executives soon approached Tariko from the nearby headquarters of Martini & Rossi. They reached an agreement with Roust Inc. (which Tariko had founded in 1992) to distribute Martini vermouth in Russia. When the first consignment arrived by truck at the Eliseevsky supermarket in Moscow, an energetic young man was there to unload it: Tariko himself.

Despite the astronomical price – the equivalent of about US$50 at today's prices – people started to buy. First a bottle per day was sold, then five, then ten. Soon Roust had the necessary distribution network in place to supply Martini to other large supermarkets. By the end of the first month, Roust had sold more Martini vermouth in Russia than Martini & Rossi had sold there in the entire previous year. Extremely pleased with these results, Martini & Rossi signed a deal making Roust their importer for Russia. By 1994, Roust had established itself as Russia's leading importer of upmarket beverage alcohol products. The company then enlarged its product line to include, among others, Johnnie Walker scotches, Smirnoff vodka, Gordon's gin, J&B scotch, Bailey's cream liqueur, Metaxa liqueur and two brands of French champagne: Veuve Cliquot and Krug. In 1998, Roust became the largest importer of Martini vermouth in the world, with a volume of 1½ million nine-liter cases per year.

Roustam Tariko was smart enough to realize early on that he did not have the experience to run such an increasingly complex and profitable business on his own. He decided that he wanted his organization to be based on Western management systems and organization, rather than the old Soviet way of doing business. He says that he adopted a deliberate policy of associating with major foreign companies for two reasons. The first was to learn from the Western companies and use them as models. He worked very closely with Martini & Rossi executives in the beginning, some of whom he still considers to be his mentors. He also frequently called on advisers at Goldman Sachs, McKinsey and PricewaterhouseCoopers. The second reason for his association with Western firms was the protection he suggested they would provide against corrupt and criminal elements in Russia. By working in the 'shadow' of powerful Western companies, according to Tariko, Roust was less vulnerable to the influence of regional syndicates and the Mafia.

As he began to set up his organization, Tariko's natural inclination was to gather an executive team that he could trust, who would be as dedicated to the success of the company as he was. Tariko felt that the best way for him to do this was to put his best friends in key positions. He called on five of his oldest friends – all of whom, like Tariko, came from the same small city in Tartarstan

– to help him run the business. Tariko's friends were strategically placed in key managerial positions.

One of the friends in this group, Igor Kosarev, shared perhaps the most important role with Tariko in the early days of Roust. He was the director of Roust, Moscow. Kosarev and Tariko's roles were separate but complementary, creating an executive dyad at the top of the company. Tariko explained:

> In the beginning, I focused on establishing relationships with foreigners, and Igor established the relationships we needed with the government. Though he didn't have strong marketing and HR skills, he was essential in establishing the operations of the company. Igor was able to work with government officials. I am a Tartar, so I couldn't develop the kind of friendships with Russian officials that he did. He's a native Russian, so he's similar to them. He followed a classic Soviet career path before joining Roust. He worked for the government, for the Communist Party, and for the Moscow Pravda. He met Yeltsin regularly when Yeltsin was mayor and then First Secretary of the Communist Party. I never wanted to work for the government, so I struggled with the travel agencies and the Italian companies.
>
> Igor benefited the company enormously in the early days, because he could solve almost any problem we ran into with the government. He was very creative in that area. We quickly became the most successful importation business in the country, mainly because all our products passed the border with no problem. The government trusted us. Igor also managed our relationship with the tax authorities. If you didn't have a good relationship with the tax authorities, every 10 days or so a policeman would come to your office asking for a bribe or causing trouble. But Igor was very tough and well connected, so we never had to pay any bribes.

According to Tariko, these special links to government officials, strengthened by the payment of required taxes, served as a 'roof' for the organization, protecting it in areas that the 'shadow' of Tariko's Western allies didn't reach. For example, several years ago the Mafia threatened a top executive of Roust in St Petersburg. Igor appealed to his special government contacts for help. They gave him a phone number to pass on to the people who were threatening the St Petersburg executive. 'We gave them the telephone number, and we never heard from them again', Tariko said. 'The government people probably said something like, "Don't touch this company because it's under government control". The government looks at the bottom line; if a company is paying a lot of taxes, they protect it. Igor got us out of many difficult situations like this.'

RUSSIAN STANDARD VODKA

By the late 1990s, Roust Inc. had become a tremendously successful import and distribution business. However, Tariko was not one to rest on his laurels. He realized that distribution skills were not enough. He decided that the logical next step for him, after distributing foreign brands for so long, would be to begin marketing and advertising these brands himself. He negotiated with Bacardi Ltd and proceeded to create an in-house advertising and marketing division in Roust to promote their brands. Through this experience, he became interested in brand management and focused on this area with advice from McKinsey.

At the same time, he realized that he now had the experience and organizational structures in place to allow him to create his own premium alcohol brand, made in Russia. In 1997 he formed a company to develop and produce what would be called Russian Standard vodka – a product designed to conquer not only the domestic market, but also to challenge the popularity and market position of Stolichnaya and other established premium brands all around the world. To exploit the brand management experience he had gained with Bacardi, he decided that Russian Standard would eventually evolve into a brand management organization.

Once again Tariko was taking on a major challenge. The domestic alcohol market, oversaturated already, was plagued by slim profit margins and onerous taxes. Government policy toward the production of alcohol and spirits partially accounted for the lack of major capital investment in the industry, the deterioration of quality standards and the loss of traditional expertise. The few new development projects and production launches were mostly for regional markets, and all focused on medium or low price ranges, where demand was highest. Few companies dared to enter export markets, and even fewer succeeded. Added to this was the enormous problem of building a robust distribution network in a huge country where involvement with regional distributors, intermediaries and even criminals was difficult to avoid, and robbery and hijacking were common.

Though aware of all these problems from his experience importing and distributing Martini & Rossi products, Tariko was confident that if anyone in Russia knew the ropes, it was he. He decided to focus on the consumers he knew – drinkers of premium alcoholic beverages – and to launch a top-quality vodka for both domestic and export markets. The design and quality of the bottle, label and cap were also developed to support the premium vodka image, though for the packaging components the company had to go to foreign manufacturers to meet its stringent quality requirements.

The launch of Russian Standard vodka was successful, and the new product quickly gained a significant market share in the domestic market, even beating arch-rivals Finlandia and Absolut. It did well in its export debut as well: it was launched in Italy in March 2000, and stocks intended to cover demand for a year and a half were depleted in one month. By 2003, Russian Standard vodka was fast approaching sales of 9 million liters and was available in 16 countries outside Russia. Tariko's greatest subsequent challenge would be success in the North American markets, and ultimately to build a worldwide brand. Ironically, acceptance by Western markets would give the Russian Standard brand a kind of cachet that would make it an even more desirable product in Russia and Eastern European countries.

RUSSIAN STANDARD: A BUSINESS MODEL IN SEARCH OF MEANING

The creation of Russian Standard vodka marked the beginning of the transformation of Roust Inc. Parallel to the creation of Russian Standard vodka, Tariko began to think about developing a business model for his growing organization. He wanted to create a model that would allow steady evolution – and, even more important, stability – for the organization, even in periods of economic crisis. He could see that all around him (in the late 1990s) Russia was crumbling. Geographical borders were fluctuating; the government was unstable; the economy was in ruins; the ruble in freefall. Worse yet, he felt that Russians were suffering psychologically. As they lost their status as a world power and the pride that that status entailed, standards of various kinds declined or disappeared: moral standards, political standards, quality standards. Targeting the consumer market, the Russian Standard brand would promote new products and services that would recall the high standards of Russia's pre-Revolutionary past, while at the same time becoming a symbol of a new Russia.

Tariko's vision, developed in the early days of Russian Standard, would be that the brand should reflect *central* Russian values, in the way that Coca-Cola represents the central values of Americans: freedom, friendship, and so on. If all would go according to plan, he hoped that the Russian Standard brand would be linked to Russia in the way that Mercedes *is* Germany, Coca-Cola *is* the US, Sony *is* Japan, and Christian Dior *is* France. To him, these products are seen as tangible symbols of the industriousness and intelligence of the people, or the prosperity and technical superiority of the nation. Tariko explains:

> The products people buy are like a mirror of themselves. There are three values that we look at in brand management. We can talk about them as a triangle of values that any premium brand will have. On the bottom, you have *functional* values. For example, Coca-Cola's functional values are: 'sweet brown drink, red can'. The next level is more complicated; it reflects *expressive* values. They show with whom we identify. Taking Coke again, the expressive values are 'young, American', etc. On the top of the triangle are *central* values. For Coke, these would be things like love, freedom, patriotism, friendship, and so on. Generic brands are different from premium brands because they don't try to reach people at the level of central or expressive values. Like washing powders: wash quicker, whiter, whatever, but that's it. If you drink Coke, though, you're saying, 'I'm free; I'm part of a community'. That's why it's so difficult to compete with Coke. It's a simple product to produce, but it's very difficult to recreate those central values. I'm interested only in brands that have all these three values. I'm not interested in brands that don't communicate central values.

The choice of Russian Standard as the name of the vodka as well as the brand management company was an obvious one. Russian Standard would ideally not only gain a large market share of loyal consumers won over by the quality of its products and services, but would encourage Russians to raise their standards in other areas of their lives as well. Russian Standard would become a benchmark, synonymous with top quality and with honest, fair business practices with consumers. Above all, it would be truly *made in Russia*. Tariko codified this in a way that could be communicated to his employees and customers:

> Our philosophy is made very clear in our vision statement, which is posted on all our walls. We say that Russian Standard is not just a brand; it's a business model that unifies people. There are five key principles. The first is the overriding principle of our company: 'Create new value instead of redistributing existing assets'. The second is very practical, almost moralizing: 'We are fair and thus rewarded with trust'. We emphasize that it's a big advantage to be honest. It's practical and useful, because if people trust you, business is easier. It's quite an important principle for us. The third principle is purely about our positioning: 'All we create is solid and beautiful'. We will produce only beautiful services or products. Not necessarily expensive. The fourth principle: 'We build the future on the bedrock of the past'. The fifth principle: 'We are working for the prosperity of Russia. We are a Russian company'.

The Russian Standard Company was set up under the watchful eye of Roust Holding Limited to produce and market its vodka, along with a line of other products and services to be identified and developed. Roust Inc., the distribution business, was also moved under the umbrella of the holding company. Other products for development by the Russian Standard Company Tariko initially considered were caviar, perfume, or a clothing line, all of which would meet international expectations for quality. Later, however, Tariko reconsidered his plans about, for example, going into the caviar market. He explained that in order to get the quality he was looking for he would be forced to kill too many fish. His strategic plan for the Russian Standard Company would not change however. He continued to look for new ideas.

RUSSIAN STANDARD BANK

The fallout from the August 1998 financial crisis in Russia provided an opportunity for the organization to expand in a new direction, and for Tariko to test his business model. He felt ready to multiply his skills and broaden his interests. In 1999, with the help of McKinsey advisors, he came to the conclusion that there was a niche market in Russia for a bank that would have 'good assets, normal assets from a financial point of view'. He decided to start a bank that would operate according to Russian Standard principles. The bank's main focus would be on consumers.

Through McKinsey contacts, he met several experienced Russian bankers, many of which came from now bankrupt first post-communism banks or from the Central Bank of Russia. Russian Standard Bank opened in June 1999. As of early 2000, it was already ranked at about 45 out of the 800 banks in Russia in terms of capital, with 170 employees.

The strategy for the Russian Standard Bank initially included both business-to-business and business-to-consumer services, but eventually concentrated on the retail side. Consumer lending and credit cards for Russian citizens were declared top priorities. (Tariko says he eventually wants to be the 'GE Capital of Russia'.) As consumer confidence in bank savings accounts was very low in Russia in the environment following the 1998 financial crisis, the Russian Standard Bank initially only loaned money, but did not have any deposit accounts. Later, with return of trust of banking institutions, deposit accounts were introduced. The target market at that time was identified as Russian middle-class borrowers, and the maximum amount of credit was initially set at the equivalent of US$500. Similar small-lending programs in Latin America and Eastern Europe, and the first analysis of the Russian Standard program, show this type of program to be profitable and fairly low-risk; and Russian Standard Bank executives assumed that an individual wouldn't disappear with such a small amount.

Tariko's emphasis on Russian Standard core values of stability and fair practices is still in effect as an important element of the Bank's strategy:

> In the past, Russian banks have lacked the focus on market research that is essential in the consumer-goods arena. They were notorious for long queues and surly cashiers. Without listening to their customers' needs, they were unable to offer excellent, customer-oriented service. We believe that our strength in creating innovative, creative marketing approaches is a powerful advantage in building a customer base and creating market value.

In the early stages of the Bank's growth, Tariko actively courted foreign banks to become the main shareholders, partly because they are important cornerstones in a stable banking structure in Russia. He initially intended to increase the US$25 million already invested in the bank by US$150 million in foreign investment over the next four years. He feels that if the bank is financially sound, with significant foreign stakeholders, that grounding will inspire confidence in its clients. Tariko describes Russian Standard Bank as something like a new paradigm in Russian banking – based on a distinctive corporate culture, with internationally acceptable accounting and practices compatible with a position in international finance.

Developing a truly independent private bank in Russia is not an easy task. As in any economy, banks are strategically important targets for government control. But Tariko appears once more to be using a balance of power to good effect: foreign equity and a large customer base should protect against government or other undue influence. In addition, Tariko says he will see that ties to the government are kept friendly but distant: 'Russian Standard Bank has had a very positive response from foreigners already, because they are willing to work with independent institutions while most of the big banks in Russia used to be associated with the government. They see our bank as a viable alternative. And our bank has been phenomenally successful. We have now a leading position in consumer lending.'

In February 2003, the International Finance Corporation (IFC), the private sector division of the World Bank Group, made a US$ 10 million equity investment in the Russian Standard Bank, the only IFC equity investment in a Russian bank after the 1998 financial crisis. In December 2003, IFC signed an agreement to provide a three year US$ 40 million ruble-linked revolving loan to the Russian Standard Bank.

In an IFC press release on December 10, IFC's Director for Central and Eastern Europe, Edward Nassim, said, 'Russian Standard Bank is an innovative partner and a pioneer of consumer finance in the country. Russian Standard Bank is growing fast and by providing flexible financing, IFC will support its new growth targets.'

RUSSIAN STANDARD ON-LINE: AN INTERNET BUSINESS EXPERIMENT

The paint had hardly dried in Russian Standard Bank when another business opportunity fell into Tariko's lap. In the summer of 1999, friends from Goldman Sachs told Tariko that they saw him as the person to build an on-line Internet service in Russia. Tariko, who had already been thinking about the Internet, became intrigued by his friends' suggestions.

He began by developing a web portal, Russian Standard On-line. Realizing that a portal would have to be linked to services, he cast about for ideas. An idea about establishing a cyber grocery emerged. 'People have to eat, so if anything could get them to use the Internet, the cyber grocery would', Tariko thought. Moreover, he thought this would exploit the synergies between his divisions – Roust, the importation and distribution division; Russian Standard Company, the product development division; Russian Standard Bank; and Russian Standard On-line – his organization, it seemed, could capture a large share of the developing business-to-business and business-to-consumer market in Russia, and serve as a major distributor for Western companies. To develop his on-line business, Tariko hired a team of successful ex-consultants from major strategy consulting powerhouses.

Unfortunately, this project did not work out, like many other Internet bubble ideas worldwide. Tariko describes a combination of what he calls objective and subjective reasons:

> Objectively, this is a tough business, requiring a lot of investment. Subjectively, I didn't have enough force to succeed. I saw the vodka and banking businesses growing, with limitless opportunities. Simultaneously, my Internet business was developing a lot of difficulties, but I just failed to push hard enough both in terms of human resources and investments necessary.
>
> There were some strategic mistakes made in our B2B business. I had underestimated the extent to which consumer market was 'black'. I had believed that this market was 20–30 per cent black, but it happened to be much more black than I had expected. So these Internet projects were my major disappointments. I decided to leave this business and closed the B2B and B2C e-commerce companies. I lost a considerable amount of money, and I had to say good-bye to all the people who were working there.

After dismantling this project, Tariko threw his energy into growing his three remaining businesses: distribution of premium imported beverage alcohol brands; Russian Standard Vodka and the development of other Russian Standard branded products; and Russian Standard Bank.

BUILDING A BRAND MANAGEMENT ORGANIZATION

With a desire to make his firm a 'billion dollar company within 10 years', Tariko concentrated his efforts on making Russian Standard a global umbrella brand. He wanted to emulate companies like Virgin, GE or Disney who successfully brand products and services from different categories under the same name. In 2001 he conducted a survey on the essence of the Russian Standard brand in order to eventually convey it to the consumers. After several months of contemplating research reports; meeting with notable Russian media and arts personalities; customer focus groups; and chance encounters during his travels all over Russia, an overall brand strategy was born. In essence, Tariko decided, the brand 'embraced the past...and inspired progress'.

This search for the essence of the brand helped Tariko refine his businesses. First, he transformed the distribution of imported premium alcohol brands. Little by little, this business was becoming less interesting to Tariko. Although still considerable in terms of volume and revenue, it was in fact tangential to the organization. This shift correlated with changes in Roust's relationships with its suppliers. Bacardi-Martini set up its own distribution in Russia in early 2002.[1] Although distribution of Bacardi-Martini's products had brought in 50 per cent of the company's profit and up to 60 per cent of turnover, the dissolution of the partnership turned out to be a blessing. Both in terms of profit and turnover, Russian Standard vodka quickly made up for the lost income from Bacardi-

Martini products. Tariko explained: 'We used to be an importing company that produced and sold its own vodka as well. Now we have become the Russian Standard Vodka Company that also distributes foreign brands.'

As far as the bank is concerned, Tariko's belief that consumer credit would be a good business turned out to be true. The bank grew to an organization employing 1500 people with offices in Moscow and 12 other cities by early 2003. It was expected that by the end of 2003 the organization would have twice as many employees. For the first time in Russian history, it was possible to set up a line of credit in no more than 15 minutes, at a bank branch or directly at an electronics or home appliances store. For the first time in Russia it became possible to get a real credit card (debit cards have been available since about 1993). For Tariko it's a symbolic change – a new life-style choice has been made possible thanks to his bank.

The Bank's website says:

Our Bank is dedicated to the principles implicit in the name Russian Standard. The essence of our philosophy lies in declaring, and then practicing, new standards for doing business in Russia:

Creation

We are creating wealth, not merely redistributing it.

Trust

We operate honestly, and have the trust of others.

Perfection

Everything that we create is of high quality and dependable.

Experience

We are building the future while remembering the lessons of the past.

Patriotism

We work for the benefit of Russia.

Vodka and banking make an unusual cocktail, not always easy to blend. In January 2000, an advertising campaign was rolled out to promote the Russian Standard brand. The emphasis was on fixing in consumers' minds the concept that Russia has a past rich in splendor and tradition – a past from which Russian Standard brands draw inspiration, while at the same time firmly looking toward the future. Stereotypical images of Russian were contrasted with new 'standards' which were supposed to be common in contemporary Russia but still unknown to the world. Tariko told us:

Standards are like traffic lights; it's possible to drive without them, but watch out! Russia is like a country with no traffic lights. We want to say to Russian consumers, 'We have beautiful things in our country that were made in the past, but let's move forward'. Our advertising campaign reflected this. For example, on one side of a billboard, you saw a *matrjoshka* [a Russian doll]. It's a symbol, but a boring one. So on the other side of the sign was a beautiful Russian lady dressed in a modern way. She looked very self-assured, as if she knew where she was going. The copy line read: 'Standard Russian – Russian Standard.'

However, despite high expectations on the part of Tariko and Russian Standard executives, the 'Standard Russian – Russian Standard' campaign did not have a significant impact on vodka sales. Moreover, the management and some customers of the Russian Standard Bank resented it. They felt it was inconsistent with the image of seriousness and trustworthiness the bank was supposed to convey. As a result, Tariko decided to stop the 'Standard Russian – Russian Standard' campaign. As explained by a marketing executive from Russian Standard:

> The campaign, which was originally developed for international markets, was stopped in Russia because, although we perceived it as clever and funny, some people felt it was disrespectful of Russia's past and culture, like *matrjoshkas*, *babushkas*, etc. But more importantly, Russian Standard is much more than vodka. Russian Standard is about a Russian ideal, something that embraces our past, but inspires progress. That is the Russian standard. The initial campaign was clever, but fell far short of the real essence of the brand.

GETTING ORGANIZED

As the organization grew, Roustam Tariko tried to loosen his control of Roust Trading Ltd and its divisions while also trying to build a top-performing management team with a strong entrepreneurial orientation. There were some growing pains. The organization had to evolve from an exciting but messy new venture run by a group of somewhat inexperienced friends, to a more professional enterprise with systems that would permit rapid but stable growth.

A self-described micromanager and workaholic, for many years Tariko remained directly involved in strategic and operational issues, and was also the key decision-maker. All managers responsible for the various company functions and activities reported to him. The divisions used very strict IT tracking systems; all tasks and deadlines were entered into the system and all managers provided daily progress reports. (This was later reduced to weekly reports.) This information was forwarded directly to Tariko. He used to check out the system almost every morning, staying at the center of all activities and taking the pulse of the organization regularly. He sent e-mails to managers when he had a question or concern, following up with phone calls and scheduled meetings if necessary. Backing up this strict system with a less rigid personal touch, Tariko tried to be accessible for informal meetings and discussions. He also filled a cross-coordination role, serving as a liaison between all functions. He maintained an exhausting schedule, working from home and in the office until well into the night, with time off only for a run and a working dinner.

Although Roust was quite centralized by Western criteria, Tariko believed that there was much more trust between him and his subordinates than is the case in most Russian companies, and relationships were more informal. No matter how lowly or lofty the position, Tariko used to interview every job applicant himself, looking for ambition and evidence of an ability to learn. The interview process was unhurried, with emphasis on getting to know the candidate and, within certain guidelines, creating a position to fit their strengths and interests. Most employees were young, though Roust also tried to hire experienced professionals in positions that required them. Most of the employees were (and still are) on first-name terms with each other and with the boss, and Tariko insisted that people use the familiar *ty* as opposed to the more formal *vy*. Unlike the typical Moscow businessman, said colleagues, Tariko asked for, listened to and valued others' opinions (or, at least, it seemed so).

By 2000, changes in the nature and scope of business called for a change in management. Although Tariko's original group of five close friends served him well in executive positions, their strong ties to him made the situation complex. In the early 'crazy' days of Roust Inc., Tariko said, the close bonds he shared with his old friends served the company as a kind of corporate culture. They were all young, with little Western business experience, but they could count on their loyalty to each other and the company. As Roust Inc. grew, Tariko focused on hiring competent outsiders to accommodate the company's rapid expansion while, as he admits, neglecting the development of the skills of his original group of friends. For instance, one of the friends initially took care of the accounting function in the organization. However, with growth and more challenging tasks ahead Tariko realized:

> He is an old-style accountant. In order to work in Roust, you need Western type skills, which is why he isn't number one any more. He isn't chief accountant of the holding company, but of Roust Inc. He didn't evolve with the organization, picking up Western skills along the way; probably because he was working too hard (and I'm responsible for that).

Both Tariko and his friends realized that their positions needed to evolve to keep pace with the further development of the organization. On one hand, they had always been big supporters of the business and had worked very hard. But on the other hand, they were conservative and didn't want to loosen control. They did recognize the need to grow, from a start-up led by a group of friends who knew and trusted each other, to a more professional organization with a corporate culture that would instill and enforce the organization's values.

In order to resolve these problems, Tariko implemented a certain amount of organizational restructuring:

> Most of my original friends have changed positions to support me in starting up new businesses. All these guys are good for start-ups; they don't mind sitting in rooms with nothing, instead of beautiful offices. They don't care about comfort, big cars, whatever, because they've already 'made it' several times over. I use them because it's quite difficult to bring in someone from the outside at the very beginning. Imagine that you're a top executive at Coca-Cola, and I try to convince you to join a start-up company. On the other hand, people with a lot of outside professional experience are best for established businesses.

Tariko believes that the problems he faced were evolutionary in nature. In the first phase of an entrepreneurial start-up, the founder typically invites three or four friends and relatives to help launch the new business. This business is held together through friendship ties, regardless of the fact that there are bosses and subordinates. However, if the business is successful and the complexity of the organization increases, structures based on friendship may hinder further development. Eventually, the owner becomes less involved in day-to-day operations, and has less control over executives. This is the moment when, in Tariko's opinion, problems start. He says it is difficult to identify talented managers who can be entrusted with taking care of the 'cherished baby' the owner has been nurturing for several hectic years. Still, Tariko acknowledges, at a certain moment the entrepreneur must find the courage to admit that he can't handle the business alone:

> Take the bank, for instance. We hire between 50 and 100 people every month, to fill positions at all levels in the bank. I came to a Bank employees' party and saw 1500 people there. Soon we will have 3000 people working for the bank. It's a different scope of HR challenge.

For Tariko, a successful business requires a delicate balance between people and money. Sometimes the business is making a profit, but hasn't got the right people. Or, on the other hand, you've got good people, but do not have enough money in the coffers. This is a constant set of challenges for the owner. In 2003, Tariko said:

> I don't want to run day-to-day operations of the business. In the past I did 150 per cent of the day-to-day operational work; now I do about 30 per cent. I dream of doing zero per cent operational work! I want to have self-sufficient people who can make their own decisions. I am steadily moving in this direction. I see my task as finding the right type of business for us; creating a strategy for developing such a business; then building the right structure for execution of the business plan. My primary skills

are in selection of the right business opportunities, developing a strategy, and then launching the strategy.

I know what I'm good at: developing ideas, calculating how much money is needed to implement them, and finding the right people – I think this is my major leadership function. This is from the professional point of view. From a personal standpoint, I think the main challenge of leadership is the need to inspire the people around you. People work not only for money, and not only for the Russian Standard idea, but also because they are part of a good team. There must be a good atmosphere in the company. Creating this corporate culture is one of my major tasks.

In a 2002 interview with a Russian newspaper, Tariko said 'we' more often than 'I': 'we want', 'we have done'. In reality, the 40-year-old Tariko was still very much in control of all his organizations.[2] Although the three Roust Holding companies (Roust Inc.: distribution of alcohol with an annual turnover of about $100 million; Russian Standard Vodka: with turnover of about $60 million, and Russian Standard Bank with assets of over $200 million) were run by separate boards, all of them were chaired by Tariko. Two years later, in 2003, Tariko, however, said that the organization was less of a one-man-show. He commented:

The guys who manage both Russian Standard and the Bank are very competent people. There some things that I don't even understand any more. I only look at the budgets and see that they have spent $12 million on a project. I no longer ask why they spent $12 million instead of $11 million. All I ask is about how to make them interested in spending $11 million.

However, finding the right people to run the show has turned out to be a difficult task. Tariko hired and then fired many experienced top managers, Russians and foreigners alike, including two bank chairmen, CEO for the group, and, ironically, the HR Director, who was supposed to help deal with personnel issues. Tariko even mentioned that his organization had developed a bad reputation with the executive search and recruitment consultants. He offered the following explanation of the situation:

The first factor is very objective: we are a fast growing company. Take, for example, Goldman Sachs. People are constantly being kicked out of Goldman Sachs, and nobody criticizes the company for that. It's accepted that those people just don't work well enough to reach their targets. I let people go for the same reason; because they fail to run as quickly as I would like them to. They are incapable of doing that. There are some people who can't work very intensively. They feel very unhappy if they have to, they start having problems in their families, banal things like that. They don't want to work around the clock, they don't want to be totally concentrated on what they are doing. For such people it is very difficult to breath in a company like ours, where the growth rate is 300 per cent per annum. People who can't hack it are the ones who want to have a more normal life.

The second reason is related to the complexity of the business we are in. Imagine that you are interviewing a person. He/she has graduated from a good university, has got good experience in a Western company; the track record is good, everything seems to be OK. Unfortunately, after this person starts on the job, you find out that he/she is not capable of meeting our requirements to the fullest extent. The person just can't invent the type of advertising campaign I am looking for, or he fails to be able to calculate the default rate to the very detail. It might be that they are just lacking creative or mathematical skills. No matter how detailed the job interview, it is impossible to guarantee in advance whether the person will be able to do the job.

For example, a person might come from a business where they were designing Mercedes, thinking that they will be doing something similar in our organization. However, I am constantly building new businesses. In other words, I am inviting the person to join a start-up business in which neither of us has previous experience. It may happen that skills-wise this person fails to meet my needs.

The third factor contributing to my decisions to say good-bye to people is the development factor. Very often people whom I need today will no longer be necessary for me tomorrow. People who can manage a $30 million business, start having problems when they need to run a $100 million business. And the people who can run a $100 million business wouldn't have joined me when I had a $30 million business, because the company was too small to interest them.

For example, in my bank today I need people with completely different skills from those whom I hired just one year ago. In normally developing countries you see a similar situation, but it typically takes place over a five-year period, and when people leave five years after they joined the company, nobody is surprised. In our case, with a 300 per cent growth per year, we do what other companies do in five years. That's why a person may become less useful here very quickly.

The fourth factor that I have to mention is that ironically, because Russian Standard is a marketing business that tries to reach people on an emotional level, the public seems to have a strong reaction to negative news about Russian Standard. Several times when well-known executives left Russian Standard, people reacted as if it were a scandal. Partially, it's the fault of the people who are leaving; partially it's the fault of the press. Mass media love scandals. If a top executive at a steel mill was fired, nobody outside of the factory would even pay any attention.

As Tariko came to realize, the difference between Russian Standard and a steel mill is that Tariko attracted (and sometimes fired) people who were well-known in the elite labor market for Russian executives. As experienced managers were still scarce, the career moves of people of such caliber were monitored and actively discussed in the Russian business community. Russian Standard's 'revolving door' reputation did not help Tariko to attract the talent he was looking for. Inside the company some top managers even placed bets on how long they or their colleagues would be able to stay in the organization. On the other hand, those who had been in the organization for at least 12 months tended to stay on for a long term. Tariko said:

The transition and restructuring was painful. I understand that I caused damage to some people, because I made a mistake in selecting them, or, maybe, they made a mistake in their decision to work for me. I paid for this, and they paid for this as well, and I regret that.

Now my task is to turn around the public view of this situation. Some executive search companies still consider us to be rather scandalous and risky for top managers. I need to address this issue publicly. Overall, however, my feeling is that the crisis is over. The crisis was related to the transition from a one-man show to a corporation. Taking into account that this process involves people's careers, it can't happen without some damage to me and to them. But, if you look at our businesses, you'll see that all this is justified. At the end of the day, the results of the business are good.

What attracts them to my company is that we offer them a future. I can tell them that if they work in a foreign company, they'll probably never make it to the top. It's unlikely that, in the near future, there will be a Russian at the head of an American or French global organization, for example. The competition for these top jobs is much tougher. I tell young, high-potential Russian executives that if they work in Russia, they'll advance farther and faster. I've never even considered leaving Russia myself.

To succeed in his company, one needs to be a talented individual. Here is how Roustam Tariko defines talent:

Talented people enjoy what they are doing because they've always wanted to do it, and they know that they do their job well. It doesn't matter where they work. They're self-sufficient, and they behave differently: they don't participate in office politics; they don't feel hurt when someone says something unpleasant; and they are usually relaxed. It's very interesting to watch these people. I can tell very quickly if a person is talented or not. I see how many ideas this person generates. A good manager can generate one idea per year, but an exceptionally talented person can generate 300 ideas. Such a person will spend a longer time in our organization.

Tariko acknowledged that talented people may suffer from lack of persistence in putting their visions into practice. He formed teams that provided a supportive structure for the creative people. Because his businesses had a high return on investment, he could afford to create teams in which there was a certain amount of overlapping responsibility.

Talented people are often lazy. They can't implement their ideas. Such people also run risks because they don't bother to do the necessary preparation. I often put three solid managers in a team with one highly-talented individual; a team like this is able to consistently put good ideas into practice.

Tariko also realized that to motivate his executives to invest their ideas and talents in his company, he needed to provide them with tangible rewards.

First of all, beginning in 2001 I started designing corporate governance principles that protect my employees and me. For example, compensation agreements with top managers are now clear and much more predictable for both the individuals concerned and myself. So I am much more relaxed now than I was a few years ago.

In general, his compensation strategy for top management was to pay more than market average and offer financial incentives, such as bonuses that may reach the equivalent of their annual salary. Tariko signed agreements with several managers at the Russian Standard Bank offering them shares if objectives were met. Following recommendations from McKinsey, he offered shares to people who successfully contributed to the market capitalization growth of his organization by 50 per cent or more. He is ready to give up to 20 per cent of shares in his banking business to employees. Tariko acknowledged that not all employees believe that taking shares in the bank is such a good deal. Some of them opted for financial compensation instead (bonuses may be equal to annual salary). Tariko, nevertheless, believed that short-term incentives such as salaries and bonuses are not enough for creating a successful bank. He wanted managers to be motivated for at least five years ahead.

In his alcohol distribution business, on the other hand, he shared profits with his top managers, because the trading company per se has almost no value. For example, if the two star brands, Russian Standard Vodka and Johnnie Walker, were taken out of the operations of the distribution company, its value would drop tenfold.

In Tariko's opinion, one of his achievements is that he managed to transfer his passion for the Russian Standard brand to his employees:

> Many people wouldn't be working here if it weren't for the Russian Standard brand. They love the brand. And I don't think that I am the only one who owns it. In reality, this brand belongs to all Russians who see in it a lot of positive things that have happened, are happening, and will happen in our country. That's why the people working for the organization see through this brand that yes, we, Russians, are educated, and that we can be successful. People understand that legally, it's Roustam Tariko who owns the brand, but de facto it belongs to them. They built it, they are developing it, and they take good care of it.

ROUSTAM TARIKO HIMSELF

Who is Roustam Tariko? What drives him? No organization can be analysed without a close look at the inner theatre – the early developmental influences – of its founder, and Russian Standard is no exception. It is, after all, the founder's energy, enthusiasm and charisma that are the source of corporate culture. Tariko has all those traits in abundance, wrapped in a complex personality that is not without contradictions.

Tariko was born in 1962 in Menzelinsk, a city in Tartarstan. His mother divorced his father when Tariko was one, for reasons that were never made clear to Tariko. His mother held a prominent position in the local Communist Party, traveling frequently. However, she seems to have been able to compensate for the lack of a father in the household, as well as for the little time she had in her busy schedule for her son. Because Tartars are a very unified group who form tight-knit communities, Tariko was raised as the adored child of a loving matriarchal extended family.

Tariko remembers being a self-sufficient and confident child. After seeing an old picture of himself, taken when he was seven years old and just starting school, he reflected:

It's a beautiful picture. I look so proud of myself! I clearly knew that I had a good future. I was so surprised, looking at the picture, to see that conviction in myself as such a young boy. I always thought that it was only with experience that you could start to say to yourself, 'Ah-ha, you could be lucky! You have enough skills; you're smart'. But looking at that picture of my first day of school, I can see now that I thought those things about myself even then. It's probably because of my mother; my mother loved me so much.

His first business venture was at 16, as a singer in a rock band along with his would-be business partners. Through his mother's connections, their group became the official rock band of Menzelinsk, playing everything from disco evenings to weddings. They went by the melodious name of 'Vocal Instrumental Group of the Palace of Culture of Menzelinsk'. Hardly the Beatles, but Tariko did earn the generous salary of 70 rubles per month.

It's obvious that Tariko draws a great deal of strength from these happy recollection. For all his present drive and ambition, he evidently relies heavily on his past and on long-established contacts for stability and security. Not only are some of his closest colleagues his school friends from Tartarstan, but he also tries to apply lessons learned as a boy to his business and personal life as an adult:

The family is the most important influence. How much love did you get from your mother when you were young? I know what keeps me strong: I grew up with a huge amount of love from my mother. You have a lot of stress when you're young. Either you see your mother's face everywhere, and so it's okay, or you don't, and it's quite devastating for a child.

I interpret charisma as how much you can love people – how many of them you have the energy to love. It goes in degrees. One man loves only his dog; another his dog and family; another his dog, family and neighbors; and so on. But how do you find enough energy to love hundreds or even thousands of people in your company? ... Thinking back to my childhood, I see that I'm quite happy and successful because my mother dedicated so much energy to me. And I'm using it still.

Tariko is an intense man whose mind always seems to be racing. He gives the impression that he's taking in not only everything that's being said, but everything in the room. He's also a good, reflective listener. He's obviously driven, and his conviction when he talks about his vision for Russian Standard is convincing. He talks quite easily about himself, apparently unafraid to examine his own strengths and weaknesses. He's keen to learn from others at all levels but goes to the top for his primary professional advice. He's also a talented linguist, speaking fluent English and Italian. He's often compared to Richard Branson; and while he concedes that there are similarities, he also insists that his vision and business model are unique, suited to success in a turbulent nation.

When asked about his leadership philosophy, he explained that his 'love of beautiful things' and his 'hopes for Russia' are what motivates him. He's obviously proud of the organization he has created, and has very clear ideas on the development of the architecture and leadership of his organization:

> When I started my business, I acted intuitively. My personal excitement and interests drove me. When I began, I wasn't able to express why I was working with Martini instead of selling shoes, for example. Only later did I understand that aesthetics provided a lot of excitement for me, so that's why I moved to premium goods.
>
> Russians like to buy premium goods, but they don't have a track record of producing very beautiful products. Producing premium goods takes about 10 times more effort than producing average goods. You need not only money and organization, but also experience. Many nations have brands that are symbols, but Russia no longer does. There aren't many things that we build well in Russia any more, and that's our tragedy. Someone once said to me, 'Always have big objectives'. So I'll strive to make the brand that will be recognized by the world as a symbol of Russia. It would be one of the happiest days of my life if someone came to me and said, 'Your brand helps us to understand Russia'.

As enthusiastic as he was about his organization, Tariko was keenly aware of the need to establish a strong and self-sufficient culture, along with systems that could survive without him. He also knew that while he had mastered a delicate balancing act between the powerful forces at play behind the scenes in Russia, he had to remain vigilant. 'The challenge is that it's not just about me any more. The consequences of my decisions now affect a lot of people. This troubles me a lot. I'm responsible for a lot of people, people who have changed their lives because of me, to work for me.'

With his business growing, Tariko started thinking more about the social responsibility he held as a head of the organization. He was convinced that in his consumer-oriented business the notion of social responsibility was closely related to the trust in the minds and hearts of his consumers. With vodka, for instance, the trust is related to being sure that after consumption of his product, people will wake up without unpleasant feelings (he even joked that Russia, a country that is well-known for its high volumes of vodka consumption, would be healthier if people drank Russian Standard rather than cheap, low quality vodka). With the Russian Standard Bank, responsibility meant assuring clients that the information they shared with the bank when applying for credit would not be sold to a third party. With a new idea Tariko was entertaining, a life-insurance company, responsibility lay in making sure that the organization remained permanently stable and solvent.

RUSSIAN STANDARD OF LEADERSHIP

Is there a Russian Standard of leadership? In Tariko's opinion, it is still in the process of development. However, he envisions certain elements of this Russian Standard of leadership. Tariko believes that Russian leaders corresponding to this new standard will be cosmopolitan and patriotic at the same time. Russian leaders, well-educated and well-versed in international business practices, will be difficult to take advantage of in the international arena. They will be as competitive as their colleagues from any other country. With Russian businesses now expanding beyond Russia, being able to cooperate and compete on equal footing with business leaders from other parts of the world has become a necessary part of everyday life. Tariko opposes the view actively lobbied by, for instance, newly emerging Russian business schools that are trying to convince their potential students that in order to do business in Russia you need to study in accordance with a 'Russian MBA curriculum', rather than getting a quality international business education in the West. On the other hand, the patriotic feature of the Russian Standard of leadership means that people will be proud of being Russians, and proud to offer Russian-made goods and services.

Tariko explains:

> Look at this combination of words 'Russian Standard'. By definition, the word 'Russian' has a Russian language root in it. 'Standard', on the other hand, comes from Latin, so this word is international. We want to be Russian, but at the same time, we do understand what the standards are. We are capable of speaking the languages of other people.

Tariko thinks that, although they are not there yet, Russians are moving in the right direction. He wryly observes that Russians meeting each other abroad no longer avoid each other by crossing to the other side of the street, as they used to do just after the perestroika years. In January 2003, while he was in Thailand, he found out that the host of the traditional Russian expatriates' Christmas party was not in Thailand that year. In order to keep the tradition of a Russian Christmas in Thailand alive, Roustam threw a huge party, which attracted many Russians. There was Russian music, Russian food and drinks, naturally including the Russian Standard vodka. What he now describes as a hobby – throwing Russian parties abroad – is turning into a savvy brand marketing strategy for Russian Standard, for Tariko as a model Russian businessman, and for Russia.

LOOKING FORWARD

Tariko often reflects on the future, wondering what's ahead for his organization and what path his own personal development will take. Fantasies about the longer-term future for the organization vary in scope: from launching a low-proof alcohol drink for young adults to starting a life-insurance business and to launching a new airline.

Regarding his business moves, Tariko listens to advice from just about anyone, from professional consultants to taxi drivers and seatmates on airplanes. He's had many influential mentors, including his cousin Nelia Nuriahmetova (who helped him through his degree in economics from Moscow State University), businessmen from Martini & Rossi (whom he has described as father-figures) and senior partners from McKinsey. He's also always had the courage to trust his own judgment. His comments on what lies ahead:

> The future is unknown, of course. For now, I'll stay opportunistic, laying the foundation for whatever comes up. I have a top that I keep on my desk. You ask it a strategic question, then you spin it on a kind of chart, and it lands on *yes, no, today* or *tomorrow*. It's just a joke now, but it shows how far I've come; in the early days, I made a lot of decisions based on intuition. But now I'm starting to understand not only *what* I'm doing, but also *why* I'm doing it. Before I understood what was happening on the professional side; now I'm beginning to understand the deep internal triggers that motivate me. I took a seminar for top executives at INSEAD in which people in positions like mine are encouraged to look at issues of leadership and life balance. What I got out of that seminar has been very helpful from a psychological point of view. Now I understand why I'm so successful, why I work so hard, what I should do next.

He puts it as a priority to attract, develop, and retain executives capable to allowing him to concentrate on the future:

> I want to focus on the vision, implement it, explain to people how serious it is. But I don't want to be like the emperor who thought he was wearing beautiful clothes but was really quite naked. That's why I'm also somewhat of a micromanager: I don't want to have a beautiful vision that fails because of bad performance. If you look at Communism, you see that in theory it was a perfect society, but it failed because people had to wait in breadlines. If what the leader communicates in terms of vision doesn't fit reality, it's a lack of integrity. Customers and people in the organization become cynical, and finally people don't believe anything the leader says. It becomes a nightmare for the organization.

For the foreseeable future, Tariko will continue his high-risk, rapid growth development strategy:

My strategy is common for start-ups: you take more risk in exchange for higher potential returns. I don't see any way for my company to grow quickly without getting into new markets or risky products. Take the bank's consumer loan program. I could carefully analyze P&L and come up with a program to gain 5–10 new clients per day, and in 5 years I would have less than 1 per cent of the market. The other possibility is: I don't worry about the default rate, I go for 100–150 clients per day, and I quickly gain 15 per cent of the Russian market. I am going for this second option.

Finally, he intends to continue his own development:

Concerning my own future development as a leader, I know how to handle the business professionally, positioning the product, business processes, etc. Now I want to work on my relationships with the top managers, who will then be responsible with me for the second tier, and so on. Everybody has professional skills and human skills to a certain degree. I've been building my professional skills. Now I need to build my human skills. In financial terms, I'm capable of handling millions of dollars responsibly. Nobody will misuse our money. Now I need to learn how to handle hundreds or thousands of people.

However the company grows, the guiding principles won't change. I'm trying to keep young Russians in Russia. Brain drain is one of the tragedies of the country. Not only that, but many Russians are wealthy; there are many millions of dollars outside of Russia. I think that this money must come back. The time has come for Russians to invest in Russia. I'm working to build something in Russia. I hope that people will follow my example.

NOTES

1. Upravlenie Kompaniei (2002), 'Owner's task is to 'push' for the last 20%', RCB Publishing House, January.
2. Prosvetov, I. (2001), '*ROUST* is a large and powerful machine...', in: KOMPANIA, No. 5 (201), 11 February, 2002, 22–6.

Commentary: Roustam Tariko and Russian Standard

In many ways, Tariko seemed to be representative of the archetypal Russian entrepreneur. In talking to him, we wanted to have a better idea of what makes him tick, and to uncover the rationale underlying his leadership style. In preparing this case, we spent many hours interviewing and observing Roustam Tariko and his friends and subordinates in his company's headquarters in Moscow. In addition, we were fortunate enough that Tariko participated in Manfred Kets de Vries' top management seminar 'The Challenge of Leadership': an intensely personal program in which top executives examine their own personal style and leadership behavior. During three one-week-long modules spread out over a half-year period, Tariko and his peers (other CEOs) analysed their personal developmental experiences, critical events in their career, and major organizational and personal concerns. Given this close contact (in his case much more personal than with the others), he helped us to identify some significant events in his life that have contributed to his success, as well as some developmental areas that he would need to work on.

Interestingly enough, in studying the background of many entrepreneurs, wherever they come from, the themes of illness, separation, divorce and death in the family seem to be quite common.[1] Tracing their history, we find that the fathers of many male entrepreneurs are frequently absent (whether literally or emotionally) while they tend to have strong, supportive but, at times, very controlling mother figures taking care of them. Furthermore, we can frequently identify entrepreneurial-like role models in the family, with one of the parents playing that role being the most obvious example. In addition, as children and adolescents, these people often demonstrate the first signs of their entrepreneurial disposition by getting engaged in small ventures, be it selling the services of a school band, trading in stamps, or running a car wash service. In many cases, at that period in their lives, some of them take on early leadership positions, like being in charge of a group of boy scouts (in Russia being a leader in the Komsomol organization), running a student newspaper, or being the captain of a football team.

Reflecting on these findings concerning the family constellation of entrepreneurs, the comments of Roustam are interesting:

I grew up surrounded by many caring women, interestingly enough, my mother played more of a father's role with me. The ladies who took care of me, and later my cousin Nelia, played more the mother roles. When I was older I used to get up with my mother at 6:00 in the morning when the official car and driver would come to pick her up. The driver would give me some gas from her car for my motorcycle. I could have waited until the gas station opened at 10:00, and I had money to pay for gas. But I liked to wake up with my mother, and I liked the idea of taking some gas from her car.

My mother was very warm and affectionate with me. Though she was very busy, I knew she loved me. She would often go on business trips, sometimes for up to a month, but she always sent many packages of sweets and toys. I felt very safe and protected, although my situation was unusual.

Freud once said that when the child is the mother's favorite, he cannot lose. The person retains that triumphant feeling, that confidence in success that will often bring real success with it. Roustam Tariko often speaks of his mother and her strong love for him – about her belief in his abilities. However, although he says he felt very protected, it must have been confusing for a young child to have a mother who was constantly appearing and disappearing, no matter how much she loved him. To complicate the picture, there was the issue of an absent father. And to add to this strange mix of players, there was also the confusion of the mother–father roles and the other female figures in his life.

As is the case for many people, Roustam may have been reconstructing a memory of a perfect childhood, seeing it through rose-colored glasses. It is possible (and he is here one among many) that he is remembering that period of his life with more positive memories than actually would have been the case.

We could speculate that when growing up, Tariko may have experienced a certain amount of bewilderment with a father he never knew and a mother who was always hard at work. For a small child, such experiences can be difficult to take, creating a selective memory – a way of dealing with the frustration of not having these key people around. It is quite possible, given the experience of bewilderment and loneliness, that his close inner circle of friends, whom he dealt with from the age of seven, would take on the role of a substitute family. Some of these people still play an important role in his life.

The absence of his parents may have marked him in another way. It may have led to a lingering fear of abandonment, which in turn may have affected his attitude toward the making of commitments. He hangs on to old friends who in many ways seem to have outgrown their usefulness in his growing organization. Furthermore, we can hypothesize that he views making commitments as a very serious matter. In the context of making commitments and establishing a family, Tariko is also a realist. He knows how difficult it is to be an entrepreneur – to create and build up a business – and have some kind of balanced lifestyle at the same time.

After being a big fish in the little pond in Tartarstan, Tariko's arrival in Moscow may have been a rude awakening for the young man. Not only did he come from a far-flung, non-Russian province, but it also turned out that his education was inferior to that of the people in Moscow. He recalls feeling very awkward and uncertain when he first arrived in that city. He failed his university entrance exams the first year. This proved to be the shock that galvanized him, however. He was fortunate that his cousin Nelia (who is his mother's age) took charge, prepped him to retake the exams, and got him through his degree program. It could be that it was the validating encouragement of this cousin – which began during this low point in his life in a significant way and has continued to this day – that boosted his sense of self-worth and positive self-esteem, giving him a second chance at personal development.

His move from the provinces to Moscow provided the push that made Tariko recreate himself. Driven by his desire to make a mark, he made a small fortune while working with Emanuela – a story that has taken on a whiff of legend. Later, he would model himself after the Italian businessmen who became his first business mentors and father figures. He soon found luxury items to be 'motivating', probably because he wanted his association with these kinds of products to be a mirror of *himself*. Such identification certainly has a positive effect on a person's sense of self-esteem. It would seem that along with creating Russian Standard as a brand associated with specific high class values, he is also branding himself; developing and marketing 'Roustam Tariko: Russian Entrepreneur'. Russians are at the top of the pecking order in the Russian Federation; Tartars are often discriminated against, or stereotyped as terrorists or peasants. Roustam took the boy out of Tartarstan, and has also effectively taken Tartarstan out of the boy.

As has been indicated earlier, many male entrepreneurs (for various reasons, one possibly being an escape from an overdominating mother, combined with the absence of a male figure who could set boundaries) appear to be allergic to authority; they do not always function very well in structured situations. In a world perceived as somewhat uncontrollable, they prefer to be in control themselves. They like to be the ones who provide the structure. They want to call all the shots. Take the entrepreneur's natural desire to run the show, combine this with a Russian tendency to centralize power to prevent instability, and one has the makings of a determined leader who may be inclined toward micromanagement. Unfortunately, the kind of micromanagement that can be a key to success in the early phases of the growth of an enterprise can turn into a burden if some of these once essential tasks are not delegated to others at a later stage of an organization's development. For organizations to grow and flourish, empowerment and delegation are the keys.

We can find elements of such behavior in Roustam Tariko. Early on, he adamantly refused to follow his mother into a career with the Communist

Party, even though undoubtedly she could have cleared an easy path for him. He wanted to be his own person. He wanted to be in control. And this theme of control has been a red thread throughout his life. It has made him very successful but, if not carefully managed, given the rapid growth of his empire, it could also become his Achilles heel. In spite of his great need for control (and his awareness of this need), Tariko has the saving graces of being an extremely good listener, and a leader who treats his employees fairly. He also has a reputation for being willing to back down when proven wrong, even if it means changing his own ideas. Contrary to many self-centred leaders he is always prepared to take advice and act accordingly. And, most importantly, he is prepared to laugh at himself, a good indication of sound mental health.

For many entrepreneurs, their enterprise becomes a highly emotionally charged entity and can be viewed as an extension of the self. It is not merely an enterprise; it is an intrinsic part of the entrepreneur's identity. Starting a business, and being successful in it, enables the entrepreneur to be part of a virtuous cycle. Tariko's organization is definitely an extension of him (beginning with the name), and in some ways helps to bolster his self-esteem. Like many other business leaders, he likes the visibility that comes with success. But, unlike many other entrepreneurs, he does not exhibit a tendency toward depression or mood-swings; both his leadership style and personality seem to be quite stable. He has found an effective way to deal with inevitable ups-and-downs that are part of life's journey.

As a leader, he radiates self-confidence; he can be inspiring. But he can also be enigmatic, putting on, if he wants to, a quite convincing poker face. This is the kind of behavior that we also noticed in many other Russian executives. Over the course of the half-year that he participated in 'The Challenge of Leadership' seminar, it became obvious, however, that behind the façade Tariko is quite an emotional and sensitive person. But he has learned to control and hide his emotions very well, when the occasion warrants it. Although he is restless, very intense and impatient, he makes an effort to remain polite and focused, even though this is not always easy for him.

Tariko's enthusiasm and curiosity have helped him to overcome his previous lack of business experience. He has chosen competent working partners who give him sound advice, helping him to overcome the myriad of difficulties that Russian entrepreneurial businesses face. (We mentioned earlier the latent insecurity about their educational background that we observed in many Russian CEOs.) Tariko, however, is the kind of person who has taken pragmatic steps to improve his business competences. He is an eager learner. He has worked closely for many years with high quality consultants from McKinsey and Goldman Sachs who have acted as executive coaches. Some of them have described him as an unusually open-minded and creative individual. Furthermore, he has built bridges with various business schools to attract the best and brightest to his organization. He can deal with adversity as he has weathered well the realities of failure of some of his ideas. Fueled by a creative mind, he emphasizes the importance of issues that are of a pioneering nature in Russia: brand management, communication, consumer behavior, reputation and image, guiding principles, reliability, teamwork and the development of his own leadership skills.

What could be of concern (and here he is not alone among Russsian business leaders) is that if something were to happen to Tariko, the survival of his organization might be endangered. Though he is working on developing a strong layer of second-in-command executives and is slowly removing himself from a cross-coordinating function, the systems aren't yet in place (and the brand isn't well established enough) that the firm could carry on without him. He still has lingering micromanager tendencies, and given his extremely high demands cannot always keep top executives. His company is known for a high turnover of executives in senior management positions – a problem that he recognizes. At the same time, he desires to foster a corporate culture that generates creativity (a commodity that's particularly fragile in a Russian company). He wants to foster the kind of creative corporate culture that would flourish even without his presence. Presently, he has created a high performance organization run by a number of young, workaholic executives who seem to have little time for a balanced life.

Both the strengths and the weaknesses of the Roust/Russian Standard group are evident, and as in most entrepreneurial firms, they arise from the same source: the founder himself. Roust *is* Roustam Tariko, regardless of his advancement to a more decentralized governance of the organization. The organization reflects the energy, drive and intensity of its leader. It is a product of his vision that can serve as a sort of beacon of excellence in the turbulent Russian environment.

NOTE

1. Collins, O.F. and D.G. Moore (1970), *The Organization Makers: A Study of Independent Entrepreneurs*, New York: Meredith; Kets de Vries, M.F.R. (1996), 'The anatomy of the entrepreneur', *Human Relations*, **49** (7), 853–83.

5. Mikhail Khodorkovsky: *chelovek c rublyom* (man with a ruble)

Throughout 2003, the trials and tribulations of Mikhail Khodorkovsky, Russia's richest man and the former CEO of Yukos, the second-largest Russian oil producer, captured the attention of the media, business community, politicians, and researchers and educators in Russia and abroad. His own actions, and the actions that were taken against him, provoked waves of speculation about the future of the global energy industry and Russia's political and economic prospects.

Early in 2003, it looked as if Khodorkovsky's personal and professional life were going according to plan. He announced his intention to step down in 2007 as CEO of Yukos, a company with a market capitalization of $26 billion. The treadmill of work was getting to him – in 2003 he worked up to ten hours a day, six days a week – and he said that he didn't want to be working so hard after the age of 45 (a milestone he will reach in 2008). Khodorkovsky's disclosure of his retirement plans was the first announcement of that sort made by an oligarch in the history of the new Russian capitalism, and it sparked strong rumors (which he denied) about his ambitions to succeed President Putin when the latter's second term expires in 2008.

Then, on 22 April 2003, came a second announcement, when a smiling Khodorkovsky and Evgeny Shvidler, CEO of Sibneft, Russia's fifth-largest oil company, revealed an agreement to merge their companies into a giant oil producer with an estimated $45 billion market value. YukosSibneft would be the biggest of the Russian oil companies, producing 30 per cent of the total Russian oil output. (The second-largest company produces around 18 per cent). A combined Yukos and Sibneft would hold the world's fourth-largest combined oil reserves. The scale and timing of the deal made it an event of global importance; the new company – if the deal went through – would be able to compete with ExxonMobil, Shell and BP.

According to the terms of the deal, Yukos would pay core private shareholders of Sibneft, including the notorious Roman Abramovich (one of the most influential oligarchs during Yeltsin's era and currently governor of Chukotka), $3 billion for 20 per cent of Sibneft and exchange another 72 per cent belonging to the group for the shares of Yukos proper (not more than 26 per cent). Khodorkovsky would become the CEO of YukosSibneft while Shvidler, long-time associate of Abramovich, would chair its board of directors.

Both the financial terms of the deal and the new composition of shareholders received mixed reactions in the Russian media and business community. Over the past few years Khodorkovsky had developed a reputation as Mr Corporate Governance of Russia, promoting principles of transparency, protection of minority shareholders' rights, and separation of executive and oversight bodies. Under his guidance, Yukos had become a model Russian corporation with a fully transparent shareholder structure and a board of directors dominated by independent members, comprehensive financial reporting, and strong investor relations efforts.

Sibneft, on the other hand, had a reputation as being one of the *least* transparent oil companies, with a history of shareholder rights abuses, corporate wars for assets, and outdated accounting and reporting systems. Its shareholder composition had never been clear; some Russian mass media speculated that former Kremlin kingmaker Boris Berezovsky was still a part owner of the company.[1]

The combination of Khodorkovsky's announcements left the Russian and international business communities puzzled, but it was not the first time the oligarch had surprised the world with an unexpected move – and in the past, such moves had always brought him significant dividends. And the surprises were not over yet.

On 26 October 2003, masked commandos from the Russian Ministry of the Interior stormed Khodorkovsky's plane, which had just landed at Novosibirsk airport, and arrested him. He was rushed back to Moscow where he was jailed. The prosecution charged him with tax evasion, embezzlement of assets and fraud. From his prison cell, Mikhail Khodorkovsky expressed his resolve to prove his innocence, and announced that he was resigning as CEO of Yukos. He also approved later, as a shareholder, the end of the merger negotiations between Yukos and Sibneft. Many observers concluded that Khodorkovsky's career in business was over – but not quite the way he had planned it only a few months earlier. But it would be a mistake to write off Mikhail Khodorkovsky too soon.

A MODEL (BUT VERY AMBITIOUS) SOVIET YOUTH

In the summer of 2002, then-Yukos CEO Khodorkovsky went to visit the Yukos-sponsored 'New Civilization' camp for young Russians. Participating children spend two weeks organizing and working in 'Newlandia', a society with its own parliament, private entrepreneurs, and common currency (the 'rudol'). The children learn about the democratic process by levying taxes and passing laws to govern their society. In addition to various government jobs they can choose, they can also opt to run for election to parliament or become entrepreneurs.

Only one boy made any serious rudols that summer, ending the two weeks as a rudol millionaire (compared to the average profit of a few hundred rudols). He did it by finding loopholes and working very hard – making an initial quick profit on a business venture, then amassing a 'fortune' by lending money at high rates to the eternally strapped Newlandia parliament. The other children in the camp had chosen steady, but poorly paid, government jobs over the hard scrabble life of the Russian entrepreneur. The realities of the camp paralleled life in Russia; mirroring the choices of their parents, most of the children said they thought it was better to work for the government than to strike out on their own. Khodorkovsky might have been thinking of the citizens of Newlandia when he commented at the 2003 Davos conference that he was alarmed that so many young Russians wanted nothing more than to pass the civil service exam, which at best leads to a meager but steady salary of about $200 per month. He said, 'Does this not tell us that society is projecting some sick ideas on our youth?'[2]

Khodorkovsky is well placed to know that only a few very determined and fortunate Russian entrepreneurs make it all the way to the top, and even then they remain vulnerable to the actions of government officials, as he has learned the hard way.

Mikhail Khodorkovsky was born to a typical family of Soviet-era engineers in Moscow. Like many of the young people of his age group, he grew up in a cramped two-room apartment. His parents worked at Kalibr, a plant that manufactured high-precision measurement instruments. Although his father supplemented his salary by moonlighting in other jobs, there was never enough money for the small luxuries of life. During school vacations, Mikhail helped the family out, earning a little money sweeping streets or doing carpentry work. In his free time, he practiced martial arts. Despite the hours spent working during vacations, he was a good student. In high school he was selected for an advanced chemistry class, and after graduating in 1981, he went on to the Moscow Chemical and Technological Institute.

As a student, Mikhail was very active in the Komsomol organization (the Young Communists League), which operated under the Communist Party's guidance and united almost all Soviet youth aged 14 to 28. The principal objective of Komsomol (which had over 40 million members at the end of the 1980s) was the political and moral upbringing of new generations of Soviet citizens. Well equipped for that task, it had a powerful nationwide apparatus with hundreds of thousands of full-time bureaucrats and its own mass media, production, recreation and entertainment facilities worth billions of dollars. After earning a degree in 1981, Khodorkovsky worked for a short time as a chemical engineer, and also as a Komsomol boss. In short order, he was elected second secretary of the Komsomol committee for the Frunzensky district (one of the 31 boroughs in Moscow).

About that time, Komsomol organizations were given the right to set up economic entities, and many began to explore various new opportunities that had emerged with the reform-minded Gorbachev government's promotion of *khozraschyot*, an economic model based on self-financing. Many of the Komsomol organizations went into business for themselves, running cafés, discos, travel agencies, and the like, funding these ventures initially with loans or subsidies from their own coffers. Komsomol organizations that managed to turn a profit were allowed to retain (and use as they saw fit) any proceeds they made from such ventures. It was understood that some of the profits ended up in the pockets of the young Komsomol organizers.

Secretary Khodorkovsky saw a challenge and went for it. The self-financing proviso turned out to be a tremendous opportunity not only to advance his own career, but also to, for all practical purposes, mint money – and legally, too. Opportunity plus political connections plus huge ambition: this was the secret formula that Khodorkovsky and a few other entrepreneurial Russians, men who would become known as 'the oligarchs', used to build their own private empires in the so-called Wild East.

Legend has it that the ambitious young deputy head was anointed by Communist Party bosses, and perhaps even the KGB, as their front man for their experiments in capitalism. Khodorkovsky himself once admitted that nothing could be achieved in those days without patronage and political sponsorship. The undeniable fact is that Khodorkovsky far surpassed his original masters, whoever they might have been.

Khodorkovsky's first venture, with several partners, was a youth café that did not do well, largely because it was not in a prime location. He then founded the Center for Scientific and Technological Creativity of the Youth. Officially, the mission of this (and many similar) Komsomol-related organizations founded under the self-financing proviso was to disseminate scientific and technological information via books and other publications. Recognizing, however, that there was an interesting loophole in the Soviet economic system, Khodorkovsky decided to increase the Center's profits by expanding its function to include consulting services. This strategy would enable him to convert discretionary funds available to many factory directors.

Under the Soviet economic system, wages were centrally regulated and were always paid in real money; commodities, on the other hand, often changed hands between companies via 'virtual cash' – a State subsidy that could be 'traded' but could not be converted into real money. State-owned companies that accumulated excess virtual funds were not allowed to convert that credit into real-money income. However, they *could* pay for services using this virtual cash. Khodorkovsky realized that 'red' directors could wire their virtual funds to the Center (as they eventually did to many similar companies' accounts as well) in exchange for 'consulting services'. They received some of the cash back, gaining real money, and Khodorkovsky also profited, because fully self-financed organizations such as the Center did not have the same restrictions on turning the virtual money into cash. The directors had the added comfort of knowing, when they dealt with the Center, that they were working with 'the authorities', because of the Komsomol connection. They felt good about dealing with Khodorkovsky too: people described him in those days as honest, very hard working, and never flashy. The result was that the young man was literally making money out of nothing.

In the summer of 1987, Khodorkovsky's Komsomol superiors told him that he would have to choose between a career in the upper hierarchy of the organization and going off on his own to continue his 'self-financing tricks'. Khodorkovsky amazed everyone by announcing that he would continue his entrepreneurial efforts. He later said he knew that people thought he was crazy, given that a career within any Soviet organization was expected to be much more secure, not to mention more profitable, than any self-financing venture. Later, after he had made an initial success of his venture, some of his older friends reminded him that they had lived through an earlier period of *khozraschyot* in the 1960s – a liberalization that was later repealed. Many people who had tried to exploit that earlier trend towards a market economy had ended up in jail. Khodorkovsky explained, 'I did not remember this! I was too young! And I went for it.[3]'

And then, not long into his self-employment, things got *really* serious. Sooner than his competitors, Khodorkovsky understood that the business of transforming virtual money into hard cash would not last much longer. He decided to put what remained of his virtual money to work, first exchanging it for foreign hard currency with Soviet export companies, then buying products from foreign companies with his new currency, and finally reselling those products in Russia, with astronomic margins, for virtual cash (and thus beginning a new cycle of virtual-to-real-cash conversion). The most popular product category was personal computers, and his most frequent customers were huge state-owned companies. Rumor has it that Khodorkovsky and his friends were also producing counterfeit stonewashed denim clothes (of well known Western brands), which were fashionable at the time. There may have been other opaque types of business activities under the roof of the Center for Scientific and Technological Creativity of the Youth as well, including imports of counterfeit cognac and vodka. As if all that wouldn't keep a person busy enough, the Russian magazine *Profil* reported that Khodorkovsky combined the development of this first business with moonlighting as a carpenter *and* studying in the evenings for a second degree from the Moscow Plekhanov Academy of National Economy![4]

Although it is difficult to separate fact from fiction regarding Khodorkovsky's business activities in the late 1980s, a few things are clear. He had no financial capital to start with and relied on other resources. His ingenuity, intelligence and determination played an important role, but he also built on his people skills in two distinct ways, both of which helped him throughout his business career. First, he developed and maintained enduring ties to his original scientific colleagues, his new business partners, and his Communist Party and Komsomol superiors (who apparently enjoyed working with the energetic man and his associates, whom they referred to as *rebyata*, or 'young fellows').[5] Second, unlike many other entrepreneurs of the perestroika era, he managed to build a team early on that followed him throughout his subsequent business initiatives. Having started out together as a group of students looking for self-financing opportunities, this team continued to work with Khodorkovsky on his later, grander ventures. The team members have never let one another down, though they treat outsiders according to the principle, 'If one parrot dies, we'll buy another one' (that is, outsiders are disposable resources).

MENATEP BANK

Foreseeing the imminent end of his 'virtual money' business, on one day in 1988 Khodorkovsky walked into Zhilsotsbank, a specialist branch of Gosbank, the central bank of the Soviet planned economy, and asked for a loan so that he could continue some of his other business activities.[6] Bank officials turned him down, explaining that they could give credit only to other banks. Undaunted, Khodorkovsky set up a new banking entity, The Commercial Innovative Bank for Scientific and Technological Progress, with the help of connections within Gosbank. The newly created Commercial Innovative Bank then purchased the Center for Scientific and Technological Creativity of the Youth, which Khodorkovsky renamed Menatep-Invest (Menatep being an abbreviation for Interbranch Scientific and Technological Programs). Gosbank, when approached by Menatep for a loan, agreed to finance Khodorkovsky's ongoing computer import business. Even Khodorkovsky himself seemed amazed that he was meeting practically no obstacles from the Soviet system. His success seemed almost too good to be true. But it *was* true: Khodorkovsky opened a new business, Menatep, and turned a new page in contemporary Russian business history.

Initially, Menatep did little more than finance Khodorkovsky's trading and currency businesses, but later the business became an authorized intermediary for government financial credit to state-owned companies. Menatep took money from the government, loaned it to enterprises, then collected their payments and returned the money to the government. Khodorkovsky invented and used a financial model that allowed him to hold on to the cash long enough to use it to make a profit for himself. The experience honed his already impressive skill at maintaining excellent relations with government authorities. Rumors about his connections circulated widely at that time.

Mikhail Khodorkovsky was growing not only ever more wealthy, but also ever more wily. His next step was to tap into huge piles of cash sitting under the mattresses of millions of Soviet citizens unable to use their savings in the deficit-stricken economy. He started an advertising campaign, unprecedented in the country, to get people to invest in his bank, with a core message, 'Buy shares in Menatep and get rich'. To explain to Soviet citizens at large the advantages of capitalism in general, and the merits of Menatep in particular, Khodorkovsky and a colleague published *Chelovek c rublyom* (Man with a Ruble). Released in 1991, the year that the Soviet Union ended, it was a heartfelt defense of capitalism, designed to interest people in investing. Khodorkovsky was no longer recognizable as the earnest Communist youth he once was – although the new bank's culture reflected the reclusive, low-key nature of its founder, who still wore jeans and flannel shirts to work. Nevertheless, years later, Khodorkovsky remarked, 'If the old Mikhail had met the new one, he would have shot him'.[7]

On the heels of the Soviet Union's collapse, Boris Yeltsin's government introduced privatization-oriented market reforms in Russia. In 1993, Anatoly Chubais, head of the privatization effort, engineered a vouchers-for-shares scheme in which Russians could receive privatization vouchers worth 10 000 rubles. These vouchers could then be exchanged for stock in the industry of their choice, or put to work in an investment fund. Again Khodorkovsky was quick to see a potential for profit: with many Russians daunted by the prospect of making such a choice in a new and nebulous investment environment, Menatep was able to buy up huge quantities of privatization vouchers, thereby gaining access to valuable assets in such industries as plastics, metallurgy, textiles, chemicals, and food-processing. The big prize was still ahead, however.

By 1995, a handful of Russian entrepreneurs – the new breed of oligarchs – had accumulated monetary and material assets worth hundreds of millions of dollars and gained enough political weight to move on to the sacred cow of the Russian economy: raw material-extracting companies. Exempted from the vouchers-for-shares program, these companies were now privatized via a 'loans-for-shares' scheme. In this scheme, proposed by the oligarchs and agreed to by a cash-hungry government, some of the largest enterprises were transferred, via auction, to those private investors offering the highest price (a total that could, and in most cases did, include loans and future investments). The government entrusted a number of banks controlled by the oligarchs to conduct the auctions. In the manner of all foxes guarding henhouses, those oligarchs had feathers in their mouths (and new assets in their pockets) when the Russian state sold such assets as Norilsk Nickel, Tumen Oil, Severstal, Svyazinvest, and Sibneft.

Menatep was put in charge of handling the bids in the privatization auction for Yukos Oil, then the second-largest oil company in Russia (and the fourth-largest in the world). Russian oil directors had a reputation for being a caste apart, never letting Moscovites, ex-Komsomol boys, or 'New Russians' into their oil fields (which, being located primarily in the northern parts of the country, were also geographically removed from Moscow's control). Nevertheless, Khodorkovsky – who had no experience in the oil industry, but recognized its huge cash-generating potential – managed to appropriate Yukos in the privatization auction, working out what the Russian mass media later described as one of the most unusual and audacious deals in the history of Russian privatization. Though a number of other large Russian financial-industrial groups made aggressive bids for the company, the winning bid was made by a company controlled by Khodorkovsky himself. Other, higher bids had been disqualified on 'technical grounds', but there was no evidence that Menatep had broken any existing Russian laws in acquiring its stake in Yukos. In trying to find foreign investors, Khodorkovsky had personally approached a number of Western investors, but was turned down by all of them on the grounds that the risks, given the approaching presidential elections, were too high.

Khodorkovsky and his partners paid $350 million (in loans and promised investments) and acquired $3 billion in debt. (Yukos at that time did not include the Eastern Oil Company, which Menatep took control of in 1997.) The partners now had a 78 per cent share of Yukos, a fantastic bargain considering that two years later, when Yukos shares began trading publicly, the market capitalization had reached $9 billion (which included other acquisitions that Yukos had made in the meantime). Khodorkovsky made no secret of the fact that Yukos would be a cash cow for Rosprom, the financial industrial conglomerate he set up as a holding company for Menatep's industrial assets. By that time Rosprom had interests in about 100 different companies, spanning a wide range of industries. Shifting his primary interest to the development of Rosprom, Khodorkovsky stepped down as Menatep's CEO (remaining its chairman, however). In 1997, he assumed the job of Yukos' CEO.

This period was the nadir in Khodorkovsky's relationship with both foreign and Russian investors. He later said about that period that if an individual conducted business in Russia in a Western manner, he was simply 'torn to pieces and forgotten'; and yet the traditional Russian way of doing business was no longer acceptable, even within that country's borders. For example, Menatep's minority shareholders – Russians – complained that the company's management, with Khodorkovsky at the helm, lacked transparency, efficiency, and a focus on profitability. The situation was even more difficult for foreign partners. For example, the American oil conglomerate Amoco had reached an agreement in 1993 with Yukos (before Khodorkovsky took control) to exploit one of Russia's richest oil fields, but soon found itself in an arranged marriage with Khodorkovsky after Menatep's purchase of Yukos in 1996. Khodorkovsky didn't like the deal that had been worked out in that earlier agreement and asked Amoco to put in more money for a smaller stake. Amoco executives refused to renegotiate, believing that documents they had in their possession backed them up. However, Khodorkovsky said that he specifically asked to see a signed contract that would require Yukos to continue negotiations with Amoco, but to his surprise, no such document was ever shown to him.[8]

Either way, this type of situation was fairly common. Westerners were caught in a bind; they wanted Russian oil, but they found it extremely difficult to trust the oligarchs in control.

Then came the 1998 Russian financial crisis. The Moscow office of Menatep Bank went under when the government devalued the ruble by 400 per cent and defaulted on its debt. Khodorkovsky transferred the bank's remaining funds to Menatep St Petersburg, which was still solvent, but he had to deal with angry creditors there – among them, several foreign banks whose loans to Menatep were secured by Yukos shares.

Khodorkovsky tried to work out a three-year repayment plan, based on income from oil exports rather than Yukos shares, but two of the creditors refused. In a still controversial sleight-of-hand, Yukos threatened to make a share offering that would effectively dilute the creditors' stake to the extent that those shares would hold little remaining value. Some people claimed that at the same time, Yukos assets were moved to off-shore shell companies – claims that have always been disputed by Yukos. In any case, seeing that they would be left empty-handed, the creditors backed down and agreed to sell their shares to Khodorkovsky. The share offering was cancelled, and the assets were brought back into Russia. Khodorkovsky (with some core partners) regained control of Yukos.

BUILDING A COMPETITIVE BUSINESS

In his early days, Khodorkovsky built successful businesses from scratch, inventing new business models and using to his advantage loopholes first in the Soviet planned economy and later in the chaos of the emerging Russian market system. He competed the way that seemed best to him then: in an open fight. Yukos was a different story, a new challenge of unprecedented scale. Formed in 1993 by combining several Siberian oil production facilities, Yukos had 11 000 wells badly in need of repair and 90 000 employees waiting for unpaid wages and dreaming of pumping more and more oil at any cost. The accounts were less than transparent, and the company had a debt of almost $3 billion. Yukos moved swiftly to lay off 11 000 employees and divest non-core businesses, such as a cigarette factory the company owned, but it was still far from maximizing its production capacity.

Khodorkovsky, who likes to repeat that he isn't an oilman, developed a strategy tailor-made for Russia: combining advanced Western technology with an inexpensive Russian workforce and depreciated equipment to produce oil efficiently at a cost that Western companies couldn't match. Through an alliance with the French company Schlumberger, Yukos began to upgrade well technologies and information technology systems, with the goal of increasing production by 50 per cent by 2005. Yukos hired scores of expatriates for key posts, including a chief financial officer from Schlumberger, and brought in some younger-generation Russian managers from Menatep and other of Khodorkovsky's businesses.

The drastic cost-cutting measures began to pay off fairly quickly, but the Russian financial crisis of 1998 threatened that early success. Khodorkovsky responded with a new restructuring program, which set a trend for other Russian oil companies to follow a few years later. Yukos spun off many services and centralized the management of the remaining services, splitting 'upstream' and 'downstream' operations (that is, drilling/extracting and refining/marketing) into separate business lines. At the same time, the company continued to invest in modern technology, both in the core business and in management systems. These moves soon paid off: the net income of Yukos rose to $2.5 billion on sales of $7.2 billion in 2000. In 2001, Yukos increased production by 18 per cent. In 2002, Yukos achieved phenomenal results, increasing oil production to 69 million tons, revenues to $11.7 billion, and net income to $3 billion. It became an industry benchmark in Russia, both in its operating results and in its management systems.

Having mastered oil company management, Khodorkovsky looked forward to new challenges and was clear about what he wanted for Yukos. In an interview with the authors of this book in 2002, he said:

> In three years [Yukos] will have finalized everything within Russia in terms of efficiency, and we'll start testing ourselves outside Russia. And five years from now we'll have many features of an international company, but completion of the process of building an international company will probably take place in seven to eight years. In parallel with that, we'll have to carry out diversification of our business, moving from oil to energy. In ten years' time, we'll be a stable energy company, like British Petroleum.... I have been following that role model for five years now.

The 2003 merger with Sibneft looked like an important step toward achieving this vision.

CULT OF TRANSPARENCY

Despite Mikhail Khodorkovsky's sojourn in jail, Yukos serves as a model Russian company, with visible standards of corporate governance. Khodorkovsky said that the late-1990s battles with minority shareholders forced him to understand what corporate governance was all about and to realize how important it is to any public company. However, although Yukos was doing well, as recently as 2001 he felt that it was still undervalued on the stock market because, as he acknowledged, there was a lack of trust on the part of investors. He said, 'In part, this [distrust] can be removed by improving transparency, and we are working in that direction.'[9]

Signaling a move to internationally recognized standards of corporate governance, Yukos adopted GAAP (Generally Accepted Accounting Principles) and published three years of GAAP-standard accounts in 2002. Khodorkovsky invited experienced foreign businessmen, such as former vice-presidents of Crédit Lyonnais and Phillips Petroleum, to sit on the Yukos board. The Yukos website provides extensive and daily updated information about the company, stock market quotes, production volume and corporate plans. Investors' briefings and conference calls have become routine for the company.

One section on the Yukos website (added in 2003) was devoted exclusively to corporate governance. The first subheading was 'Principles and Priorities':

Yukos Oil Company believes strongly in the same principles of corporate social responsibility that are recognized in the majority of developed countries today, and is committed to putting them into practice in all aspects of its activities.

Yukos' challenge is to ensure social stability and promote development in all spheres of life in the regions where it operates. In doing so, the Company does not attempt to replace the government and the vital role it plays in socio-economic development. Our contribution to the government's social policy is limited to creating jobs and paying taxes.

Nevertheless, Yukos plays an active and significant role, both materially and otherwise, in addressing the most acute social problems in its regions, while at the same time encouraging the local populace in developing initiative and independence.[10]

The statements above were accompanied by a photograph of Khodorkovsky and UN Secretary-General Kofi Annan shaking hands just after they signed the UN's Global Compact initiative. By signing this agreement, Khodorkovsky committed Yukos to observe international standards in the areas of human rights, labor and the environment.

Yukos is evidently still focused on improving its reputation with Russians – among them, its own employees – and the world. In addition to addressing Principles and Priorities, the Yukos website also includes sections on Knowledge, Effectiveness, Cooperation and Responsibility, with each section sending a clear message about Yukos being a responsible corporate citizen. Khodorkovsky had a special 'image committee' within the organization, headed by him personally. Though the committee was initially formed to counter Khodorkovsky's reputation for unfair asset-grabbing, it spontaneously dissolved as it became apparent that Khodorkovsky's image in the press had improved. The board of directors, for their part, quickly moved to address issues of corporate governance, persuading the business community that 'Yukos is a transparent company' and burnishing Yukos' image in the eyes of the employees of the organization.

Following the motto 'Yukos – a transparent company' (an unusual slogan for a Russian business), Khodorkovsky disclosed details of his ownership of Yukos (he controlled 36 per cent of shares) in 2002, a move that was welcomed by analysts: 'It's a first for one of the oligarch groups, and it will have a powerful and beneficial emulation effect for all the others'.[11] Somewhat disingenuously, Khodorkovsky said, 'Now we understand how business is done in the West. As a shareholder, I earn money in dividends and with the increase in the market capitalization of my company.'[12] This philosophy worked well for Khodorkovsky. In 2001, *Forbes* magazine listed him among the world's 538 billionaires, with a net worth of $2.4 billion. In 2003, he became the wealthiest Russian, his personal fortune topping $7 billion.

Khodorkovsky's drive for sound corporate governance and Yukos' solid financial results paid off for other shareholders as well. The company became a star of the Russian stock market, helping it to become one of the best performing markets in the world in 2002–2003. Yukos' capitalization grew from $21 billion in December 2002 to $30 billion in July 2003. But Khodorkovsky believed that Yukos was still undervalued by international standards: its market capitalization to income ratio was around 8, while global players such as Exxon and BP had a ratio in the range of 18 to 21. The reason for its undervaluing lay in the perceived risks inherent in doing business in Russia.

BUSINESS AND POLITICS

Since his early days as a Komsomol entrepreneur, Khodorkovsky has understood the importance of political connections in Russia and has made a great effort to nurture his network in the corridors of power. The acquisition of Yukos made those connections even more important. Oil is the principal Russian export and major hard-currency earner for the government. The industry is still heavily regulated and taxed by Russian law, but it's also – and probably more importantly – regulated by informal interventions of key government officials, including the president. Khodorkovsky was open about the importance of the existing political network. He said, for example, that while the Sibneft deal was being negotiated, 'governors of concerned regions, ministries, the prime minister, and, of course, the president were informed about our intentions ... and we immediately received an approval'.

In the 1990s, direct lobbying was the most important tool in dealing with the government, and Khodorkovsky excelled at it, winning not only Yukos but many other assets. At the time, he had powerful contacts in high places. One of Khodorkovsky's former partners was one of Putin's deputy chiefs of staff.[13] However, times have changed. Khodorkovsky described the new realities of Russia in the following way: 'Previously, we were all focused on the cash revenues of our business, since no one believed that the situation would last. Now that things are stabilizing, people are more interested in increasing the value of their property.'[14]

That objective requires structural changes and improvements in the overall business environment – improvements that will reduce Russia-specific risks and increase the capitalization of Russian companies. Instead of fighting one another for access to the almighty Russian president to gain some short-lasting favor, as in the Yeltsin years, the oligarchs decided, at the turn of the millennium, to unify their efforts and attempt to bring about changes to the economy at large.

In 2000, Khodorkovsky was one of the key figures involved in seizing control of the Russian Union of Industrialists and Entrepreneurs (Russian acronym: RSPP), previously a dormant association of red directors. The group's new leaders now use the organization as a platform for direct dialogue with Russia's president and government. Khodorkovsky became one of the members of its governing board and the head of its international affairs committee; and he was an always-present participant in regular meetings with President Putin.

Re-elected in 2000 for a four-year term, Vladimir Putin presents a sharp contrast to his ailing predecessor, Boris Yeltsin. Always youthful and sporty, Putin is trying to provide new momentum to the Russian economy. He is a confirmed believer in a strong state and strong government, and is determined to change the dynamics of government–business interactions in Russia. Putin has made it clear that Yeltsin's practice of making political decisions with oligarchs and giving favors to selected financiers is over. Direct dialogue between President Putin and the oligarchs has been phased out by more bureaucratic forums such as the 'Council on Entrepreneurship' under Prime Minister Kasyanov – a council of which Khodorkovsky was a member. The council meets regularly with the premier members of the cabinet to discuss the oligarchs' proposals for economic and legal reforms. Khodorkovsky called the president and his own oligarchic peers 'counterparts' in the dialogue about Russia's economy. He praised Kasyanov's government as the most liberal and professional in modern Russian history.

This 'dialogue' has yielded positive results for the Russian economy, the government, and, to a large extent, the oligarchs. Under oligarchic pressure, the Russian parliament adopted a flat income tax rate of 13 per cent and reduced corporate profit taxes and mandatory social security contributions. Tax collections have significantly improved with these changes, allowing for some extra government spending on social issues and defense. Helped by favorable oil prices, the Russian economy grew for three consecutive years, the ruble appreciated, and inflation stayed under 14 per cent. The RSPP adopted a 'Charter of Corporate and Business Ethics' and set up a Commission on Corporate Ethics, which serves as an effective out-of-court settlement body for Russian businesses.

These various developments notwithstanding, the power equation for the oligarchs changed in the early 2000s, as the rise and fall of Khodorkovsky shows. Political analysts and sociologists have different opinions about the underlying reasons for Khodorkovsky's misfortune. Some refer to his open financial support of liberal political parties; others suggest that the Kremlin detected his rumored plan to put into the New Duma over a hundred deputies loyal to Yukos and Khodorkovsky, from all parties, to form a powerful lobbying force; others recall the oligarchs' meeting with President Putin in which Khodorkovsky openly criticized the government for its corruption. Some analysts believe that the anti-Khodorkovsky campaign had a purely economic rationale – a number of powerful people from Putin's entourage might have been eyeing Yukos' assets. Privately, Russian oligarchs complained about Khodorkovsky's unwillingness to 'cooperate' with the government, and about his stubbornness, which they felt could negatively affect the balance of power between big business and government in Russia. Whatever the real reasons were, and there must have been more than one, the prosecutor's office decided to hit hard: it opened ten criminal cases against Yukos shareholders and executives. Two of them were found guilty of tax evasion and given suspended sentences. At the time of writing, three others are in prison waiting for court hearings, and two are at large with search warrants issued again them. President Putin stayed clear of the case, repeating that it was a purely criminal, not a political, affair.

'KREMLINESQUE INTRIGUE' IN WESTERN ATTIRE?

Khodorkovsky, in his interview for this book in 2002, admitted that the most efficient business is a one-person entrepreneurial venture. Every multi-person enterprise brings with it inefficiency. However, because some tasks require the efforts of more than one person, organizations will always exist.

The extraction and refining of oil necessitates an organization of considerable size. At the time of its acquisition by Khodorkovsky (via Menatep), Yukos had a legacy of inefficiency at all levels in the organization – along with huge potential. Khodorkovsky was obsessed with the notion of achieving organizational efficiency in order to make the most of that potential. Although he met with some resistance – managers in the oil fields wanted to continue drilling new wells instead of increasing the output from existing wells, and heads of regional operations wanted to keep their huge support-services infrastructures – his goal was to keep only the most efficient employees and businesses. As Khodorkovsky said in his interview:

Approximately 10 or 20 per cent of us, working in large corporations, provide the other 90 per cent of the world with goods and services. And the motto for all corporations is the same: 'efficiency'. If you can't work better than somebody else, then go to the street [i.e. get out]. If I can find someone who is cheaper than you are – go to the street. This is not a very benevolent corporate culture.

The remaining 80 per cent of the workers have a much easier life. The other categories of workers – bureaucrats, medium-size businesses, etc. – all have a much less stressful kind of job. You can find idlers [within corporations], but they are a weakness within the organization. That's why my task is to build an efficient organization. All the areas where I can't be the most efficient have to be divested.

Khodorkovsky created a strictly hierarchical organizational structure. In our interview, he explained that his company could be depicted as a combination of three pyramids: one dealing with upstream oil production, the second in charge of downstream production, and the third taking care of the financial, staff and corporate affairs. Within each pyramid is a modified matrix structure: 'What we are trying to achieve is that within the framework of the pyramidal structure, we build what I call an 'electron cloud'. In a good pyramid you have an electron cloud of people who are not tied to individual atoms'.

Within each strictly delimited pyramid, according to Khodorkovsky, no deviation is permitted from standard operating procedures at the lower levels. He said:

For God's sake, no deviation from the procedures! If I see deviation from standard operating procedures at a low level, I need to catch the deviant immediately and put him in an upper level position or, if I have a sufficient number of people there, kick him out. Because if I leave him where he is now, this person starts getting involved in what during Soviet times we used to call *ratsionalizatorstvo* [a term that meant internal improvement activities, or intrapreneurship]. This was a special word with a positive connotation. This process would be called something like *rationalization* in English. It referred to the people who put forward new ideas.

Now imagine a situation when I have oil production going on for twenty years. Statistically, every ten years I could have a build-up of sulfur, which could cause an explosion. I don't know when exactly this sulfur build-up is going to occur during this period of ten years. That's why there is a written procedure saying: 'Purge the [oil] reservoir every six months'. Then this innovator, or *rationalizator*, comes in. He sees that there is *no* sulfur accumulating in the tanks. He sees that he's been observing the cleaning process for several years, but there has been no accumulation of sulfur between cleanings. He gets into the tanks a few times, and then he says: 'Look, guys, I have made some calculations here; if sulfur build-up continues at this rate, then it means that we can do the cleaning once every two years, rather than every six months'. So he starts doing it once every two years. After that I have an explosion of sulfur at, say, a reservoir at my Sergievskneft production facility. I start to dig for causes, and find a *rationalizator* there.

Because of his strong belief that people should obey rules, Khodorkovsky felt that many jobs required employees who might be described by staff psychologists as 'dumb but reliable'. When asked what kinds of jobs there are at Yukos for graduates of the world's top business schools, Khodorkovsky replied that out of 110 000 jobs, he could offer approximately 3000 positions to engineers and business school graduates, people who 'have attended all the classes and taken notes of what the professors were saying in a good handwriting'. Such people could be hired for jobs in which they would be paid decently and would 'feel just fine'. Khodorkovsky said:

> I'll tell these people 'You are never going to make a lot of money at Yukos, but [on the other hand] I am not going to force you to think. You will only have to do exactly what you know how to do. If you have to do something different, you will be retrained first'.
>
> For some people [with real talent and potential] I have 70 [top] jobs. For the whole of my company there are 70 jobs like this. If you are ready to compete for any of those 70 jobs, then we'll be happy to consider you. [There are not 100 or 200 jobs like this], as I don't need that many top people. These are very expensive people, and I need to produce my oil cheaply.

To motivate the talented people within that 70-person cohort, the company offers above-market salaries for professionals. Khodorkovsky looked for key people whom he considered to be the best on the global market. In fact, he claimed that for these positions he is willing to consider only the top five professionals in a given field. As a result, his talent search extended beyond Russia in recent years. Yukos currently hires top executives from Schlumberger, Amoco, PennzEnergy Corporation, Crédit Lyonnais, Phillips Petroleum, and other such companies. There are now more than 50 Westerners working in the Yukos headquarters building in Moscow. The company can also boast of significant local talent – people whom every headhunter in Moscow and beyond would dream of capturing.

Khodorkovsky said that money is a key element in the motivational system within Yukos. However, he strongly believed that benefits and perks should *not* play a significant motivational role in an organization – a theory that goes against the grain in Russia. He believed that people should work for a fair wage or salary and should then be able to make their own choices in terms of how to spend the money. Social benefits at Yukos are not as extensive as they are at some other Russian companies. The official company policy is to provide them only if they are not available (for a price) elsewhere. Khodorkovsky said: 'The most important thing an individual has is his or her freedom, and money constitutes the material foundation of freedom. If an individual is tied up by social benefits, this is non-freedom.'[15] As far as Khodorkovsky is personally concerned, he is not motivated by the desire to earn more money: 'I have enough money to last for ten of my lives'.

Despite Khodorkovsky's disdain for social benefits, Yukos has one of the most advanced human resource management systems in Russia. It was recently recognized as such, winning the Grand Prix of 2001, an HR management contest in Moscow. The HR division's major focus is on recruiting, training and developing technical and managerial expertise. The company has set up a whole department at a technical university in the Siberian city of Tomsk to train engineers for its oilfields, thereby creating a corporation-wide pool of young employees with high potential. (Yukos finances the relocation of its employees from Siberia to Central Russia). In addition, it has set up assessment centers for thousands of its middle managers.

Yukos also takes employee communication seriously. Unlike most Russian organizations, it has an employee-friendly website that provides a lot of information about the way people at Yukos work, study, develop their skills, spend their free time, and participate in charitable activities, with illustrations provided by children of Yukos employees.

The website has a section called 'Family Album', which includes stories about the lives and careers of about three dozen Yukos employees from different parts of the country. There are also stories, with pictures, about people who have worked in Russia's oilfields and refineries from World War II to the present. They all illustrate the Yukos motto: 'Employees of various Yukos enterprises make one family – the Yukos family'.[16] The tone and style of the stories bring a feeling of déja vu to older readers: they hark back to Soviet-era articles about worker dynasties, loyal to the same plant for several generations; or accounts of 'heroism at work' that the Soviet Press used to produce in large quantities. Still, the notion of 'family' as used by Yukos' corporate-image designers is quite revealing: we see who the father figure is in the family and how he watches over his family members, despite his conviction that 'money rules'.

The website also has a lot of information about philanthropic and disaster relief projects supported by Yukos. Among many others, Yukos sponsors scores of children's homes and orphanages in the regions in which it operates. Khodorkovsky and his top executive team personally provided financial backing for an orphanage. Top executives spend time with children from this orphanage, and many executive team meetings are held close to the location of this facility. Although these activities began seven years ago, no effort has been made to publicize them.

In Moscow, a city where job opportunities for qualified individuals are relatively bountiful, Yukos is considered the employer of choice. Westerners and Russians coming to work for Yukos bring with them the most advanced oil-exploration and business techniques. However, according to a former Amoco executive who leads Yukos' exploration team, in order to succeed, new executives have to learn to live in a management culture that 'remains distinctly Russian, permeated with Kremlinesque intrigue'. This executive says,

'The only way you can survive [at Yukos] is if you have a few key people in the organization – Russians – watching your back against disloyalty by other Russians'. He finds the Yukos top management 'tough and smart', and adds that working for Yukos is like being involved in 'the extreme sport of the oil industry'.[17]

SERIAL ENTREPRENEUR OR GLOBAL CEO?

Khodorkovsky said that he once had an argument with his father about whether a diffident person can be a successful business leader, or whether one needs to be emotional to be successful in that job. (Khodorkovsky apparently said yes to the former; his father, no.) A leader in an organization, he said, should not be emotional, because personal sentiments lead to feelings that prevent the leader from getting rid of ineffective businesses. Therefore, in Khodorkovsky's opinion, a detached leader is very necessary for a mature business.[18] Khodorkovsky sees himself as an entrepreneur, with the type of leadership profile that is particularly useful to the organization at the stage of creating a business and growing it.

In any case, Khodorkovsky is known to be a calm person. As one of the top managers in the organization said: 'I never saw [Khodorkovsky] angry. Irritated, yes, but not angry'. When asked if he ever has temper tantrums and throws phones at people, as some red directors have been known to do, Khodorkovsky told us: 'In order for me to get angry, I must desperately want something, but at the same time be absolutely helpless in terms of achieving it. Beyond the boundaries of my own family, I never face such situations'.

He explained that he never gets angry with subordinates, because if an employee is not doing his job correctly, it's not the employee's fault; it's his own. The problem is that he, Khodorkovsky, selected the wrong person for the job or failed to explain some necessary procedure well. 'If it is impossible to explain [that procedure] to him [in such a way that the job gets done properly], then ... I fire him.'

However, as CEO of Yukos, Khodorkovsky did not fire people easily. In 'Kremlinesque intrigue' – style, he created a so-called Administrative Reserve department, with a capacity of 30 positions. At the time of writing this book, this 'Corporate Siberia' counted seven people in it. The concept of such an 'honorary exile' was well mastered in the former Soviet Union, where high-level executives and governmental officials who had made mistakes were transferred to positions with lofty titles but no authority in governmental institutions, research and teaching organizations, or embassies in the smallest of the third-world countries.

Khodorkovsky ran Yukos in an informal way. While he remained involved in investment, sales and HR decisions, he no longer signed documents or negotiated with buyers and suppliers.[19] Describing his major task as that of coordinating the actions of managers, Khodorkovsky prefered not to spend too much time in the office, restricting his workload to 50 hours per week.

A voracious reader, and an observer of world-famous politicians and executives, Khodorkovsky seems like a man who has achieved what Abraham Maslow called 'self-actualization'[20] – that is, becoming the best one can be. He believed that it is the self-actualization dimension of work at Yukos that motivated his top-level managers and allowed the organization to squeeze them dry. Khodorkovsky commented:

> Obviously, top managers work at the self-actualization level. The 'squeezing model' is built around the concept of constantly encroaching on a person's desire for self-actualization. [At Yukos] you constantly feel the breath of the person 'in line' behind you. The issue is not that the runner-up will necessarily take your position. It's that tomorrow that person may get ahead of you, and then you'll no longer be number one. You'll just be number two. For that, comparing yourself to the [external] competition is very useful.

As for Khodorkovsky himself – a man who still prefers a turtleneck to a suit and tie – he in many ways remains a young man who has not yet lost his youthful desire to change the world.

Khodorkovsky called himself a crisis manager, saying, 'Changing from a Russian company to an international one ... getting mixed up in a new fight – now that's interesting'[21] And, given the progress at Yukos, he gained a respectable track record in crisis management.

However, as we described above, Mikhail Khodorkovsky faced the greatest crisis of his career in 2003. In early July, his closest associate (and president of the Menatep group) Platon Lebedev, was arrested on charges of wrongdoing during the privatization of a Russian mining company in 1994. Prosecutors searched Yukos' offices and charged some of its employees, including the head of security, with a range of crimes from tax evasion to plotting murder. Yukos' stock plummeted at the time. Then in September, Putin addressed the issue head on by announcing that there was no political motivation behind the scandal, and said that his government would not reopen investigations into the privatizations of the 1990s. By mid-October, Yukos shares had fully recovered their historic high.

But the situation was still very unstable: in late October, Khodorkovsky was arrested on charges of fraud and tax evasion, and the Russian stockmarket plunged 10 per cent. On 4 November, 2003, Mikhail Khodorkovsky abruptly resigned as CEO of Yukos. In a statement from his prison cell, Khodorkovsky said he was resigning in order to protect Yukos and his employees from 'the blows directed at him and his partners'.

Khodorkovsky's replacement was Simon Kukes, a US citizen of Russian descent, who was a former CEO of TNK-BP. Kukes had joined Yukos in the summer of 2003 to become chairman of the board, and also became CEO after Khodorkovsky's resignation. In his first two months on the job, Kukes vowed to strengthen corporate governance and the operational independence of management from shareholders, and to press ahead with the Sibneft merger. In a bow to the government, he promised to revisit Yukos' aggressive tax optimization strategy.

The brilliant YukosSibneft merger was in jeopardy, however. With the imprisonment of Khodorkovsky, Sibneft's founder (and owner of Chelsea, the English soccer club) Roman Abramovich saw his chance to take the upper hand in the deal. Sibneft demanded top management jobs and a greater equity stake for their company. When Yukos executives refused to reduce their company's equity stake, Sibneft announced that it would suspend the merger. *The Wall Street Journal Europe* reported that Abramovich was considered a 'trusted ally of the Kremlin, who has several times taken over assets from tycoons who have had a falling-out with President Putin.'[22]

In February 2004, when news broke about the definite YukosSibneft demerger, some observers thought that the shots were being called from the cell in Matrosskaya Tishina prison.

But people still wondered, who could possibly replace Mikhail Khodorkovsky, and how? In an analysis of the announcement made by Khodorkovsky regarding his retirement (long before his arrest), the Russian business daily *Vedomosti* reminded readers that there had been only three (more or less) successful cases of business leadership succession in Russia thus far.[23]

Once again, Mikhail Khodorkovsky had done the unexpected. By the end of 2003 he was no longer CEO of Yukos, but his influence was undoubtedly as powerful as ever. What would the future hold? Russia, and the world, waited and watched.

NOTES

1. Source for 'Boris Berezovsky was still a part owner': Patricia, Kranz, (1998), 'He's got the oil. Now can he make money?' *Business Week* International Edition, 2 Feb, Number 3563, p. 19. Source for the shareholders composition and a reputation of being non-transparent: Gotova, Natalia and Yuri Khnychkin (2001), 'Sibneft's President Strongly Recommends Not to Mix The Company and Its Shareholders', *Kompania*, 28 May, Number 166, pp 12–13.
2. Aris, B. (2003), 'Land of Bureaucratic Opportunity', *The Moscow Times*, 30 January.
3. Hoffman, D. (2002), *The Oligarchs: Wealth and Power in the New Russia*, New York: Public Affairs, p. 107.
4. Profil, 21 November, 1998, No. 43 (115).
5. Hoffman, D. (2002), *The Oligarchs: Wealth and Power in the New Russia*, New York: Public Affairs, p. 107.
6. Hoffman, D. (2002), p. 119.

7. Slevin, P. (1991), 'The New Soviet Up-and-Comers Trade Party Line for Bottom Lines', *Miami Herald*, 18 August.
8. Klebnikov, P. (1998), 'Russian Roulette', *Forbes*, 20 April, **161**, (8), 136–7.
9. Bahree, Bhushan and Jeanne Whalen (2001), 'Russia's Yukos Starts to Win Over Its Doubters', *Wall Street Journal*, 4 May, p. A13.
10. www.Yukos.com.
11. Whalen, J. (2002), 'Russian's Richest Man Discloses Worth', *The Wall Street Journal Europe*, 21–3 June, pp. A1, A8.
12. Klebnikov, P. (2002), 'The Oligarch Who Came in From the Cold', *Forbes*, 18 March, **169** (6), p. 110.
13. Klebnikov, P. (2002), 'The Oligarch Who Came in from the Cold', *Forbes*, 18 March, **169**, pp. 110–12.
14. Ibid.
15. Khnychkin, Yu (2002), 'Osnovnuyu Stoimost Sozdayut Predprinimatelskiey Mozgi', *Kompaniya*, 12 August.
16. www.Yukos.ru.
17. Whalen, J. (2003), 'An Unlikely Exporter of Russian Capitalism Goes With Profit Flow', *The Wall Street Journal Europe*, 16–18 May, pp. A1 and A5.
18. Shmarov, A. (2001), 'Russian Managers: Special Project of Expert Magazine', *Expert*, 1 October.
19. Bushueva, E. and E. Osetinskaya (2003), 'Khodorkovsky otmeril sebe srok', *Vedomosti*, 4 April.
20. Maslow, A. (1943), 'A Theory of Human Motivation', *Psychological Review*, **50**, 370–96.
21. Whalen, J. (2003), 'An Unlikely Exporter of Russian Capitalism Goes With Profit Flow', *The Wall Street Journal Europe*, 16–18 May, pp. A1 and A5.
22. Whalen, J. (2003), 'Yukos Would Cede Management Jobs to Rescue Merger', *The Wall Street Journal Europe*, 2 December, pp. A1, 4.
23. Bushueva, E. and E. Osetinskaya (2003), 'Khodrkovsky otmeril sebe srok', *Vedomosti*, 4 April.

Commentary: Mikhail Khodorkovsky and Yukos

In July 2003 Mikhail Khodorkovsky was officially admitted to the top league of global business leaders – he was the first Russian to participate in the annual informal Sun Valley summit of top business leaders in the US along with Bill Gates, Warren Buffet, Jeff Bezos and the like. *Fortune* magazine ranked Yukos as number one among the 500 largest corporations in the world in the 'return on investment' category and number two in 'return on sales'.

Around the same time back home in Russia, Russian prosecutors arrested Platon Lebedev, Khodorkovsky's long time associate and president of his holding company Menatep for alleged fraud during the privatization of a medium-sized fertilizer-producing company back in 1994. The prosecutors questioned Khodorkovsky himself as a 'witness' in this case. In an officially unrelated event, prosecutors began an impromptu audit of Yukos finances and searched its Moscow offices with the help of masked police armed with machine guns. Immediately, Yukos' market capitalization shrank by almost 20 per cent as investors' sentiment about Russia switched from 'very positive' to 'deep concern' in a matter of days. Only a few months later, Yukos' share price rose again to recover its historic high, after Putin spoke about the positive effect of Khodorkovsky's support of politics in September 2003. By late October, Khodorkovsky was in jail.

Khodorkovsky's resignation from his position as CEO of Yukos in November came as a surprise to the world, and yet Yukos insiders said that Khodorkovsky had apparently been putting a more independent management structure into place long before his problems with the government erupted. One executive said, 'It is clear he was expecting [the arrest] to happen. He'd said over and over, "You guys are going to have to figure out how to get along without me."'[1]

This continuing drama illustrates that Khodorkovsky's influence on the Russian economy could hardly be overestimated – just as his personal and his business vulnerability should not be underestimated. In that sense, Russia's richest man epitomizes the iconic symbol of Russia, an eagle with two heads. Reflecting the current state of affairs in Russia, the eagle's one head looks forward to the market economy and a liberal society, while the other head keeps gazing at the totalitarian past, when the State controlled every aspect of life from cradle to grave. Khodorkovsky's stature and accomplishments are unique, but at the same time very illustrative of the new breed of entrepreneurs, who over the last 15 years built businesses of all sizes and profiles on the ruins of the centrally planned economy. Some people draw analogies to 19th century America, where 'robber barons' controlled resources to their tremendous personal, and sometimes political, advantage. (We will look more closely at these similarities in Chapter 10.) Other people think of Khodorkovsky as a kind of fearless conquistador, opening up new worlds. In any case, Khordorkovsky typifies a new way of life for Russians, and not one that is accepted by all.

WEALTH AND INDEPENDENCE: A BUSINESS MODEL

Khodorkovsky's behavior and career are in some ways typical of entrepreneurs from any country, but they also reflect specifics of the economic and political situation of the late 1980s–1990s and Russian national culture. Khodorkovsky never had a great business idea along the lines of Amazon.com, Starbucks or Microsoft Windows. Instead, he was very opportunistic, and indeed rather indifferent to the nature of the business he was in, up until the time he fell in love with the energy sector. However, he always knew what he wanted *from* his business, and he built, acquired or disposed of companies with this vision in his head. Like many other Russian entrepreneurs of the 1990s, who grew up with chronic shortages of most essential goods and the all-dominating shadow of the State, two themes were central to Khodorkovsky's empire creation: wealth and independence. The relative importance to Khordokovsky of these two themes may have changed at different points in time, and their juxtaposition caused complicated twists in strategy, but they have always guided his thoughts and deeds.

Khodorkovsky's business models continually evolved to reflect both his changing environment and his place in the world. That evolution was unprecedented and remarkable because it occurred within such a short period of time. He started off by finding loopholes in the disintegrating Soviet economic systems, and making money out of air. Business models were simple and easy to copy; the time horizon for his new ventures did not exceed a few months; and decisiveness and speed were major competitive advantages. Khodorkovsky exploited the artificial nature of Soviet ruble and price systems; the existence of various foreign exchange rates; the deficiencies of the banking system; the closed nature of the Soviet economy; and his own connections. He was one of the first to recognize something others failed to acknowledge: the Soviet State did not control *all* of the country's resources, because its citizens had piles of idle cash that they could put to work. Only a few years later, hundreds of businesses following the same strategy – borrowing from the Russian population to finance business (primarily trading operations) – collapsed, ruining millions of families, but Khodorkovsky by that time had extended his time horizon and engaged himself in privatization of State assets. His strategy was crystal clear: acquire anything that could generate cash at the lowest possible price. His group Rosprom ended up owning more than a hundred companies from various industries.

While early financial and trading operations ensured Khodorkovsky's financial independence, reselling and milking of privatized assets allowed for bigger deals and long-lasting wealth. He moved on to oil to follow the Soviet state's strategy of pocketing easy cash by selling low-cost crude at the world market. Khodorkovsky acquired Yukos because he envisioned it to be a cash-generating machine that would pump out profits for decades without much intervention. With annual net cash flows measured in billions of dollars, Yukos met his expectations. Nevertheless, Khodorkovsky soon embarked on a new voyage of discovery – into the world of stock markets and shareholder value, where 'paper wealth' serves as a universal measure of success and importance. Cash lost its magnetic appeal for the man. Khodorkovsky decided to build a world-class company with a market capitalization that would rival that of British Petroleum (BP) or Shell. It would be financially transparent – a vision unprecedented for a Russian business and requiring a dramatic shift in strategic thinking and operational philosophy. Khodorkovsky made this shift quickly, but recognized that it would take time to change others.

Of course, the collapse of the Soviet system, market reforms in Russia, and especially its opening to the world, played an important role in the evolution of Khodorkovsky's business models, but he also was an active agent of these changes. Khodorkovsky was not only opportunistic in dealing with the business environment, but actively shaped it to meet his own needs. Among other things, he founded the first commercial bank in Russia; instituted (along with other future oligarchs) loans-for-shares auctions and sales of the largest natural resources-producing companies; pushed for reductions in personal income tax and in the mandatory sale of export hard currency proceeds to the State; initiated a country-wide campaign to promote corporate governance; and ensured Parliamentary support for the Code of Corporate Ethics. Without a doubt, Khodorkovsky – with the help of his political and business allies – directly shaped the economic landscape of modern Russia.

Management of his environment was always very high on Khodorkovsky's agenda and he was very blunt about this aspect of his leadership role. The Komsomol youth organization must have been a good training ground for Khodorkovsky. Until the time of his unexpected imprisonment he was good at making friends in the corridors of power and putting friends into important government jobs. He concluded alliances with fellow businessmen, and just as easily broke them. He used existing organizations to push new ideas, and created political 'Special Purpose Vehicles', short-lived groups and organizations to lobby his agenda. He was able to mobilize the business community and mass media, and made quiet deals with people at the very top. In the early years Khodorkovsky fought his enemies using all available means. Later he said he realized the advantages of dealing with differences in a civilized manner; he was one of the early proponents of the Commission on Corporate Ethics, the unofficial oligarchs 'court'.

The move toward increasing Yukos' market capitalization widened Khodorkovsky's influence to include Western investors and analysts. Khodorkovsky assumed this almost unheard-of role with his usual determination and soon became a habitué of top-level global events, a darling of Wall Street, and personal friend of financial and industrial moguls. In his usual manner, Khodorkovsky did not limit his effort to promoting Yukos, but actively advocated Russia's attractiveness for global investors, and worked hard back home to improve it. His interest was pragmatic: to increase Yukos' capitalization. But the results of his efforts have been far-reaching.

The government investigation into Yukos' finances in 2003 therefore, must have seemed like a personal affront to Khodorkovsky. For his entire career, he was on the offensive, carving Russian politics and economy to his taste. Now for the first time he was under direct fire. He had to defend his freedom, independence and wealth. The arsenal in his possession was impressive, but so was that of his opponents, and the outcome was far from certain.

LEADER WITH A RUBLE

Almost from the beginning, Khodorkovsky had a closed circle of trusted associates who served as an advisory council for his business projects – what could be called a Russian-style executive team. However, Khodorkovsky admired successful business professionals, and his council of friends was slowly replaced as his principal source of advice by Yukos' board of independent directors, and Yukos management meetings became dominatated by professional executives with no connection to Menatep. Khodorkovsky seems to have avoided one of the most common mistakes of successful entrepreneurs: clinging to old buddies and yea-sayers long after the organization has grown out of the start-up phase.

In fact, Khodorkovsky sought advice from business professionals, including expatriates, earlier than most Russian oligarchs. Attracted by the expatriates' functional expertise, Khodorkovsky first placed them in technical positions in his organizations. There he could control them; he was initially suspicious about their good intentions, and he doubted their ability to operate in the complex Russian environment. However, as the time passed and many of them proved to be effective and trustworthy, Khodorkovsky gave them more elbow room. They gradually extended their presence to the senior management positions. At the time of his arrest, several of Yukos' top executives, including the COO and CEO, were Americans, who were less likely to be indicted by Russian prosecutors. Khodorkovsky's personal evolution and self-reflection also supported this trend; he believed that being a successful entrepreneur didn't mean being an operational manager, and so he began to withdraw from daily operations. He was a fervent admirer of executive talent; he searched the globe to hire the best people, and treated them like stars within his company.

On the other hand, Khodorkovsky had a somewhat Taylorist approach to managing the rest of the organization. He believed in specialization, strict working procedures, control and monetary rewards. Moreover, Khodorkovsky is an introverted man, not the kind of charismatic leader who inspires rank-and-file employees with fascinating visions and enthusiastic speeches from the oil rigs. He preferred to lead Yukos from his Moscow office through a very hierarchical management structure. This approach turned out to be successful in improving Yukos' efficiency and correcting problems of poor discipline after its acquisition. Therefore Khodorkovsky regarded this management structure as universally appropriate for large organizations with many thousands of employees scattered over many locations.

The bright people he hired for the top jobs at Yukos, however, usually had a different view on effective management practices. As the degree of delegation within Yukos increased, these people tended to translate their views into practice, even though they did not always air their ideas in the CEO's presence. The influx of experienced executives with a global outlook, and young MBAs had begun to transform Yukos into a very different company from Khodorkovsky's structural model of a pyramid with miniscule individual cells and vertical lines of communication. They have built one of the most advanced HR management systems in the country; created leadership development programs; partnered with business schools to improve management training; and opened a department at a technical university in Siberia. Employee communication programs have reached a scale unprecedented for a Russian company of that size. Social initiatives directed inside and outside the company confirm its reputation as the employer of choice in Russia.

This transformation has not been easy, as it clashes with the old Yukos culture of secrecy, distrust, excessive control, subordination and risk-avoidance, which dates back to the years of fighting for control and survival. To some extent Khodorkovsky was a part of the problem. Even though the CEO tried to project a casual, modern image, he was always escorted by intimidating bodyguards, never left his isolated office to wander around, and rarely smiled or told jokes. The security department is still one of the most powerful in the company and it will probably stay that way for years to come, remaining a countervailing power to modern HR practices.

THE SUCCESSION CONUNDRUM

Yukos (and some of Khodorkovsky's earlier enterprises) always stayed ahead of the Russian competition by pioneering new ways of doing business. Now Yukos has joined the transparent corporate governance campaign – but the competition is launching similar programs and will eventually catch up with Yukos. As the experience of oil giants such as BP indicates, the next step for Yukos may well be the creation of a flatter organization with autonomous production units, profit and loss responsibility pushed down the line, strong horizontal links and a culture of innovation, support, delegation and personal accountability. While he was CEO, however, Khodorkovsky did not see a need for this kind of transformation.

Given Khodorkovsky's leadership style and the demands on Yukos to transform itself into an ever more modern organization, we had predicted that the transition from Mikhail Khodorkovsky to a new head of Yukos promised to become one of the most intriguing pages in the unfolding history of business in the New Russia. Khodorkovsky's announcement of his retirement in April 2003 triggered intense speculation about leadership succession at Yukos. Skeptics cited the poor track record of leadership succession in Russia: recent specific cases of failed top management changeovers and owners returning to run their business, and Khodorkovsky's young age and natural thirst for power. Optimists, however, threw back some heavy arguments. Khodorkovsky was both intelligent and experienced; he understood what he wanted and what he could do. A well-thought-out game plan had always been behind his decisions – if his desire to find a replacement for himself was not a result of an emotional spark of fatigue or satiety, then there was no reason to imagine that it would not be carried out as rationally as his previous moves had been.

Many elements necessary for a smooth transition were already in place. Khodorkovsky had a good track record of selecting effective top executives. In choosing and developing his successor, he would build on advanced HR technologies, the experience of his board members and a powerful network of global connections. The job he offered would interest the most ambitious and talented executives worldwide. As Khodorkovsky had consistently reduced his direct involvement in Yukos management and delegated power to hired hands, he would probably have been able to avoid the typical founding entrepreneur's 'I had to return to save the company' syndrome. He had solid experience in dealing with talented executives, including expatriates, and understood their expectations and work habits. And, last but not least, he operated within the model of long-term value creation, which required organizational renewal, including at the very top.

Khodorkovsky had, in theory, everything he needed to prepare an adequate successor: money, personal experience and a network of connections; a pool of talented managers in Russia and abroad to choose from; and plenty of developmental tools.

With hindsight, it appears that Khodorkovsky had gone much farther to prepare for an eventual succession event, including a catastrophic one, than anyone had realized. In the end, his resignation could be seen as his only option, but given the care he took to put a stable management structure in place, his decision can also be seen as an example of the last, good thing a CEO can do to save his organization.

On the other hand, observers of Russian business and politics agreed that Simon Kukes, though himself a highly experienced executive, would not be able to match Khodorkovsky's abilities in the areas of leadership in which the former CEO excelled: his envisioning and strategy development; his iron-fisted control of the diversified energy conglomerate; his flexibility in the unpredictable world of Russian politics; and his management of the shifting relationships between business and government. It appears that Khodorkovsky's succession plan reflected his leadership philosophy and style. He took care of the institutional side of the equation by putting in place systems which functioned semi-autonomously, but he was less focused on the need to develop leaders internally and had to bring Simon Kukes into Yukos from the outside.

Khodorkovksy would pay a high price for not having developed strong internal leadership. His defense campaign appeared to be purely legalistic, and while he was in jail the Russian government succeeded in winning over public opinion with populist anti-oligarch rhetoric. At the same time, Yukos began to distance itself from its former leader as the situation worsened. When the YukosSibneft merger was cancelled, there was a real danger that Yukos might lose some of its assets or even be dismantled.

Some experienced executives left the company after Khodorkovsky's arrest, and employee morale in general appeared to be low. When asked what they thought about his arrest, many workers in Nefteyugansk, a town with a Yukos oil-drilling facility, said that it served Khodorkovsky right. They claimed that Khodorkovsky had given them nothing but nice uniforms. People had already forgotten that before his arrival, wages had not been paid for months. Furthermore, under Khodorkovsky, wages were relatively high, and there was an overall improvement in the living conditions in Nefteyugansk.[2] Now their future was again in question.

Who would handle these and other complex issues? Would Simon Kukes, as CEO and Chairman of the Board, be up to the challenge? Would Khodorkovsky have behind-the-scenes influence from his prison cell, or would his energy be devoted to negotiating with the government for his freedom?

Khodorkovsky said from prison that he was leaving Yukos to devote his time to his Open Russia foundation, and to building an 'open and truly democratic society in Russia.' Opinion in the Western press was largely supportive of

Khodorkovsky; in fact there was even some grumbling that if the trend toward 'state capitalism' in Russia continued, then perhaps the country should be forced out of the economic Group of Eight.

At the time of this writing, we could only speculate on the outcome. Would Yukos be forced into bankruptcy? Khodorkovsky's fate would depend on the direction Putin's near-certain second term would take. There were signs that Russia might turn toward another 'winter period': the populist themes of Russia's uniqueness, superiority and special destiny in a hostile world were re-emerging; the central government was strengthening its power; and the special services were gaining disproportional influence. The New Duma was dominated by Putin's 'pocket party' which had no specific ideology, but used the slogan 'together with the President'. Liberal parties could not clear the 5 per cent barrier to gain entry to the Duma. The economy looked good, with growth at 7.5 per cent in 2003, but the Yukos situation, similar threats to other companies, and Putin's rhetoric about fighting economic inequality made the business community nervous.

If these trends were to culminate into a new course towards an authoritarian, state-dominated, populist Russia, Mikhail Khodorkovsky might be well advised to find a better use for his entrepreneurial talent outside his homeland.

NOTES

1. Whalen, J. (2003), 'YUKOS Executive Pledges Continuity', *The Wall Street Journal Europe*, 30 Oct, pp. A1, A10.
2. Ostrovsky, A. (2003), 'Yukos workers shed few tears for jailed ex-boss', *Financial Times*, 17 November, p. 20.

6. Ice and flame: building a NYSE company in Wild Russia

An unusual group was having dinner at Le Carré Blanc, the best French restaurant in Moscow, one evening in May 2002. Other patrons gazed at them with undisguised interest. The youngest of the group, an American impeccably dressed in a dark suit, white shirt and designer tie, leaned back in his chair and slowly sipped his wine. With the help of an interpreter, he was listening intently to an older Russian man. The Russian, in an open-collared, short-sleeved blue shirt, dominated the conversation. His energetic gesticulations were hard for other diners to ignore.

The two men were the founders, and for many years had been senior executives, of VimpelCom, a Russian cellular operator that had grown in less than 10 years from conceptual idea, to small family-like company, to $2 billion NYSE-quoted corporation with 5.5 million subscribers.

These two men had had countless conversations since their first meeting in October 1991, but this one, in the Moscow restaurant, was different from all the others: it was their first meeting as *former* executives of VimpelCom. A few hours earlier, Augie K. Fabela II, the young American, had stepped down as VimpelCom's chairman of the board. His dinner companion, the Russian Dr Dmitry Zimin, had resigned as CEO a year earlier. Both had cut their ties to a company that had been the center of their lives for more than a decade.

Zimin leaned across the table towards the younger man and spoke insistently: 'But Augie, why did you leave VimpelCom? The principle shareholders wanted you to stay on. Yes, they may have had a different opinion six months earlier, but when we met recently they all asked me to help them convince you to stay on as chairman. Okay, I'm 69 and it's time for me to go – I don't measure up to the new generation – but you're only 36! Why should you leave when your achievements are so visible?'.

Indeed, VimpelCom had recently returned to the black, under Fabela's leadership. After nine quarters of losses following Russia's financial crisis in August 1998 (excluding a stockprice bubble in early 2000), the company had shown a profit in the first quarter of 2002. Its incremental market share was now higher than its major competitor's; it had accumulated a $300 million war chest for regional expansion and financial analysts were strongly recommending its stock to investors.

Fabela smiled and reached for his glass: 'It's over, Dim. It was a great journey, but it's over. It's time to move on'.

TESTING THE WATERS

The 'great journey', as Augie Fabela II called it, had started on a rainy afternoon in October 1991 in the still-existent Soviet Union, when he and his father, Augie K. Fabela I,[1] respectively chairman and CEO of Plexsys (an Illinois-based manufacturer of cellular equipment) disembarked at the Moscow Sheremetievo Airport. For the previous six months Augie II had resisted an invitation from a Lebanese-American fellow entrepreneur to make a reconnaissance trip to post-Communist Russia and discuss opportunities for a joint venture to sell and manufacture Plexsys equipment there. Pushed by his father, Augie II finally agreed to a visit, 'just to discover a new country', he said – a country that would soon become his home-away-from-home.

A series of meetings with people from MAK-Vimpel, a military-industrial conglomerate, didn't leave Augie II impressed. Various images lingered: Russians dressed in similar gray suits and dark ties sitting around a long table, talking about how their company could manufacture anything in the world from missiles to cellular phones if they just could get some seed money. Augie's casual observations of Russian reality were more enlightening. Even though the country was going through a severe depression, there were some expensive cars in the streets and there were local customers at hard-currency restaurants. What really struck him, though, was that none of these apparently well-to-do customers had a cell phone!

The Fabelas already had experience operating a cellular network in a country other than their own – Colombia – and they felt that Russia offered great potential for their business. But Augie II wasn't sure, however, that working in the mysterious Russian environment without local expertise would be possible. He and his father decided to invite some Vimpel executives to the US to visit Plexsys' production facilities and see cellular telephony in action. Having provided an opportunity for each side to learn more about the other, they could then discuss potential cooperation in Russia.

Struggling with unfamiliar names, Augie II managed to communicate to the Russians that their delegation should include one colleague in particular, a man who had intrigued the Fabelas during their visit to Moscow because of his intelligence and drive. This small, older man, whom the senior Augie called 'the professor', was obviously passionate about his ideas: when he wanted to make a point in a meeting, he pounded his fists on the table. After the Russians' visit to America, that first impression was confirmed, and both Fabelas knew that they had to work with him.

EMBRACING CAPITALISM: FROM ANTI-MISSILE SHIELDS TO PERESTROIKA COOPERATIVES

Augie and his father were right to be impressed, although at the time of his visit to the US in February 1992 they didn't know that 'the professor' was Dr Dmitry Zimin, department head at the Applied Radio Research Institute (RTI in Russian) and a CEO and principal shareholder of a number of small businesses. With almost four years of experience, he was a rare 'veteran' entrepreneur in the newly emerging Russian markets, but none of his ventures had yet become a real success.

After completing his Ph.D. at the prestigious Moscow Aviation Institute, Zimin had joined RTI to work on developing radio systems for the Soviet military. He made a significant contribution to the design and construction of the Soviet anti-missile radar system, published dozens of scientific articles, and trained many successful scientists.

Zimin's background was modest. He didn't remember his father, who had perished in a gulag in 1935, when Zimin was only two years old. His mother, who came from the noble family of Alexander Guchkov – famous for receiving Czar Nicholas II's abdication – worked as a typist. They lived in two rooms with Zimin's grandmother, aunt, and her husband, sharing the bathroom and kitchen of an eight-room apartment with five other families. Young Dmitry was quite adventurous at an early age. He started to assemble his own radio receivers at the age of 12, played cards and chess (a life-long passion) for money, smoked, and rode motorbikes.

As a young man, he loved to move fast, be it in a car, a motorboat, or on skis (water and alpine). In the 1970s, with friends who were fellow skiers, Zimin built four ski lifts near Moscow. Even as an older man, he retained his love of speed and adventure. After acquiring a new Mercedes 420 in 2002, he tested it by making a trip to Minsk (700 km from Moscow), driving at 200 km per hour. As a Soviet citizen working for the military in the 1970s and 1980s, he wasn't allowed to travel to foreign countries, but he read everything he could get his hands on about travel and adventure abroad. Later, as a successful entrepreneur, he would travel extensively.

Zimin was an energetic and intellectually curious man, and the tense, bureaucratic atmosphere of the Soviet work routine in the 1970s and 1980s drove him crazy. He was constantly looking for an escape. It was no surprise to anyone that he was one of the first to start thinking about alternative business activities in 1987 when Mikhail Gorbachev authorized private enterprise in the form of *cooperatives* – companies owned by at least three people. Zimin said, 'In those days we had great engineers working for the military. I wanted them to work for the general population, to design and make things useful for everyday life. I also wanted them to have freedom to do things their own way. Of course, I wanted this freedom for myself, too'.

Zimin assembled a team from among his RTI colleagues and formed VimpelCom, a company whose purpose was to find practical applications for the radio technology they were experts in. Zimin's employer provided some initial funding in the form of office space and some cash. Zimin and his colleagues received just over 15 per cent of the new company's shares, with the rest going to RTI and its parent company, Vimpel.

To Zimin, getting industrial partners like these was a real coup. It seemed to him to be a good deal for everybody. There was no way he could have foreseen the trouble that would come from the 'sleeping' shareholders: they would later sell their stock to Sistema, a newly emerging Russian financial industrial group (with interests from telecommunications to insurance) and principal shareholder of MTS, a Russian GSM operator and a major future competitor for VimpelCom.

But at the outset, Zimin was confident that he had the right partners. Having gained investment capital, he began a search for the right business to go into. His vision was simple: produce something that people would buy. In rapid succession VimpelCom manufactured radar detectors for speed-loving drivers, designed satellite equipment, and attempted a joint venture with French giant CSF Thompson to develop satellite television. None of these ventures was successful, however. Zimin later admitted that he and his colleagues didn't really understand what the market was all about. In fact, this was one reason why a short time later Zimin joined forces with the more experienced Fabelas, father and son.

GETTING READY TO PLAY RUSSIAN ROULETTE

If the Fabelas had picked a winner in Zimin, it wasn't by chance. Augie II was only 24 when he first met Zimin, but he was already a seasoned entrepreneur who had worked with many partners. Contrary to what most of his middle-aged Russian counterparts thought, Augie was anything but 'green'.

The grandson of a rancher, he was the third child of Augie Fabela I, a Mexican-born engineer, and his wife, a Colombian-born nurse. His father was tireless in his search for new businesses, jobs and life challenges. The senior Fabela took his wife and two infant daughters to the US – Augie was not yet born – with $12 in his pocket and no specific plan for how to earn more or feed his family. At different times he had owned convenience stores, a gas station chain, and a race-car engine repair shop. He worked hard and the family moved often in search of better opportunities, but none of Fabela I's businesses ever turned into anything big. The family had to struggle and during the 1976 recession, when the only job Fabela I could get was filling tanks at a gas station, all the family members, including the teenage children, went to work. Augie II was too young to get a job, so he was responsible for housekeeping and family meals.

With his father always busy, little Augie spent a lot of time with his older sisters and his mother, a devout Baptist. A quiet homebody who disliked the boisterousness of outdoor games, he was nonetheless fascinated by his father's energy and drive.

When Augie Fabela I founded an engineering company, his son, who was 13 at the time, participated actively, doing office work and even negotiating and closing deals over the phone. From that time on they were business partners.

Augie II preferred helping his dad to attending school – to the point that his parents were afraid he would never graduate from high school. But in junior high he realized that good grades were important, and he earned his diploma at 16. To his own surprise, he was admitted to Stanford, Harvard and Northwestern, none of which he knew much about. He chose Stanford: 'It was far away and it just felt like a great place'. The shy 16-year-old boy from the Chicago suburbs went to California with two dreams: to overcome his shyness and to learn about the world. Sleeping only three or four hours a night and taking every international course in the curriculum, Augie finished his undergraduate work in two and a half years and earned a master's degree in international relations in another 18 months. He forced himself to participate in discussion groups, political campaigns and academic research groups. He experimented with learning Japanese and Chinese. He also made a two-week trip to the Soviet Union, even though he had nothing to do with the Slavic department at Stanford. During that trip he witnessed the consequences of changing money with a black marketeer: he saw the man arrested and beaten on the spot. He visited a Jewish refusnik in a little apartment in St Petersburg – a man whose name a Slavic studies professor at Stanford had given him – and he walked snowy Moscow streets crowded with large numbers of people in uniform.

Instead of going back to the Chicago area after graduation, he did two summer internships and took a marketing job with the largest media conglomerate in Japan, where he worked for two years. In addition to his full-time employment, Augie started a Japanese wine-importing business.

In 1989, after his return to the US and to his father's firm, Augie felt that the time was right to strike out on his own. With his sister, he acquired the information-technology division of their father's engineering company. Since no bank would extend a credit line to two siblings in their early twenties with no resources, they financed the business using their personal credit cards. The business took off and by 2002 had reached around $10 million annual sales.

In parallel with the IT business, Augie II started another company offering employee-leasing services. In 1990, while moving their engineering company from Chicago to Quincy, Illinois, to benefit from favorable tax incentives, the Fabelas came across Plexsys, a small cellular equipment manufacturer. At that time it was trying to develop markets in Latin America, where Augie's father had worked for quite some time. Both father and son felt that cellular telephony had tremendous growth potential. Plexsys had a great product but no international experience, so the fit with the Fabelas was perfect. The Fabelas signed an international marketing agreement with Plexsys and later found a way to do a leveraged buyout of the company. At the time of the buyout, Plexsys had around $4 million in annual sales. Two years later it had grown to $20 million in sales, all through international operations. In 1994 the Fabelas got out of the business, selling it to Comsat International, which managed to bankrupt the company within a year and a half. But by then Augie Fabela II was up to his ears in a new venture – VimpelCom.

A ROUGH START

Initially Augie and his father went to Russia to look for opportunities to sell (and to set up a joint venture to build) small switches for cellular networks with limited coverage. But after seeing the poor state of the cellular industry there, the Fabelas sensed an opportunity for providing cellular telephony services and decided to concentrate their activities in that area.

As noted earlier, after their visit to Russia in October 1991 (and after the Russian delegation's visit to the US in 1992), the Fabelas decided that they wanted Dmitry Zimin as a partner, even though he saw operational activities only as a way to develop a manufacturing business. Zimin later recalled, 'There was no demand for the radio equipment we could build, so we had to become an operator to earn money to support engineering activities'. The Fabelas convinced Zimin that they should work together. The deal was simple: VimpelCom – owned by RTI, Vimpel and Zimin & Co, and managed by Zimin – was to become a vehicle for penetrating the Russian market. Zimin assured his partners that he had full control of the venture and that he was free from other shareholders' pressure. The Americans would provide the initial financing, the marketing, and financial and management skills. VimpelCom and the Russians would be in charge of technical expertise, strategy, and the political connections necessary to secure the operating licenses. The Fabelas decided between themselves that Augie II would represent them in the Russian project.

SETTING UP A PARTNERSHIP

Wireless telephony, as a service available to the general public, had its start in 1991 in St. Petersburg. Earlier, the Soviet Ministry of Telecommunication had decided that the country would develop two European cellular standards: NMT and GSM. The first GSM license for the Moscow region, by far the most attractive market in Russia (given its almost 15 million inhabitants), was awarded to Mobile TeleSystems (MTS) in 1993.

In 1996 Sistema Telecom became a majority owner of MTS. Sistema had emerged from the ruins of the Soviet economy in the early 1990s when future oligarch Vladimir Evtushenkov turned the Moscow City Committee on Science and Technology – which he headed as a state official – into his private enterprise. Using city connections, the industrious bureaucrat privatized many lucrative Moscow businesses, such as insurance and microelectronics. Sistema Telecom was one of his successful bets, and MTS his favorite company, which he nurtured and protected with great interest. (VimpelCom would soon catch his attention as well.)

Cellular communication had a slow start in Russia; by the end of 1992 the only Moscow network had 6000 customers. Bulky and extremely expensive handsets ($2000 a piece) and limited coverage restrained demand for the service in the initial stage. MTS was more careful than its only competitor and developed a wider network before it started selling services in 1994, but despite Deutsche Telecom's involvement, the consortium lacked marketing savvy at start-up.

By the time the Fabelas and Zimin got their act together, Moscow officially had no frequencies available in either the 450 or 900 MHz bands, so both NMT and GSM options were closed to VimpelCom. Plexsys, which still belonged to the Fabelas, was a manufacturer of analogue equipment produced to the American cellular standard known as AMPS, operating in the 800 MHz band. Zimin and the Fabelas decided to gamble on the AMPS standard, despite the Ministry of Telecommunication's decision in favor of two European standards. And so the competition for licenses began.

Zimin, with his unique ability to work the system, was invaluable. Augie II remembered: 'At that point Zimin took the lead. He was the one who went out and got the license to build a network and import AMPS equipment'. Had only the Americans been involved, the licensing hurdles would have been insurmountable.

In the early 1990s, the Russian military controlled the 800 MHz spectrum required for AMPS operation. However, Zimin was able to convince the top brass that VimpelCom wanted to give work to the Russian engineers who had helped build the Soviet anti-missile shield. The Ministry of Telecommunication proved to be much tougher, however: 'I spent a week waiting in a Deputy Minister's reception office,' Zimin recalled, 'only to get a five-minute meeting and an unequivocal response: "Over my dead body!"'

He was undeterred by the rejection. 'I finally managed to meet Vladimir Bulgak [the Minister]', he said. 'My principal message was this: The country is talking about military facilities' conversion to civil needs, and the military are ready to clear some frequencies in 800 MHz. Let's jump on it.'

After long deliberation and many meetings with Zimin, Bulgak announced that AMPS would be a 'regional standard' and issued an operational license to VimpelCom for the city of Moscow.

Augie II and Zimin had learned a critical lesson about the importance of frequency spectrum for cellular telephony – and a lesson about negotiation and diplomacy. Since VimpelCom had no influential shareholders with direct government links (unlike its competitors), Zimin took on the task of nurturing relationships with the government and military officials responsible for spectrum allocation. He became a frequent visitor to the corridors of power and would continue to be so for years to come.

Soon after obtaining the AMPS license, Zimin created a separate company, KBI, and obtained a GSM-1800 license for Moscow. Zimin suspected that the main reason the authorities awarded VimpelCom and KBI the licenses was that they wanted 'to silence us – they didn't expect us to survive'.

BEELINE: RIDING THE WAVES OF RUSSIAN CAPITALISM

In 1994 VimpelCom started its test operations in Moscow, installing four Plexsys base stations and one mini-switch, which allowed them to provide services in a limited area of downtown Moscow. The Russian economy was in a deep depression, with the GNP shrinking by 5 per cent per year and inflation running at 500 per cent, but to the founders' surprise, their stock of 100 telephones – much more elegant than their competitors' briefcase-like models – sold out at $5000 apiece (plus subscription fee) in one day. Sales assistants at the department store where the first phones were sold were getting $500 bribes from customers desperate to get to the head of the queue. Gangsters, politicians and businessmen alike were begging Zimin for the phones. By year end VimpelCom had 3000 customers and a severe capacity shortage.

VimpelCom started to look for network expansion. With no cash on the balance sheet, no access to commercial loans, and no strategic shareholders, the company looked pretty unattractive to investors. However, Zimin's charm and Fabela's persistence paid off: Ericsson signed an agreement providing facilitating credit for suppliers. Zimin and several VimpelCom managers pledged all or a portion of their shares to Ericsson. In 1995 the company acquired $36.3 million of equipment from Ericsson, an acquisition that allowed it to roll out a full-scale digital AMPS (D-AMPS) network in Moscow and the Moscow region.

Staffed primarily with former engineers and scientists from RTI, VimpelCom was a technology- rather than customer-driven company in the early days. Augie II said, 'When we had network problems, network engineers would literally shut the network down to work on it, and their excuse would be: 'Don't worry about it. Russians are used to it. In any case, this is much better than what they had before'.

Given that attitude, there wasn't much to differentiate VimpelCom from its competitors. Fabela quickly realized that by focusing on service and marketing, VimpelCom could become a leader in the still-dormant market. However, the concepts of customer service and satisfaction, sales commissions and advertising were as foreign to VimpelCom managers as was the English language at that time. Fabela took responsibility for that part of the business, determined to change the company's mindset, while Zimin concentrated on political and technical issues. Quite quickly VimpelCom had its salesforce trained in new customer-support strategies, and a customer service center was made available 24 hours a day, seven days a week. Fabela also tried to set up a separate sales company with another Russian partner-company, which turned out to be a less-than-savory organization. When that partnership turned sour, he was advised to leave Russia for a while. He did so, fearing for his safety. As Zimin said: 'I think he learned a good lesson from that experience: that he shouldn't mess with anything which is Russia-specific'. From that point on, Fabela left all external activities to his Russian colleagues, concentrating on building the marketing and sales functions of VimpelCom.

Fabela brought in Liz Hamburg, a former associate from the Japanese media giant he had worked for, to help VimpelCom with marketing and sales. He also hired a number of young people to work with her. Fabela and Hamburg, an American with a marketing background, strongly believed that VimpelCom needed a trademark. They proposed the idea to senior management, arguing that customers would respond to an image that was friendly, nice, comfortable and light – quite the opposite of VimpelCom's heritage as a military research institute.

Zimin's initial reaction was negative. He and the other Russian managers believed that their superior engineering system needed no advertising effort. Zimin saw work on a trademark as a waste of their time and feared that putting huge investment into its promotion would be like 'heating the stove by burning bank notes'. He finally agreed to participate in weekly brainstorming sessions on the brand, but only reluctantly. At one very emotional meeting a brand name was eventually selected: BeeLine. Though they went along with the choice, Zimin and the other Russian managers were simply humoring Fabela and Hamburg; they didn't believe that there was any value in a brand name. So while Hamburg made sure to use the brand name in all promotion, Zimin went out of his way to criticize the 'waste of money' and the childishness of using a bee for a company logo. Fabela said later, 'Zimin was quick to adapt and understand the concept of service, but it took him a full year to accept the BeeLine brand name, and to understand the value and strength of a brand name and the need to differentiate our company'. (By 2000, BeeLine was one of the most recognizable trademarks in Russia, and if Zimin ever put a tie on, it was a BeeLine tie.) Later, Zimin would say that Hamburg was 'one of the most important people in Vimpelcom's history', who 'turned our brains upside-down'.

Powered by the BeeLine brand name and a superior network, VimpelCom soon moved ahead of the dormant competition. The company positioned its services as high-quality, premium products for the new Russian elite. Everybody who was somebody (or who pretended to be somebody) had to have a BeeLine phone. The new elite was receptive to buying handsets at $1000 and to making full use of the phone service: their usage yielded a record ARPU (average revenue per user) of $323 a month by 1996. By the end of 1994, BeeLine was represented by a large distribution network of licensed dealers. Zimin and Fabela knew that VimpelCom was a viable company – year-end revenues were $30 million and profits were $9.5 million. Incredibly, 1995 was even better: net income rose to $27.6 million on revenues of $101 million. Zimin and the other managers were featured in the Russian and international press, which portrayed them as the human face of the new Russian capitalism.

Given Zimin's and the VimpelCom engineers' superior technical skills, building and putting into operation the first D-AMPS network in Moscow (and later expanding to GSM) was no great challenge. On the other hand, keeping his job as CEO and keeping control of VimpelCom soon would be another matter.

THE FIGHT FOR CONTROL

Concentrating on operational activities, neither Zimin nor Fabela gave much thought to the ownership structure of VimpelCom, which had remained unchanged since the company's incorporation. The Fabelas had brought into VimpelCom some Plexsys equipment that they had purchased personally, and some cash, both of which were entered as 'loans' on the company books. None of the other shareholders – Vimpel, RTI or Zimin and his associates – had contributed any kind of equity. However, VimpelCom's success had not gone unnoticed, and one day Zimin and Fabela woke up to learn that they had a new shareholder, Sistema, which was rapidly acquiring telecommunication assets in and around Moscow and which controlled MTS, one of VimpelCom's main competitors. Its founder, Vladimir Evtushenkov, one of the most powerful businessmen in the country, had earned a reputation as the 'business face' of Moscow's powerful mayor, Yuri Luzhkov. Using their influence and in keeping with the best traditions of early Russian capitalism, Sistema had persuaded the managing directors of Vimpel and RTI to sell their VimpelCom shares.

VimpelCom was now in bed with MTS, which made Fabela and Zimin very uncomfortable, to say the least. Fabela remembered:

> We ourselves put in, through our own investments, around $2 million. We contributed all that without having any stake in the company, because we believed it shouldn't have any foreign ownership so it could get the benefit of a purely Russian company in getting the licenses. We trusted our partners, and then we found that Vimpel had sold its shares to Sistema. The heads of RTI and of Vimpel got $50 000 for their transactions. For that relatively small amount of money, they had handed over control of assets worth hundreds of millions of dollars. This kind of transaction was typical at that time.

Zimin recalls that period as a critical point in his relations with Fabela. Both men wanted to develop the business, although they had no precise plan for how they would do this. They *did* know, though, that they couldn't control development with Sistema involved. Even though Sistema didn't move in immediately to seize management control, Zimin understood that he wouldn't be able to maintain the freedom to run VimpelCom the way he wanted over the long term. And since Sistema had bet its money on MTS, its managers would use VimpelCom as a cash cow in the short run or even merge it with a GSM operator. Neither of these scenarios was acceptable to Zimin, who by that time had discovered the pleasure of being his own boss. Fabela knew that, as he owned no equity, he would be thrown out of the company sooner rather than later.

So in 1995, Fabela went back to the US to attract new investors to buy out Sistema. Together with his father they created a 'special purpose vehicle', FGI Wireless, and Augie II and Hamburg went on the road to sell 50 per cent of it. It was Fabela's first serious fund-raising exercise, but the young man was convincing, the cellular industry was booming, and his plan to have 10 000 customers in Moscow by the year 2000 looked aggressive enough for investors. Most of all, as Fabela described it, Russia seemed to be a potential Eldorado – especially to American investors, who were 2000 kilometers away (and hadn't yet been shaken by the Russian financial crisis to come in 1998). Institutional investors such as Templeton Emerging Markets Fund and Soros Fund signed up, as did many individuals. Together, the funds and individuals contributed $12 million to FGI Wireless, enough to buy 45 per cent of VimpelCom from Sistema. However, as Fabela recalled,

> Just before we closed the deal, Sistema realized that $12 million was too low. But we had already anticipated that, and by the time they tried to change, the shares were in the escrow account. That taught me a lesson that allowed me to identify early the single weakest point for a Russian businessman: greed. It was tremendously strong in those days, and still is tremendously strong. And as long as you throw out some factors to let them exercise their greed, they don't think of anything else. They lose focus.

After the transaction Sistema still owned 40 per cent of VimpelCom; FGI Wireless owned 45 per cent, with Zimin and his partners owning the remaining 15 per cent (and therefore holding the deciding vote). Given Zimin's explosive character and tendency to change views, Fabela feared that VimpelCom was under serious threat of falling back into Sistema's hands. The balance was very fragile. Fabela decided that he needed to buy Sistema out completely to protect the company from Zimin's unpredictability.

ZIMIN THE CEO

The casual observer would never recognize in Zimin – with his old suits, outmoded glasses, mischievous smile and modest office devoid of bodyguards and glamorous secretaries – the head of a large Russian business. At management meetings he often spoke about Mikhail Bulgakov's novels and the theory of homeostasis, and he never used the foul language so typical of Russian executives. And yet, as CEO, Zimin was the real center of decision-making power at VimpelCom. Different factions of senior executives fought for his attention and approval. Having no business education or experience, Zimin borrowed strategic ideas from his colleagues, from theoretical physics, and from Russian discussions of Western economic theories. A stoic adept at competition, he wanted to run two independent D-AMPS and GSM networks, first as different companies and later as competing divisions of VimpelCom.

Zimin liked to manage by wandering around the company. He was always an attentive listener. He was also an impulsive decision-maker, sometimes acting unwisely on what he heard as he wandered. Many ill-fated VimpelCom initiatives, such as the creation of a research lab to design new handsets and to develop in-house software products, resulted from his ad hoc conversations with employees. By 1998, VimpelCom had on its balance sheet a car repair shop, a restaurant, land bought for the construction of houses for employees, and interests in dozens of small companies. Lured by extremely high returns (up to 100 per cent), Zimin – against Fabela's advice – approved multi-million-dollar investments in Government Bonds (GKO), which at one point in 1998 were bringing more profits to VimpelCom than its operating activities, but which collapsed in August 1998.

Despite Zimin's somewhat eccentric leadership style, the overwhelming majority of VimpelCom employees saw their CEO as a superman who fulfilled their aspirations for meaningful work and a decent living, protected them from inflation by paying dollar-denominated wages, and from foreign capitalists by keeping control of the company. They took pride in working for the first officially acknowledged post-Soviet millionaire, who was putting in 14 hours a day to build a high-performance organization. Having chafed under the meticulous rules and regulations of their former military bosses, they admired Zimin's openness and simplicity, his sense of humor, even his rumpled old-fashioned suits and professorial glasses. They enjoyed casual tea parties with the CEO – impromptu events at which poetry was recited and global problems were discussed. Only a few years before, they had all dreamed together about creating something new and exciting. Zimin had led them through tough times, and now their dreams had become reality. VimpelCom was more than a place to work for a majority of its employees, it was a second family. Zimin was very proud of having 'workers' dynasties' as he called them, at VimpelCom – his own wife, three brothers-in-law and son worked there, and many other senior and rank-and-file employees worked alongside their own family members.

The 'old guard', as Fabela called Zimin's long-time associates, exercised significant influence over him, slowing and politicizing the decision-making process. Recognizing that sluggishness, Zimin tried to get rid of some old guard employees, but most of his efforts were incomplete: people were simply shuffled around rather than taken out of the organization. Zimin knew – and often publicly acknowledged – his shortcomings as an operational manager, and he sincerely wanted to delegate significant powers to the second line of management. But just as those powers were easily delegated, they were easily taken back when he felt that others threatened his control over VimpelCom.

In line with Zimin's desire to have the best and the brightest and to professionalize management, VimpelCom attracted a number of high-flying Russian and expatriate executives and specialists. However, most did not stay long, citing the conservative and highly politicized culture of the organization, along with Zimin's erratic management style, as major reasons for their departure. Zimin was known for changing his decisions many times a day. For example, once, after a long and expensive search, he hired a chief operating officer – only to inform the bewildered man that his services were no longer required at noon on his first working day.

And yet, despite many operational and tactical mistakes, Zimin always picked winning strategies – starting the cellular business, securing GSM frequencies, introducing (albeit with reservations) the BeeLine brand, going public (see below), switching to GSM from D-AMPS and creating a mass market, bringing in strategic partners, and investing in the regions. As Augie Fabela said,

> It rarely took him more than six months to get to where VimpelCom's CEO should have been, which for a 60-year-old man who has no business background whatsoever is amazing. So I knew that as long as I was patient enough and I started the sales pitch and education process, within six months he would come to the right answer. In between, he would do all kinds of ridiculous, crazy things, but he always came to the right answer.

NEW YORK STOCK EXCHANGE: TAKING IT TO 'THE STREET'

Fabela doesn't remember when and how he came up with the idea of taking VimpelCom public, but the more he thought about it, the more it seemed to be the best way to solve his problems with Zimin and Sistema. Sistema had finally realized that the company couldn't control Zimin, and its general strategy was to get out of any business it couldn't fully control. VimpelCom needed money if it was to buy Sistema out, and the best way to get that money and keep control of the company was through an IPO. Fabela recalled: 'I had never done this before – I didn't know if it *could* be done – but I was sure that this was the best way to consolidate and control the Russian partners'.

Over dinner in early 1995, at Moscow's first pizzeria, Fabela presented to Zimin his idea of taking VimpelCom public on the New York Stock Exchange: 'I painted a picture of how this would create much more wealth and value for him and other shareholders'. Zimin listened attentively, asked a lot of questions, but didn't say yes or no. He took the issue back to his long-time colleagues and minority shareholders, who had become VimpelCom managers. Their reaction was unequivocal: Zimin was an idiot to waste time and money on getting involved in the US stock market, given that VimpelCom was growing extremely fast and bringing in hard cash. Zimin went back to Fabela and told him that he, Zimin, didn't believe it would ever happen. He thought that VimpleCom should concentrate on operating activities. Zimin's Russian managers pressured him to hold that line, doing everything possible to make sure he didn't change his mind. But Fabela also kept up the pressure on him.

While Fabela looked at VimpelCom's IPO project as an opportunity 'to do something unique, that we hadn't done before', and create value for himself and other shareholders, Zimin saw things differently. His own first priority, in the early days, had been to find work for himself and his men, to put their brains and hands to productive use. When VimpelCom became operational, he insisted that its employees had decent working conditions and salaries, and that customers were getting good service. As the company grew and matured, he developed his vision for VimpelCom as a kind of super-organization, more efficient than leading international operators, pursuing a wide range of activities, providing high-quality services, employing top Russian talent, paying high wages, and playing an active role in the local community by supporting scientific research and education. He wanted VimpelCom to become an exemplary company for the new Russian society. Even though his ideas about the specifics of the company changed over time, ranging from building American-style houses for all VimpelCom employees to creating a research institute within it, he was always certain about one thing: to implement this vision he had to be in charge.

Sure as Zimin was of all this, Fabela never gave up on his plan to go public. He talked about getting Sistema out and replacing it with passive financial investors; about 'cheap' stock market money for capital investment; and about the historical importance of being the first Russian company on the New York Stock Exchange. What finally won Zimin over was a scheme invented by Fabela that allowed Zimin to keep control over the post-IPO structure of VimpelCom through preferred stock (that is, stock that had voting rights but no economic value). After signing on to Augie's vision, Zimin became an avid supporter of the IPO, tirelessly promoting this initiative within and outside of VimpelCom.

With Zimin's new enthusiasm, from late 1995 VimpelCom concentrated on preparing for the IPO. Implementing the plan was a nightmare. Fabela concentrated on the American exercise and managed to get from the NYSE and the SEC such unusual favors as a waiver on the requirement to have three years of GAAP financial statements. But his part was easy compared to Zimin's. When VimpelCom's CEO and finance director showed up at the Russian Central Bank, its officials couldn't understand what the executives were talking about – and when they finally did understand they didn't know what to do about it. It was the first time a Russian company had proposed selling shares on the US stock market. Almost nobody at the bank, the Ministry of Finance, or the Ministry of Telecommunication was supportive, but Zimin – with his energy, charm, exceptional empathy, and recently acquired knowledge of Russia's power structure and the rules of their game – prevailed.

On 15 November 1996, 18 months after Fabela and Zimin's pizza dinner in Moscow, a smiling Zimin waved to the crowds from the balcony of the New York Stock Exchange. The slightly rumpled engineer – wearing a VimpelCom cap and his trademark professorial glasses – was now the first official *multi*millionaire in the new Russia. The IPO had been ten times oversubscribed, with opening-day trading at $30 per share (the subscription price had been $20.50). The sale brought $53 million into VimpelCom's coffers. VimpelCom was now a Russian company valued at $530 million, providing services to 56 000 subscribers, with annual sales of $200 million.

Zimin owned 45 per cent of the company and FGI Wireless 19 per cent, with 36 per cent belonging to the new public shareholders. Zimin remained CEO and Fabela became chairman of the board.

THE CALM BEFORE THE STORM

From a small start-up with a messy shareholder structure and an uncertain future, to a regional telecom powerhouse quoted on Wall Street, VimpelCom had definitely arrived. From 1995 to 1997, it was one of the most profitable Russian companies. The horizon looked bright; there was no hint of the brewing financial storm that would soon hit Russia. In the company's 1997 letter to shareholders, Fabela (as chairman) and Zimin (as CEO) summed up their past success and future vision in glowing terms:

ANNUAL REPORT 1997 – (EXCERPTS FROM) LETTER TO SHAREHOLDERS

We are pleased to report that our growth and success continued in 1997, our first full year as a publicly-traded company. In 1997, we strengthened our leading position as the premier cellular communications provider in Russia. In many ways, it was a celebratory year. *Russia Review*, a bi-weekly magazine dedicated to reporting on Russian business, hallmarked our success in 1997 by awarding us the title of 'Company of the Year', ahead of Russian oil and gas giants and major Russian banks. Quite an accomplishment for a startup company that only commenced operations in 1994.

Operationally, 1997 was a record year. We experienced a surge in our subscriber base, which grew over 95 per cent to more than 110,000 subscribers. Despite increased competition in the Moscow cellular market, we maintained our leading market share of over 50 per cent at year end 1997.

…

Meeting the Challenges in 1998

Our challenges for 1998 are straightforward. We must continue to sustain and manage the continuing growth of our business and strengthen our position as the leading cellular communications provider in Russia. Our energies are focused on these challenges. … We look forward to a bright 1998!

VimpelCom entered 1998 with two networks: D-AMPS covering almost all of the Moscow region and some adjacent areas, and GSM-1800 with limited coverage in the city of Moscow. VimpelCom significantly extended its roaming area for D-AMPS customers as the new regional companies were opening their operations across Russia. GSM customers, on the other hand, didn't have access to roaming. D-AMPS services, sold under the BeeLine name, brought in the lion's share of revenue, while GSM, originally seen as cheaper cellular telephony for city-dwellers, couldn't expand its client base. Even as GSM confirmed itself as a uniform standard in Europe, growing numbers of traveling VimpelCom customers were unhappy not to be able to roam there. VimpelCom's competitor, MTS, supported by its second shareholder (Deutsche Telecom), woke up and intensified its marketing efforts which included advertising of international roaming capabilities. VimpelCom faced a dilemma: should they keep pumping money into the D-AMPS network, or should they change strategy and start a massive network build-up and promotion of GSM services?

Pulled in opposite directions by pro-D-AMPS and pro-GSM factions within VimpelCom, Zimin was unsure which way to go. The company worked on developing both standards, unable to make a final decision.

DEVELOPMENT VERSUS CONTROL

The choice was finally made in favor of GSM, whose revenue represented 95 per cent of VimpelCom's total $160 million in the first quarter of 2002. One of the decisive factors in winning Zimin's support for the GSM project was the firm stance in favor of that pan-European standard of VimpelCom's new shareholder, Norwegian operator Telenor.

At the beginning of 1998, VimpelCom had started discussions about potential cooperation in Russia with some global cellular operators, including Telenor, a then state-owned telecom company providing fixed, cellular and satellite telephony and Internet services in Scandinavia, Eastern Europe and Asia. Telenor had minority ownership in three regional cellular operators in the Russian Federation and was eyeing the lucrative Moscow market.

Although at that time Zimin was exploring joint venture options to develop capital-intensive regional licenses and was not particularly interested in bringing new shareholders into VimpelCom proper, Fabela was. The younger man was seeking a foreign company that could ensure proper management of VimpelCom, limit Zimin's tendency to rule arbitrarily, and bring more credibility for Western investors. Thus it was Fabela who drove the negotiations with interested foreign operators. He also had a personal agenda for seeking a foreign link: he wanted to get out of VimpelCom: 'It was an exit for me. I had done it all; I took the company to the New York Stock Exchange. It was time to move on'.

But the August 1998 financial crisis changed everyone's priorities. Western operators abruptly broke off negotiations leaving VimpelCom on its own, with all its licenses and no cash.

Following a 400 per cent devaluation of the ruble and the Russian government's default on its foreign and domestic debt, many banks froze their operations. Within a few weeks, VimpelCom lost over $60 million that it had invested in government bonds and ruble bank deposits. The situation was soon critical. VimpelCom had over $200 million in dollar-denominated debt and only about

$16 million in cash. As the crisis deepened, customers began to drop out: from August 1998 to March 1999 VimpelCom's customer base shrank from 140000 to 116000 subscribers. Worse, market research showed that rival company MTS was increasing the number of its subscribers, luring away many BeeLine customers.

Zimin spent days and nights at company headquarters, talking to the senior staff and rank-and-file employees. The latter seemed to stay cool, knowing that their CEO wouldn't let them down. The former concentrated on trying to find solutions. Tactics were clear: the company had to tighten its belt and renegotiate vendors' contracts. Zimin refused to reduce dollar-denominated wages and resisted staff reductions, agreeing to them only after months of discussion. Beginning in March 1999, Vimpel let over 400 people go (many of whom were later rehired), granting them generous severance packages. In addition, construction activity was frozen, some service companies were spun off, marketing and sales expenses were cut, and investment projects were put on hold. These and other severe budget restrictions were monitored via weekly management reviews. In January 1999 VimpelCom entered into a $27.8 million standby two-year credit arrangement with Sberbank, Russia's largest bank, with Zimin's stock as collateral. With that financial support the near future of the company was ensured, but its strategic prospects looked gloomy. One senior VimpelCom executive recalled: 'We could continue to serve our remaining customers and pay vendors and employees, but we didn't have a viable business strategy. Crisis distracted everybody's attention from the fundamental question of development.'

Made doubly cautious by the company's financial position, a strong faction of Zimin's old guard insisted that VimpelCom should drop its GSM expansion plans and concentrate on what it already had. The opposing 'RTI gang' – Zimin's buddies from the old days as RTI – advocated severing D-AMPS and investing whatever the company had into building a dual-band GSM network. Endless heated meetings, dozens of quickly forgotten firm decisions, and hundreds of personal insults culminated in Zimin fully committing the company to GSM.

Fortunately, negotiations with Western operators had resumed in the months following the crash. Finally, Telenor offered a modified proposal to acquire a minority stake in VimpelCom. As was often the case, Fabela felt that it was a great opportunity and Zimin was skeptical, concerned about losing control. Three months of intensive negotiations produced a compromise deal structure: Telenor would buy newly issued VimpelCom stock to achieve a 25 per cent-plus-one share. And it was willing to pay a 15 per cent premium on the market price for that block of VimpelCom shares. After the new issue, Zimin would have 34 per cent of the voting shares. The two principal shareholders (Zimin and Telenor) would sign an agreement allowing Zimin to nominate six candidates to the nine-member board of directors; Telenor would nominate the remaining three.

In addition, the agreement stipulated that Telenor would send five Norwegian executives to VimpelCom.

The signing ceremony was scheduled for 29 December 1998 at the Moscow Palace Hotel. The Norwegians organized a banquet, but Zimin asked them to cancel it. The event itself wasn't cancelled, but Zimin arrived late. With his wife at his side, he announced to Fabela that he refused to lose control over *his* company and wouldn't sign the agreement. Fabela, keeping cool, pulled Zimin into an empty office and shut the door. The Norwegians didn't understand what was going on, and none of the Russians could (or would) explain.

Half an hour later, Zimin emerged from the office with a sour smile on his face, slowly approached the signing desk, carefully inspected the golden pen, took a deep breath, looked around, found Fabela's face and held his gaze, and signed. When it was over, a smiling Zimin stood up and turned to Telenor's vice-president: 'Henrik, where is the promised banquet?'. Soon the long table was covered with delicacies, and the festivities (replete with toasts and jokes) went on into the night. Having made his point about who was in charge, Zimin relaxed and became the life of the party.

The first part of Telenor's $163 million investment reached VimpelCom's account in May 1999, a few months after Telenor's five 'on-loan' executives had gone to work in Moscow. Looking back several years later, Fabela remembered:

> [The Norwegian executives] didn't offer the complete package of experience that we really needed here. My feeling was that VimpelCom would be in trouble with them alone. They couldn't control Zimin, which means my investment would have been jeopardized, and even worse, the company I started would never attain its true potential.'

Fabela decided to reverse his earlier decision to cash out. He would stay on as chairman and keep the two parties together. Telenor's deal had boosted VimpelCom's stock and brought in some cash for GSM development, but the company's problems were far from over.

In June 1999, VimpelCom started a massive marketing campaign for its new BeeLine GSM products and services. There followed almost three years of (for Russia) unprecedented and innovative marketing and PR efforts to reestablish the primacy of the BeeLine trademark and beat MTS in the Moscow market. A prime example was the 'phone in the box' promotion: for the first time VimpelCom offered reduced-price handsets with a prepaid card. By making cellular telephony available to the mass market in Moscow, VimpelCom managed to penetrate new – and very receptive – market segments, such as young adults and small and medium businesses. VimpelCom also promoted aggressive price cuts. However, the new customers came at a price: the company reported a loss of $39 million in 1999 on sales of $226 million, whereas MTS's profits were estimated to be about $50 million for that same year. MTS was more attractive to business customers who were lured by GSM roaming capabilities – many of them switched from VimpelCom. VimpelCom was forced to heavily subsidize phones to reach a new market niche with much lower ARPUs (monthly revenue per customer).

While VimpelCom struggled with new product development, MTS started to develop GSM networks in the regions. VimpelCom's regional licenses required it to begin services no later than the end of 2001. The company didn't have enough cash; its strategic shareholder, Telenor, was unenthusiastic about regional development and required management control in exchange for investments. Fabela started a new search for a partner interested in developing the Russian regions. In the summer of 2000 VimpelCom was very close to reaching an agreement with a large international operator, but at the last moment the deal fell apart.

At the same time VimpelCom began to feel increasing pressure from the new Minister of Telecommunication, with strong links to a St Petersburg-based competitor, who started to question VimpelCom's right to the 900 MHz spectrum in Moscow and attempted to block use of that spectrum. The Norwegian Prime Minister intervened and the incident blew over, but the threat of further action remained.

Both Zimin and Fabela were extremely concerned. As Augie Fabela said:

> The Russian environment had changed. Zimin was a very talented guy when it came to dealing with the old establishment. He did a great job at being accepted and being able to navigate it. He actually did great even with the next generation, which is one step older than the current generation. But it was clear that he just wasn't going to be able to offer the same sort of support to VimpelCom in the future.

When one of the largest Russian financial conglomerates, Alfa Group, expressed an interest in cooperating with VimpelCom in regional development, both Zimin and Fabela welcomed it as a great opportunity for the company. 'We needed a Russian institution to protect us going forward in the same way that the NYSE had protected us in the past', observed Fabela.

Dramatic negotiations lasted more than seven months, first between VimpelCom and Alfa and later between VimpelCom, Alfa, and Telenor. Zimin, who had stayed out of negotiations during previous partner deals, spent a great deal of his time participating in the talks, and Fabela wholly immersed himself in the process. When the deal finally went through, it took the team 22 hours to sign the agreements.

Shortly after the signing ceremony on 30 May 2001, Zimin transferred his CEO's baton to Jo Lunder, a Telenor-grown executive who for the two previous years had worked as VimpelCom's COO and had quietly managed to free the company of most of Zimin's old guard. Zimin not only gave up his day-to-day involvement, he also chose not to nominate himself to a board position.

Even though some of the 'old guard' remained in the company, Zimin's era at VimpelCom was over. Not having groomed a successor for himself, from then on he would remain just another passive shareholder.

Fabela stayed for another year as chairman of the board, 'to make sure that they [Alfa and Telenor] worked together', as he put it. This mission succeeded in spite of the very different backgrounds of the two strategic investors, and despite their initial concern about Fabela's potentially divided loyalties and his disproportional influence in the company.

The year 2001 turned out to be quite successful for VimpelCom. The company dramatically increased its customer base, significantly regained market share in the Moscow region, almost doubled its revenue, and for the first time in two years turned a handsome profit (net income of $11 million on revenue of $427, EBITDA of $148 million). The company also launched regional operations and secured all its licenses, raised $250 million in non-secured bond offerings, brought the transition from D-AMPS to GSM near completion, and wrote off the D-AMPS network. Furthermore, it reestablished its high profile in the business community. In May 2000 VimpelCom was recognized as Russia's number-one company in corporate governance by Brunswick UBS Warburg; in March 2001 it was ranked number one in corporate governance by the Moscow Institute of Corporate Law and Governance; and in November 2002 BeeLine GSM was named brand of the year by the Russian independent rating organization 'Brand of the Year'.

EPILOGUE: BACK TO THE DINNER TABLE

Fabela raised his glass and smiled at Zimin: 'Let's drink to our ten-year-long adventure and its success, Dim.'

Zimin: 'Success? I still can't figure out how I could work with you, Augie, and how you could work here in Russia, without knowing anything about the place, without speaking the language.'

Fabela: 'I always rely on God. If it's God's will that something happens, it's going to happen; I just need to work. If it doesn't happen, then I will have learned along the way.'

Zimin: 'And how did we manage to get along? Remember when I was trying to get rid of you?'

Fabela: 'My dad always treated me with tremendous respect as an equal. Always. And with your relationship it was the same thing. I have tremendous respect for you. Primarily, for your ability to adapt to change and for the speed with which you adapted to change.'

Zimin: 'Well, you were a young boy when I first met you. Very ambitious and not always attentive, but you learned along the way. You helped to save VimpelCom from Sistema, and you should take full credit for taking VimpelCom to the NYSE. Without you VimpelCom wouldn't have been the same.' He paused and added with a smile: 'It could have been better, but definitely not the same....Well, enough of the past; let's drink to the future!'

NOTE

1. The Fabelas referred to themselves as Augie I and Augie II, rather than Augie Sr and Augie Jr.

Commentary: VimpelCom's founders

Leadership is usually seen as a lonely business, Russian leadership even more so; the notion evokes images of such larger than life mavericks as Peter the Great or Mikhail Khodorkovsky who dominate their followers and foes alike. VimpelCom's story proves that autocratic – and some might say idiosyncratic – leadership is not the only kind that exists in Russia. On the contrary, as Danone's experience with Bolshevik shows, acquisitions can be integrated smoothly. And as the story of Zimin and Fabela proves, joint ventures can be long lasting, effective, and extremely beneficial for the organization and the leaders themselves. The unique dynamics of Zimin and Fabela's partnership offer a number of valuable lessons for business leaders worldwide, but especially for Russian entrepreneurs striving for a global reach, and foreign businessmen eyeing the still mysterious Russian market.

Both Zimin and Fabela have competencies associated with effective leadership: both men are visionaries; they have a high level of positive energy and effectively pass it on to their followers; they see the global interconnected world; they frame events in a positive way; they are persistent and stress-proof. Early in their separate careers, they demonstrated that they could be successful in various undertakings requiring leadership. But neither one could have led VimpelCom to its present heights single-handed. Fabela did not have enough charisma, extroversion, local and technical knowledge, social sensitivity, ability to build and maintain social relationships or flexibility. Zimin lacked knowledge of such market economy fundamentals as competition, marketing, branding, finance, customer relations. In addition, the impulsive and volatile Zimin often lost his concentration, and his patience, in high-level corporate negotiations.

However, by combining their intellectual, social and emotional capital, creating an executive role constellation, Zimin and Fabela produced a leadership dyad that could have hardly been matched by any other Russian telecom executives, including those who individually had much stronger leadership potential and by far greater access to various resources, especially political support.

VimpelCom's leaders provided a broad organizational vision for an 'innovative, always ahead-of-the-competition business with social meaning' and enriched it with very specific content at different stages of VimpelCom's development:

- service-company (initial stage)
- cellular operator with superior network, service and brand (1995)

- first Russian corporation to be quoted on NYSE (1996)
- socially responsible enterprise (1997)
- Russian company with international standards of performance and quality (1997)
- GSM operator providing services to the masses (1999)
- nation-wide GSM operator (2001).

Under Zimin and Fabela's leadership VimpelCom employees transferred these visions into the new realities for themselves and the environment in which VimpelCom operates. Zimin and Fabela set very ambitious goals like taking the company public in less than a year, and surpassing a GSM competitor that dominated the market, and did everything they could and a little more to achieve those goals. But the leaders never attempted to do its alone; in critical moments they always managed to rally VimpelCom's stakeholders – employees, shareholders, customers, vendors, and financial institutions, some government representatives – behind the company cause.

Unlike the leaders of some other organizations we studied, the Zimin and Fabela pair never let their company stagnate, continuously changing its business models, technology, operational processes and bringing aboard new executives with fresh ideas and superior skills to stay ahead of the fast changing environment. Not all innovations worked, some hiring decisions turned out to be wrong, but the fundamental result is there – VimpelCom became a model for other Russian companies. It was also one of the first Russian business to recognize the importance of modern corporate governance not only as an instrument to protect minority shareholders rights and attract financial and strategic investors, but also as an effective management tool adding value to the organization. VimpelCom set the trend which many Russian corporations later followed, and became a training ground for some independent directors who later joined other Russian organizations where they promote a philosophy of sound corporate governance. VimpelCom led its Russian competitors, suppliers and distributors to the new standards for corporate customer service; vendor financing; financial transparency; use of modern financial instruments such as bonds, convertible bonds and syndicated credits; hiring of expatriate managers and specialists; and management of investor relations.

Their external orientation distinguishes VimpelCom's founders from many Russian business leaders, but they are more than attentive watchers of the business environment who try to predict developments or react to them. In the true spirit of effective leadership they initiated and managed such important environmental changes as the introduction of a new cellular standard in Russia, extension of the radio spectrum available for cellular telephony, and legislation to allow for the sale of pre-paid cards.

Each of the founders made his unique contribution to the successful leadership partnership by not resting on, but *building* on his intellectual and social capital. Charismatic Zimin was a principal channel for transmitting their vision to the organization, exciting its members with new challenges, and at the same time providing a comfort zone for the employees. He has become a kind of mascot, a symbol of VimpelCom's values of innovation, development, and respect for employees, independence, organizational commitment and loyalty. Zimin played the role of a caring father, who is soft and attentive with his kids and always alert to protect them from stronger street bullies. His knowledge of Russia's political system's workings and national culture, contacts within the military, superior technical knowledge, extroversion and perseverance allowed Zimin to build extremely valuable social networks outside of the company. His openness to new ideas, risk propensity and intuition ensured that VimpelCom undertook successful change programs at critical moments of its existence.

American serial entrepreneur Augie Fabela initially brought experience to VimpelCom that none of its competitors could match. He assumed the role of VimpelCom's link to the rest of the world, which later expanded to the growing Russian financial sector. To a large extent Fabela instilled at VimpelCom the culture of a well-developed public company, and installed management systems supporting it. He led his older partner in forming specifics of the organizational vision at different stages of VimpelCom's development. Fabela's boldness, focus and negotiation skills played a central role in ensuring the financial stability of the company, and its independence and development. Avoiding the limelight, Fabela played the role of private executive coach to many of VimpelCom's key executives, including its CEO.

VimpelCom's founders had complementary sets of competencies and leadership styles and their combination produced impressive results. But this partnership's formation and development was not a rosy story of a first love. How these two very different people learned to work together is probably the most intriguing part of the story. At the time of their first encounter, Zimin was clear about what he wanted, 'to be my own boss, a good father to my colleagues/ subordinates, use my technical skills and build a recognizable enterprise'. Fabela had his own vision for the Russia's project: 'value creation by building a cellular company'. Good luck put them together, but their willingness to assimilate each other's vision, and Augie's readiness to play 'secondary' roles, are factors that allowed them to work together. They started out of need (if not desperation) for each other; they worked together as a well-functioning team providing leadership to thousands of people; and they ended up as friends. Rephrasing Soviet poet Vladimir Mayakovsky's verses about Lenin and the Communist Party, VimpelCom employees say: 'When we say 'Zimin' this includes Fabela; when we say 'Fabela' we include Zimin'.

The partnership went through the stages of cataloguing each man's personal leadership shortcomings; accepting the other's superiority in some specific areas; convergence of individual visions for VimpelCom; development of working mechanisms for interaction; and the building of trust. Failures resulting from unilateral actions and successes produced by each side facilitated the two first stages; joint wins ensured the next two. Initially the partners' trust was purely opportunistic and limited to certain areas. The partnership became stronger and more effective as its members learned new skills and enriched their mental models. Collective work transferred initial trust to a deeper, emotional level and extended to all areas of professional life, and for Zimin even to his private life. Zimin's curiosity, openness and learning ability played a key role in his acceptance of Fabela as a trusted equal partner; Fabela's emotional intelligence and patience greatly facilitated this process. Ironically, the two men always communicated with each other through interpreters.

Their relationship is a unique situation in which a person in his 20s and early 30s became an extremely successful mentor for his senior partner, who had nearly reached retirement age. Surprisingly, the recipe for that success is not different from current leadership development wisdom – respect for the mentee, openness and empathy with his work, advice rather than direct commands, continuous dialogue, praise and constructive feedback. Like any good mentor, Fabela had the skills and experience Zimin needed, and as an exceptional mentor Fabela influenced his senior partner's attitude and actions.

In turn, Zimin played the role of a caring tutor for Fabela, often unconsciously managing the latter's exposure to realities of Russian business life, introducing him to new people and traditions, taking care of the practical aspects of his Russian existence. Alongside Zimin, Fabela matured and in spite of his shyness became a prominent figure in Russian telecom industry.

Even with all the crises and setbacks they met along the way, Zimin and Fabela very successfully played visionary and architectural leadership roles in creating their business, rallying people from different constituencies to implement their vision and building a rational and dynamic organization. However, as it often happens with entrepreneurs and Russian leaders, VimpelCom's founders failed in another important task: leadership succession. They did not train or even identify a successor before they left the company. When Jo Lunder left the CEO's position in the summer of 2003, VimpelCom's board had to go outside the company to search for his replacement.

Will a new CEO take VimpelCom to new heights and at the same time preserve its uniqueness, which so far served as its strategic weapon? Both founders keep their fingers crossed.

7. Frontstep Russia: a high-tech start-up and survival in a new 'time of troubles'

It was 29 December, 2000, the day of SOCAP's corporate New Year's party. Traditionally the biggest holiday of the year for Russians, the New Year's party was also to be a big performance day at SOCAP[1] that year. Almost all of the company's employees had prepared short performances for the party: some people would sing; others had planned skits. The biggest event, however, was still a well-kept secret, even as the party unfolded.

Maria Ilyina, General Director and founding partner of SOCAP, was going to dance, and her big moment was fast approaching. As the previous act finished up, she adjusted a ruffle and clicked a castanet softly. Then her cue came and she burst onto the stage. Her employees were astonished to see their boss performing a passionate and perfect flamenco dance.

Maria Ilyina threw herself into the dance, heart and soul. She had much to be happy about. This party was particularly special for her. It heralded both the eve of the first year of the new millennium and the beginning of a new period of development for SOCAP, Ilyina's company. A Russian firm that localized, sold and installed enterprise resource planning (ERP) systems, SOCAP had been established and was now co-owned by Maria Ilyina, Nickolay Oladov, Vladimir Musin and Olga Mikhailova.

Maria Ilyina and her key employees, who were primarily young technical university graduates, had struggled together in the mid-1990s to build SOCAP during a period of economic and political instability in Russia. Maria Ilyina had motivated them not with money, as there was little to be had, but by her contagious enthusiasm for the company and its tremendous potential. And that approach had worked: her employees had worked hard, satisfied for many years with the reward of the prestige they earned as part of a high-tech start-up.

But just a couple of months before the December 2000 party, Ilyina had faced a nascent mutiny. Her employees had begun hearing about peers working in Western subsidiaries in Russia whose compensation packages included higher salaries and better career development programs than their own – and this while the Russian economy was stabilizing and SOCAP was increasingly profitable. Discontent began to grow within the halls and cubicles of SOCAP. Finally, in October 2000, employees of the Consulting Department – who carried out enterprise resource management software installation work at client sites – requested a meeting with Ilyina. They asked to hear about the future of the company, wondering specifically how it would affect their careers, their salaries and their opportunities for career development.

Maria Ilyina agreed to the meeting, although she had little idea what to say or how she might placate her employees. She was confronted with a challenge that was simple to understand yet difficult to resolve. Her best employees, young people who had gained a great deal of experience in her company, were being tempted by the siren songs of larger, wealthier Western organizations in Russia; and yet SOCAP simply did not have the financial resources to match the salaries the Western organizations could pay. Ilyina understood what this implied – SOCAP was in danger of losing large numbers of its best employees – and she feared that this brain drain would be disastrous for the company. How could she keep her valuable employees happy at SOCAP?

Unable to make concrete promises for the future at the meeting, Maria Ilyina simply listened to her employees' concerns and promised to look for solutions. Over the next few months, she made good on that promise, acting on some of the employees' requests. In December 2000, several days before the New Year's party, she called a general meeting at SOCAP. She presented the company's mission statement and outlined her vision for the next several years, then handed out envelopes with new salary figures and announced employee bonuses. There was a general feeling of satisfaction among employees – a feeling that Ilyina had listened to their concerns – but everyone was aware that the progress they had seen was only a beginning.

Now, as she danced at the New Year's party, Ilyina was filled with a sense of joy and relief: she felt that she had bought herself and her company some room and time to grow. But in the new year she would have to face the difficult task of taking her company from a start-up culture to a more stable, systemic organization that could produce increased revenues. The only way to stay ahead of the competition was to have the best products and provide the best services – and the only way to achieve those goals in her industry was to hire and retain the best people.

As her dance came to an end, Ilyina said to her astonished colleagues, 'Now you see that I would be able to earn my living even *without* SOCAP!'. Everyone in the room laughed and applauded, but they knew that SOCAP was Ilyina's life. One of the company's old-timers proposed a toast: 'Here's to not only the greatest general director but also the most desirable woman in Moscow!'.

THREE GOOD FRIENDS AND ONE GOOD PRODUCT

In 1992, Maria Ilyina (then 32 years old), Vladimir Musin (35), and Nickolay Oladov (31) were working together at Interquadro, an Italian–Soviet–French joint venture for software development and computer technology. One of the very first Western–Russian joint ventures, Interquadro was among the few high-tech companies where technologically savvy Russians like Ilyina, Oladov and Musin could gain business experience. The three future founders of SOCAP worked together on many projects and saw each other often after business hours over a cup of tea or a beer to discuss projects and console each other about their boss's latest cruelty.

The three all had extensive computer programming experience. Nickolay had worked as an engineer, database administrator and a programmer at a large Russian plant. Before joining Interquadro, Vladimir had earned a Ph.D. in physics and mathematics at the Moscow Aviation Institute (MAI), one of the leading technical universities in the former Soviet Union; and as part of MAI's applied projects he had participated in development and production of mobile laboratories for environmental monitoring. Maria Ilyina, who had also graduated from MAI with a degree in applied mathematics, had gained her information-technology experience working for various research institutions of the former Soviet Union.

Working for Interquadro in the early years of the rebirth of capitalism in Russia was difficult. Because competition for capitalist jobs was high, the leaders of organizations such as Interquadro could afford a rather cavalier attitude toward their employees. As Nickolay recalls, the attitude of their Interquadro boss was hardly reassuring: 'There are millions of you here [in Russia]. If you don't like your job, the door is open. I'll find other people'. And yet few employees walked out of that door. At the dawn of capitalism in Russia, working in a Russian–Western joint venture was very prestigious indeed, and the salaries were high compared to the rest of the country. Furthermore, joint ventures were the first types of organizations in which Russians could become familiar with Western management styles, and young people like Maria and her friends were eager to gain such experience.

While developing an internal project related to implementation of management information systems at Interquadro, Maria and her colleagues worked with Slavo,[2] a small French company that sold software packages to Interquadro for its internal needs. Maria, Vladimir and Nickolay saw an opportunity to sell Slavo's products to other companies in Russia and suggested that they represent the firm. Slavo agreed, and thus began the trio's initial amateurish efforts at entrepreneurship. Though they were still working as full-time employees at Interquadro, they managed to moonlight, creating ties between the French provider and their own Russian clients. Maria Ilyina recalled:

> I think that we managed to do what we did because we were so naive. We really believed that we had an opportunity to help Russian industrial enterprises rise from their knees by providing them with modern management tools. Unlike most Russian

entrepreneurs, many of whom have grown into influential and extremely rich people now, we didn't have any government-related connections or starting capital generated by Communist Party or Young Communists League-related circles. We just kept going straight ahead.

When we started out, we had our office in a corner of Nickolay's apartment. The three of us sat in his apartment and sold software systems to the largest Russian enterprises. Our three first projects involved one of the largest oil refineries (a monster in the Russian oil-processing industry) an ore-enriching plant that employed 40 000 people, and a nuclear power plant. All we owned as a business was in the apartment: three computers, a software package in need of translation and localizing, and three people.

Within a short time, the enterprising friends had made three successful sales worth a total of about one million dollars. The entrepreneurs started to believe that there was sufficient demand in the market for their products to support a full-time effort on their part. This early success was the motivation the three partners needed, and it was not long before they decided to leave Interquadro.

Maria, Vladimir and Nickolay combined their limited personal savings and established their own company in 1994, set up to be the Russian equivalent of Slavo, their French partner. Within a few months the trio was joined by Olga Mikhailova, an Interquadro colleague with a computer programming background, who helped the three entrepreneurs in their marketing efforts and soon left Interquadro to become one of the shareholders in the new group. The three original founders of the company each held a 30 per cent share, while Olga, joining later, got 10 per cent of the ownership.

All of the financial operations were handled directly through Slavo's office in France. Acting as representatives of the French company, Maria Ilyina and her associates had to learn a lot (and quickly!) about running the business according to French rules, although they constantly had to adjust both product and process for the conditions of living and working in Russia.

The four partners spent much of their time frantically translating the software products from French into Russian. They had to do this work very quickly, because the clients needed their systems urgently. Ironically, only Maria was fluent in French; the rest of the group had to rely on her and whatever help they could get from dictionaries. A distribution of duties emerged naturally: Maria and Nickolay were responsible for the technical development and client training, while Vladimir was responsible for sales and Olga took care of after-sales service. Fortunately, although their software packages were new to Russian enterprises, they were not overly complicated to localize and to use.

Despite the encouraging response from clients, the partners knew that their situation was risky. Their personal incomes were still quite small, and the cash flow often dried up from a mere trickle to a drought. Years later Maria Ilyina found an old journal containing her notes about the company's financial situation in the early days. Among the entries there was one that said: 'Loan Vladimir 20 dollars for food'. All of the partners had families to provide for, and it was not at all clear whether the new venture could eventually offer a stable source of income to its owners. Nevertheless, the partners never gave up the idea of helping industrial enterprises. They made a conscious choice to forfeit business opportunities in the more lucrative banking sector (although one of their early information-system sales was to the bank where Ilyina's husband worked) so that they could keep working with manufacturing enterprises.

During that first year, the initial software implementation projects were completed successfully and new clients signed contracts. In early 1995 the company hired its first employees – mainly students from the Moscow Engineering Physics Institute (a premier Russian technical university), who worked as part-time programmers – and finally moved into a real, though modest, office.

Despite their early success, Maria Ilyina and her colleagues soon began to encounter problems. By the mid-1990s major competitors, SAP and BAAN, were establishing their presence in Russia. The competitors' sales, customization and implementation systems for Manufacturing Resource Planning (MRP) software were heavily supported by their international branches, which was not the case for the Russian company. Slavo was unable to provide such a support to their Russian partner.

The final blow to the partnership came in mid-1995, when Slavo experienced severe difficulties related to their operations in France. Although Ilyina and her partners were making money in Russia, the French company was about to go bankrupt. Coincidentally, the partners' former French boss from Interquadro had started the process of acquiring Slavo in France. That was a big (and unpleasant) shock for the four entrepreneurs, because they had absolutely no desire to have any relationship with their former boss. Slavo's problems in France severely affected the company in Russia, because Russian clients paid the French company directly for services rendered by Ilyina's company in Russia. The problems in France would freeze, or even swallow up, the money earned by the entrepreneurs in Russia.

In order to get their money back, the Russian entrepreneurs had to learn the intricacies of the French legal system and solicit help from a French lawyer. Unfortunately, the Russians did not have any documents confirming their rights to the money owed them. In the turmoil and ecstasy of the initial entrepreneurial flurry and the technical work related to translation and localization of software, the then-inexperienced owner–managers had not thought about properly documenting every aspect of their relationship with their foreign partners. A strong belief in personal ties and personal commitments, inflated somewhat by early Russian media publications with an idealized view of the morals and ethics of Western businesspeople, was the foundation of their relationship. The French lawyer, surprised at the informality of the agreement, asked them to look through all of their papers and find at least *something* on which he could base a claim. Luckily, Maria Ilyina and her colleagues managed to find a piece of paper – an old, already yellowed fax message – that would help them to get part of their money back. Ilyina said of the hard lesson this experience taught them:

> The failure was like a tragedy, not because we had to face the reality of the capitalist world, but because we saw how people in the West betray each other. We had believed that the way business is done in the West is the right, honest one, and that people there are trustworthy and reliable, and that it's only in Russia that people are unreliable. We had thought that all the best in terms of business behavior was there, in the West. And when we saw all the *merde* and all the dirt of business in the West, saw all the commitments being broken and everyone trying to save his or her own interests at all costs, it was a much stronger blow than loss of our money. We couldn't overcome this blow. All of our conversations with the top management of Slavo weren't really about money, but rather about their deceit, their betrayal. I remember very well the feeling of terrible disappointment. We had believed virtually every word they said, and we had worked on the basis of complete trust. That's why we hadn't thought about documenting everything at that time.
>
> We didn't know how to look into the eyes of our clients in Russia, how to tell them that there would be no further versions of software, no upgrades, no technical support because of the problems with the French software provider. We promised that we would change the software system installed for a new one, and we eventually kept that promise.

Competitors in Russia immediately took advantage of the situation and started to disseminate information about Slavo's serious problems in France. The four Russian partners were not daunted, however: rapidly gaining experience as they wrestled with their problem, they set about finding a new supplier. They soon struck a deal with another French company, SOCAP SA, that was in the same business and was accustomed to dealing with the same types of clients. They arranged to substitute SOCAP's software for the Slavo programs at their clients' sites, and they got permission to use SOCAP's name in Russia.

All was not perfect, however. SOCAP specialized in first-generation MRP systems, which were quickly becoming obsolete. Ilyina and her colleagues soon realized that they had to move in the direction of ERP (Enterprise Resource Planning) systems. These management tools, more powerful by far than MRPs, cover almost all aspects of modern production organizations. Unfortunately, the Russians' small French partner did not have the resources to invest in the development of new software products, and that inability to focus on development soon caught up with them: less than a year after the beginning of their cooperation with the Russian entrepreneurs, SOCAP started experiencing internal problems in France. The entrepreneurs' inevitable separation from the French company was peaceful. Vladimir Musin recalled: 'The people from SOCAP France treated us fairly, but still the situation was not in our favor'.

Once again, software systems would need to be changed at the clients' sites. Once again, Maria Ilyina and her associates would need to find a partner in the West. Who would it be this time?

They first looked for a potential counterpart in France, where their previous partners had come from. This was a natural impulse, given not only the company's history but also Ilyina's fluency in French and her passion for France and French culture. But as they weighed their options, Maria and her colleagues realized that they would be better off dealing with a *global* software manufacturer, one that had experience in both Europe and the US. They wanted to join a Western company whose dynamism matched their own.

The search for a new partner took SOCAP Russia about a year. Finally, in December 1996, they signed a licensing agreement with SYMIX, an American company with offices in Paris. (The latter was an important search criterion, given that Ilyina did not speak English.) This time Ilyina and her colleagues (having learned from their own history) organized themselves as a separate legal entity in Russia. They managed to keep the old name, SOCAP, however, in order to maintain market recognition.

SOCAP RUSSIA

The agreement proved fruitful, as evidenced by the rapid growth of the next 18 months. During that year and a half, SOCAP gained valuable experience with the new ERP software system, translating and localizing it for Russia, and signed many new contracts.

Then, in August 1998, the deep financial crisis paralyzed Russia. Many companies suddenly found themselves virtually without money. The national currency dropped dangerously, from six rubles per dollar to 20. SOCAP had to adopt drastic measures to survive. When calculating its fees, for example, SOCAP used an exchange rate of ten rubles per dollar – half the official rate – giving clients this break so that they would continue planned software projects rather than drop them altogether. Some losses had to be borne, however: even with SOCAP's reduced rate, some of the payments from this difficult time took years to collect.

However, despite the hardships, not a single SOCAP employee, and there were over 30 of them by that time, was laid off. The employees were told very frankly what the situation was. As Vladimir Musin recalled:

We told them that the payments were being made to us at the exchange rate that was below the market, that we were not getting enough money. We told our people that we would do everything possible to be able to pay wages and index them when possible. However, we could not keep the wages tied to the ruble–dollar exchange rate. If money started coming in again, we would try to increase salaries. We frankly told our people that these were the conditions, and they accepted them.

SOCAP's avoidance of layoffs was unusual. Because the financial crisis affected almost every Russian company, late 1998 and early 1999 saw layoffs in nearly every Russian organization. SOCAP, on the other hand, took advantage of the abundance of available talent. They found and hired several good people whom they needed for the execution of contracts that had been signed prior to the crisis, affirming what was (and would remain) one of the founding partners' guiding principles: their people were their company's most important asset.

THE PEOPLE MAKE IT HAPPEN

Walking into SOCAP's office south-west of Moscow,[3] a visitor today would have the impression of a university campus. Young people are in the majority, some in suits and ties but most dressed far more casually.

From the very beginning, SOCAP was oriented toward hiring young people, for two reasons. First, Ilyina and her colleagues could afford only inexperienced people in the early days; they could not pay well enough to attract anyone but young university graduates or even students. Second, there were not many ready-made specialists for the type of work that SOCAP endeavoured to undertake in the market, and Ilyina and her colleagues thought that it would be easier to train young people. Ilyina recalled the firm's decision to hire students as employees:

> I don't think that there was any emotional foundation underlying this decision. It's not that it's more interesting to work with young people, for example, or that there's a more dynamic feeling of life. The decision was much more pragmatic: young people are an inexpensive resource, and each of them is a *tabula rasa*. In the type of business that's just emerging in Russia, one with neither history nor experience, the most logical decision is to hire people with a good potential, who don't require high salaries, and turn them into what we want them to be turned into.

From the very beginning, most of the people working at SOCAP were dynamic and enthusiastic about their job, starting with the partners themselves and extending even to the part-time courier who moonlighted to deliver mail. Everyone enjoyed the newness of both the process and the product: nobody else was implementing management information systems in Russia at that time; these were new technologies aimed at helping to manage enterprises in a new way. Ilyina found that students and young graduates were ready to forego bigger earning opportunities elsewhere in exchange for an opportunity to learn at SOCAP. She explained:

I like people who can immerse themselves with full self-determination and self-sacrifice into something they like to do. There are many people like that in computer programming. Information technologies are very good for exercising the mind. People who are involved in such work can come to a state of fanatic engagement – they don't notice the time, they don't care about money. I like such people. There are lots of them in our company.

As Nickolay Oladov explained, these young people were ideal for SOCAP. For the most part they had few family obligations and little debt (because most higher education is still free in Russia). They were eager to learn and ready to accept SOCAP's way of operating. But there was a downside as well: top managers had to invest a great deal of their time in mentoring the young people.

One of the biggest training challenges was helping new employees learn how to deal with clients. It was difficult for many Russian clients to accept professional advice from young people, especially in the more traditional Soviet-style organizations, because in the Russian business culture, gray hair was often seen as a symbol of reliability and dependability. Many Russians believed that young people, simply because of their age, could not and should not be taken seriously as business partners.

Young consultants often found themselves in difficulty with clients who were up to twice as old as they were. In one tough situation, Ilyina had to go to the client's office and discuss the work done on their project under the supervision of one of SOCAP's 'senior' consultants. The consultant himself, however – a young man – did not dare enter the office. During the meeting he periodically peered through a small window in the door in an effort to figure out what was going on.

In another situation, an employee in whom the company had invested heavily in terms of training – and who had just reached the point at which payback from that investment could be expected – resigned from SOCAP, explaining that his parents had just 'arranged' a nice job for him with Gazprom, one of the largest Russian corporations. Ilyina was very disappointed by this employee's decision to leave. On the one hand, she felt betrayed, but she also felt sorry for him: 'He just doesn't understand that he'll be an invisible pawn in that monster company, while he could be a very respected and successful consultant with us.'

This illustrates the crux of Maria Ilyina's challenge during this formative time. Many of her employees were like children. 'They want it all,' Ilyina said, 'and they want it now'. As one consultant said: 'Maria fusses over us as if we were children. For her, we are young, inexperienced kids, and therefore she pays a lot of attention to us.'

In general, employees genuinely enjoyed working for SOCAP. However, they were also very ambitious, and they were looking for visible career growth, primarily up the hierarchical ladder. The company tried to respond to these ambitions by creating titles for enterprising workers. Soon there were a surprising number of 'senior consultants' and 'department heads' to be found at SOCAP, most of the former and many of the latter still in their early twenties. Surprisingly, some of the senior consultants had less than two years of overall work experience!

Rapid advancement created problems with perceptions of fairness. When considering promotions and appointments within the company, Ilyina and her associates always took into account how promotion of one person would affect that person's colleagues (especially loyal employees who had been with the company from the very beginning). As an extreme example, at one point a new department had to be set up in order to accommodate the need to promote one employee who would otherwise have been passed over for a peer.

On the whole, the employees themselves liked this fast-moving culture. One young senior consultant said:

> The 1998 crisis showed I had picked the right company to work for. I didn't lose my job, and there was even more work after the crisis than before. Quick development of the company also led to a quick promotion for me: after just six months on the job I was already running my own projects. Top management trusted me at first because there wasn't anyone else to do the work, and then because I demonstrated that I could do the work.

ONE BIG HAPPY FAMILY?

As the company grew, the employees and the partners worked together to improve their software. In the early days they were located in a slightly dilapidated office under the roof of a Stalin-era high-rise in Moscow, its ceiling so low that people regularly hit their head against the beams. Their enthusiasm for this opportunity to create something useful and to contribute to the economic rebirth of Russia, their shared experiences of crisis and success, and the close physical proximity of everyone in the small office soon led to the development of a family atmosphere in the company. Everyone was on a first-name basis and used *ty*, a pronoun reserved in the Russian language for addressing peers, close friends and relatives. Indeed, some of the old-timers recall that they used to call Ilyina *'Tyotya Masha'* (Aunt Masha), using not only the family label but a diminutive nickname reserved for informal relationships. Reflecting the family atmosphere, employees often ate lunch together, and they enjoyed spontaneously organizing birthday parties and informal holiday gatherings.

Through the time of the 1998 crisis and into the new millennium, the company, which by 2002 had around 55 employees housed in a modern office, retained a democratic start-up culture, something that at the turn of the century was still quite unusual for a Russian organization. However, the partners were not sure how they could, or even if they should, continue to foster this kind of corporate culture. Vladimir commented:

> When we had five or ten people, there was no distance between the owners and the rest of the people in the company. However, with growth we should be distancing ourselves more from the employees. It's difficult to do this with young people, however; they don't understand it. They still see us as a small company where everyone uses *ty*. Fortunately, this familiarity doesn't cause too many problems with work. It'll disappear when we grow. I don't communicate with the youngest employees that much anymore, so they won't have the same expectations.

Undeniably, as SOCAP grew, the organization's needs began to change, and this had a direct effect on the corporate culture. With the software development tasks largely resolved, at least for the time being, the partners needed to look for people with a different set of skills – people who could work directly with clients, implementing and facilitating software opportunities. These client-contact consultants had to be businesspeople who understood the context of clients' needs: accounting, taxation system requirements, production, logistics, and so on. They also had to be experienced and autonomous, since with growing ranks the partners had less time for mentoring. Vladimir recalled:

> We had always been a step or more ahead of our clients, because we read more, we visited more places outside Russia, and we had had more experience with the corporate culture of Western companies. However, at a certain point we felt that the clients started to catch up with us. We felt that we didn't have enough professional skills and knowledge among our consultants.

People with such skills existed in large Western organizations present in the Russian market (in the Big Five consultancy companies, for example), but they were still unaffordable for SOCAP. Once again, finding people with little experience but solid theoretical knowledge seemed to be their best solution. SOCAP decided that economics graduates of Moscow State University would be their best source of new consultants. Nickolay Oladov said: 'We could no longer rely on graduates of technical universities. We felt that people without an economics-related background weren't as strong as we would like them to be from the point of view of understanding the business.'[4]

The MSU graduates coming to work for SOCAP were a different crowd than the programmers who for years had come from the Moscow Engineering Physics Institute. Ilyina and her partners noticed that, on the one hand, they brought in more knowledge and had sometimes had internship experience in Western companies; on the other hand, they had a better idea of their own job-market value and had higher career aspirations. Nickolay Oladov told us:

They saw themselves as professionals, which wasn't yet totally true for some of them. Nonetheless, we could see that we would have to create better reward and development systems for them. We had just never paid attention to this before. We used to motivate people by paying them what we thought to be competitive salaries. We're a small company; we can't offer much career growth. There's not much vertical space for people to move up the ladder. We've started to think about it now, though. Professional development is also important now, because our people are asking for it. Understanding what we should be able to offer these people is a task we have to address.

The influx of economics-trained employees with higher expectations brought change to SOCAP. With the growth of the company, and the branching out into a new kind of employee, SOCAP's 'family' atmosphere began to fade. This bothered many people in the company, especially those who had been there the longest. Recognizing their concern, Ilyina tried to organize events to bring people together. Once she 'put the whole company on skis', for example: everyone was given a day off – a day that they called a Healthy Day – to ski together at a nearby ski resort. Another time, the whole company got together at Ilyina's dacha for a winter party.

Ilyina explained her perspective on the issue of cohesiveness as follows:

I think that we can keep the family atmosphere in SOCAP, because the company has just about finished the employee growth cycle. In European offices of our partner companies, the number of employees is similar to ours. The cycle of sales and implementation of our product warrants having 60 people as an optimal number. So I think that with about 60 people we can keep the family feeling in the organization. We're developing traditions in our company. We have people who are young in age but already have a relatively long tenure in the organization, which means that our traditions don't get covered with mothballs or die, but rather live in dynamic development.

WHAT ABOUT THE BOTTOM LINE?

But as SOCAP passed out of the exciting start-up phase, employees began expecting more than just a wild ride and a family culture as their main rewards. The influence of the MSU graduates – who had heard about career growth and professional development from recruiters at their school and in their human resources management classes – had started to spread in the company. From prospective employees as well as from staffers, the partners started to get questions about career development opportunities at SOCAP. However, when asked about what was meant by 'career development' and what they expected from SOCAP, many people seemed to be at a loss for an answer, or answered in very general terms. For example one employee, when asked about career development, responded with what seemed to be a request for a better supervisor: 'I'd like to have a person in the organization with whom I could sit down to discuss the issues I'm facing when managing a project, discuss my problems, and get advice, learn some new tools, see how I can do more sophisticated things, and grow professionally.'

The confusion many employees felt was exacerbated by the fact that most of the consultants and programmers at SOCAP had never been employed anywhere else and therefore could not make concrete comparisons with other organizations. Although recruiters tried to poach some of them, most of the employees wanted to stay with SOCAP. When asked what might induce them to leave, many mentioned money. One programmer was offered twice his SOCAP salary elsewhere, and he left (though reluctantly). According to his old colleagues, the thing he missed most at his new job was 'the atmosphere of SOCAP'. Another employee who left SOCAP to join a competitive company asked to be taken back by SOCAP after a few months – and he was. Ilyina thought of these incidents as positive examples of the real advantage that SOCAP's culture had over other companies.

For several years, SOCAP's management handled the poaching problem on a case-by-case basis. Ilyina usually heard about offers that were being made to SOCAP's key people from these people themselves, and she could (and generally would) then make a counter offer. However, by 2000 it was becoming obvious that people wanted to hear more than just a higher figure.

As she began to think seriously about this growing dissatisfaction among employees, Ilyina realized that whereas undefined reward systems were a part of the problem, there were also weaknesses in SOCAP's system of hiring new people.

According to Vladimir, department heads, in consultation with management, made most hiring decisions. However, the four partners discussed and had the last word regarding all of the *top* positions. Decisions on hiring needs were made in accordance with the planned budget for current projects. There was a de facto strategy committee that discussed, among other things, the staffing and resources required for specific projects. Committee members tried to coordinate requirements and budgets to see what salaries they could pay and whether they could afford to hire a new person or not, but the fit between need and budget was not always perfect. As Vladimir said: 'Sometimes we couldn't afford to hire someone but we did anyway, because we saw a strategic need. We might have an important contract soon – and if we did, we'd need consultants for that project. It takes time to prepare a consultant'. Compounding the problem, Ilyina learned that SOCAP had a reputation for being a great company, but one in which people had to work hard without adequate compensation.

AN EARLY NEW YEAR'S RESOLUTION

Matters came to a head in October 2000, when the consultants requested the meeting with Ilyina that was described earlier. They wanted to hear about the future of their careers, their salaries, and their development opportunities. Ilyina realized, hearing the passion in their presentation, that things would have to change.

From the time of that meeting until the New Year's party, Ilyina focused on her response to pressure from the employees and on the growing number of personnel problems the company faced (including potential turnover and a lack of qualified personnel to staff the most important projects). She concluded that it was time for SOCAP to undertake a serious effort to improve its own business.

Ilyina understood that management theory-savvy employees of the Consulting Department drove the requests for career opportunities, training and strategic planning related to human resources. Many of them, in parallel with their work, were pursuing master's degrees in management at Moscow State University or the State Management Academy. Though some of the programmers had picked up jargon related to career planning and development, most of them seemed perfectly satisfied with the status quo. The only concern they had was the amount of their salaries.

As for the consultants' concerns, Ilyina knew that many were well-founded. Up to that point, the owner–managers of the company had each continued to fulfill multiple roles beyond general management; and they and key employees selected approaches from popular management books and Western university texts on strategy and marketing, human resources management and business development. Ilyina realized that while SOCAP's corporate culture was important, it was not enough. In her response to employees, announced just before the New Year's party, she promised to make adjustments to keep the wages in line with trends in the labor market and to reevaluate salaries once a year. She knew, however, that these were only stop-gap measures.

It was time, Ilyina concluded, to launch an internal development project to improve the company's structure, motivation of employees, and career development options. Her 'baby' had definitely grown out of the start-up phase, and they had managed to survive in a new time of troubles.[5]

A VISION AND A MISSION

Ilyina recognized that the October 2000 meeting at which employees expressed their concerns for the future was a significant focal event that had brought structural weaknesses to light, and she initiated rapid change in response. She told us:

> It was not possible to continue managing the firm in the old way. We had a 'family-like' discussion of our problems in that meeting; in order to move forward, after that conversation with our employees we started an internal development project in late 2000. With the help of both internal people and a wide assortment of external consultants – ranging from a big Western firm to business school students – the company went through an analysis of its organizational structure. This included optimization of project organization and staffing; assessment of employees' skills and drafting of a professional development program; analysis of the working environment and measures to increase motivation; and improvement of internal communication and performance evaluations.

One of the major concerns of the external consultants helping SOCAP focused on internal organization of the projects within the firm. Although most of the company's professionals had been put through a project management course designed by a Western consulting firm in the past, some of the basic elements of project organization were lacking in the organization. For example, SOCAP had no coherent approach to measuring the amount of employee time spent on a specific project. There had been attempts to introduce time sheets in the Consulting Department in the past, but they had died after only a few weeks because people did not understand the need for such records.

Yet another problem the consultants identified related to the system of professional development of employees. Some employees were encouraged to take company-sponsored classes to earn internationally recognized qualifications in management systems, while others received no support or even encouragement from the company. Various employees through the years had made enthusiastic attempts to introduce employee-development courses – courses in business English, for instance – but each attempt soon lost momentum. Compensation issues, another problem in the eyes of the workers, were a complete nightmare for management. Although SOCAP tried to monitor the market, such monitoring was limited to hearsay evidence. Topping the list of problems identified by the consultants was the lack of a clearly developed vision for the company and a mission statement that would satisfy the employees.

To address these issues, the top managers went to a resort area for several days to work uninterrupted. They worked out a mission statement that was presented to SOCAP's employees in December 2000:

> Our mission is to provide a high level of professionalism and the world's best information technology to our clients, and effective business practices for SOCAP.

Introduction of the mission statement was particularly important to the Consulting Department employees, most of whom had learned about the concept of mission statements at university, and who were responsible for communicating SOCAP's mission to their clients.

At the same time, management announced the firm's projected financial goal: to reach a turnover of about 6 million dollars and about 10 per cent of the market of midsized enterprises by 2003. However, as was made clear at the meeting, SOCAP was never going to be a large organization.

REBUILDING FROM THE GROUND UP

Ilyina and her partners focused next on some of the hierarchical and structural weaknesses of the company. One of the first major moves was to appoint Nickolay Oladov as acting Director of Consulting. SOCAP first tried to find an outside director, preferably with Big Five consulting experience. However, they could not find a suitable candidate in Russia: they could not pay well enough to convince a well-established person with the security of a job in a stable, wealthy company to switch to the young and still risky SOCAP. Thus it was decided that Oladov would act as Director of Consulting for the time being.

SOCAP also merged several of its departments, thereby reducing the number of positions at the department-head level. This shift was made in parallel with the introduction of a 'pyramid of experience', an organizational format that placed a large number of associates at lower levels, and a decreasing number of more experienced employees at higher hierarchical levels. Maria Ilyina and her colleagues initially had concerns about valuable employees whose earlier-granted 'titles' would now be taken away. However, several took this development as a relief, preferring the professional side of their work (programming or consulting, for example) to the managerial responsibilities that their added epaulettes had demanded. Still, concerned with potentially hurt feelings, Ilyina decided to give these 'demoted' employees a 'senior' title addition. Salaries were not negatively affected by the reorganization.

Addressing its reputation as a place where people work hard for little financial reward, SOCAP restructured employees' salary levels at the end of 2000, giving substantial raises to most of them. In addition, the company introduced a system of bonuses to be determined on the basis of the semi-annual performance evaluation. Bonuses would be paid six months after a positive evaluation in order to optimize the company's cash flow and serve as a short-term retention tool.

The firm also introduced a personalized training and development budget for its key employees. These employees could spend their budget allotment getting training and internationally recognized qualifications in enterprise resource planning. One employee who constantly complained about his salary was given an option to take a cash bonus in the amount of his personal development budget.

It was also made clear to him that if he chose that option, he would receive no further support in terms of company time, assistance or money to study and earn a qualification in ERP systems. After thinking about his alternatives, the employee chose the personalized development budget over cash.

Understanding the need to beef up its marketing and sales function, SOCAP launched a search for a highly qualified director of marketing. Ilyina managed to recruit Pavel Karaulov, a Russian with a US MBA and work experience in the United States. Karaulov had studied for his graduate degree in business on the Edmund S. Muskie fellowship, a program founded in 1992 for development of high-potential professionals in the countries of the former Soviet Union. While the first graduates of the program wanted jobs in multinational companies, current graduates were tending to choose Russian businesses. Pavel Karaulov was attracted to SOCAP by both the industry and the company itself. He praised SOCAP's emphasis on precedent-based sales, an approach that relied on the company's clients as its best source of new contracts. As Karaulov pointed out, using clients as 'sales representatives' was a sign of successful relationship management in the company.

For Maria Ilyina and the other co-owners of SOCAP, the arrival of Pavel Karaulov was quite a milestone. This was the first time that they had managed to hire someone who had worked outside Russia, and they had found the process very educational. Their search for such a professional had shown them that they were still lacking in some critical skills – skills in recruitment, interviewing and selection – and seeing that lack, they had worked to learn how to position themselves to candidates. It was no longer enough to radiate enthusiasm to attract people to SOCAP, they had discovered, especially when they were dealing with experienced individuals with high expectations. It was no longer enough to try to impress people with what Maria Ilyina thought to be their comparatively opulent (for Russia) company offices. She had also found that some of her old approaches to handling recruitment interviews had to be changed. For example, she had to stop telling job candidates about the problems they would face at SOCAP, because that honesty was frightening people off.

Once Pavel Karaulov was on the job, he was given free rein in restructuring his department. He said later about his job description:

> I pretty much had to invent it myself. They said, 'You're in charge of everything, and we look forward to your work. You have your MBA; you have finance knowledge; you have marketing experience; so please help us align the company, put together a marketing strategy, manage our marketing budget, etc'. I had to decide what to do first.

Because more income had to be generated from the consulting activities to cover the company's promised improvements, Maria Ilyina and her colleagues focused serious attention on the development of their Consulting Department and its professionals. The need to have a strong executive as the head of the Consulting Department was becoming increasingly compelling, especially given that Nickolay Oladov (the co-owner serving as the de facto head of the department) needed to concentrate his attention on localization of the new ERP systems being brought to the market. His technical brilliance and unique expertise were necessary for the product development side of the business. At the same time, consultants needed someone they could learn from, and the company needed someone who could streamline project management in the organization.

Having succeeded in finding her director of marketing in Pavel Karaulov, Ilyina embarked on a search for a director of consulting. From a generous field of applicants, she finally had to choose between the top two short-listed candidates – a seasoned, 40-year-old senior manager from a Big Five company, and a 28-year-old manager who also had Big Five experience. It was a tough choice. Although the 'gray hair' preference in Russian business favored the older person, Ilyina felt that the young spirit and dynamism of the company would not be a comfortable environment for this seasoned professional. She opted instead for the enthusiasm and persistence demonstrated by the younger candidate, Kirill Sidorenko.

General 'town hall' meetings with all the employees were now a tradition at SOCAP. That format, which had worked well in 2000, was used again at the general meeting in December 2001. The new organizational structure was presented to employees at that meeting, along with some changes in the area of human resources. The firm had never had a dedicated HR professional, as Ilyina reminded employees; the company's accountant had handled any compliance issues related to labor legislation, such as maintaining the bare minimum of labor records, while the owners had fought fires related to personnel issues in the organization. Recognizing the need to have an executive responsible for human resource issues, the partners had decided that Olga Mikhailova, the minority co-owner, would be in charge of the Human Resources Management Department; and they announced her new assignment at the town hall meeting. Olga, whose expertise lay primarily in the area of programming, testing and client support, acknowledged that this new role would be a challenge for her: 'It's my job, and I'll do it to the best of my abilities. But I'll need to learn a lot, as this is a totally new field for me'.

AUNT MASHA

Maria Ilyina herself remained the uncontested 'Chief Emotional Officer' and a driving force behind all the changes. When asked to describe her leadership style, Pavel Karaulov said:

Well, the silly word 'charisma' comes to mind. One of our friends said that whenever she talks, she turns you into a zombie. You say yes to her requests, but then when you replay the whole conversation back to yourself, you don't understand *why* you said yes. In other circumstances you would never have said yes. It works with clients too; she can close a deal like no one else, and that's a gift.

Ilyina felt that the credit for her success in the company and in her life was due to the people around her, although her life had not always been easy. She remembered:

Several times I was just kicked out of the house by my parents, as a child, with a bag of my belongings. I took this seriously, thinking that they were really throwing me into the street. And that was a punishment for some really minor misdemeanors.

My mother was a very strong and severe person, and my father was always scared to disagree with her openly. Even when he disagreed when her, he never supported me. And this all happened despite the fact that I was a good child: reasonably intelligent and well-behaved. I still can't understand why it was necessary to apply the kind of measures my parents did.

Ilyina's parents influenced her view of the Soviet society in which she grew up. Her mother was a well-educated historian, and her father was in the military. The government had executed her maternal grandfather for disagreeing with the political regime. Ilyina's family had a comfortable lifestyle, but they held strong anti-Soviet views.

I had a lot of pressure in terms of political views as a young child. It was a heavy burden. There was a conflict between the outside world and the views held at home. I read forbidden things, including restricted documents my mother had access to; there were political discussions I couldn't repeat at school. I read Solzhenitsyn at a very early age. I learned a lot about the Soviet regime. I was very much involved in dissident activities when at school, and I attended a lot of meetings of dissident circles. I was constantly immersed in this milieu. I still have painful memories about this.

As is often the case with strong entrepreneurial women, Ilyina was an only child who was closer to her father than to her mother. She said:

I have always liked men – as friends, as partners, and as lovers. I have always paid attention to them. I think that men are easy to deal with. Since my childhood I have been surrounded by them as friends, acquaintances. ... And I still surround myself with men in my business.

I strongly believe that a woman can manage to run a business like ours only when she is supported by great men working with her. My value is in keeping all the men working together.

I think that I can find compromises in various difficult and ambiguous situations better than a man could. It's easier for a woman to accept and acknowledge her mistakes and apologize. I do this regularly; I manage to manoeuvre people and make them work toward achievement of a common goal.

Nickolay Oladov described her as 'a fountain of spontaneous ideas and emotions'. Ilyina said her main role in the organization is that of 'idea generator':

> My employees tell me that new ideas are born here, in my office – ideas about new projects, new markets, new products, new relationships, new approaches. That's the role I see for myself. I also get people to work together on the new ideas.
>
> What we're lacking in the organization is someone to keep me grounded, to remind me of reality. For a long time Nickolay played this role – but I could control him too easily.... Our new Director of Marketing is a very down-to-earth, realistic person, and I think that he'll be able to provide the balance we need.

Pavel Karaulov's first impression of Ilyina was that she was very willing to learn and grow. He felt that he could say no to her if necessary, but there were others who did not dare:

> I think that some people try to avoid confrontation with Maria. Her personal feelings about someone influence her opinion, no matter what that person has done for the company. But what I see is her willingness to understand why a person's response is a no and not a yes.
>
> And when we come to a mutual agreement on something, I can be almost positive that the agreed-on thing is going to happen, for real. It makes Maria very angry when people violate agreements – when they fail to do what they should, or what they promised.

Ilyina acknowledged that one of her strongest points is her ability to attract attention to and interest in her business from people who would otherwise probably not even notice the company. She often gets informal advice and help from busy and successful businesspeople who are caught up in her enthusiasm and readiness to learn and try out new things in her company. The strength of the company's management, in Ilyina's opinion, is that she and her colleagues use these contacts as a learning opportunity. Unlike many other Russian owner–managers, they have come to an understanding of the need for professional managers and consultants for the success of their business.

Other executives in the company commented that Ilyina is not always objective. One noted:

> 'External casing' – top-notch clothes, nice tie, manners, family, good education – is very important to Maria. She evaluates people according to these standards. When something goes wrong, she attributes it to a person, rather than finding an objective reason.
>
> It's very difficult to talk about any rules of the game when dealing with Maria, because in fact this is a game without rules.

FRONTSTEP CIS – BECOMING PART OF A GLOBAL COMPANY

On 23 March, 2001, SOCAP announced that its name would be changed and that the organization would formally become a part of Frontstep, a holding company headquartered in Ohio, USA, which owns SYMIX. After three additional years of successful licensing partnership with SYMIX (they had been affiliated since 1996), SOCAP would receive direct investment from its partners in exchange for a percentage of shares in the firm and would become part of a global company. Frontstep CIS,[6] as it would now be known, would still be managed in Russia by its current top team. Furthermore, given the conditions in Russian business, the company would need to maintain its identity as a Russian entity: some big clients were military-industrial complexes whose management was not particularly keen to deal with 'foreigners' or 'foreign companies'.

At a press conference held to announce the changes, Ilyina said that the transformation of the Russian company SOCAP into Frontstep was commensurate with the quality of SOCAP's activity in localization and implementation of enterprise-resource planning systems in Russian enterprises. The new status of the firm, as a representative office of Frontstep, meant both new opportunities and new challenges for the company.

For Ilyina, being part of Frontstep would help her company strengthen its position in its traditional areas of expertise – providing enterprise resource planning solutions to furniture, printing, food-processing, machine-building, instrument and packaging industries. It would also open new opportunities for the company – for instance, in the retail trade. The new status of the company would allow it to implement solutions for clients more quickly and would allow management and clients alike to profit from the expertise of Frontstep's managers and specialists.

There were human resources consequences as well. The fact that Ilyina's company had become international had, on the one hand, significantly increased the interest of potential job candidates by mid-2002, with Olga Mikhailova receiving a steady stream of résumés. On the other hand, recruiters and competitors were increasing their efforts to court Frontstep's employees. Furthermore, the skills of the employees had become an urgent issue. It was no longer enough to be internationally minded and to speak fluent English. Employees needed to correspond to the standards of a global company in a variety of ways. This would affect recruitment, selection, development and retention of employees. About this issue Ilyina said:

> My own criteria for assessing people in terms of professionalism are benchmarked against the Big Five companies. Offices of the Big Five present here may be better or worse than their overseas counterparts; however, I can see that the level of people

in these companies is higher than anywhere else. These companies have clearly defined corporate cultures, policies and procedures, and they have well-defined training and development programs for their people. My goal is to be like these companies. That's why I impose similar requirements on our people: aside from encouraging them to develop their professional skills, I tell them how they should dress, how to communicate, and how to behave when they're at a client site. Big Five organizations are a benchmark for us in terms of work organization, career plans and development programs.

But was this Big Five benchmarking really the best vision for Frontstep, Russia? Would a Big Five structure be the right corporate model for Ilyina's company? What would happen if the family culture and entrepreneurial dynamism of Frontstep were to be reined in by more rigid control and reward systems? Would the company have to pay Western-level salaries to attract and keep top employees? Would Ilyina herself be happy in such an organization?

As one sales manager put it:

The positive advantage we have compared to Western companies is the type of atmosphere we have at SOCAP. The relationships are warm and informal, and for me, as a Russian, this is a plus. It's always pleasant to work in a company where you're treated not with 'cold professionalism' but with 'warm professionalism'.

However, the foundation of mutual trust that's used for building relationships within the company may be the reason for some of the disorganization we're facing. People get confused without clear policies and procedures, and that makes the processes more complicated.

Were there alternatives that Maria Ilyina had not yet considered for Frontstep's development and growth as an organization? Could she pull together the best Western management ideas and then merge them with effective Russian leadership practices? Rather than joining the foreign Goliaths, could Ilyina dare to be the David who beat them at their own game?

NOTES

1. SOCAP was the company's name until it was changed in mid-2001 to Frontstep.
2. The name of the organization has been changed.
3. The company has been in this new office since early 1998.
4. The decision to hire people from MSU was also likely motivated by the fact that Maria's son, Dmitry, had graduated from that school and had gone on to a lucrative consulting job with a well-known strategy consulting firm.
5. The original 'Time of Troubles' (*Smutnoye Vremya*) was a period of political crisis in Russia from 1598–1630, when foreign intervention, peasant uprisings, and pretenders seizing the throne caused major socio-economic disruptions.
6. CIS, or Commonwealth of Independent States, is a confederation of 12 former Soviet Republics, including Russia.

Commentary: Maria Ilyina and Frontstep

The case of Frontstep CIS contradicts the common concept that entrepreneurship in Russia is close to impossible unless a person is connected to illegitimate activities, has old Communist party ties, or access to scarce resources. Chronologically and developmentally, therefore, Frontstep is a newer business than Roust Inc., Yukos, or even VimpelCom in that, as far as we know, the founders were working on their own, from the beginning. Maria Ilyina's start-up is a typical 'garage' type, one of the first in the new wave of high-tech companies drawing on the Russians' scientific and engineering skills.

The problems faced by Frontstep are not significantly different from those faced by any growing start-up. Because the company relies heavily on the human capital of its employees, issues of motivation, development, and retention of talented personnel have become crucial for the company's survival and success. Leadership challenges are typically tackled through charisma of the General Director with inevitable positive and negative consequences for the organization – a situation that we also saw in Roustam Tariko's organization, described earlier.

With no 'old Soviet' money or seed money provided by international organizations, the personal stakes for Maria Ilyina and her fellow founders of Frontstep CIS were particularly high. That the group was successful has much to do with the fact that their entrepreneurial activity was directly related to their professional and educational background, that is, computer programming. Despite this link, however, they (like many entrepreneurs starting a business related to their professional background) struggled with the subsequent need to move away from daily professional challenges in the direction of managerial responsibilities. Even entrepreneurs who are perfectly prepared for technical work and its challenges often discount the significance of their lack of business experience or skills in general management spheres such as strategy, finance, marketing or HR. As problems arise in these management spheres, so do disillusionment and frustration.

In the early days, Maria Ilyina and her partners dealt with the problem by turning management over to others and sticking with their own knowledge base. They felt, as many technology-based entrepreneurs do, a tremendous relief when freed from their managerial responsibilities. Unfortunately, such an option is not always available to owner–managers. In that case, entrepreneurs need to develop their own management skills. This case shows that employees who have received a better management education than their employers can push the owners of the organization in the direction of refocusing on core skills or in the direction of learning new managerial skills.

Another interesting focal point of the Frontstep story is the naive belief that is typical of entrepreneurs in the early years of capitalism in Russia. Maria Ilyina and her associates, in their start-up days, bet their company on their Western partners' good will, honesty, and inclination to keep commitments. With their over-idealized view of partners in general (and foreign partners in particular) they succumbed to the entrepreneurial tendency to underestimate potential threats to their business. As a result, they failed to keep proper records of their activities and agreements with foreign counterparts until convinced of a harsher reality by their own experience. The disillusionment that Ilyina faced is just one type of frustration an entrepreneur might have to deal with. In this particular case, the company managed (perhaps because of Ilyina's charismatic influence) to stay afloat and continue its activities regardless of the problems and losses incurred. Not all companies are so fortunate.

In the case of Russian entrepreneurs, the over-idealization of partners may reflect a need to fill in the vacuum related to lack or loss of ideals. As a child, Ilyina had been heavily exposed to anti-Soviet views and dissident moods. Because the Soviet reality had been heavily criticized in her youth, she tended to see the West as a better place in all respects, including business practices. This case also demonstrates a resource-based approach to forming relationships with the foreign partners by Russian entrepreneurs: given that Ilyina is fluent in French (and speaks no English), the company has looked for partners primarily in France; and even when striking a deal with an international company, they prefered to work through their Parisian office.

The story of Frontstep CIS demonstrates the staffing challenges typical of modern entrepreneurial organizations in Russia. From Ilyina and her partners' experience we can clearly see the pros and cons of the option of hiring inexpensive individuals and developing them into fully-fledged professionals. Many small businesses in Russia follow the model of looking for cheap labor. The intangible costs to the entrepreneurs include their own time and effort necessary for coaching less experienced people, as well as their sense of personal loss (more acute because of the greater emotional attachment) when employees choose to leave the company.

The collectivist mentality of Russians is reinforced in Frontstep by the family-type atmosphere: the owner–managers play the role of 'parents', coaching and educating individuals and stepping in when trouble develops and 'naughty children' fail to behave as expected (as when Ilyina intervenes on behalf of one of the consultants to resolve a problem for him). When certain individuals are promoted to important-sounding positions that they are unequipped for, they are forced to ask their 'parents' for help. On the other hand, from the standpoint of dealing with traditional Russian organizations, the case underlines the importance of 'gray hair' in dealing with traditional, bureaucratic organizations or Red directors.

Maria Ilyina wants her people, particularly consultants, to be as skilled as employees of the world's leading professional services firms. Her own son is the same age as most of her employees. He successfully works for a world's leading consulting powerhouse; Ilyina seems to have the same expectations for her employees. The employees, on the other hand, expect training and development opportunities, coaching, and career progression comparable to those of the consultancy powerhouses. Both sides (employees and employers) failed to live up to the mutual expectations. On the one hand, a strategy of hiring less expensive people didn't allow Frontstep to really compete with the international professional services firms for the best talent available; on the other hand, developmental opportunities at Frontstep CIS were much more limited than in the companies Ilyina benchmarked her people against.

Ilyina's solution was to hire managers with experience gained in international professional services organizations. It should be noted that the trend in many Russian organizations is similar: to stick to a cheaper hiring option when dealing with the majority of labor, but to be ready to pay for knowledge and skills of managers who have benefited from developmental opportunities provided by multinational organizations.

Maria Ilyina is a person with a vision. As a leader, she develops a vivid description of the company's future, new markets, products, customers, and so on. She knows how to speak to peoples' collective imagination. She is the driving force behind innovations in the company, and its emotional engine. As discussed in the opening chapters of this book, in many Russian organizations, despite the lessons of the bloody past, the desire for strong, even autocratic leadership continues to influence organizational life and practice. In the case of Frontstep, we see instances when the owners of the organization have to intervene on behalf of their employees in relationships with clients, and family-type relationships with employees expecting protection from 'parents' when trouble develops. The danger lies in development of learned helplessness – that is, the inclination to wait for instructions to come from above and employees' failure to think for themselves. Ironically, this could in fact prevent employees from developing into the consulting professionals Ilyina wants them to become.

Ilyina recognizes and plays to the importance of her male colleagues as she pursues success. She deliberately uses her femininity to gain buy-in and cooperation from both clients and co-workers. In the Russian culture, the gender roles for women include caring, family values, weakness, and reliance on men. Ilyina seems to use what we might call 'mental seduction' as a way of getting the support and approval from people around her. She also brings a motherly touch to her relationships with the employees, which often turns to jealousy on her part when an employee moves to a different company. Although not acceptable in many other circumstances, this approach seems to be working well in the context of the Russian culture.

Her colleagues describe Maria Ilyina as a charismatic leader. Weber's original definition of charisma involves endowment with divine grace and authority that is neither tradition nor legal/rationality based.[1] This is certainly true in Ilyina's case, as she held no previous Komsomol or Communist post of importance. Charismatic elements arise from a complex psychological interaction process between the leader and the followers, binding them together. In forming a perception of the leader as a charismatic person, followers find an outlet for assuming responsibility for the chaotic world around them. The charismatic leader, empowered through the projective forces of the followers, becomes the recipient of other people's ideas, fantasies and wishes.[2] In the case of Frontstep CIS, employees form a special bond with Ilyina who (in their eyes) encompasses their expectations and fantasies and absorbs problems when they develop. A similar bond exists to a lesser extent in some of the other companies we describe in this book, but it seems to be strongest in Frontstep, perhaps because the organization is still small enough for Ilyina to develop a personal relationship with almost all her employees.

However, charismatic leaders may lose a firm grasp of reality and fail to distinguish fact from fantasy, and may fall victim to their own sense of grandiosity. Charismatic leaders may also become exploitative of others. Another danger is that if idealized leaders fail to meet the expectations of the followers, there may be a reaction of rebellious hatred on their part.[3] We did see a potential mutiny at Frontstep that Maria Ilyina was able to disarm. Although there is no evidence that these phenomena will occur within Frontstep in the future, it is worth keeping in mind the dark side of charismatic leadership.

As has been mentioned earlier, effective leaders play two roles – a charismatic one and an architectural one. Envisioning comprises the heart of the charismatic role: leaders must have a compelling vision, they must involve all employees in the visioning process, and they must empower the employees to implement that shared vision. Ilyina is unusually effective at the first one of these tasks. She develops a vivid description of a future state that conveys a fundamental reason for the company's existence, and she manages to provide meaning and create group identity. However, she is less effective at the second role. The architectural role of the leader involves design of organizational structure, and the implementation of control and reward systems. If these two roles are not aligned, the company can expect problems. To her credit, she is aware of her deficiency in taking on the architectural role, and she relies on her co-founders and on expertise of hired managers. Recognizing limitations and looking for help from others is one of the qualities that many other Russian entrepreneurs, unlike Maria Ilyina, still have to learn.

Like many other leaders mentioned in this book, Maria Ilyina relies, through a conscious choice or belief in serendipity, on her employees' need to belong to a good organization that is involved in achieving a great cause. She excels at managing meaning. One of her major recruitment and motivational tools is the argument that her company is helping Russian industry get up from its knees through application of modern management software and management principles. She and her associates are proud of being involved in Russian 'real sector' (industry) development. 'An interesting job coupled with a great cause' is the carrot that she has used for years to motivate and inspire her staff. Survival, together, against all odds is another rallying theme. Finally, having suffered from promises made but not kept, 'Make a promise and keep it' is an internal business ethics principle that she tries to instill in all of her staff.

To her credit, Maria Ilyina is not afraid to acknowledge that there are still many things she doesn't know – a very good indicator of the future success of her company, since learning takes place after first acknowledging a need for further development.

NOTES

1. Weber, M. (1922/1963), *The Sociology of Religion*, Beacon, NY: Beacon Press.
2. Kets de Vries, M. (1988), 'Origins of charisma: ties that bind the leader and the led', in J. Conger and R. Kanungo (eds), *Charismatic Leadership: The Elusive Factor in Organizational Effectiveness*, San-Francisco: Jossey-Bass.
3. Kets de Vries, M. (1988), 'Origins of charisma: ties that bind the leader and the led', in J. Conger and R. Kanungo (eds), *Charismatic Leadership: The Elusive Factor in Organizational Effectiveness*, San-Francisco: Jossey-Bass.

8. Troika Dialog

In late 2001, Troika Dialog, one of Russia's first investment banks, led a consortium of investors in an historic deal to acquire 49 per cent of Rosgostrakh, a former insurance monopoly in the Russian Federation. Rosgostrakh is a huge organization, with branches spread across Russia's 11 time zones. In 2001 it collected an amount equivalent to approximately 30 per cent of the market in Russia. Still partly owned by the Russian government, Rosgostrakh is another of the post-Soviet 'sleeping bears'; this one undoubtedly waking up, but not yet fully active.

Troika Dialog, on the other hand, is powered by young, highly motivated investment bankers, who built Troika from an office with four unpaid associates into an organization with an enviable clientele – and a reputation for fair practice – both inside Russia and in the international investment community. Founded in 1991, it has the longest operating history of any Russian banking and securities firm. It provides investing and financial advisory services to Russian and foreign companies and is a leading domestic capital raiser. It quotes nearly 150 securities on the Russian Trading System, which it co-founded, and manages portfolio investments of around $10 billion. *Euromoney* magazine, among others, has consistently ranked Troika Dialog as Russia's best investment bank and best securities firm. In 2001 it had 350 employees in Moscow and four regional branch offices. It also has a subsidiary in the United States.

Troika's CEO and president, Ruben Vardanian, joined Troika in 1991 when he was 22, as one of the original associates. By 2001, he was the undisputed head of the company both in practice and in perception: he was the chief dealmaker, the organizational architect, and a father figure to his employees. He too has collected his share of accolades. To cite a few examples, the American Chamber of Commerce in Russia named him Businessman of the Year in 2000, the World Economic Forum singled him out in 2000 as one of the 100 global leaders for tomorrow, and in 2001 *Fortune* magazine named him one of its 25 'Leaders for the Future'.

Ruben Vardanian's interest in Rosgostrakh – the acquisition was his project from start to finish – was multifaceted:

- It was *commercial*: Rosgostrakh's unmatched retail network would be a perfect distribution system for Troika's financial products, such as mutual funds and its clients' shares and/or bonds. Vardanian thought that if he could succeed at making this network effective Troika, as Rosgostrakh's partner, would have a huge long-term competitive advantage over other investment banks, both foreign and Russian.

- It was *strategic*: Vardanian believed that revitalization of a company such as Rosgostrakh would strengthen the Russian financial industry and benefit the Russian state and society at large: 'If I can make this company liquid [attractive to financial investors], I will be able to say that the market economy has triumphed in this country'.
- It was *profit-based*: the acquisition would be good for Troika. Because it was an attractive investment in a private equity project, Vardanian and the other Troika shareholders saw it as a value-creation opportunity: 'You get in with a consortium, restructure and clean up the organization, and then get out at much higher valuation'.
- It was also *personal*: Vardanian didn't hide the fact that Rosgostrakh excited him as a change-management exercise: 'Troika is my baby and my home; it nurtured me and I nurtured it. With Rosgostrakh it's different. It's the Soviet system's baby, and turning it around will be a huge project – but a fascinating project.' The scale of the project was immense – Rosgostrakh had 60000 employees with an average age of around 50, and a string of unresolved problems in towns and cities all over the map, from Kaliningrad in the West to Vladivostok in the East.

The deal looked good to Vardanian and so Troika went ahead with it. After complicated negotiations with representatives of the Russian government (the sole shareholder), Troika and its investment partners, who included a foreign private investment fund, agreed to buy 49 per cent of Rosgostrakh for $41 million.

In early 2002, when details of the deal became public – and Vardanian and his partners had already begun to think about how to manage this sleeping behemoth – the situation took a couple of unexpected twists. First, as the deal made its way through the convoluted approval process, the Russian government added a clause that was tough for Troika to digest: it would pocket the consortium's money but made its approval of the sale contingent on Vardanian becoming Rosgostrakh's CEO. On top of that, the Bank of Moscow, Troika's major shareholder, openly (and unexpectedly) criticized Vardanian for engaging Troika in risky long-term investment projects in 'the regions' (that is, outside of Moscow and St Petersburg). The bank had not been officially consulted on the deal because Troika had no board of directors, but it weighed in because of its majority ownership and demanded that Vardanian step down as Troika's president and CEO if he was to be involved in the running of Rosgostrakh.

This didn't match Vardanian's vision for the long-term development of Rosgostrakh and Troika, and he refused to release the reins of the latter. Troika's management openly expressed their unequivocal support for Vardanian, threatening to resign en masse if the Bank of Moscow voted him out at the shareholders' meeting. Tempers grew hot and the situation became very tense.

Vardanian believed that he had three alternatives:

1. He could step down as Troika's CEO and concentrate on Rosgostrakh.
2. The Bank of Moscow could buy out Vardanian and the rest of Troika's management (who owned 13 per cent of Troika), and replace them with other investors. Vardanian would then be free to leave Troika altogether (taking some executives with him) and create a new investment bank.
3. Troika Dialog could buy out the Bank of Moscow, thereby negating its vote, and Vardanian could become the head of both Troika and Rosgostrakh.

The first and second scenarios looked much easier to implement and would not require any significant financial resources from Troika, but either one would mean that Vardanian would sever ties with an organization that he had devoted his energy to building from its inception in 1992. The third alternative was attractive but trickier than the others. Management had a call option for 30 per cent of Troika's stock, granted in 1997 when the Bank of Moscow became a shareholder, but that wouldn't be enough to gain control of the company: the Bank of Moscow would still own 56 per cent of Troika's shares.

If management chose the third option, Vardanian would have to come up with a sizable sum of money (much more than he had personally) *and* convince the Bank of Moscow to cash out. If they chose either of the first two options, Troika would have to quickly plan for a future without Vardanian – which would be easier said than done.

AN UNCERTAIN FUTURE?

For many years, the common denominator of all the organizational processes at Troika – those governing hiring, controlling and rewarding employees, and developing strategy – was Vardanian himself. He has had such an enormous influence at Troika from the start that some might regard him as a dictator. All his mentors and subordinates do not, however, share that assessment, one of whom said, 'His values, not his will, rule this company and energize its employees'. His assistant says that she 'adores' her boss for his 'kind and trusting behavior'. Vardanian himself is philosophical: 'Sometimes people tell me that I'm a dictator here. They say that Vardanian makes all the decisions.

The good *and* bad thing about Troika is that people sometimes think that I'm like a father who will take care of them – in the sense of chiding them as well as looking after them. I never yell at people,' he says, laughing, 'but I can speak in a very quiet and terrible way'.

Whether one sees him as a loving father, a caring older brother, a liberal monarch, or a benign dictator, Vardanian has always been visible at Troika. One feels his presence even when he's not in the office, in the family-like, friendly atmosphere on the trading floor and in the company offices. Employees of all ranks seem to enjoy shaking hands, exchanging hugs and trading smiles or jokes with their powerful president, who resembles a teddy bear more than a dictator. One of Troika's veteran employees put it bluntly: 'Ruben's charisma is 70 per cent of our company'.

This would help to explain the atmosphere of euphoria and anxiety at Troika in late 2001 after the negotiations for Rosgostrakh were announced in the company. On the one hand, it was an historic deal and a tremendous opportunity. On the other hand, if Vardanian were forced to move to the top position at Rosgostrakh and leave Troika, Troika employees would lose their charismatic leader and 'father'. The question that no one wanted to ask was nevertheless on everyone's mind: what would happen to Troika if Vardanian left?

Ruben Vardanian felt tremendous pressure from two fronts: as chief executive he had to respond to the concerns of Troika's major shareholder, the Bank of Moscow; at the same time, as Troika's 'spiritual leader' and chief architect, he could hardly imagine life without his colleagues and the institution he had built. If he took either of the simpler options – move to Rosgostrakh or leave Troika to start a new bank – he would anger or disappoint half of his stakeholders, including himself. That left him with the third solution: buy out the Bank of Moscow.

KEEPING CONTROL OF TROIKA

The first few months of 2002 were very stressful for Troika Dialog employees. The growing Russian stock market required ever-increasing attention and concentration while uncertainty about the organization's future pervaded the offices and the trading floor. Would Vardanian move to Rosgostrakh and leave Troika to one of the company's star executives? Or would the Bank of Moscow install its own Troika CEO? If Vardanian sold his share of Troika and started a new bank, who would he take along?

Vardanian had already reached a decision in his heart; now he needed to bring his company to consensus. The atmosphere was strained and Vardanian knew that delay would hurt performance but he refused to rush. He needed to take the time to hear the collective wisdom of his management team and gain the team's unequivocal support for his decision. To that end, he scheduled many formal management meetings, informal discussions with veterans, and one-to-one conversations with key people. He built consensus around his vision: to keep control of Troika by buying out the Bank of Moscow. He wanted to run both organizations, Troika and Rosgostrakh. Vardanian was convinced this would ensure that Troika gained maximum benefits from potential synergy, and would give Troika a freer hand in transforming Rosgostrakh.

Executive shareholders (there were 20 at that time) committed personal funds to the deal but realized that they needed far more money than they could amass to complete the transaction. Vardanian was entrusted with the task of conducting negotiations with the Bank of Moscow and finding outside investors. This time, though, he made it clear from the outset that no potential new investor, no matter how healthy its bank account, would be allowed to take control of Troika.

The negotiations with the Bank of Moscow began fruitfully enough but soon stalled despite Vardanian's charm and exceptional negotiation skills. Andrey Borodin, president of the Bank of Moscow, didn't formally reject Vardanian's proposal to buy the bank's shares, but he set such an unrealistically high valuation for them that the deal was all but dead. Vardanian then discovered that the Bank of Moscow was also privately offering its shares to some of Troika's competitors – at a more reasonable price. Vardanian realized that he wasn't going to get anywhere by himself; he needed to apply additional, and stronger, levers of influence.

Fortunately, preliminary talks with potential investors were more encouraging than his negotiations with Borodin. What Vardanian envisioned as the right shareholder structure had Troika management as the controlling shareholder, with a number of minority shareholders, both Russian and foreign. Contrary to common practice, he wanted his Russian partners to be 'physical persons with names and bodies, not Bermuda-registered corporations'. Vardanian described his ideal partners as 'personalities who were well-known, respected and rich, but who represented various interest groups'. Working through his personal and professional network, Vardanian found that his approach wasn't as crazy as most people thought: there were in fact high-profile business figures willing to join him and rich enough to pull off a buyout. This encouraged Vardanian to pursue the buyout solution.

One potential Russian shareholder became very enthusiastic about the Troika project and helped Vardanian by working the system. In response to efforts by that interested party, the Bank of Moscow softened its position and agreed to sell its 86 per cent stake for $50 million, with $15 million to be paid immediately and $35 million deferred until 1 January 2005. To finance the deal, Vardanian provided options for 32 per cent of Troika's stock to five prominent businessmen, 70 Troika employees, and Troika's long-time shareholder Hansa SA (representing the financial interests of the Opel family), increasing the total pool of both shares and shareholders. If Vardanian could pull the deal off, he and his management team would control 58 per cent of the company.

In finding a way around his setbacks in negotiations with the Bank of Moscow and the Russian government, Ruben Vardanian once again proved he was a man to be reckoned with. In 2003 he found himself at the head of two very different organizations, each presenting widely opposing leadership challenges.

EARLY SOVIET TRAINING FOR LEADERSHIP

When he took control of Rosgostrahk in 2003, Ruben Vardanian, then only 34, already belonged to the elite clique of new Russian capitalists. He was a member of the so-called 'oligarchs' club', that is, the Bureau of the Russian Union of Industrialists and Entrepreneurs (RSPP). His name regularly appeared on the covers of international and Russian business magazines. Oxford University invited him to mentor MBA students and in 2001 *Fortune* named him one of the most promising young global leaders. Many young Russians aspired to reach his level of success.

Vardanian was exemplary from a very young age as (perhaps surprisingly) a model youth in the Soviet system. He was born into a middle-class family in Yerevan, the capital of Armenia, which at that time was one of the Soviet Republics. His parents and grandparents belonged to what was called the 'Soviet intelligentsia'; they all had graduate degrees and white-collar jobs. Because his mother's parents resided in Tbilisi, the capital of Georgia, young Ruben spent a lot of time traveling between the two cities. He was steeped in two different cultures – Armenian and Georgian – both highly valuing human intellect and family ties, but strikingly different in their approach to life. He learned to integrate the two cultures: the hard-working and tragic Armenian side, and the joyful, lighthearted Georgian side.

Although he enjoyed a caring family atmosphere at home, Vardanian wasn't a homebody. He fooled around with other kids, went regularly to the basketball club, acted in the local children's theater, and managed despite all these activities to be the best student at school. He also found the time to look out for his friends. He hated lies and aggression and was known to fight bullies in the streets to protect his friends: 'I could beat up some people. I was very strong physically. When I was small and I had to fight someone older than me, I would jump on him and start beating him and crying at the same time'.

Some friends joked that Vardanian reached the highest point in his leadership career at the age of 14 when he became the head of a Pioneer organization – a Soviet organization for children aged 10 to 15 – at 'Artek', a huge, elite institution of the Soviet Union. Artek hosted top Pioneers from all over the country (Vardanian included) in 45-day shifts. He later became a head of the Komsomol organization at school.

Ruben's mother was a researcher with a demanding work schedule, so in Ruben's early years he spent a lot of time with his father, a professor of architecture, whom Ruben called 'a very talented, very unique person'. He also spent time with his maternal grandmother and his older sister who 'was like a second mother' to him. Many of her friends later became his, setting a life-long trend of having older acquaintances and associates. Following his sister's example, Ruben read at an early age many of the books from their extensive (5000 volume) home library, including Erich Maria Remarque's novels and Erich Fromm's *Escape from Freedom*, his favorite book at that time.

At the age of 17, Ruben graduated from high school with a gold medal, the highest academic achievement granted in his school system. Being admitted to university would clearly not be a problem, but making a choice among possible institutions would. He wanted to realize his dream of going to Moscow, as his parents had done years before, but they preferred to see him attend university in Yerevan. 'They said that I was too young, that I would never come back. Armenians are expected to stay and marry Armenians as we're a small nation. I had a discussion with them and they refused to let me leave Armenia.' One of the family's friends helped young Vardanian by convincing his parents that Ruben was mature enough to live in the capital, reminding them of the times young Ruben and his sister had lived by themselves while their parents worked in Africa on a two-year contract. Vardanian later had to admit that his parents had been right on at least two counts: 'I didn't go back,' he said, 'and I married a non-Armenian'.

When Vardanian passed the entrance exam and became a student at Moscow State University, he felt as if he had already done the most important thing in his life. The remainder, from that young perspective, seemed to be pretty straightforward: 'I knew that I would be a student, then a post-graduate student, I would become a professor, and I would later return to Armenia. It was very clear. I would become a Communist party member. It was a predetermined, 30-year-long career path'.

However, life in the Soviet Union at that time meant dealing with some decidedly negative realities – realities that made the Communist route look less appealing:

> By Soviet standards my father had a very high salary, but living in Armenia, having a high salary wasn't enough. People depended on unofficial perks. For example, some professors took bribes or charged students for exams. My father refused those 'additional' earnings. On the one hand, we were part of the elite but on the other hand we were always borrowing money from friends.

Money was always been in short supply.

Vardanian's first summer job with a student construction company reinforced his impression that being a cog in the Soviet system wouldn't be as rewarding as he had hoped. 'When I earned my first thousand rubles, my father was making 300 rubles a month. I was a student and my father was a professor, and I was making several times more than he was. Something was wrong.'

Then, quite unexpectedly, Vardanian's path took a new turn – one that inspired further self-reflection. In 1985 the Communist Party leadership decided that NATO's military threat demanded a greater Soviet defense readiness and thus, beginning in 1986, all university students became eligible for the military draft. Normally, people think of a two-year mandatory stint of military service as lost time at best, but not Vardanian. He was lucky again:

> Officers used to get a lot of magazines. I was only a lowly grunt, of course, but I had a friend who was a postman, so before the officers got their magazines, *I* would read them. In addition, my sister's father-in-law sent me Samuelson's *Economics*. After I read that book, I realized I had other career options. I started to think about my life, about what I wanted to do, whether I wanted to leave or stay in Russia.

REBIRTH AS A CAPITALIST

In 1988, after completing his mandatory two-year military service, Ruben Vardanian returned to the School of Economics at Moscow State University. It was as if he now had a whole new life – one in which capitalism was an option. The imminent collapse of the centrally-planned economy had become evident to most independent-minded Soviets, and Gorbachev's economic reforms had made it possible for private individuals to start their own businesses.

With empty pockets and vague ideas about his future, Vardanian dove into the rarified atmosphere of perestroika with endless discussions about everything from milk shortages and the advantages of a market economy, to socialism with a human face, to the meaning of life. While some students exploited their newly-acquired freedom of speech to the fullest extent, others were already busy making a few rubles or even dollars at cooperatives or joint ventures. Like those entrepreneurs, Vardanian also thought about earning a decent living and providing for his parents but the joint ventures and trading operations that other young people were mostly involved in didn't excite him. He was looking for something less trivial and more challenging. He wanted to put his brain to work: 'I decided that I would find a way to earn a steady, generous salary, but in an honest way'.

Vardanian's later successes were built, in his view, on a foundation of luck, hard work, and the intervention of the right people at the right time. He remarked: 'To be honest, I wasn't the best, but people liked me because I had good relationships with them. And I got higher scores for that; I got additional points for that. I was very lucky'.

One of his first fortunate encounters was with a professor of economics who helped to focus his intellectual search with her revealing course on market economies and public companies. Her enthusiasm was catching – Vardanian soon felt passionate about them too:

> At that time we had GOSPLAN [the State Planning Committee], a centrally-planned system of goods allocation, but I knew that that wouldn't last forever. I thought about how I could find my place in the changing environment, how I could be successful, and how I could be paid very well. And I wanted to have some kind of advantage over others.

Investment banking attracted Vardanian's attention, thanks in part to his somewhat clandestine exposure to economic journals while he was in the military, as an area where intelligence and hard work could bring significant rewards. He applied for and received an individual securities broker's license from the Russian Ministry of Finance – only the third person in Russia to obtain such a license (no. 00003) – and he was ready to go. However, he faced one significant challenge – there were no investment banks or stock markets in Russia.

Then, in 1991, a serendipitous meeting with Peter Derby paved the way for Vardanian. Derby was an American entrepreneur who had gone to Russia to open Troika Dialog, an investment bank, which he incorporated in 1991 with $35 000 founding capital. The two men talked for hours after their chance encounter. Afterwards Vardanian, still working to complete his university degree, said to himself:

> I can try investment banking with Troika for five years. If there's no market economy in Russia in five years, I'll get out and do something else. For me, it was a question of time: whether I could wait for future developments or not. I wasn't engaged, I didn't have any obligations, I didn't have kids, so I could afford to give it a try.

And so Vardanian, only 22, started to work for Troika Dialog without a salary, while finishing his studies at Moscow State University. Troika had three other employees at that time.

The young Vardanian had grandiose dreams, but even he could hardly have imaged what the future held. If he had looked into a crystal ball in 1992 and asked to see an image of the company 10 years hence, he would have seen Troika Dialog as the undisputed leader of the nascent Russian investment community, with 350 employees in Moscow, New York, Ekaterinburg and five other cities. Vardanian himself would be a shareholder and the president and CEO not only of Troika but of another organization as well. Of course the young man had no crystal ball, but he did have intuition, self-confidence, and continuing luck, which he put to good use over the next 10 years. Vardanian would never regret gambling his future on Troika.

VARDANIAN INC.

Vardanian joined Troika in part because he felt no rush to become a millionaire. Instead, he wanted to build a sustainable business that would bring not only money but respect:

> In spring of 1992, I became general director of Troika Dialog, and a partner. There was another co-director, a woman. It was more like a freelance business than real investment banking. We were like a consultancy. A year later we faced a conflict of interests: I wanted to build a real brokerage company, an investment bank, but she wanted Troika to continue as a freelance consultancy. After serious discussions, she decided to leave and I stayed in the company, intending to build a brokerage firm. We had 20 people and enough money to stay afloat until November 1993. I thought that we should take that opportunity. It was our big chance. I remember opening the first brokerage account on 26 April.

In short, Vardanian wanted to build a business in an industry that didn't yet exist 'by going where nobody else would go'. In a period of mass privatization when Russia was known for shady loans-for-shares schemes, Vardanian's vision for his organization was unusual: 'I wanted to show that we could make money without being crooks'. (Although at the time some might have cynically shaken their heads on hearing this, Vardanian did gain the respect and trust of the Russian and international financial communities and later was publicly recognized with several prestigious international awards.)

One day in 1993, Bernard (Bernie) Sucher, who had had 10 years of experience on Wall Street and was in Russia to do missionary work, dropped by Troika to ask if he could open a brokerage account for $20 000 with the company. This was an unthinkably large amount in those days and the proposition scared Troika's staff to death. They asked Bernard to come back the next day when Vardanian would be in. The two young men met the following day and talked for many hours about Russia, business, investment banking, and life in general. Vardanian's simple vision of helping his country by building a 'normal' enterprise fired Bernie up. He stayed with Troika for eight years, not simply as an investor but as Vardanian's partner and mentor, sharing insights about the investment business. Following a disagreement with Peter Derby, then the principal owner, Bernie left Troika in 1996 but returned in 1997 to help Vardanian with organizational restructuring.

Following Sucher's advice, Vardanian had Troika concentrate exclusively on securities, denying all requests for consulting services. Troika held its first auction of government bonds (GKO) and became a leading trader of privatization vouchers (titles to ownership given to all citizens of the Russian Federation as equivalents of their individual share of the public property accumulated by the Soviet state). As a sign of Troika's growing reputation, the first foreign bank opened an account with Troika in 1993.

By early 1994, the Russian voucher market was booming and Troika Dialog was acting as an agent to a number of leading international funds and brokers interested in privatization auctions. At the same time Troika began to advise foreign investors looking to acquire equity in Russian companies. That summer, when the vouchers expired and the market ceased to exist, several international investment houses retained Troika on mergers and advisory mandates. The shares market picked up as the vouchers market ended and Troika was among the most active traders in the new market. In addition, the firm took on its first serious public fight for stock market integrity, taking a counterpart to court for failing to honor a trade agreement. The case was lost but a precedent with a strong ripple effect was set.

In 1994, Troika Dialog made its first profit, $4 million, and Vardanian paid the first bonuses to his staff. These two events made him think again about the future:

> I said to myself, Troika's made 4 million dollars. You proved that you can build a good organization. You can achieve some good results in this environment. Okay, what more do you want to do? There was quite a serious discussion going on in my mind about what I wanted to do next!

For the short term, Vardanian decided, Troika would continue to 'build a normal business for a normal country', adding new accounts, services and staff. In 1995 it opened its first regional branch (in Nizhny Novgorod) and co-founded the Depository Clearing Company, with Vardanian as one of its supervising directors. In 1996, the National Association of Brokers and Dealers (NAUFoR) was created, and Vardanian served as a chairman of its board in 1997–1999. Troika invested heavily in research, building a foundation for its future status as the best financial research company. As the business grew, Troika added new employees, hiring people with varied backgrounds: foreigners, Russians who had studied or worked abroad, and former scientists, painters, government officials and operational managers. One of the latter category, Bernie Sucher's former driver, became a successful broker.

In 1995 Troika Dialog was publicly recognized for the first time as Russia's leading domestic broker when *Euromoney* rated it 'Russia's Best Investment Company'. The company retained this title for the next four years and won many other awards from international institutions such as the World Economic Business Forum in Davos and *Central European Magazine*, among others.

As Russian financial markets heated up, Vardanian wanted not only to take advantage of the growth but also to establish an institutional framework for the sustainable development of the industry in the years to come. Troika expanded all types of domestic services and set up Troika Dialog USA in New York City to meet the Russia-focused needs of the North American institutional investment community. In 1996 Troika established a sister company, Troika Dialog Asset Management (TDAM) – the first in the Russian Federation to develop domestic asset management. In 1997 Troika Dialog co-founded the Moscow Stock Exchange.

Troika's principal shareholder, Peter Derby, recognized Vardanian's leadership by promoting him to the position of CEO and president of Troika in 1996 and allowing him to become a minority shareholder. In 1997 Derby decided that it was the right time for him to cash out his own original $35 000 investment. The market was very responsive to the idea – Troika had nine offers for Derby's shares from five Russian banks, including the huge savings monopoly Sberbank, the Bank of Moscow, and four large globally-recognized international financial institutions. Derby was decidedly pro-Western, fearing that Russian investors would try to change Troika's course and might even refuse to pay him. Vardanian had a number of talks with Derby and convinced him to involve other Troika executives in the decision-making process. Vardanian applied a 'scientific' approach to choosing a buyer, asking executives to rate each prospective buyer on two dimensions: 'attractiveness for shareholders as physical persons' and 'attractiveness for Troika as an institution'. All but two of the 25 participating managers rated Donaldson, Lufkin and Jenrette (DLJ), the American investment bank, as the best choice for them personally, since it offered the highest price and would have certainly honored its financial obligations. However, all of them selected the Bank of Moscow as the best option for Troika, and thus the overall winner. Peter Derby agreed to the selection.

Vardanian explained their choice:

> We felt that it was imperative for us to work for the whole market rather then to sit in the pocket of a big group. That's why we rejected offers of three banks of Russian industrial-financial groups; they would have significantly limited our work. Sberbank was too big, slow, and unpredictable. Bank of Moscow was a young, ambitious institution without any investment banking division. They regarded participation in Troika as a financial investment, not as an enlargement of their operational infrastructure. This was very important for us.

For the same reason, Vardanian didn't want a big foreign bank as an investor, fearing that such an institution would use Troika as an 'entry ticket to the Russian market' and swallow Troika into its global operational structure.

The new shareholder fulfilled its financial obligations and paid approximately $56 million for 86 per cent of Troika. Vardanian and 27 other Troika executives, who had 'worked for free for five years', cashed out some of the shares that had been granted by Peter Derby just a month before the deal. Derby sold his stock and Troika management retained the remaining 14 per cent. The Bank of Moscow confirmed Vardanian as the company's president and CEO and kept a low profile. For many years very few people, even in the Russian financial community, knew who the real owner of Troika was.

The next year, 1998, promised to be even more successful. Troika Dialog set up its Clearing Brokerage Department, a service that would allow hundreds of regional participants to deal safely with the financial crisis that lay, unseen, just ahead of them. Troika also grew the volume of operations with domestic securities, including Government Bonds (GKO). The company also won a large-scale advisory mandate to serve as a financial consultant to VimpelCom, Russia's largest cellular operator, for its $163 million deal with Telenor AS of Norway.

Through all these changes Troika grew fast – faster than the company could adapt its systems and people, as it would turn out.

REINVENTING THE BUSINESS

The financial crisis struck in August 1998 and almost wiped out the securities market in Russia. The ruble was devalued by 400 per cent and the government defaulted on its financial obligations.

How did Troika fare through all this? According to Bernie Sucher: 'Troika was psychologically and organizationally much better prepared for the 1998 crisis than its competitors....[I]t smelled the danger [of the Russian securities market overheating] as early as late 1997, and had taken some precautions'. Vardanian didn't share his assessment. He thought that Troika management made a number of serious mistakes that could have been avoided.

True, Troika had felt the first signs of the market's overheating by late 1997 as returns on many traditional instruments started to decline. However, to preserve the overall profitability of the business, Troika made a decision to move into high-yield government bonds (GKO), an instrument it had previously regarded as too risky. Then in August 1998, the GKO market collapsed.

A second error occurred in the summer of 1998. In July Troika invited Andrey Illarionov, a prominent Russian economist (later on economics advisor to President Putin), to speak to the firm about the Russian economy and prospects for the financial markets. Illarionov had been outspoken in predicting a severe crisis in government finances and possible ruble devaluation. Vardanian had many meetings with his senior managers to discuss that forecast. Some suggested getting out of all Russian monetary assets and preparing for the crisis by cutting expenses and concentrating on secure foreign securities. Others saw no real danger. Discussions were long and sometimes heated but in the end the majority (and Vardanian) voted to continue operations with Russian securities, including GKO, effectively ignoring Illarionov's advice.

A five-year-long lease contract for luxury office space in downtown Moscow, signed at the peak of the real estate market at the end of 1997, added another heavy burden on Troika's cash flow when the government stopped servicing its debt and the ruble collapsed in August 1998.

By the fall of 1998, the financial markets in Russia resembled an arctic waste in the middle of winter – cold, dark and lifeless. Many domestic banks and investment houses went out of business, international banks closed their Moscow offices, equity investors were sent packing. Troika lost over $6 million. The company had about $20 million in cash left after the initial collapse – and hard choices to make. Closing down, as some people suggested, was never a real option for Vardanian. He considered two alternative strategies:

- A traditional after-crisis austerity program – slashing costs, minimizing all sorts of market exposure and waiting for better times.
- An unorthodox go-ahead program – using momentum to get ahead of the competition by continuing with a full range of services, hiring the best professionals and picking up new clients who had been dropped by the retreating international banks.

After long discussions with his managers, Vardanian realized that the first strategy wasn't viable in Russia, with its small market and unpredictable future. Without actively recreating the now defunct market, Troika wouldn't last for more than two years. Vardanian was convinced that the only way to go was the high-risk route.

After receiving shareholders' approval, Troika's management moved swiftly to introduce its restructuring program: expanding research and sales activities, energetically engaging in work to change Russia's image as a 'land of lost opportunities', hiring idle investment bankers, and aggressively working with medium-sized Russian companies to package and present them to international investors. Troika made some cost adjustments as well, reducing a number of support staff and cutting operating expenses (and even some salaries). The latter was an extremely difficult decision, made after long deliberations. Vardanian felt strongly that all employees should take equal cuts but was persuaded by his Western colleagues that the salaries of the traders, who were the key money-makers in the company, shouldn't be reduced. After learning of this injustice, one group of company employees rebelled – the traders themselves – who demanded the same pay cut as the others! Of course, Vardanian couldn't refuse.

In February 1999, with the Russian financial industry still suffering from an after-crisis hangover, Troika sent its sales and research people to the United States to present a realistic picture of the new Russia to foreign investors. The trip was very well received and won Troika many customers. A number of foreign companies retained Troika as a consultant and agent for recovering assets held by troubled Russian companies. Troika published many industry-specific reports during this period, laying down a solid foundation for its reputation as a leader in Russian markets research. Vardanian himself was very active, attending conferences and speaking about new opportunities in Russia. Troika's bankers spent a lot of time with a number of medium-sized Russian companies, working to make them attractive to foreign investors.

Vardanian's strategy paid off. In 1999 Troika made a number of important equity transactions, including Telenor's acquisition of a blocking stake in VimpelCom, and Protek LLC's UK purchase of Flagship, a Russian billing software company. Troika also brokered debt settlements for some important Western clients and entered a new area of financial and investment consulting to foreign companies, assisting Philip Morris and International Paper in their Russian market expansion.

In 1999, Vardanian hired a new CFO for Troika – Michael Flood. Flood joined Troika after retiring from PricewaterhouseCoopers. He had originally gone to Moscow in 1995 to assume leadership of the financial institutions practice of Coopers and Lybrand (which subsequently merged to become PricewaterhouseCoopers). On his retirement a few years later, Flood wanted to stay in Russia and 'help a Russian company'. Following his first meeting with Vardanian, Flood knew which company this would be – Troika Dialog. Flood remembered their first encounter:

Ruben shared with me a simple vision – which he didn't call a vision then, just a story. He said that Russia was his home and he wanted to live and die here. He wanted his children to live here, not somewhere else. And he said, 'Yes, it's a shitty country today, but imagine what it could be if I did honest things and others followed'.

This attitude was exactly what Flood was looking for and he never regretted his choice, calling Vardanian 'one of the smartest guys I ever met in my life' and 'somebody with great intuition, which I had thought impossible to find here [in Russia]'.

By 2000 Troika was back in the black without having touched a reserve fund set up by the shareholders after the 1998 crisis. The company advised VimpelCom in a $225 million convertible bonds issue, acted as underwriters in Telenor's $120 million purchase of Russian telecom operator Kombelga's stock, and arranged for the first ruble-denominated bond issue for Samaraenergo utility ($30 million). Salaries were raised to pre-1998 levels and bonuses were paid again. Hansa SA acquired from the Bank of Moscow a 5 per cent stake in Troika Dialog – another indicator of Troika's success. The American Chamber of Commerce in Russia recognized Ruben Vardanian and Bernie Sucher as Businessmen of the Year 2000.

Judging by its accomplishments and accolades, Troika Dialog had become a unique institution on the Russian landscape, known for taking a strong lead in shaping regulation of the securities market and behavior norms for business in Russia. Indeed, as early as 1992 Vardanian had started to use international auditors at Troika, against the wishes of his associates who felt that he was crazy to pay thousands of dollars to foreign auditors to confirm what everybody at the company already knew. But Vardanian persisted in his push for transparency and high standards of corporate governance, believing that the industry was in a 'long-term game' and in that game 'what is good for Russia is good for Troika Dialog'.

Business was back to normal and many people at the company felt they could relax, but not Vardanian. He had proved to the world, and to himself, that one can build a successful business in Russia without being a crook. But even with that proof in hand he had no plans to take a long-dreamed-of sabbatical. He was too concerned with Troika's future growth: 'Troika is a successful company within a small industry. The entire industry made $400 million revenue in 2000. We made $60 million. Great results! But our expenses are around $45 million, most of them fixed. We'll be successful only if the industry becomes much bigger'. And so he committed himself to growing the industry even more.

Some of Vardanian's older and more experienced mentors thought that he had a more personal ambition as well: 'Ruben would like to see Troika offices in every major country, becoming a Russian Merrill Lynch', said one. Vardanian laughed on hearing that. His ambition as of 2002, however, was to see Troika offices in all major Russian cities, making it the Merrill Lynch of Russia.

A WORLD-CLASS ORGANIZATION WITH RUSSIAN PERSONNEL

In the early 1990s Russia could have set world records for the relative youth of many of its government officials and business executives. But even in that crowd 24-year-old Ruben Vardanian, the general director of Troika, stood out. He always seemed to find himself at the head of groups of people older than himself. Even in 2003, at 34, he was the youngest senior executive in Troika.

Fortunately, Vardanian enjoys working with senior people (thinking of them as mentors) and with people from different backgrounds. Having become the top executive at a very young age, he spends plenty of time consulting his colleagues before making a decision. 'Especially the first few years, I wanted to be sure

I was giving enough thought to my final decision.' The diversity at Troika is evident and continues to be a priority there. For example, even skeptics who complained about seeing too many Armenian names in the company telephone directory shut up when they ran into an HR executive of Azeri origin in the hall.

Vardanian has been a great champion of modern management tools and Western productive values from the word go. He believes that in Troika Dialog he built a 'Russian organization with an international way of thinking' and credits the early presence of expatriates and the significant role they played in the company's growth with having an extremely positive impact on Troika's management systems, culture, and Russian staff.

To ensure long-term development and stability, Vardanian put a high priority on designing effective organizational structures when he took the helm. Inspired by some of his mentors, as early as 1995 Troika had in place formalized budgeting, an annual business planning process and periodic performance reviews for all employees. In 1999 Vardanian and his management team instituted a strategy development process which included one- and five-year strategy planning, quarterly two-day off-site strategic sessions attended by key people, and company-wide discussions of growth strategies.

Vardanian also focused on the 'soft' side of organizational development. In 1994, he and Bernie Sucher put together their first version of Troika's values manifesto. They called it 'Our Identity'. 'Our Identity' played an important role in Troika's life: all new employees memorized it, and it was often referred to during strategy meetings or when people faced ethically or strategically challenging situations. Vardanian saw it as the glue that kept Troika employees together, and it has been continually updated and enriched by the employees themselves. Another document created around the same time, 'Rules for Everyone', served a very practical purpose in the early days. Bernie Sucher wrote it to educate Troika employees in productive behavior on the job. It contained such simple concepts as 'Be on time'; 'We win or lose together so don't ever say, "That's not my problem"'; 'Make your car requests in advance'; 'Alert management to problems – real or potential – immediately'; and 'Write short summaries of your business trips and meetings'. According to Vardanian, the rules had a tremendous impact on everyone: people learned them and dramatically improved their work efficiency. Later, the rulebook's existence was nearly forgotten as the rules became second nature – just another part of the general business culture at Troika. One problem persisted, however: management could not convince everybody that a ringing phone should always be answered, even if it isn't one's own.

The best systems and strategies break down quickly if an organization doesn't hire the right people. Knowing this, Vardanian made recruitment a serious business at Troika. Every candidate would go through an intensive series of interviews. For many years, there was also a unique Troika twist: Vardanian met each potential employee. He says he has no scientific recipe for picking the right people: 'I believe in intuition. And many times when I saw a good person I would say, "I don't have a job for you but I want you to join us and we'll find a position for you."' He admits that this approach became more problematic as Troika grew and matured. However, his message to potential recruits is still the same today as it was in the early days: 'I tell people that it's challenging working here. You're building something unique and you're building it by yourself. It's not like somebody is deciding for you what to do and how to do it.' Vardanian acknowledges that at least one thing has changed over the years, however:

> When people came to Troika in 1994, they had to accept on faith that I was the right person to lead the company. By 2003 I could say that I'd been managing Troika for 10 years, so no one questioned what we do. In the early days it was very difficult to convince people that Troika was a good place to work or do business.

The thorough recruitment process is complemented by a semi-annual performance appraisal, which is taken very seriously by everybody in the company. As recently as 2000, Vardanian was still reviewing 130 people, spending almost 20 per cent of his annual time budget on that task. Troika also began experimenting with 360-degree evaluations and other standard performance tools, with Vardanian and his staff putting into practice what they had learned about management development from seminars hosted by leading Western business schools and from management journals. At the beginning of 2002 Troika had 350 employees working in offices in Moscow, St Petersburg, Rostov, Nizhny Novgorod, Samara, Ekaterinburg and New York. Vardanian believed that he should stay as close to those employees as possible, although the amount of direct contact he had with people was inevitably declining: 'Though I still know everybody in the organization, I can conduct performance reviews with only 40 or 50 of them now. I did reviews with all of them until last year'.

Although Vardinian himself now has less of a direct influence, training is a high priority at Troika to which a budget of around half a million dollars is devoted every year. Not surprisingly, Vardanian himself is a real champion of professional development, beginning with his own. Unlike many of his compatriots, he takes the term *leadership* very seriously and is a devoted reader of books and articles on the subject. In 1992, he attended training sessions at Banca CRT in Italy and spent two months at Merrill Lynch's Emerging Markets Training Program in New York. That was followed by two courses at INSEAD: Value-Based Management and Negotiation Dynamics. In 2001 he completed the General Manager Program at Harvard Business School.

Aligning himself with modern management trends, Vardanian has slowly liberated himself from operational duties, giving others increased responsibility: 'I try to commit people to a jump to a new level. In the past, a lot of departments reported directly to me. Now, only four departments report directly to the president'.

Although Troika was an early Russian front-runner in investing in employee education, the firm is not at the top of the compensation scales in the Moscow market, although its salaries are fairly competitive. Vardanian preaches long-term value creation and wants his employees to participate in the process: 'I believe strongly that in investment banking you should have an opportunity to become a shareholder. It's difficult to get people's commitment to a long-term view if at the same time you don't give them shares'. Eighteen Troika executives were shareholders in 2003 and the company is preparing a new stock option plan that will include more.

Because long-term planning requires a stable workforce, Vardanian has also taken care to create a sense of security at Troika. Personnel turnover rates are far below those at other investment banks. Troika has its own system of dealing with low performers:

> We don't fire a person immediately when we find that he isn't fitting in. We try to give him a second, even a third, chance. What happens is that low performers initially get isolated within the company. They're still in, but at the same time they're out of the company. This is quite painful for everybody. We have to take steps to remedy that.

When people regain ground it makes Vardanian very happy: 'I had a great guy, one of the top people in the company, who was twice close to being fired because he couldn't find his position in the organization. And I'm happy that I didn't make him go because he's one of the key people now'. When improvements don't follow, as was the case with one senior executive whose professional incompetence was tolerated for over a year, Vardanian suffers from the inevitable firing as if it were a personal blow.

Vardanian doesn't like to fire people. On the other hand, he sometimes encourages Troika's *best* performers to leave. He all but forced one of his closest associates to take up an offer from Merrill Lynch in 1996, convinced that Troika couldn't provide that employee with equal challenges and growth opportunities. Vardanian believes that people and organizations often grow at different speeds and therefore can't always satisfy each other. As a result, some people have to leave, though they might come back at a later stage when a new challenge emerges. And they often do – Troika has an extremely high rate of return employment.

People are occasionally fired from Troika, and not necessarily for poor performance. For example, after a long period of deliberation, Vardanian sacked one of Troika's most productive managers, an American woman:

> She said that she came to Russia to help Russia, but people were having a hard time dealing with her. She said that at the Chicago Bulls, people don't talk to each other but they still win championships. I answered that I don't want to work for the Chicago Bulls. Okay, maybe I won't win the NBA championship and I might regret that, but I don't want to work for a company like the Chicago Bulls. I spend 10 or 12 hours per day with the people at Troika, and if I didn't speak with them it would be terrible for me. She thought that this was wrong; I thought that she was wrong. I asked her to leave.

VARDANIAN: ORGANIZATIONAL ARCHITECT OR ENLIGHTENED MONARCH?

CEO Vardanian keeps his door open and encourages all employees to drop by, although he admits 'some people come in more often than others'. He takes pride in answering all his e-mails and phone calls, even though those tasks add a heavy burden to his 15-hour workdays. He feels that such responsiveness is important not only for his employees but for himself:

> I think people get respect here at Troika. I think this is one of the most crucial things in this country. Here the government doesn't respect people, the old system didn't respect people, and people themselves don't respect each other. There's even quite a significant lack of self-respect. But I respect people. I know that people are good inside. I believe in that strongly.

Vardanian believes that his role as a leader is to reinforce this belief and make it a part of Troika's corporate culture:

> Every day you need to prove what you say. I think worthless slogans – like some in the old Communist system – are a big problem. As soon as you start doing things differently from what you claim to believe, you destroy everything. So each day I try to show people that we're in the same boat, that I'm not a big boss who has a separate life.

Involvement and empowerment have a very specific meaning at Troika. The company's managing directors enjoy a great deal of autonomy in running their business and making operational decisions. That autonomy isn't formalized but the directors go to Vardanian only when they don't know what to do. He explains, 'They're allowed to take as much power as they can handle. It's their decision. I want to give a lot of independence to the partners'.

Vardanian's habit of consultation and consensus-building with senior managers is a key element of Troika's corporate culture. During the summer of 2001, for example, over 70 people participated in a number of sessions devoted to the discussion of the company's future. Their sole task was to clarify Vardanian's new vision of Troika as a half-billion-dollar company. Even with smaller issues, Vardanian takes full advantage of other people's experience and works on getting consensus. He recognizes the pitfalls of his leadership style but is willing to sacrifice high-speed decision-making in favor of building support: 'I try to create a consensus, or at least make people listen to ideas. Of course, this means we postpone some decisions but it makes us all more comfortable when we have to make tough ones'.

Vardanian has always placed personal communication at the top of his list of effective management tools. Casual information sharing, an integral part of the routine at Troika, takes many forms, from lunchtime discussions to cigarette breaks. However, there's also a system of formal meetings designed to ensure a common understanding of Troika's business values and objectives, its problems and achievements. For example:

- Weekly staff meetings attended by all employees to review the current state of affairs, learn of major events, and hand out birthday presents.
- Top-management weekly meetings to discuss current issues.
- Monthly meetings held with key people and top executives to discuss results and pending issues.
- Quarterly strategy sessions for top-level management.

Twice yearly, all employees (and their family members) attend two-day sessions off-site to socialize and to celebrate prizes given to best employees (three cars awarded in 2001) and 'veterans' with five years' seniority (commemorative watches).

Vardanian has remained a central figure in this system, attending all meetings and regularly making speeches: 'We talk about what's going on in and around Troika – good news, bad news. It's very difficult to do this every week but I still introduce new employees, mention employees' birthdays, and hand out presents'.

AT THE CROSSROADS

By all accounts, Vardanian himself leads a well-balanced life. Being a very likable person, he easily makes friends outside of the area of his business interests. His best friend, for example, is Dr Mark Kurtzer, a Moscow surgeon, Chief Physician (Center of Family Planning). Vardanian also maintains ties with Alexander Tsekalo, pop singer and comic actor (whose 'first Russian musical', *Two Captains*, Vardanian helped finance). He also has dreams that have nothing to do with business, among them plans to learn French and take up hang gliding.

His personal agenda was already full at the time of the Rosgostrakh deal in 2002: promoting entrepreneurship in Russia, traveling the world, and participating more actively in parenting his two children. (He married in 1996.) He said that 'having good kids is the most important thing for me' – but contributing to the development of a strong and stable Russian economy is an almost equal passion.

Vardanian knows that there is still much work to be done on that front, but he's optimistic, since he feels that he knows how to get where he wants to go. He believes in fair play, long-term goals and entrepreneurship: 'We need to show that ordinary people can become entrepreneurs and be very successful in Russia'. He has already succeeded in creating at least one role model – Ruben Vardanian.

TRAINING A DINOSAUR TO DANCE

Troika had become a well-structured organization with satisfied employees. Vardanian turned his attention to Rosgostrakh, albeit with some reservations. Just after the deal with Rosgostrakh, Vardanian said, 'Troika still continues to grow and develop. We're not yet at the stage when I can feel comfortable that it's working like a real company. We're still the organizational equivalent of a kindergarten'. Undoubtedly, the new challenges at Rosgostrakh would make serious demands on Vardanian on both the professional and personal levels.

Freedom from the Bank of Moscow wasn't the only positive outcome of the highly publicized deal to acquire Rosgostrakh. Vardanian explained: 'We ended up with great shareholders. Immediately after the deal, in June 2002 we formed a board of directors which is probably the most capable board in Russian financial industry'.

Troika's board of directors at that time was indeed a unique composition of skills and personalities. Ronald Freeman, Member of the Investment Committee for the Doughty Hanson & Company European Property Fund, a former First Vice President of the European Bank for Reconstruction and Development (EBRD), CEO of Schroder Salomon Smith Barney International and Senior Engagement Manager at McKinsey, sat on the board along with Valentin Zavadnikov, Anatoly Chubais' former deputy at UES (Unified Energy System of Russia) and Chairman of the Industry Committee of the Russian Federation Council (the upper chamber of parliament), Danil Khachaturov, Chairman of the Board of Directors of Rosgostrakh and former first vice president in charge of finance for Russian oil giant Slavneft, and Georg von Opel, representing his family fund Hansa, and Ruben Vardanian.

But the most colorful and controversial figure was Troika's (non-executive) board chairman, Alexander Mamut. By far the most influential person among Troika's Russian shareholders, Mamut was a member of the aforementioned 'oligarchs' club', the Bureau of the Russian Union of Industrialists and Entrepreneurs (RSPP), where he heads a working-group on the finance and securities market. Mamut was one of the most influential Russian businesspeople in the late 1990s but in 2001 stepped down as chairman of the board of MDM Bank, one of the most aggressive Russian financial industrial groups, to concentrate, in his own words, on 'something else'. In 2002, along with fellow oligarchs Anatoly Chubais, Oleg Deripaska, and others, he became a shareholder of the newly formed TV-6 television channel. Although Mamut's name has often been mentioned in connection with business and political scandals (such as Russian money-laundering through the Bank of New York, sales of unpaid Russian loans to developing countries, privatization of the oil company Sibneft by Abramovich and Berezovsky and Boris Yeltsin's re-election in 1996), he almost never talks to the press and keeps a low public profile. However, none of those accusations have ever been proved officially. Some Moscow rumors credit Mamut, who holds 10 per cent of Troika's shares, with the whole deal's design and implementation as well as with providing financing to Troika management. Mamut has not commented on those rumors.

Despite some grumbling that Vardanian 'sold his soul to the oligarchs', the Russian financial community has welcomed Troika's stake in Rosgostrakh. Evgeny Yuriev, president of Aton brokerage, said, 'We can only be happy for Troika. Alexander Mamut is known as an experienced professional and skillful lobbyist. When such people enter the stock market it will help the whole industry'.

Vardanian looked forward to the challenge of working with a new board and wasn't concerned about its potential interference with the way he ran Troika and Rosgostrakh. He welcomed professional directors with high expectations. He felt that Troika needed 'some discipline and sharper focus on results' and believed that the directors would be an invaluable source of strategic advice. Significantly, however, the fact that he and his management controlled a majority of the stock ensured that any potential attempts by the new board to fundamentally change Troika's unique culture would probably be defeated. As a sign of the board's alignment with Vardanian's perspective, one of its first decisions was to approve the 'Code of Conduct and Ethical Business Practices', which codified his values of transparency and fair practices.

In 2003, Vardanian told us that his role as CEO of Troika hadn't fundamentally changed, even though he had delegated additional powers to Jacques Der Megreditchian, managing director, Capital Markets, and Pavel

Teplukhin, president of Troika Asset Management, allowing them to manage their respective lines of business more independently. His responsibilities at Rosgostrakh left Vardanian less time for Troika but he still served as its public face, chief strategist, and chief corporate culture officer. Some employees who worked closely with him think that Vardanian spent too much of his precious time on low-value-adding activities, objecting to the fact that he still 'discussed personal problems of a junior banker for hours' and interviewed all candidates for positions of any importance.

Upon becoming Rosgostrakh's CEO, Vardanian immersed himself in the new organization. Only a few months later his schedule had shifted to what he considered 'normal': his 'dear family' (Troika) took about 60 per cent of his working time, while his 'project' (Rosgostrakh) took up the remaining 40 per cent.

Vardanian decided at the outset that Rosgostrakh needed an 'organized management' approach, a hierarchical organizational structure and formal systems and procedures to deal with the large numbers: 'You can't manage an organizations with staff spread over 11 time zones by walking around and shaking hands'. To bring those changes about, Vardanian applied a classic change management strategy to Rosgostrakh. He started by bringing in about 20 new managers from Troika as well as other dynamic Russian organizations, both from inside and outside the financial industry, to head key departments and subsidiaries. He then hired McKinsey to help with business and restructuring strategies. The joint work between Rosgostrakh's new management and the McKinsey consultants resulted in 12 cross-company strategic projects, including a new organizational design, a common IT-platform, a corporate 'university', an incentive compensation system, and local recruitment. Rosgostrakh began to evolve from a messy amalgamation of regional and lower-level legal entities to a two-tier structure with corporate headquarters in Moscow and 10 highly autonomous 'daughter' companies reporting to it – seven covering Russia's administrative super-regions and three covering Moscow and the national republics of Bashkorostan and Tartarstan.

In addition to being the organizational architect, designing management systems and procedural disciplines, Ruben Vardanian acted as the charismatic leader of Rosgostrakh, with a motivating message: 'The most important thing today is to spread hope and enthusiasm into grassroots Rosgostrakh organizations, to convince them that the company has not only a glorious past but also a bright future'. When he took over Rosgostrakh, the overwhelming majority of employees were already extremely loyal to the company – it is the only employer in many regions where it has an office and is thus crucial to local economies – but people were deeply frustrated with years of mismanagement and power abuse. However, they seemed to accept the restructuring at Rosgostrakh with little resistance.

Vardanian knew that new management systems alone couldn't change employees' work habits. Therefore, he quickly began to build a new corporate culture, integrating employees' existing loyalty with new standards for performance and development. In November and December 2002, Vardanian spent every weekend personally discussing business plans with management teams from all 80 Rosgostrakh branches. He says it was 'a tough exercise for them, not so much about the numbers but because it required a change in attitude'. During these weekend sessions, Vardanian identified some key people to develop, others to monitor for a while, and some to be removed immediately. He revived Rosgostrakh's internal radio system, allowing him to broadcast simultaneously to the organization's 80 offices, from Tchukotka to Kaliningrad. A new all-company newsletter presented Vardanian's vision of Rosgostrakh as 'a modern financial institution, present throughout Russia, providing quality services to an ever increasing number of customers, and attractive jobs with development opportunities for employees'.

There was one other great unknown, however. The Russian government still owned a majority interest in Rosgostrakh. Even though it had vaguely announced its intention to sell off another 25 per cent of the company, the timing and conditions of the next auction weren't clear. Rumor had it that other firms, some of them Troika competitors, were preparing to attempt a buyout. Vardanian believed that it was in the interests of the state to further privatize the company, which badly needed new investments. He saw consolidation of ownership in the hands of today's minority shareholders as a guarantee of this future capital inflow and fast operational restructuring.

In his first six months on the job, Vardanian visited over 20 Rosgostrakh branch offices, including such exotic locations as Yakutsk and Tchita. The long-haul flights between locations gave him time for self-reflection. He thought more and more often about his next project, which was slowly taking shape: charity. Vardanian closely followed progress in this area in Russia:

> We have 'pieces' of charity – some people doing something here and there. Recently rich folks like Zimin [founder of VimpelCom cellular telephony company] have begun setting up their own charity foundations. But they're all amateurs. Western countries have whole charity industries with detailed rules and regulations, and the effectiveness of their charity is much higher. We need to develop a charity industry as we have developed a financial industry here in Russia. That's what I really want to do.

When would that time come? He said he didn't know. His personal assistant complained that Vardanian was trying to 'embrace the unembraceable'.

Vardanian's personal assistant may have had the first glimpse of her boss's future taking shape when, on 26 February 2004, Rosgostrakh's board of directors accepted Ruben Vardanian's resignation as the company's CEO, and elected him as its Chairman. The board replaced Vardanian in the CEO position with Danil Khachaturov, who had served as Rosgostrakh's Chairman since 2002.

Why the unexpected change of leadership? Was it a question of fit, with Vardanian not being the right operational leader for the long term? Perhaps it was because although during his 22 months as CEO Vardanian had reorganized Rosgostrakh into a well-performing insurance company with fast growing revenues, he did not realize his ambitious goal of creating a nation-wide financial services organization. Nevertheless, the Russian financial community was still positive about Vardanian's leadership of Rosgostrakh; Alexander Koval, President of the Russian Insurance Union said, 'Thanks to Vardanian, Rosgostrakh has changed significantly for the better'.

In any case, Vardanian's new position will probably give him more time to focus on Troika Dialog. Or will he focus on the charity industry in Russia? Or...?

Commentary: Ruben Vardanian and Troika

A Moscow journalist once called Ruben Vardanian a 'golden boy of Russian capitalism'. Certainly Vardanian's age, his story, and his reputation at home and abroad evoke this image. However, even if it once held some truth, he has long outgrown that 'boyish' image. And at first glance, he doesn't even look truly golden – the business he runs and only partially owns is miniscule when compared to the empires built by Khodorkovsky and other Russian oligarchs; his personal wealth hardly compares to that of the new Russian billionaires. And yet both Vardanian's business and his cause have greatly benefited from his disproportionally high influence in the Russian business community.

Vardanian's success is exemplary and unique for Russia. Unlike all his fellow members of the oligarchs' club (the Bureau of the Russian Union of Industrialists and Entrepreneurs), Vardanian did not build his business by privatizing assets of the Communist State. He started from scratch, like many less visible and unheralded entrepreneurs of the 'second wave'. But Vardanian accomplished much more than many of his peers. Not only did he create a successful enterprise, but (with some other players) he also founded the new industry of investment banking in Russia. With a focus that was very unusual for Russia in the 1990s, he stuck with his initial strategy and ignored hundreds of other seemingly lucrative projects with quick paybacks and sky-high returns.

Vardanian succeeded by working on three things: himself, Troika, and the environment his organization operated in. The interplay between these success factors is remarkable and enlightening.

When 22-year-old Vardanian entered the business world, he already had some of the competencies of an effective leader. He was curious and open to change, learned fast from diverse sources and situations, looked forward rather than backward, and was well read. He was good at influencing people. He was intelligent, patient, determined. He also knew he wanted 'to make money with his brain', in other words, to become wealthy by controlling his destiny and preserving his integrity. He was open to ideas from the world outside Russia. Because the Russian economy was in a state of constant flux, Vardanian looked at the environment as a soft construction material for his life rather than a rigid containing factor, the view he preserves today. His ability to see the big picture – his helicopter view – has guided him ever since.

Vardanian created Troika to be a viable organization through which he could implement his broad but specific vision for his life. He first concentrated on developing industry-specific skills, having realized that the investment industry could be a driving force for a market economy. He believed that new standards, including ethical ones, would emerge and spread into the other branches of the Russian economy. But as the market began to demand more and more professional services from Troika, Vardanian had to immerse himself in organization building. His vision of Troika as an ever-present market leader, profitable business, and transparent and reliable partner for customers, employees and even competition guided his work. Vardanian understood his own shortcomings in general management skills, and he worked to overcome them. Like many effective managers he developed an ability to learn from all sources available: management books, professional training seminars, casual conversations, people he met at social events. But his unique trademark was his ability to learn from people who work for him. Vardanian searched for people who could mentor him, and hired them into his organization.

While building Troika, Vardanian strengthened his natural leadership competencies and developed new ones such as empowerment and delegation, team and organizational culture building, providing feedback and rewarding people, and not the least his emotional intelligence. Over time, his leadership style took shape. Leadership by example, direct contact with employees at all levels, and intensive communication became his preferred leadership tools, and became the foundation for a strong corporate culture.

At the same time, his limitations as a leader and their potential consequences for the business became more apparent. His search for consensus at any cost, risk minimization, and exaggerated involvement with employees' needs – in the comfortable culture of a big family with an attentive brother as a CEO – could threaten Troika's competitiveness both in the short term (speed of decision-making) and long term. To his credit Vardanian recognized these issues and tried to compensate for personal weaknesses with organizational arrangements; he delegated more and more decision-making authority down the command chain, introduced some P&Ps to govern the internal life of Troika, and created a powerful and performance-oriented board of directors.

During the years of rapid growth, deep crisis and recovery, Troika Dialog took a different purpose in Vardanian's mind and value system. From an instrument to achieve his personal vision, it became almost a 'living creature'. Vardanian created a new organizational reality, reflecting his vision, values and fantasies. Therefore Troika had a high intrinsic value to its chief architect, and to him, it was not disposable, whatever the financial benefits could be.

With Troika Dialog firmly on track by the year 2000, Vardanian changed his leadership focus toward the market environment. He pushed for new securities market legislation, a higher level of transparency in Russian business, and the introduction of effective corporate governance models. As a member of the Union of Industrialists and Entrepreneurs, he worked out such important changes in the legislation as the introduction of a flat income tax, new customs regulations, and a reduction of corporate profit tax. In making these changes, Vardanian used and developed his emotional intelligence skills, integrity and personal convictions to bring other business leaders and government officials to his way of thinking. Even though his vision of Russia as a 'normal country' is not yet realized, these steps are encouraging.

Parallel to improving the business climate, Vardanian also grew his own organization. He engineered the unprecedented acquisition of Rosgostrakh, intending to transform the failing insurance giant into an enterprise responsible for Troika's sales in the outer regions, and eventually turning Rosgostrakh into a valuable business on its own. Vardanian's clear vision for the project, his reputation and rich social network allowed Troika not only to accomplish the deal, which by far exceeded its own financial resources, but to keep management control over the new venture. In the same manner Vardanian ensured that one of the cornerstones of his vision for himself – control over his own destiny – stayed intact, through a management and outside financial investor buyout of Troika's majority shareholder. His desire to control his own destiny may have been one factor in his decision to resign his CEO position at Rosgostrakh.

Vardanian had earned a reputation as one of the most effective and candid business people in Russia. However, he faced enormous managerial as well as ethical challenges to consolidate his status. As Rosgostrakh's CEO he headed an organization with geographically dispersed operations; 50 000 low-skilled employees, many of whom had reached retirement age; a decrepit infrastructure; and ridiculously low efficiency. To deal with these challenges, Vardanian brought in dozens of successful managers from organizations very different from Troika. Many of them were used to tough directive leadership from the top, and exercised this leadership style themselves. They subscribed to values of quick material gains, assertiveness, and individualism rather than Troika's values of fairness, cooperation, and long-term development. Was Vardanian frustrated in his effort to transform the organization he acquired and the people he recruited?

His initial strategy was to shift his focus to Rosgostrakh without releasing Troika's reins. He had to find a balance for managing two organizations, which diverged in virtually everything, including business, size, age, stage of development, and culture. But even Troika was no longer the same; it now had active minority shareholders on the board of directors, with their own expectations for the company. Moreover some of them had a particular reputation in the Russian business community, and many observers questioned Vardanian's ability to preserve Troika's and his own integrity under new pressures.

We can only speculate on Vardanian's decision to step down; was he unprepared to tackle these and other challenges he faced? He had not done a major organizational transformation before; his general management experience was limited to one relatively small organization; he had not turned existing businesses around; he had always thoroughly selected and personally mentored his key executives; he had never worked with a professional board. Perhaps his favorite leadership tools were less effective with people used to authoritarian management and less educated and demotivated employees. He hadn't mastered a command and control leadership style. Vardanian lacked some skills required for his new tasks at Rosgostrakh. He was uncomfortable with quick centralized decision-making; he prefered development to firing; had never downsized even in bad times; was weak in formal multilevel planning and control, and organizational system design and building for a multidivision organization. He didn't like working under severe time constraints, and his resistance to stress was limited. But Ruben Vardanian's reputation was not dimmed after he stepped down from Rogostrakh. He had a unique ability to push himself to new heights by learning new competencies and leadership behavior. Optimists would argue that this is what made him a successful business leader, and this drive should serve him well in future situations of change. By March 2004, Ruben Vardanian was back to self-development, and set himself no limits.

9. World Class heroes for Russia

> World Class fitness centers have given us the gift of harmony in body and spirit. Before, we used to persuade ourselves that physical appearance is not important, as a human being is made beautiful by rich internal content. That's right – an internal content makes one beautiful. However, the human body is a home for one's soul, at least a temporary one. Why then should a beautiful soul waste its time in a house that is falling apart? World Class is the founder of the fitness movement in Russia. It was the first to offer unique fitness and health improvement programs (about 55 in total) that miraculously rid us of everything unnecessary – extra kilos, illnesses, complexes and fears.[1]

When we first read this description of World Class fitness centers in a Russian magazine, we found it somewhat incredible. 'Miraculously rid us of everything unnecessary' … sounds good, sign us up! But seriously, we wondered, what kind of organization is this, and how does it work?

The concept of fitness was never a marketable commodity in Communist times. Generations of Russians had grown up accustomed to the Soviet-era exercise experiences. They all had been – at least once – to state-owned sports facilities for the masses. These were inexpensive or even free, but permeated with what was called the 'Soviet horrors'. They were small, dirty and infested with cockroaches. The fitness machines were cobbled together with whatever parts were available, and placed in tiny rooms without air-conditioning. The swimming pools were dirty and unattended, and last but not least, the locker rooms stank. In those days, the dubious attraction was to spend no more than 45 minutes in the over-chlorinated water of a dimly-lit indoor swimming pool, to be followed by a shower which might or might not include hot water. Not surprisingly, only the hardiest people would put themselves through this kind of arduous experience, so at the time the word 'fitness' itself was quite a riddle to most Russians.

And yet World Class fitness centers, the first of which was opened in 1993, caught on very quickly. It was obvious that the founder had tapped into a pent-up demand that no one else had foreseen. World Class was the first, and is still the most successful, chain of fitness clubs in Russia. What was the secret behind its success? What kind of a person would come up with such a 'crazy' idea in the first place?

We looked forward to meeting Olga Sloutsker, the fencing champion, entrepreneur, lobbyist and founder of the World Class fitness centers. When we finally arrived in her office (which is plastered with Helmut Newton's large photographs of very muscular nude women), we soon realized that she is as dramatic and driven in person as she comes across in print. When we asked her to elaborate on her strategy for World Class fitness centers, her comment was, 'Look, I am not a greedy person. I don't have a crazy mentality, thinking I want to rule the world, so I don't worry about the competition. I simply tell my staff that we're No.1'.

Being number one is all that counts for any athlete, amateur or professional. There's nothing worse than being in second place. For Olga Sloutsker, a former world class Russian athlete whose impressive accomplishments never quite matched her father's ambitions for her, is being number one in her industry a form of redemption?

The strongest red thread that runs through the tapestry of Sloutsker's life is her desire to elevate herself, her staff at World Class, and the Russian people in general, to the status of 'hero' – free of extra kilos, complexes and fears. She has shaped her own role as that of the undisputed boss and head coach, who speaks with a firm voice of reason for the good of her team as well as society at large. She also thinks of her gyms as a new kind of club, where leading Russian businesspeople and politicians can meet, relax and discuss the future of Russia, while being pummelled and pampered by the best fitness professionals the country has to offer – some of whom are also former Olympic athletes. Comparisons with the ancient Roman Baths of Caracalla would perhaps not be too far-fetched, as that grandiose complex of pools, solariums and libraries was also started by an entrepreneur who found a way to profit by bringing together the diverse populations of Rome in a common pursuit of physical and intellectual development.

A FENCER IN A BATHING SUIT?

Olga is an only child, born in St Petersburg (formerly Leningrad). Her mother was a gynaecologist, and her father was a lawyer. Olga described her father's relatives as being very influential. One of her great-grandfathers shipped grain from Canada; another was involved in tin goods manufacturing. Her grandmother often talked about her studies in Switzerland and about her imported car, the first in town. Olga credits her own success, and in particular her financial acumen and ambition, to the influence of her parents and grandparents.

> My parents were not Communists. They insisted that I should respect the Soviets and our country, but not the Communist vision of society. They are both intellectuals. But I was always under extreme pressure to excel in sports, which did not leave me much time and energy to develop my own intellectual side.

But I did take their lessons to heart. My parents believe in taking pragmatic risk based on detailed calculations. My father's slogan is 'Risk should be smart'. Take risks in business, but estimate how much cash you have available, do a market survey…I do not want to fly high without first doing solid calculation of my chance of success – in order not to fall after the first trial run.

Olga's father and grandfather were devoted sports fans. They could easily answer any sports trivia question, like 'Who ran as a sprinter for the USSR during the Olympic Games in Mexico?' The two men would take Olga with them to watch soccer and basketball games in the local stadium. Olga's father had come of age during the Nazi blockade of Leningrad during World War II; his own dreams of athletic glory, therefore, had been cut short. Both he and Olga's grandfather hoped that their girl would be a great athlete, making up for what they themselves had missed.

One day when Olga was eleven years old, her father stopped by the new sports facility under construction in their town to sign her up for swimming lessons. He gave her name and phone number to the administrators. They told him to bring Olga in several months later, when the facility would be officially opened. A few days later, he called them to ask if he should buy Olga a new swimming suit. Their response surprised him: they laughed, and told him that she wouldn't really need one to learn fencing! What Olga's father had taken for a future swimming pool was in fact a fencing facility.

Olga took to fencing – like a fish to water – and she soon learned to do it well. She was competing at the local level by the time she was twelve. She was sent to a state-run boarding school for young fencers, of which there were only two in the USSR at that time, where promising children from all over the country went to study and train with professional coaches. She worked hard, training twice a day. She felt obliged to do well for her team, her coach, and her home city. She hoped to be selected for the USSR fencing team, but in spite of her hard work, she never made it.

Olga graduated from the Lesgaft State Academy of Physical Culture with a degree in physical education. In 1988, at the age of 23, she got married, relocated to Moscow, and found herself without a job or a team to train with. Although financially she did not need to work, she felt her life was incomplete. She thought often of her parents' advice: 'It's wrong not to work. It's wrong to worry only about being beautiful'.

The idea of opening a fitness club came to Olga Sloutsker when she accompanied her husband, a prominent financier, on one of his business trips abroad. One day, out of sheer boredom, she decided to try the gym in the hotel in which they were staying. As a former member of an elite USSR sports team she was used to working with the best athletic equipment available, but she was surprised by the quality of the hotel's fitness facility. The clientele consisted of hotel guests, primarily businesspeople, who could hardly be defined as professional athletes! Nevertheless, she saw that they liked using the excellent workout equipment, and happily sought the advice of the hotel's professional fitness instructors. Sloutsker later said that in the hotel gym she felt some of her drive and energy from the old days coming back – and this inspired her to think about how she could combine sports and business to liven up the routine of her married life in Moscow. She was soon planning to open her own elite fitness center – the first in the Russian capital.

A FITNESS CRUSADE

Beginning in the early 1990s, Russia was flooded with icons of Western culture and Western brands such as Coca-Cola, McDonalds, and Marlboro, and Russian consumers eagerly bought whatever Western products they could afford. It was the widespread opinion of Russians that Westerners knew more about running businesses than they did. Sloutsker's business idea was to make Western-quality fitness centers available to all Russians, and to prove that this business model would work. She knew she would have to create a product that would differentiate itself on the market by providing the highest quality in both customer service and fitness technologies. Both concepts were new for the Russian people.

Sloutsker admitted she did not really know what she was doing when she started. A crash course in business was the beginning of a steep learning curve that included trips to international fitness conventions and conferences. She was determined that *her* fitness center would be nothing less than a 'World Class' facility.

Financing the start-up was arranged with the help of her husband; Sloutsker simply borrowed money from him. The first World Class fitness center opened in 1993 on Zhitnaya Street in downtown Moscow. Sloutsker had to import literally everything except the bare walls for her new club, including sports equipment and special flooring, doors, toilet paper holders and rubbish bins. And this even included a Western brand name – World Class. Sloutsker signed a contract with the Swedish fitness company World Class so she could use their brand in Russia. She said:

> I always wanted to provide a high quality product. To do this, you need high-quality professionals. I believe that the best way to have them is to train them; you need to invest money in education. That's the philosophy of my company. From the first day I started to educate my staff and to educate myself.
>
> Since opening the first World Class in 1993, I have made a lot of mistakes. I always tell potential clients that they can rely on my consultancy services because my expertise is worth millions of dollars in mistakes! But because we did not have

competition in the early days, I could afford to make mistakes. I lost money, but not my first place on the market, which was more important to me.

Clearly, just having a liking for fitness was not enough. More was needed. I really did not have an idea of the meaning of words like 'balance sheet', 'debit and credit', 'accounts payable'... I went to a business school and I hired a private tutor. I spent six hours a day reading business literature. I felt like my head was swelling up, but I mastered the basics of financial control, business operations and marketing. I also realized the importance of learning from our colleagues from abroad. Now I annually send my staff to the best international conventions, and I meet with industry people to see their vision, breathe their air.

I have also educated my own family. As a typical Russian businessman, my husband lived a 'snack' life. I convinced him to get rid of these bad habits and join my club.

Delighted (middle- and upper-class) Russians flocked to the new club, attracted by the international level of services and quality. There was an excellent pool with saunas, a Russian steam bath, a Turkish hamam, jacuzzis, a solarium, and a gym with Western-made machines and weights – previously unknown in Russia. There were specialized aerobics studios and a spa, all in a total floor space of 5200 square meters. It was most emphatically *not* a Soviet-type club for the masses. It was designed to be a club for people of a new Russia, for the new capitalists and their families. And it also became an oasis of Western comfort and service for expatriates living and working in Moscow. It was located literally right in the center of the city, ten minutes away from the Red Square, in a great downtown business location and a prestigious residential area. Sloutsker recalled:

When I opened my first fitness club, I thought my role – although this may sound presumptuous – was to instill a club culture in this country. Club culture did not exist in the Soviet Union. There were no real clubs, places where people who don't know each other, who have different occupations, have different nationalities or religions, come together, who are tied to one and the same place because they identify with it, because they have common interests. And that's what we've managed to build here. Building a club culture was my mission at that time.

In 1995, the Swedish partner of World Class went bankrupt and Sloutsker bought out the trade mark for Russia and the CIS (Commonwealth of Independent States). The position of managing director of the World Class center in Moscow was offered to Irina Krag-Timgren, who had been the head of the Swedish World Class Corporation's activities in Russia (St Petersburg and Ufa) since the late 1980s. Later, Olga Sloutsker and Irina Krag-Timgren parted company, and later Irina started Planet Fitness, her own chain of fitness clubs in Moscow in which World Class owned shares for some time. Although they retained some ties, the break up was painful, and is something that Sloutsker does not like to discuss openly.

And then another departure would change Sloutsker's business model permanently. Some of Sloutsker's staff left World Class that year to join a franchise of Gold's Gym opened by Americans in Moscow. Her former employees obtained the World Class client database and transferred the names and contacts to their new employer. This was a real blow both to the business and to Sloutsker personally. She later said this second defection forced her to rethink the way her business was organized, and the way she hired, trained and motivated her employees. She also decided that from then on she would be both the owner and the managing director of the World Class fitness center.

Despite these internal setbacks, within a short period of time the first World Class club became very popular. In 1997 a second $4000m^2$ World Class club was opened in a quiet residential district in southern Moscow. It has a round, split-level pool, and looks like an aqua-park with slides, artificial currents and underwater lights. This club features programs for young children and teenagers, and has more families and housewives as members than at the central-Moscow club. Within five years of opening, this club had 4500 members; not surprisingly it is busy throughout the day.

In 1997 a contract was signed for construction of a large sports and trade center in Zhukovka, Moscow's most prestigious suburb, home to many of the Russian elite, including the President, Prime Minister, high level government officials, successful businessmen, bankers, movie and pop stars. The 1998 financial crisis forced Sloutsker to reconsider the budget for construction and change the plans, but she carried on with the project. In 2000, World Class opened a new $3700m^2$ facility in Zhukovka. There again the strategy was unique, this time to focus on outdoor activities like skiing, skating, mountain biking, roller-blading, hiking, cross-country racing, open-air basketball, volleyball and tennis. This club's clientele can be described as people who have it all: luxury cars, beautiful houses with landscaped gardens – not to mention public attention and popularity. But World Class offers them something they cannot easily buy: good health. The result was an 84 per cent membership renewal rate after the club's first year in operation.

Perhaps reflecting a shadow of the Socialist legacy, the membership fee of each facility reflects the social profile of its members. While the least-expensive corporate club membership costs $850 per year, the Zhukovka membership is $4000, payable in advance. What do clients get for extra money? Space, says Sloutsker. Whereas Smolensky, the chain's smallest facility which opened in 2001, accommodates 3000 members in a $2500m^2$ corporate club, at the elite Zhukovka its 1600 members can spread out over $3700m^2$.

'MOTHER' RUSSIA

The harder Olga Sloutsker worked to develop her business, the happier she became. The fitness business suited her perfectly. She was involved in sports again; she was proving to her parents that she could be as successful as they were; and perhaps most importantly, she had something to *do* other than while away her time as the beautiful wife of a wealthy man. She had found her true calling:

> As far as I know, the people who usually own fitness clubs – and who are successful at it – are people who have been very involved with sports or previously worked in gyms as managers. There isn't much of a career ladder to climb in this business. In some cases, it's just a person who has passion for sports and who has come across the money to finance a gym. To run a fitness center, you must be a special kind of person – someone who is unafraid of freedom and comfortable making risky decisions. As for me, I have never worked for anybody. I would probably be a bad employee if somebody were to hire me.
>
> I remember the first time I looked at my balance sheet and realized that I had earned some money. I was very proud of my first income – it wasn't a small amount. At that moment I knew my future was secure.

Sloutsker is grateful to her husband for his early financial support (for which she has since repaid him), but she is proud that her business is now self-sufficient:

> My husband has his own business and busy schedule. He has no time to solve my problems, if I have any. But his advice is more than appreciated. I have never had a feeling that my husband and I are on different sides of a barricade. And I do not feel offended when I am reminded that I am a woman. It would be a mistake to forget that I am a woman.

During the period when she was working hardest on the success of her clubs, Sloutsker and her husband had a son. (He was born in the United States, the first Russian child born to a foreign surrogate mother – an event that sparked a media frenzy in Russia at the time.) Being a mother, Sloutsker says, has forced her to put her priorities in order. Unlike many career women who feel torn between their professional and family responsibilities, Sloutsker thinks she has managed to find a good balance. She calls Russia a matriarchal country, with a woman behind every successful man. But this does not mean that women are invisible. Under the Communists, women were encouraged to be active in all fields; the term 'housewife' had a negative connotation. In the post-Soviet new century, women entrepreneurs are almost as common in Russia as their male counterparts. To her delight, her career accommodates perfectly what she sees as her dual roles as a woman and as a professional businessperson:

> I think women shouldn't feel embarrassed if what they really want to do is social work, or choose goals that conform to traditional gender roles. After all, the main role for women is to give birth and nurture children. If a woman can't bring her career and family life into harmony, she should stop working or reschedule her working day.

I usually wake up at 8:00 and spend some time with my son. Later he comes to my club, swims and practices other sports. I changed my schedule because of him; I have almost no busy mornings. He is a special part of my life, because I became a mother quite late, when I was 34. No doubt he changed my life. But it was he who was integrated into my husband's and my life, not the other way around. I do not think it is necessary to spend all my time with him, to be influenced by his schedule. I can afford a nanny. My son has changed me, but I do not want him to suppress me.

He understands the importance of work. One day I told him that I wasn't going to work because I was sick. It was difficult for a 4-year-old to understand how I could not go to work. He asked, 'How are we going to live if mother does not go to work?'

Olga realizes that in the Russian culture it may be difficult for women to succeed if they are competing in business against men:

It is absolutely clear to me that men dominate in society. A woman's main task is to be a good mother, a stabilizer in a society. Men are more adventurous; they come to more radical decisions. Women are soothers; they are rational and pragmatic, less conflictual, but stronger and wiser when a conflict has to be solved. Russia has had many women leaders and governors. They were either in control themselves, or they were very influential for the Russian leaders – and I will be too!

Sloutsker thinks the man's role in society is more complicated; women do not have to prove as much as men do. As an example, she says if a woman tries to start her own business and fails, she can always return to a full-time role as wife and/or mother within her family. Thus a woman always has a choice, whereas men do not. They feel pressure from childhood onward to be tough, and to put others first: 'Do not cry – you are a man'; 'Let the girl go first'; 'You must be strong and brave'; 'You must study and work hard, and earn a good salary'; 'You must be a good husband and a good father'. Sloutsker sympathizes with them, and says sometimes she even feels sorry for them.

FOR THE GREATER GOOD OF RUSSIA

There are many similarities between Olga Sloutsker and Maria Ilyina, the general director and founding partner of Frontstep described in Chapter 7. Their underlying system of values encompasses twin desires – to mother their clients and employees, and to 'seduce' them. Their leadership style involves dispensing calibrated doses of maternal concern and correction. They try to motivate their employees to excel not by offering extravagant material rewards, but by telling them that each person's efforts will contribute to the greater good of the Russian people.

Both women lead by flamboyant example; each one has created a corporate culture that is entirely professional, but at the same time vaguely resembles a kind of crusade led by a Russian Joan of Arc. However, whereas Maria Ilyina has concentrated on consolidating her business, as Olga Sloutsker's business matures, and as other competitors enter the market, her vision has grown exponentially. Her vision – crusade – is to improve the general health of all Russians. Her battle plan has three main thrusts: to spread her expertise through consulting; to train her employees to increasingly professional levels, and send some of them – imbued with her philosophy – out into the world; and to recruit Russian politicians to her cause.

Fitness is a dynamically developing industry in Moscow, with a turnover of $70 million as of 2001. Not counting the old-style *kachalki*, or semi-clandestine weight rooms, there were estimated to be about 70 to 80 fitness clubs in the city in 2003. But no more than 40 of these clubs meet international standards. Large fitness centers like World Class may have an annual turnover of more than $10 million and have up to 3000 customers. Opening a fitness center requires investments of at least $2 to $3 million, but investors could expect to recoup their funds within about two or three years under the market conditions of 2001 and 2002.

Since its birth in 1993, the Russian domestic fitness industry has been dominated by savvy female entrepreneurs who run three of the oldest chains: Olga Sloutsker at World Class, her former partner Irina Krag-Timgren at Planet Fitness, and a third woman, Elena Dari, who runs Marcus Aurelius. These three doyennes of the trade were not the only ones to see an opportunity on the Moscow market – or perhaps it would be more accurate to say that their competitors were emboldened by the trio's early success, other entrants included international franchises such as Reebok, Gold's Gym, and Fit-and-Fun. Even Moscow's City Hall wanted a piece of the action – they set up a physical culture and sport committee to open a chain of municipal fitness centers serving each administrative district of the megalopolis. By the end of 2003, the city government intended to open ten low-price clubs in suburban areas, each offering gym facilities, body building, playgrounds, and in some cases, swimming pools.

Thus, new fitness centers popped up in the early 2000s in Moscow like mushrooms, but the market could accommodate still more. Even 100 fitness centers would be a relatively small number for a city of Moscow's size, with its estimated population of about 12 million. (In comparison, Vienna's 1.5 million inhabitants can choose from among about 1000 fitness clubs.) On the other hand, demand for elite fitness centers in the upper-price segment of the Moscow market was considered to be 60 per cent filled by the end of 2002. The sector with the most potential for growth was for middle-class Russians. Meanwhile, the regions outside of Moscow largely remained undeveloped, partly because the major Moscow chains showed little interest in regional expansion. Children's fitness programs seem to have strong earning potential; in Moscow, ten per cent of the client base was children. Another growing field was fitness consulting, aimed at advising entrepreneurs wanting to open a new club.

While Sloutsker claimed she was not interested in investing in facilities outside Moscow and St Petersburg (although she had already opened one in Almaty, the business center and former capital of Kazakhstan), she had no intention of conceding World Class Russia's pole position to any of her new competitors: 'I want to dominate the market, to be a leader, but I can do this by selling my consultancy and management services elsewhere'.

In 1999 she met with Mike Chaet, the President of CMS (Club Marketing and Management Services, USA), who conducted several workshops for World Class sales managers. Olga and Mike signed a contract to open CMS-Russia. Its motto was 'Fitness-ready-to-be-used'. If investors had the funds and desire to open a club, World Class-CMS Russia would take care of the rest. In addition to sales and marketing programs they offered fitness, service, and construction consulting.

For three years in a row the World Class network was included in IHRSA (International Health, Racquet and Sportclub Association) Global 25 – an annual review of the top performers in the worldwide health and fitness industry. World Class was the only Russian fitness club that ranked so high.

Besides World Class club operations, Sloutsker came up with the idea of organizing fitness conventions in Russia inspired by the many international fitness conventions she went to herself in the early days. Between 1995 and 2003, 15000 fitness specialists and amateurs from all over Russia and the CIS republics attended the World Class Fitness Convention. The goal of each Convention was to promote good health in general to the public and the latest trends in the world fitness industry to professionals, and also gave World Class an opportunity to showcase its achievements; Sloutsker personally delivered lectures on the business of fitness. Sending her employees to such events served as a powerful motivation and retention tool in the organization. With the best instructors running master classes, Sloutsker showed the outside world that World Class clubs were the most experienced fitness services providers in Russia, and quite possibly beyond.

Olga Sloutsker quite happily accepts that her efforts to promote fitness encourage competition. She knows the marketplace is changing, but far from being concerned by competition, she welcomes it, even indulging in a kind of maternal pride about the Russian newcomers. Many of their founders cut their teeth at World Class. She says,

> We are happy to have competition, because without it you do not improve. We trained the competitors and I am proud and happy about that; people who once worked for us created almost every new fitness club in Moscow. They keep us on our toes. But we are not afraid. We are ready.

She believes that everyone she trains will reproduce her style and culture in their own gyms. Those followers have the knowledge and the energy to be successful. She says:

> They were 'conceived' and brought up by us at World Class. They go forth to be leaders and protagonists. They open their own clubs, but they take the World Class philosophy with them. Every year many of them participate in the annual World Class Convention in order to be among the first and to receive new ideas and materials. They want to look like us!

By 2004, client retention was the only real challenge World Class faced. Despite the success of the Zhukovka club that catered to the needs of wealthy or Western-oriented Russians, Sloutsker's expansion plans required reconsidering the definition of target client base, so that the organization would be less dependent on attracting upper-class clients.

> The amount of people who can afford our membership is our number one problem. There are not enough rich people in Russia for a huge health club industry. Plus most of them do not care about fitness; they have their private yoga teachers and their psychological problems. We need middle-class growth. Today, even the lowest membership fee is out of most people's reach [the average salary in 2003 was still only $106 a month, and $500–600 in Moscow].

The problem is that Russians who grew up under Communism have a particular mind-set about exercise, and they resist paying for facilities that were free under the Soviets – even though those facilities were dirty, poorly staffed and under-equipped. Olga mentioned that some of her attempts to popularize the concept of fitness met with barbed remarks, such as 'You talk about good health for everybody, but your fitness centers are only affordable to the rich'. Thus, her problem is uniquely Russian:

> Few Russians are willing to part with some of their income to pay for exercise. In Western clubs, if one person leaves another will soon take his place. I have to train my staff to understand that we do not have this fallback. If somebody buys a membership in my clubs we have to do everything possible to keep them.

Sloutsker's solution is quite ambitious. She wants to convince all Russians that good health should be a top priority, and World Class fitness centers are the place to go to achieve it. She said:

> I constantly work on promoting a healthy lifestyle for Russians. I want our political leaders to promote health and fitness. And I do not mean just any development on the outskirts of civilization. I want us to be in the mainstream with professionals and state-of-the-art techniques.

> During the years that Yeltsin was president, there were never any sport competitions on television, because sporting organizations could not afford to pay TV channels to air them. People could watch politics, sex movies and talk shows, but not sports.

Olga Sloutsker has made it her personal mission to address this problem, in particular bringing it to the attention of President Putin. On 30 January, 2002 World Class took part in a round table discussion with Putin and other government officials, who conceded that a lack of physical activity was detrimental to the nation, and that there should be a concerted effort should be made to promote health and fitness in Russia.

> I have discussed this problem with President Putin, and made a presentation to the State Duma (the Russian Parliament). I want to succeed in making fitness a state policy in our country. This may sound a little bold, but it is one of my goals. I happened to start the fitness business in this country, and I feel my role is to develop the fitness industry for all Russians.
>
> I think it is important to have a mission. A mission turns a small bakery into a transnational company. It turns one single fitness club opened by the wife of a rich man into a chain of clubs. It turns some small initiatives into something that people see and get interested in. The mission is *why you are doing it.*

There is a pragmatic business aspect to promoting fitness – Olga has her eye on a new generation of clients:

> We are now introducing fitness classes in secondary schools. I think that a revolution can be made in secondary schools. The attitude of schoolteachers should be changed, and the way physical education is taught should be improved. I am not alone in thinking this; the Governor of St Petersburg and former vice-prime minister Matvienko [in charge of the social sphere in the Russian Federation] agree.
>
> We now need to design the techniques, the methodology, put it in a document and offer it to the country. Does the country need it? Do we need it? I am a practitioner. I know how to do it, but it's not something that we [World Class] are going to make money on. But that's today. Tomorrow things may change. Schoolchildren who take physical education lessons in school are potential members of my fitness clubs. If I don't educate the population, if I don't instill in them the need to practice fitness, I will find myself without clients tomorrow.

'WORLD CLASS, THE BRAND WE LOVE'

By 2003, World Class was a well-recognized brand in Russia, with 1200 employees serving 14000 clients. Over the years, Olga Sloutsker had hired professional managers to take on some of the responsibility for daily operations, but one event in particular convinced her that she had given up too much control. We happened to be in her office as she was thinking about the repercussions of a recent firing.

A secretary came into Sloutsker's office and quietly put a peeled orange and a cup of green tea in front of her. This is a daily routine: one hour before her workout, Sloutsker has a fruit and some tea. While sipping the tea, she talked about Boris Leonidov[2] whom she had just fired.

Boris used to be the head of sales for World Class. He had joined the company almost five years earlier, after a large multinational company laid him off during the 1998 financial crisis. Sloutsker had liked this ambitious and talented young man. She could tell that he had no clue about the fitness industry, but he seemed like a quick learner. Most important of all, he had extensive sales experience.

Boris was indeed talented. Sales kept rising after his arrival. Sloutsker was happy that she had taken a chance on the young man. With new clubs opening up, Boris' responsibilities increased, and so did the number of sales people and the volume of sales. Boris decided to enroll in one of the MBA programs offered in Moscow. Most of the MBA programs in Russia were evening programs that allowed students to combine their studies with daily work responsibilities. Sloutsker supported Boris's idea.

A couple of years later, close to his MBA graduation, Boris told Sloutsker he wanted to negotiate a new contract. He suggested that he should be made vice-president of World Class and get a considerably bigger financial package. Sloutsker listened to Boris's requests, agreeing that he had obviously done a good job of studying negotiations and presentation techniques. But she also caught herself thinking that maybe all these MBA programs were just spoiling good people:

> People somehow start to lose their head after an MBA program. They are probably *not* taught how to be loyal to the company, but how to promote themselves…Instead of applying their knowledge and skills for the benefit of the company, adapting them to the realities of business life in Russia, they end up with their head completely emptied … And then they can't adapt to the reality.
>
> They start thinking: 'Aha, I've paid my money, I've attended classes of professors from various parts of the world who have taught me various things. Now that I am back in my organization, I see that nothing is happening there, or things are developing in a wrong way.'
>
> So, what happens next, the individual starts to, excuse my language, shit on the heads of everyone else, because he is the only person with an MBA degree around here, and unfortunately that is what happened with Boris. He lost touch with reality; he has lost connections with his employees… He started to show disrespect to people around him.

This impression of Boris's disrespect towards his people had been creeping into Sloutsker's mind for some time. Although she didn't normally interfere in the activities of business units in her organization, in this case she carried out what she called an audit of the sales department's activities to see if Boris really had a part in the overall success of the sales function.

I wanted to figure out if he would be worth the salary he was asking for. How was he getting his results; what had he contributed to the success of the department. To my surprise and disappointment, none of the people interviewed by me personally and some other people who are public opinion leaders here, mentioned that he was an essential member of the team. As it turned out, his absence had in no way harmed the work of the department. It turned out that people did not see him as a leader, did not think he was creative. They did not feel he had things under control. He was present, he acted like a head of department, but he was not a leader, not a person whose decisions were accepted.

He avoided responsibility, and he didn't deal with problems. For instance, there were two heads of sales departments in two different clubs. There was a conflict of interest between them, as client groups periodically intersected. They, naturally, came to him as an arbitrator. Boris, however, said: 'You decide yourselves'. So, instead of saying 'Here is what you should do' and salvaging the relationship, he did nothing to end the conflict. This kind of thing happened quite often. He was afraid to make decisions.

Sloutsker remembered another episode that she now saw in a different light. Some time before, Boris had received approval for a new salary and bonus budget for his people. However, instead of signing a document for the payroll department that would allow automatic payment of new levels of salaries and bonuses, he preferred each month to issue a specific order authorizing a 'beyond ordinary' payment to his employees. Each time, in Sloutsker's opinion, he did this to demonstrate his power to the employees. Episodes like that started to flood her memory. She recalled instances when Boris would keep a top salesperson, who averaged $2.5 million in sales per year, in his office for hours. He would berate the individual one day, and then ignore the person for months, not even bothering to answer his e-mails. Yet another example: he would say good morning to some people in the department, while ignoring the rest of the members of his team. And now he wanted to become Vice President.

The answer to the well-planned and logically described proposal for a new position and a new compensation scheme for Boris was Olga's firm 'no'. Her conviction now was that she had given him enough. Not only was he disloyal by making extravagant demands, he didn't seem to be a good people manager. The best thing was to let him go:

He has his degree, but in terms of the human factor, there is a big question mark about him. Boris came to our organization with a good experience, and he was ambitious... but he did not understand anything about our business. We gave him a good tool, our sales system, and we gave him our product. The product already existed, and it is a good one. There was no need to reinvent the product. When he got his MBA, he lost his head. He could not clearly evaluate his contribution.

Taking another bite of an orange and a sip of green tea, Olga said that since Boris had left World Class, she had found out even more about his leadership style.

His people had been continuously afraid that Boris would decide to cancel their bonus or salary increase. They resented his differential treatment of employees, and they hated the way he would harangue them in his office. They were glad he was gone.

When asked what is different about *her* leadership style, Olga admitted that her employees are afraid of her as well – but she describes this as a 'different kind of fright':

> Employees are afraid of me, I am often told that, but they are afraid in a different way. They are afraid to disappoint me, because they see that we are all working hard, doing our best. They are afraid to let their company down. They are afraid to make me sad.

When we heard this story, we reflected that Sloutsker's persona seems to cry out, 'I am a leader! I am the one who made it all happen!' She rarely cites World Class staff members by name in media interviews. She talks about herself. She is always friendly and direct, but she is clearly an iron lady who continues to control daily operations despite the fact that she has a management team. She never carries any bags – they would interfere with her smooth walk and independent image – leaving that task to her chauffeur/bodyguard.

Indeed, World Class staff's awe of Sloutsker is apparent in the way they greet her in the corridor or lobby, transfer her phone calls reverently, serve her tea or coffee, apologize for bothering her with questions – and the way they blush when she speaks to them cheerfully, and turn pale when her voice has a steely note. She says, 'I can be hard, but I have a soft heart'.

Her assessment of herself was confirmed as we got to know her better. In our first meeting, Olga was the only one who talked. She came across as a beautiful, slightly arrogant lady, whose body language showed that she had little time to waste. She told us we would be allowed 45 minutes for the interview, and when the time was up her secretary would remind us to stop. At first, much of what she said seemed to be taken from her 'party line speech'; she said things like: 'Yes, I am very ambitious! I am a leader and a well-known personality in the country!'. But as she became more at ease, her tension disappeared, her voice became softer, her answers more personal, and every once in a while she would smile. After we broached some difficult questions, such as her split with her former partner Irina Krag-Timgren, she became more introspective and seemed less self-absorbed. She described her leadership style with a fascinating metaphor: she says she is a very emotional person so she has to lead with a 'frozen' heart. She says much of her success comes from her ability to see 'deep inside' people. By the end of the meeting we felt we had caught a glimpse of the real Olga, the charismatic team leader who had won the devotion of her followers.

Olga believes the main reason World Class has been so successful is because she is a good team leader. She is good at finding the right people for each job. Indeed, the turnover of personnel in World Class is minimal, and for every new job opening there are dozens of applicants.

> I want people with burning hearts and a strong desire to contribute to the company. The company needs educated people who want to improve themselves. I really appreciate when employees do something to please our clients and not just to please me. We have a thorough selection process for fitness instructors. Each candidate has to pass three rounds of interviewing and then go through a three month internship period during which they undergo training and take exams.

Olga is aware of the fact that her organization is an employer of choice for many candidates from the fitness industry and graduates of Physical Culture and Sports institutes (all instructors have completed specialized higher education). Standards of acceptance are very high. During their internships, candidates learn the theory and practice of fitness, methodology, planning of classes, physiology, and so on. Interns are not paid. However, training potential fitness instructors costs Olga about $500 per person.

Every year all fitness personnel have to go though an assessment process. There are two parts to the assessment process: theoretical and practical. The practical part continues throughout the year, as managers give grades according to the trainer's personal achievements. The theoretical part includes questions about fitness and the physiology of the human body. All these results go into the 'Pyramid' – a system with three levels of professional growth. Everybody is aware of the requirements for each level and, thus, knows what to work on. The levels are: fitness instructor, personal trainer, master-trainer. There are ample resources available at the Club for development: training sessions, seminars with international specialists, and international fitness conventions in Europe and the US.

Olga Sloutsker says that all World Class staff members have a similar level of motivation:

> My workers believe in the uniqueness of the company, and I mean employees from the top level down to the lowest ones like janitors. All the janitors in the men's locker rooms are men, which is unusual as most of the cleaning personnel [traditionally in Russia] are women. The janitors are attractive and physically fit. Our security people and handymen are retired military officers who are not afraid of hard work. They look neat in their uniforms, and they are respected. Employees are the face of the World Class for those who come to the clubs. They provide a clean environment: floors and walls, and lockers, and toilets, etc. From this point of view they are also involved in sales. An outside cleaning company would not be able to attract new customers in this way.

In Olga's view, it is extremely important to make sure that all of the employees are proud of associating themselves with a winning organization, with a winning brand, and with a winning leader:

> In a short period of time we opened three new clubs. I conducted a meeting with new employees of the three clubs. I put them all together in a large hall. Of course, I couldn't remember all their names, but I wanted to see their faces, I wanted them to see me. I told them that the most important thing expected of them is to represent the brand, our brand, World Class, the brand that we love, that we respect, that we wouldn't let anybody spoil. So I told them that wherever they go today – to a disco, to a fitness convention, to a fitness class, to a place where they spend their free time, or wherever – that they represent our brand, our company. They have to think not only about themselves, but they have to understand that they are a prism through which people view my company, the leader in the market.

Sloutsker believes that her people are very ambitious:

> I should say that they have leadership ambitions. We are a leader. We have never had to play catch-up. We've always been Number One. That's what I am proud of.
>
> I am a professional athlete. I know that there is a special ambiance in high-level athletic teams. People may even compete with their own team mates, but still, everyone, coaches, masseurs, athletes, are unified by some great intangible mission. That's the mission of victory, the mission of defending national colors and the honor of your country. Athletes don't necessarily talk about it, and may not express it publicly, but there is this aura of participation in a great cause, and the aura of being affiliated with a leader, a champion. It exists here at World Class. That's what, in my opinion, brings people here and keeps them here.

Still, it takes an effort on Sloutsker's part to instill a real understanding of ownership in her employees. For example, once during her daily exercise routine, she noticed some plastic cups left by clients next to the treadmills and weight machines. Automatically, she picked up the used cups and threw them into a rubbish bin. The next day, she saw cups there again. She called to a personal trainer on duty in the gym, drawing his attention to the cups. His reaction was swift: 'I'll call a janitor right now'. This was not the action Sloutsker had hoped for. 'Ownership' would mean that the personal trainer would do exactly what she had done herself the previous day: going one step beyond regular duties and seeing the big picture – taking responsibility for the organization in a broader sense. She said:

> Sometimes employees have a hard time measuring up to this very high bar set by us, the bar of responsibility. Anyone can make a mistake, but we want people to try to reach the bar. They should care about their work, and worry about failure – that's what we are trying to develop in our people.
>
> Let me give you an example. I hired an intelligentsia-type, nice young woman with a degree from the School of Journalism of Moscow State University, to work on marketing. One of her first jobs here was to set up a photography session. *Domovoy*

[a glossy family magazine] was preparing a special issue on ten years of capitalism in Russia, featuring several companies including ours. A photo session was arranged, with a famous and popular photographer. The session was to take place in our club, on a Sunday night. This new employee sent all of us a message that we had to be there at 22:00 to prepare for the shoot. I am an experienced person in all this stuff, so I came earlier. But many of our employees came at 22:00, and some who were coming back from skiing or other weekend activities were late. The person who was responsible never showed up, leaving me to sort it all out. Of course, we did the photo session, and everything went well, but she did not do her job.

You know, I can't imagine a person working for us who has responsibilities, but does not show total attention to his or her work. I didn't feel that this marketing person participated in the common cause. Of course, I summoned her in to my office and told her she needed a stronger sense of participation, of being part of the organization. I hope things are going to change.

People come to us from different companies. When they come, they are often similar to the woman I just spoke about. We later change their attitudes. I try to give them a chance. I never say good-bye the next day to an individual who makes a mistake. If a person has professional skills and is not indifferent to what we are trying to do here, than there is chance to turn that person around.

Sloutsker enlisted the help of a rather unusual kind of executive in her employee training program: a chief coach. Although there are people who are responsible for daily supervision of the fitness instructors and people who train the instructors, the job of the chief coach is about maintaining the morale of the individuals and keeping the team spirit. The idea of establishing this position came to Olga from her past experience as a member of the St Petersburg fencing team. She says that her fencing coach was an important role model for her as a leader. The coach was as a role model in another way: Sloutsker still remembers that despite a modest income, her fencing coach managed to differentiate herself from other people in small but noticeable ways, for example by dressing very elegantly and always having fashionable hairstyles. Inspired by this coach, Sloutsker says she has tried to instill in her organization the notion of being different in a positive way. This corporate culture of differentiation is clearly noticeable in the company's publications, website and advertisements.

Finally, Olga Sloutsker believes that her fitness personnel can be compared to show business professionals who all know each other and have a common dream of being hired by a leading studio and becoming stars. In the case of the Russian fitness industry, she believes, World Class is such a destination, where they become her 'heroes'.

HEROES OF THE NEW RUSSIA

In its continuous pursuit of heroes, World Class sponsored two Russian teams participating in two Olympic Games: the Winter Games in Nagano (Japan) in

1998 and the Summer Games in Sydney (Australia) in 2000. Olga Sloutsker was also a member of the Russian Olympic Committee. As a former fencer, she was delighted that the first Russian to win a gold medal during the Sydney games was Pavel Kolobkov, a Russian fencing champion.

In 2001 Kolobkov became one of the first Russian athletes to be depicted in a new World Class advertising campaign: the 'Heroes of the New Country'. Sloutsker said: 'Our country should know the faces of our heroes not only after their death, but after their victories as well. Some of the Russian Olympic champions became the public faces of the World Class clubs'.

The advertising campaign was later expanded to include not only professional athletes, but also Russian participants in the Paralympics for handicapped persons. Sloutsker proudly described how she had these people flown to Moscow to take part in the photo sessions for this campaign. When asked what she was trying to promote with it, she said that it was primarily about displaying worthy individuals. It of course also reflected glory on the World Class brand, and ultimately, on sports and fitness in general.

Speaking about her future plans, Sloutsker says:

> My plans are very ambitious and well-defined: I am not going to lose World Class's number one position in this part of the world. I would like every major city in Russia to have a World Class club. Everybody should know that the World Class Russia brand name is a guarantee of highest quality service, and an active and healthy lifestyle solution. And I want World Class to be traded on the New York Stock Exchange.
>
> God brought me into this life and gave me the chance to be a leader, and I will not waste this chance. During the next ten years my team and I will try to change the mentality of the Russian people towards a healthy, responsible way of living.

During her youth, under Communist rule, she had a strong desire to escape, to get out of the former Soviet Union, to get a better life somewhere else. Now she thinks she is bringing this better life home. Olga explained to us that even if a person is not able to change a bad situation, at least they can change their attitude – with the help of 'energy created by fitness'.

BE NUMBER ONE

The last time we met Olga Sloutsker at World Class, she recounted her previous day's experience judging young pop stars in a contest. Teenagers were doing their best on the stage, proud of their bright costumes, songs and artistic dance movements. She recalled how she had silently advised them, 'You must to try to be number one; there is no other way to grow'.

As she observed the performance from her jury box, she thought about her own life. She too had started out as just one of millions of Soviet children who had been signed up for a sports team by their parents. She believed that her goal to be nothing less than number one had made all the difference in her life.

In the early 2000s, she started to win the acclaim she always hoped for. In 2001, she was awarded the prestigious Person of the Year in the New Industry in Russia prize in a ceremony held in the Kremlin. Winners were selected by an expert council composed of well-known public figures, government officials and corporate and media CEOs. And Olga was the only woman among them. She told us: 'I deserved it! Fully and completely! Maybe this sounds arrogant, but the most important industry of all is the one that preserves health!' In May of the same year, Olga was awarded the national Olympia Prize as a leader of the new Russia. In June a new World Class club opened in Kazakhstan with the President of the country himself involved in the ceremony. The year 2003 was marked by massive celebrations of the success of capitalism in Russia. Many companies that started in early post-perestroika years have grown into successful enterprises. TV programs and glossy magazines celebrated 'ten years of new life'. Among those companies that were often mentioned in the media was World Class. It had grown to seven clubs, with an annual revenue of $23 million and profits of $9 million. One of the magazines singled out World Class as a company that has changed the way people live in Russia, and the way they treat their bodies. For the Communists, common wisdom was that only what is inside the body counts, now World Class teaches them that it is time to free the body – the container of the soul – from the ravages of the Soviet way of life.[3]

This was Olga Sloutsker's mission exactly, written large in one of Russia's popular family magazines. In a way, the article named her Head Coach. Now she is in a position to tell all Russians '*You too must to try to be number one; there is no other way to grow*'.

NOTES

1. Khodokovskaya, E. (2003), 'Mig i Vek Dlinnoyu v Desyat Let', *Domovoy*, May, 92–102.
2. Name changed
3. Khodokovskaya, E. (2003), 'Mig i Vek Dlinnoyu v Desyat Let', *Domovoy*, May, 92–102.

Commentary: Olga Sloutsker, heroine for a new Russia

Olga Sloutsker is not a typical Russian woman. Although she does seem to sympathize with the women in what can be called 'traditional' feminine roles of a homemaker (with a full-time professional job!), she is simultaneously negating such a role for herself. She isn't the first woman to find herself in the situation of depending on her husband for financial security, and not even the first Russian woman to put some of her husband's money into a business. However, Sloutsker did go beyond a pet project for a rich wife. She not only has a successful business, but also an activity to which she has ascribed a transcendental role or mission: changing the life-styles of the population, modernizing the ways children are taught physical education in school, and even improving the health of the nation.

Like Maria Ilyina, Olga Sloutsker offers a new kind of psychological contract to the employees in her organization. Sloutsker's charismatic vision is more grandiose than Maria Ilyina's however. Sloutsker believes that the chance to be a part of her team, as the leader in the fitness industry, is the factor that attracts talented fitness instructors and managers to her organization. She explains that she wants to cascade down the feeling of being a part of a combined team of the best athletes to all her staff. What seems to accentuate this effort at culture building is her observation that her people are afraid of disappointing her and letting her, her brand and her company down.

In this case, not unlike in others in this book, there are traces of ideological influences that the organizational leader seems to be using, consciously or unconsciously, as a tool in mobilizing people for the achievement of the goals ahead. Careful selection and socialization are the tools often used for culture 'indoctrination'. Sloutsker, for instance, has created a position of a chief coach, clearly borrowed from her past experience in sports. Because the chief coach's mandate is to be an educator, supporter, and guardian of morale for the instructors, Sloutsker is operationalizing her belief in the motivational forces of the 'transcendental goal' that often exists in sports competitions.

Immediately after perestroika, people in Russia showed a lot of irritation at any sign of ideological influence. Freedom that came with the dawn of capitalism meant that there was now the option of living in an ideology-free world. However, the vacuum that formed was not a comfortable state for many individuals. A need to believe in something, to be affiliated with some cause, to feel a part of a larger than life activity remained (probably coming from the pathos of the Communist times), despite the cultivation of new seeds of individualistic values in the Russian culture. The Russian Orthodox Church has not filled that emptiness. Arguably, a new expression of the generally collectivistic Russian culture can be found in employees' identification with an organization (or organization's leader), capable of providing this sense of affiliation and a rallying cry to a 'cause'. The new ideology offered by World Class offers a fertile ground for making people feel special, and helps them buy into Olga's cultural values.

As a word of caution, one should of course remember the Communist experience of having *zampolits* (deputy military chiefs in charge of morale in military regiments), and *secretary po ideologii* (ideology secretaries, or Communist party or young Communist league functionaries responsible for maintaining allegiance to the cause) – zealots who turned into chaperones controlling an individual's every move, and instruments of a Big Brother who watched for deviation from prescribed Party thinking. The lingering memories of the past could make people more cynical about buying into organizational cultural values.

Having concentrated all of the executive power and responsibilities in her hands as both the owner and managing director of the organization, Olga Sloutsker has started to focus on only the most crucial aspects of the management of her organization. Given the growth of World Class to seven clubs in mid-2003, the ambitious agenda of changing the government's approach to physical culture in Russia, and the success of consulting side of the business, Sloutsker will need to hire someone with business expertise to run the daily operations of the chain.

She will remain the leader, however, as well as the charismatic coach who motivates her fitness instructors, managers, accountants, janitors and salespeople, not to mention the clients. She may be trying to delegate a part of what she achieves with her personal charisma to other individuals, the designated chief coach being a good example. However, routinization of charisma in organizational rituals, myths, and policies and procedures is not that easy, especially if the original charismatic leader is still very much in the organization. People who report to Olga may have to play their boss like a piano, needing to be extremely attuned to her way of doing things in the organization.

For Sloutsker, the notion of fair process in the treatment of employees has become increasingly important. To an extent, concerns regarding ethical behavior towards employees may be seen as a new, emerging theme in the Russian organizations. The universalism–particularism dilemma is more difficult to resolve in Russia, however, given the overriding role of friendships in relationships. Universal rules, as applied in Western organizations, are more likely to be overruled by 'exceptions'. As a general comment, however, both in this case, as well as the cases presented in the other chapters, these new business leaders view it as important to be honest and fair with their employees.

The case of World Class and Olga Sloutsker also gives some interesting insights into the inner theater of a leader. Olga was clearly influenced by her father and grandfather, both ardent sports fans who instilled in her the wish to achieve, the drive to win. In addition, we can hypothesize that she has been influenced (through stories in the family) by her family's entrepreneurial history. Consciously or unconsciously, the entrepreneur may have been an ideal type for her, and as has been said in the chapter on Roustam Tariko, we can often find entrepreneurial role models (in whatever form) in the background of entrepreneurs.

The sport her father selected for her, serendipitously, was fencing, a sport in which she proved to excel. Fencing, however, is a sport based on individual performance. Although the team may become a champion, the results clearly depend on individuals, who are constantly on stage and whose every move is judged by jury and spectators. Like many other successful Russian entrepreneurial business leaders, narcissistic behavior is one facet of Olga's nature. She has created an organization whereby a brand, World Class, is completely identified with the owner Olga Sloutsker. The website of the organization is full of pictures of her. Her words of wisdom are posted everywhere. We can speculate that her constant refrain – World Class is the best fitness club employing the best people – is not only a great reinforcer of her own self-esteem but also that of the people working for her. And as was discussed previously, a solid dose of narcissism is clearly necessary for an entrepreneur to achieve success. Possibly Russian leaders are distinguished from their compatriots by their degree of narcissism and their sense of being destined for greatness. The potential drawback is that narcissistic leaders can be blinded by grandiosity and success. If there are no countervailing powers, it can affect the leader's reality testing. It can lead to the creation of a 'Greek chorus' of yeasayers. Furthermore, entrepreneurial types often have problems with the succession issue.

Olga Sloutsker has brought elements of Western life-style to Russia, or, more exactly, to Moscow. Beyond fitness and club culture, her great contribution has been the development of the notion of client service and client retention put into the Russian context. She clearly recognizes, however, that retaining fitness clients is not a simple task, as socio-economic reality heavily influences the spending patterns in society. At the moment, retention efforts are based on offering the highest quality, the trendiest training methodology, and a feeling of exclusiveness (for example, having the best possible trainers and sports doctors available to the clients). It should be noted that at the time of writing this book the notions of exclusivity, extremely high quality and uniqueness were being heavily exploited by the Russian advertising industry. The well-to-do section of Russian society seems to want to spend a lot on luxury goods and services. Sloutsker, however, realizes that she needs to go beyond the wealthier layers of society in search of her clientele. Given the value-for-money-minded (and spending-cautious) people that she is targeting as her clientele, there may be a need for the development of new approaches to client service and client retention.

In part, the social influence that Sloutsker is developing in Russia is geared towards securing that middle-class clientele. For instance, her attempts at bringing change to the standard approaches to teaching physical culture at schools are aimed, among other things, at educating her future customers. Could this social influence be a preparation for a new future role of a business leader? In other words, could politics eventually become a field of application for the talents and resources of Olga Sloutsker (and, for that matter, of other leaders mentioned in this book)? At the time of writing this book, the answer from most of these leaders would probably be 'no'. However, for an observer to deny this possibility would be unwise, given that Russia is entering a stage in its development where the old institutions for grooming a future political elite (from which most current political leaders have originated), such as the Communist party, Young Communists League, the KGB, and official research organizations, have ceased to exist or have lost their prominence. Business may be that particular environment where visible and (hopefully) competent individuals prepare for running the country. This is still speculation, and just one possible avenue for further growth and development of Olga Sloutsker's leadership talents. She is talking about setting the bar high and achieving the highest possible standards. What will that bar be in the future?

PART THREE

Conclusions

10. Hindsight and foresight

No one can deny that clouds are once again gathering over Russia, promising great storms.

Maxim Gorky

There is no shame in not knowing; the shame lies in not finding out.

Russian proverb

As we have seen, the collapse of Communism in the Soviet Union and the economic liberalization that followed created an unprecedented opening for business leaders. In just over a decade these New Russians built empires worth billions of dollars; transformed inefficient mammoth State enterprises into cash-producing machines; created whole new industries; and changed the lives of tens of millions of people. This book attempts to provide enough insights to answer the intriguing questions that most people ask when they consider the tremendous changes in Russia in the past decade: 'Are we seeing a new kind of Russian leadership? Can the lessons learned by the handful of successful New Russians be shared with their compatriots? Are they the right role models, as imperfect as they might be, for a stable social and economic future for Russia?' It is worth another short detour into historical context in our search for answers.

RUSSIA'S ROBBER BARONS?

Americans like John D. Rockefeller, Andrew Carnegie, Jay Gould, J.P. Morgan, and Collis Huntington and their peers were long thought of as ruthless and unscrupulous 'robber barons' whose primary goal was to accumulate personal wealth at any cost.[1] This view was criticized by later historians for being too simplistic and sometimes inaccurate, but the fact remains that there was a high level of accepted corruption in 19th century American business and politics. But was the situation then similar to what we see in 21st century Russia?

The late 19th century in the United States experienced the rise of great corporate conglomerates, in a land paradoxically devoted to the idea of laissez-faire. John D. Rockefeller, for example, realized early in his career that consolidation of the oil industry would result in much less waste. He believed that by buying up his competitors, he was protecting the industry from the disadvantages of chaos. Similarly, Andrew Carnegie pulled together horizontal and then vertical integrations within the steel businesses he dominated, by employing fair means and foul. His success, his critics were ready to point out, had much to do with the fact that he hired sharp subordinates. 'But if it hadn't been for Andy Carnegie's peculiar character,' it was suggested, 'there would have been no glue to hold the whole vast enterprise together.'[2]

Indeed, extraordinary leadership skills were the crucial factor that led to the success of the American captains of industry. Rockefeller and Carnegie, in particular, were able to select and encourage good subordinates. Carnegie was even characterized as lazy, and admitted himself that he was not so much a technical man as an organizer.[3] The banker J.P. Morgan helped to create financial order through his passion for organization. Organization appears to have been Rockefeller's greatest talent as well. In 1879, he set up the Standard Oil Trust – to stabilize the industry – which later served as a model for trusts in many other industries. Both critics and admirers of the robber barons agree that the trusts, and the holding companies that later replaced them, created a bridge between the past and the future – that is between the seemingly ethically rationalized commonwealths of the past, and a bureaucratized, syndicalist future.

What parallels can be drawn between the likes of John D. Rockefeller and Andrew Carnegie, and Russians like Mikhail Khodorkovsky, Roustam Tariko, or Ruben Vardanian? The societal context of both the oligarchs and robber barons is one in which political directions and controls move from the top down. In both situations, relative chaos ensued as a result of forceful, if not bloody, revolutions: the Jacksonian democratic, laissez-faire revolution in the US (c. 1820) and the perestroika movement in Russia. In the US it took a while for intellectuals, in concert with the Federal government, to control and channel the energies of the captains of industry and their corporations. Even now, after a century of attempts – with an insistent emphasis on a market economy, a return to a measured laissez-faire, and Enron-type scandals occurring frequently at the same time – a satisfactory response to the machinations of big business has not been entirely realized. One must wonder about the future in Russia, which after all has not inherited the history and ancient traditions of democratic and constitutional attitudes, practices and government. The main point we want to make here is that both the Russian oligarchs and the American robber barons came into influence in a period of great upheaval in their respective countries and cultures. Their actions should not necessarily be forgiven, but they should be judged in light of this context.

To speak in more specific terms, we do see similarities between the two groups of business leaders. On the negative side, there have undoubtedly been, and still are, Russian schemes as grandiose and unethical as the 19th century Americans' appropriation of state and private assets through intimidation and kick-backs in the private and government sectors. There also appears to be the same willingness on the part of some people to believe that the end justifies the means. In the chaotic late 1990s in Russia, most observers believed that modern Russian entrepreneurs were emerging in an entirely different context – they were taking control of a creaky, bureaucratic industrial society that required not *building*, but rather *transformation*.[4] But many people had serious doubts about the Russian oligarchs' ability to transform Russia. The term New Russian was often used in a derogatory sense. 'Robber baron' was too kind a term for the 'thugs' in the Russian oligarchy – 'robber' would do nicely. Unlike the American captains of industry, critics said the Russian entrepreneurs had not created something out of nothing. One American historian wrote in 1998, 'Their ruthless tactics…may resemble those of their US counterparts, but [the Russians] have yet to show a comparable ability to build and develop… It remains to be seen whether the Russian entrepreneurs build anything enduring or leave behind a comparative legacy of individual achievement.'[5]

We don't agree entirely with this pessimistic view. All of the entrepreneurs we met, with the exception of Mikhail Khodorkovsky and Jacques Ioffé, created their organizations from 'nothing'. We believe that many of the Russian business leaders we have worked with have shown courage and vision equal to that of the early American industrialists. Like the Americans, they have been criticized heavily for their methods, but as one observer said, nice guys seldom lead revolutions.[6] Whereas many people will remind you that John D. Rockefeller and Andrew Carnegie constantly reinvested profits in their companies, the Russians have a reputation for siphoning off government funds – but even this is changing in the new century. John D. Rockefeller and Andrew Carnegie, it should be pointed out, were integrators as well as builders. Finally, like Rockefeller and J.P. Morgan in their day, the new Russian entrepreneurs seem to have a genuine, gut-level desire to do whatever it takes to save their industries, and by extension their country, from chaos. All of these men have had, and will have, an indisputably tremendous influence on the development of their respective countries.

If there is one thing we're certain of, it's that time and change seem to move at an accelerated rate in Russia today. We've already remarked on that fact that it is common to see very young Russian executives who seem to have half a lifetime of experience behind them. We also believe that, like the revisionist description of the 19th century American industrialists, the Russians are proving to be good at organization and consolidation. Jacques Ioffé brought about a transformation in mindset in Bolshevik. Roustam Tariko is building an extensive distribution network and a national brand. Mikhail Khodorkovsky may or may not have a dark past, and he may or may not have had connections in the government who opened doors, but he seems to be – for whatever reason – genuinely concerned with the rationalization of the Russian oil industry.

He has already begun dabbling in philanthropy. (His perceived involvement in politics, however, appears to be costing him dearly as recent events have shown.) And there are also real examples of development: the whole *raison d'être* behind VimpelCom and Frontstep is to use existing competencies to take a giant leap into 21st century technology. Ruben Vardanian and his colleagues have virtually created an entirely new industry. The same can be said about Olga Sloutsker. We see this as evidence that Russians are also beginning to build enduring companies.

The late 19th century in America played itself out as a sort of experiment in social Darwinism. The traditional laissez-faire ideal ostensibly remained the American economic policy, though it was seriously warped by tendencies to exploitative individualism, monopolistic organization and, the pursuit of frequently quick and speculative profits. How far along the same path will the new Russian business leaders go? The answer will depend on whether they can develop and implement a new paradigm for Russian leadership.

REINVENTING LEADERSHIP WITH A RUSSIAN ACCENT

One can hardly find a less homogeneous group than Russian business leaders, who are more varied in their backgrounds, success stories, work habits and demographics than any other occupational group in the country. Our group of case studies is an indication of this diversity; it includes a 39-year-old former junior Komsomol official, a 69-year-old former rocket scientist, a former world-class fencing champion, a research-oriented computer programmer, and a 34-year-old banker who never had any other full-time job (ages at the time of writing). It also includes a Russian exile who returned home after several decades abroad, and a young man who got his start singing in a rock band and later selling chocolate. Some of them work 15 hours a day. Others spend only a fraction of their time in the office. Some excite their followers with constant walkabouts and pep talks or, in one case, a passionate flamenco dance; others prefer to deal with them through formal systems and layers of management.

The men and women leaders in these case studies have different social and professional backgrounds, come from different regions and ethnic groups, and belong to different generations. Contrary to the popular stereotypes, few of them overtly benefited from Soviet era political connections, or even specific professional expertise and training, to help them get a start. To a large extent their success is a result of behaviors that contradict many features of the traditional Russian national character. In short, they are similar to each other in that they are all different from the norm. They are the outliers. In fact, they exhibit many competencies of global leaders – they are future-oriented; systematically question and change the status quo; are open to new ideas and quickly grasp new concepts; attract and retain talented employees; and create vision for themselves and their followers. However, for each of the leaders studied in this book, we see that these and other leadership competencies have a very distinct Russian accent.

EXTREME FLEXIBILITY

Like all successful leaders of new Russia, these executives have a high level of tolerance for ambiguity. They are open to the unknown and to change, and can even work with turn-around CEOs, or lead an organizational transformation themselves. Even more importantly, they are unusually capable of changing their own mental models and the environment around them.

Mikhail Khodorkovsky started his business career in the late 1980s. At that time, his goal was simple; he wanted to make some money and he knew that to do that he needed to buy and sell goods with a mark-up, pocketing profit after every deal. In the early 1990s, he realized that controlling (not necessarily owning) an enterprise was a much better proposition – cash profits gained from such an enterprise would allow for expansion and diversification. In the mid-1990s, he pursued the privatization of assets with export potential to create stable cash-flows. By the beginning of the new century, he realized that long-term wealth creation is based on sustainable performance and business transparency for investors. This evolution is typical for successful Russian business leaders. What to say about his spectacular fall is another matter. What is quite unique about these business leaders is their search for knowledge and their ability to embrace this evolutionary model so quickly. Olga Sloutsker, Ruben Vardanian, Maria Ilyina and Roustam Tariko all specifically told us they are avid readers of Western business theories and practices – and they know their capitalists. But these are the universal rules of leadership game – to be always on the leading edge. People in our study demonstrated not only curiosity, but also extreme flexibility, rarely seen at the top of modern corporations outside of Russia.

PERSISTENCE AND RESILIENCE

Flexibility, however, does not mean softness or pliability. The people described have an incredible amount of tenacity; they are persistent and resilient. It is not easy to derail a Russian business leader from achieving a chosen goal. Means can change, but the results have to be delivered. Dimitry Zimin worked almost three years to obtain an invaluable GSM 900 license for his company: spending entire days at the Telecom Minister's offices; funding research into the frequency spectrum; seeking help from competitors; negotiating license fees to the government. Nobody believed it was possible before it was done; very few believed it was possible after it was done. This persistence and resilience come hand in hand with an ability to frame events in a positive way and to regard failures as opportunities. When, after the August 1998 financial crisis, Troika Dialog and its CEO Ruben Vardanian faced the harsh reality of a disappearing market he saw it as an opportunity to recruit the best talent and create a solid lead in market research. Such an approach is not a one-time emotional revelation, but a sustainable behavior pattern. Maria Ilyina and her associates, learning from their mistakes when dealing with Western partners and falling flat several times, not only managed to keep their enthusiasm and involvement in building a successful ERP business in Russia, but also kept promises made to clients ('Make a promise and keep it' has become one of the slogans of the company placed visibly on its website) and to the employees. What the future has in store for Khodorovsky, however, remains a wide open question.

BUSINESS LEADERS AS CATALYSTS OF CHANGE

In addition to changing themselves as the turbulent environment evolves, new Russian business leaders reshape the environment, establishing the rules of the game rather than waiting for the government to do it for them (like the American robber barons before them). Zimin forced the Ministry of Communication to accept an additional cellular communication standard for Russia, Vardanian drafted the first securities market regulations for the Russian government and pushed them into the law. To familiarize the business community with ERP systems, Ilyina invested her staff's time in a non-profit project of writing a book on ERP that immediately became a national bestseller. Olga Sloutsker launched a wide program of popularizing Russian winning athletes under the theme 'Heroes of the New Country'. Jacques Ioffé controlled the interaction between Bolshevik and Danone executives by acting as a kind of corporate culture 'translator' and integrator.

By no means are these business leaders bleeding-heart philanthropists selflessly working to improve the Russian economy. Their first priority is to shape the microenvironments of their own businesses, but their actions have a positive side effect. In the early days of capitalism, a handful of entrepreneurs pushed hard for accelerated privatization. They grabbed extremely valuable assets for themselves, but arguably also gave a great boost to private economy development in Russia. Business leaders (not only oligarchs) have become the most powerful force in fostering change in the Russian business environment. Even though some of the changes, such as customs duty increases, could hardly be called 'progressive' (or the methods by which they were achieved, 'ethical'), integration leads to freer competition and a market economy.

Controlling the environment is high on Russian business leader's agendas. Not only large business owners such as Khodorkovsky or Zimin, but people like Ilyina and Sloutsker invest heavily in managing relations with government officials, lawmakers, regulatory bodies, customers, suppliers and competitors. They create and maintain a very sophisticated network of relations, in which the leadership role does not always belong to them. However, these networks, if well managed, can add enormous value for the leader and the business. Considering relations as a major asset in today's interconnected world, Russian leaders are continuously screening the environment not only for business opportunities, but also for new potential partnerships. They are flexible in accepting minor roles in order to profit from the relationship. Zimin was ready to become a junior member of a hunting team because it included potential partners; he patiently queued to hand birthday gifts to government officials; and worked as a rank-and-file member of a radio association. Roustam Tariko, as an 'outsider', relied on his Russian friends and their highly placed contacts, but never hesitated to give elaborate parties for the friends of his friends. In the case of Khodorkovsky we could speculate that he overplayed his hand with key government officials.

EMOTIONAL INTELLIGENCE

Subconsciously or consciously Russian business leaders 'stage' their own behavior. Because they were accustomed to scanning and reacting to an unstable environment for so long, they seem to be quite good at reading the emotional state of their counterparts and using it to their own personal advantage. Vardanian, who 'never raises his voice', can be many things: a caring older brother for a new recruit lost in the system; an emotionless professional banker negotiating a contract with an old friend; or an iron-willed CEO firing a successful executive for ethical misbehavior. Maria Ilyina attracts clients, investors, business partners and employees by virtually 'infecting' them with her enthusiasm. Jacques Ioffé, Mikhail Khodorkovsky, and Roustam Tariko are described as men who never shout, but their subordinates still fear disappointing them. This application of emotional intelligence skills by Russian business leaders may be seen as manipulative, but it works extremely well.

EXECUTIVE TEAMS (AND COUNCILS OF BOYARS)

Many of the leaders we studied are also quite good at using organizational resources (people, systems, technology) to compensate for their own leadership weaknesses. For example, at VimpelCom Zimin delegated to Fabela management of investor relations, international strategic alliances, and minority shareholders. Frontstep's Maria Ilyina is open to advice coming from people around her, and often manages to get free consulting help from people interested in her approach and leadership style. Given her boundless enthusiasm, her two founding partners play an extremely important grounding function. It has made for a highly effective executive role constellation. All of the executives we met had worked with consultants, some playing the role of a mentor or coach in fairly long-term relationships.

But there is a uniquely Russian twist to the concept of executive teams as well. Quite often, business leaders compensate for their personal shortcomings with a handful of trusted collaborators. Usually, this circle works quietly, out of the limelight, to support the leader's position, but it plays an extremely important advisory role in the leader's functioning. Within this inner circle, (sometimes called '*Boyarskaya Duma*' or Council of Boyars, after the influential advisory body to the tsar in pre-Peter the Great Russia), leaders who always look highly self-confident to the outside world, share their ideas, concerns and doubts. The inner circle often works according to the 'democratic centralism' model: everybody has a say in the discussion, the leader makes the final decision, and then it becomes a law for all.

THE ORGANIZATION AS A TOOL

Being attentive to the environment, Russian leaders (unlike many of their Western colleagues) do not regard their organizations as larger-than-life untouchable sacred cows; they look much more outside and much less down the pyramid. An organization (a company with a name, legal status, assets, offices and employees) is a tool to achieve its leaders' goals, just one of the elements of a symbiotic whole, along with relationships, hard assets and personal knowledge. Organizations come and go, as the leader wishes. The real organization – the true center of power and influence – is the informal structure.

Of course, as the size of the business increases, such organizational changes become more complex. But the view of organization as an instrument, rather than a thing in itself, prevails among business leaders. The Russian traditions of high power distance and neglect for ordinary people's rights serves this purpose too. As has been pointed out, most of the entrepreneurs we studied (as in Western societies) have strong narcissistic tendencies, and their organizations remain an extension of themselves and their own desires.

RUSSIAN CHARISMATIC LEADERSHIP

Whatever a Russian leader's competencies and management style, he or she has enormous power within the organization. Followers look to the leader as a superior being who has unique rights and, by definition, deserves compliance. In all the cases studied in the course of our research, we witnessed attribution of charisma to the leaders by their followers, sometimes irrespective of the leader's will. Because the Russian people have a need for powerful charismatic leaders, they tend to create them, thereby giving Russian business leaders far greater room for maneuvering than their Western counterparts have.

Despite the difference in the scope and complexity of businesses headed by the leaders mentioned in this work, they all have one thing in common: they are actively employing the concept of a mission, or an overarching goal in mobilizing the efforts of their people.

Olga Sloutsker (World Class) talks about how feeling like a champion in the fitness industry attracts talented fitness instructors to her organization. She explains that she wants to cascade down to all her staff the feeling of being a part of a powerful team of the best athletes. A major requirement for success in her organization is team spirit, sharing responsibility for the development of the brand and the organization. Not surprisingly, she says that her people are afraid of disappointing her and letting her down. In contrast, Roustam Tariko focuses on the unifying force of his brand, Russian Standard, for both the people in his organization and the people of Russia in general. He wants the employees to be proud of promoting the brand and producing high quality products and services that all Russians can be proud of. The overarching goal is related to the well being of his own organization and Russian consumers and society at large.

Maria Ilyina (Frontstep) uses a different recruitment tool: the vision of helping Russian industry get up from its knees through application of modern management software and management principles. She and her associates are proud of being involved in the Russian 'real sector' (industry) development. An interesting job coupled with a great cause is the *raison d'être* she used for years to motivate and inspire her employees. Her mantra was similar to those of the other leaders in this book: 'We'll survive despite all the difficulties'.

Mikhail Khodorkovsky has built tremendous wealth for himself. He acknowledges that he has more than enough money for several lives. Nevertheless, he was challenged by the idea of building a world-class organization, something that would be comparable to (and hopefully better than) British Petroleum. 'Making life better in the regions where Yukos is operating' is akin to the slogans of the Communist past, but it worked as a motivator. He was also aware of rules of the business game; as the first in the Russian market to disclose the ownership structure of such a large and important organization he garnered attention and respect from analysts, shareholders, regulators, mass media, and the general public not only in Russia but worldwide. In hindsight however, we can question his political savvy. Hubris, a common disease among leaders, may have affected his decision making.

In all of the examples above, there are traces of ideological influence. This obviously remains the primary way that leaders of Rusian organizations, consciously or unconsciously, mobilize their people to create and transform their organizations. This approach to creating 'meaning' for stakeholders is interesting, given the resistance of many Russians, now accustomed to perestroika, to any signs of ideological influence developed during and after perestroika. The freedom that came with the dawn of capitalism meant that there was an option of living in an ideology-free world. However, the vacuum that was formed was not a comfortable one for individuals. A need to believe in something, to be affiliated with some cause, to feel a part of a great, worthwhile activity remained (probably coming from the pathos of the Communist times) despite new individualistic values in the Russian culture. It could be a new expression of the generally collectivistic Russian outlook; a search for affiliation or identification with a business organization (or organization's leader) capable of providing this 'greater than life' feeling and, as a bonus, a family-type atmosphere within it. The new ideology offered by organizations mentioned in this book offer a fertile ground for such optimal distinctiveness.

These entrepreneurs have found more than just an unexploited opportunity in terms of the products or services which they are bringing to the market place. They have also found, through a conscious choice or serendipitously, an unexploited opportunity to replace Communist ideology with the ideology of their business. This seems to be one of the lessons for those who wish to build a successful business in Russia that relies on mobilization of the workforce: you need to give people a sense of belonging, an opportunity to identify with a great cause, and a feeling of being part of the family, being taken care of. This is the 'messiah' role taken up by the new Russian business leaders.

In line with this view, the short-term thinking of Russian people and a long-standing tradition of '*après nous le deluge*', Russian leaders spend virtually no time preparing their succession or even reflecting on it. In fact, one of the potential negative consequences of charismatic leadership is exactly this: the failure to spend enough effort and time on developing future leaders in the organization. Consequently, in Russian businesses, power transfer often becomes a dramatic event. As was described in the case studies, all of the leaders we interviewed were struggling with this issue.

LEADERSHIP CHALLENGES FOR NEW RUSSIA

The fundamental political and economic changes of the last decade profoundly affected all strata of Russian society and laid a foundation for accelerated development of civil society and a market economy. The Communist system was dismantled to the point of no return. By the early 2000s, the private sector represented 70 per cent of the Russian economy. Price controls and consumer goods shortages are long forgotten; the ruble is internally convertible; the service sector is booming as the military industry is shrinking. The majority of the population welcomes democratic institutions and free elections. The peaceful and orderly transfer of presidential power from Yeltsin to Putin set a historical precedent for the Russia of the 21st century. Although much work needs to be done to create a truly democratic society – the creation of a free, independent press being a good example – Russia has come a long way. Many people have thrown away old dependency-based behavior patterns and taken responsibility for their lives and well being into their own hands, embarking on new lifestyles. New entrepreneurs have built more than 500 000 private companies operating in all sectors of the economy and society. After centuries of isolation, Russians are discovering the rest of the world for themselves – 15 million people traveled abroad in 2001.

Many characteristics of Russia and its people favor a successful transition toward a market economy. The country has a high literacy rate. Many of its people are extremely well educated and highly skilled. Russians are well known for their technical and artistic intellect and creative ingenuity. Furthermore, most Russians do not want to return to Communism or hard-line xenophobic nationalism, though present hardships engender a certain amount of nostalgia for the past when their empire was still intact. Many of them very much appreciate the new freedoms they have acquired only recently. Given their history of endurance, of overcoming difficulties, it is likely that they will cling to those freedoms tenaciously.

However, Russian political and business elites and society as a whole have not yet wholeheartedly committed to a model of modern civil society and capitalism. Social stability is fragile as the growing economy still disproportionately depends on energy and other raw material exports. No mechanisms have been put in place to control human avarice and the lust for power. As never before Russia needs excellent leadership at all levels of the society to deal with human, political and economic problems.

MOURNING THE PAST AND EMBRACING NEW VALUES

We chose to focus in this book on some unusual leaders. We are aware that market competition and self-reliance are not universal goals in Russian society. The resistance among older Russians to embark on real change is understandable. With the arrival of glasnost (and all the changes that followed), many people realized that in adhering to the Communist ideology, they had devoted their lives to a lost cause, but at least it *was* a cause, a collective purpose, something greater than the individual. Other members of the existing elite and many ordinary citizens are still fighting change, be it overtly or covertly, consciously or unconsciously, and remain a formidable opposing force for the future at all levels of the society, including the organizational level.

These people have not been able to properly 'mourn' the past and start afresh. In order to co-opt them into the transformation process, their confusion and fears concerning change must be recognized and addressed rather than ignored. They need help to reconcile themselves to the fact that they have been living false lives and engaging in unproductive or even immoral activities such as informing on others. The implication of having had a whole secret state within a state, made up of a large number of people managing the vast network of labor camps spread out across the length and breadth of the former Soviet Union has not yet been addressed. Only by working through these issues will a real receptivity to change be created among this group of people. And only with that new receptivity will they abandon denial, regression and obfuscation as ways of dealing with life's difficulties.

So far both the Russian federal government and business elite as a whole have failed even to recognize this problem. It is unlikely they will provide the leadership required to deal with these kinds of issues. Many, like Maria Ilyina of Frontstep, prefer to let the past be the past, and rely on 'fresh blood' of young individuals who started their professional lives under the new conditions of emerging Russian capitalism. However, some individual business leaders such as Ioffé, Sloutsker and Zimin are helping people of the 'lost generation' to find new meaning in life by putting their skills to productive use and engaging them in new capitalist ventures.

The transformation is made more difficult in that Russians have to unlearn long-held attitudes toward entrepreneurship and wealth creation. In the Soviet days when private enterprise was legally prosecuted, *biznesmen* was a dirty word, often a euphemism for *criminal* or *crook*. Even in the pre-revolutionary days businesspeople were condemned by the intellectual elite for self-serving individualism and get-rich-quick-at-any-cost capitalism. Russians need to recognize that businesspeople are essential builders in a new society. Therefore, they should be seen not as a parasitic class but as creators of employment and wealth for the population as a whole. One of the leaders that we met with during our research mentioned very astutely that in modern Russia a very small percentage of individuals create employment and earning opportunities for the majority of the nation. They need to be given both respect and legitimacy so that with time they become positive role models.

Unfortunately, some of the new Russian businessmen behave in a way that reinforces traditional negative images rather than destroying them. A major example is lack of transparency about ownership of business. Mikhail Khodorkovsky was one of the pioneers among Russian oligarchs to disclose publicly the ownership structure of his organization. And although he firmly closed the book on his more questionable early personal and professional career moves, history has come back to haunt him. Some other business leaders have followed his example, but in most other cases ownership structure remains obscure. This does not help generate a positive image of the Russian business tycoon; it does not reassure Russian or foreign stakeholders, from shop-floor workers to large investors. In addition, a heavy reliance on status symbols in the new Russia, including flaunting of material wealth, coupled with envy towards people who are better off, contributes to the negative image of successful business leaders among rank-and-file employees. Although envy is a great motivator, ostentatious behavior by business leaders does not make for a very healthy corporate culture. This kind of behavior is rather paradoxical: on the one hand, Russians want to work for successful leaders, as this gives a sense of security to them. Success is signaled by material wealth in Russia. On the other hand, they are dismayed at the earnings and overt spending patterns of wealthy Russians as popularized by the mass media.

TOWARD A THEORY OF RUSSIAN LEADERSHIP

A long history of bloody, devastating wars, the predominance of the Orthodox religion, global and local isolation made many Russians suspicious toward the outside world and everything coming from abroad. A Russian proverb says 'What is good for a German (foreigner), is deadly for a Russian'. Here is just a simple example: even among Russian business educators there is a strong belief that Russia should have its own organizational theory and derivative formation and training for future executives. There is even a national Russian standard for an MBA degree and a widely publicized idea that a Russian business education, obtained in Russia, better prepares people for work in Russian organizations. Without overcoming this deeply embedded syndrome of 'not invented here', Russians will not be able to keep up with global technical and economic progress. On the contrary, those who open up to new concepts, tools and models, whether coming from the West, East or Russia itself, will have a strong competitive advantage as the leaders described in this book have proved.

For the last ten years different factions in Russian political establishment have talked about a need to 'substitute old Soviet values' with new ones or 'develop national identity' for a new Russia. However, it's unlikely that the current political elite, including President Putin and any of his immediate subordinates, is capable of, or even interested in, actively promoting productive values for Russian society. They are too strongly linked to the traditional values and power structures, too remote from realities of life, too busy fighting political and social fires and enriching themselves to take on this Herculean task. We argue that other groups within Russian society will have to provide leadership in pushing this critically important issue on the agenda.

Social organizations such as the Club 2015[7] and its regional branches, and the Russian Association of Managers, have begun to fill the void, unifying an active, self-sustainable part of the Russian population. Members of these organizations promote change by telling their own life stories, sharing their business expertise, creating business incubators for young people, and publishing books and articles on entrepreneurship and entrepreneurs. Oligarchs unified under the umbrella of the Russian Union of Industrialists and Entrepreneurs (RSPP) make their contribution by providing loans to small businesses, financing the training for entrepreneurs, and sharing stories of their successes with glamour magazines. They use the Russian mass media (more powerful by far than their Western counterparts) to promote such values as entrepreneurship, self-reliance and achievement motivation, but they could do a lot more.

Family and secondary school education could (and eventually will) play a decisive role in instilling a productive culture in Russia. However, today neither schoolteachers struggling for survival on meager salaries, nor parents (most of whom grew up under the Communist system), can provide stellar leadership toward new values. Institutions of higher education with better trained, paid, informed and motivated teachers have to fill this gap by teaching students not only quantum physics or molecular biology, but also productive values and a positive outlook on life. They also need to insert modern business concepts into their core curriculum. Encouragingly, some entrepreneurs – including such oligarchs as Kakha Bendukidze of United Heavy Machinery, Russia's largest private heavy engineering corporation; and Vladimir Lisin, of Novolipetsk Metallurgical Plant – have become university instructors themselves, teaching entrepreneurship and strategy to undergraduate students. Slowly, but steadily Russian business schools are developing case studies depicting not only foreign multinationals' joint ventures in Russia, but also local companies set up and run by new entrepreneurs.

Influential forces are waging a battle to transform Russia into a modern, productive economy; however, one should not underestimate the inertia of the population and influence of traditional values and attitudes. This battle for the Russian soul will be decisively won when the new role model of the happy, self-sufficient Russian executive permanently replaces the former heroic icons (Red Army generals, cosmonauts, prostitutes, and corrupt government officials) in the minds of millions of young Russians. We think the new role models are likely to be, for better or worse, among the young entrepreneurs we met or heard about over the past ten years – if the Russian government and the Russian people support their activities.

CREATING A FAVORABLE POLITICAL AND ECONOMIC ENVIRONMENT

For new leadership values to become a tangible factor in Russia's development, a predictable political environment in which private enterprise is facilitated must be firmly established. Although the basic foundations of a market economy and durable democracy have been laid, the Russian political elite faces tremendous challenges. Their actions in the coming years will largely determine the competitiveness of the economy and stability of society. Not only does President Putin have a number of hot and immediate issues to tackle, from war in Chechnya to a crumbling housing infrastructure, he and his successors must also deal with larger and more profound dilemmas:

- In spite of the service sector's rapid development in recent years, the Russian economy is still hugely dependent on raw material exports. The manufacturing sector continues to shrink, contributing to increasing economic fragility and vulnerability.
- The voracious growth of the giant financial–industrial groups, which control over 75 per cent of the national economy by some estimates, raises a real issue of government's ability to prevent future monopolization and to provide opportunities for the development of small entrepreneurial companies. Russia is already lagging behind other former Communist countries in the development of this sector with only 26 per cent of its labor force working for companies with less than 250 employees versus 50–70 per cent in Central Europe.
- The Russian economy represents an extreme example of disproportional development, with Moscow attracting over 60 per cent of foreign direct investment (FDI) and over 80 per cent of added value. Only Moscow and Veliky Novgorod were rated in 2002 as regions with 'acceptable risk' for FDI. Independent surveys systematically show that the majority of entrepreneurs describe the Russian economic environment as 'hostile' to private enterprise.
- Even though bloody scenes of mafia vendettas are no longer an always-present feature of prime time news programs, contract killings and asset seizure by force are still commonplace in Russia. And corruption, the old ill of Russia, is flourishing, reaching all levels of government.

The good news is that the Russian politicians are no longer alone in thinking about these issues. As mentioned above, powerful forces within Russian society, such as big business associations, are visibly fighting to improve stability and the economic climate. Oligarchs from RSPP have an ongoing dialogue with the government on economic, fiscal and legal issues. It remains to be seen to what extent these business tycoons, who often control whole sectors of Russian economy, will go down the road of free competition, but thus far their impact has been productive: Russia has introduced a flat rate (13 per cent) income tax; slashed corporate taxes, making the total enterprise tax burden one of the lowest in Europe (31 per cent); and made small business registration more simple than in a number of Wester European societies.

In general, Putin and his government have been tolerant of the oligarchs' leadership – Khodorkovsky's imprisonment being one of the exceptions to this rule – to improve business conditions in Russia. However corrupt some of the government members may be, they are shrewd politicians with a modern mentality, who perfectly understand the benefits of a strong economy driven by private interest. It is very likely that Putin, after his second term, will pass on to his successor a more stable Russia, with clearer legislation, a robust economy and important strata of business owners and operators. He probably cannot or will not, however, do much to cure chronic Russian diseases such as corruption, favoritism and the convergence of government and big business interests. This task will require leaders of a new generation who are free not only of old ideological and cultural stereotypes, but from the demoralizing experiences of '*les années folles*' of Yeltsin's administration and Russian privatization. Only history will tell who among Russians will rise to this task, but one could easily imagine some of the leaders in this book, and indeed some of them seem to see themselves, in that role.

BUILDING A 21ST CENTURY ENTERPRISE

Many new Russian business leaders have been quite successful in building new organizations or transforming old Soviet enterprises into vehicles to turn in profits and earn returns on their investment. They have overcome many of the vices of the Soviet economic system, such as a disregard for cost and quality, lack of operational and working discipline, high absenteeism and employee turnover. However, these organizations in most cases reproduce the 3Cs model: the organization built on command, control and compartmentalization. Global competitiveness requires a very different operational model, the 3Is organization, based on information, innovation and involvement. To build such organizations is the greatest challenge for Russian business leaders of the beginning of the 21st century, and arguably the toughest challenge they have ever faced in their short, but very intensive business careers.

This change is hard not only because many elements of the previous model are heavily embedded in a Russian psyche, but also because up to now, the model worked. Why fix what's apparently not broken? Because neither Russia Inc., nor any independent Russian company, can remain in isolation from the global market – if they don't take control of their own economy, and compete on an equal footing with foreign partners, the competition will overrun them no matter what entry barriers are created. So change is inevitable.

The 'heroes for a New Russia' in this book (as Olga Sloutsker might call them) have demonstrated high adaptability and skills in managing change. Their organizations have gone through transformations and today have many elements of the 3Is model. This work is not complete, but the trend is impressive and encouraging for others. Their experiences can be distilled into some key learning points:

- To compete in the global world, Russian organizations should develop competencies mastered by their international rivals – speed and flexibility, customer-orientation and productive innovation, information sharing and continuous learning. New leadership, values, organizational practices and systems are required to create and operate such companies.
- Trust is the underlining feature of modern organizational practices. However, the general level of trust in today's Russian organizations is quite low. Employees don't trust their colleagues from other departments; middle management doesn't trust employees, and senior executives don't have confidence in their direct reports. This particular organizational feature represents the single largest threat to Russian businesses competing in the age of information, innovation and virtual teams. Russian leaders have to learn to instill a climate of trust within their organizations and among their external stakeholders, just as they successfully learned to wear stylish suits, to open their books to international investors, to listen to market analysts and management consultants, to answer media questions and even declare their personal income. This new competency will greatly strengthen their businesses' ability to grow not only domestically, but also globally.
- Trust is part of an equation that creates constructive dialogue, commitment and accountability, leading to better results. Trust forms a foundation for another organizational practice Russian business leaders need to learn: empowerment and delegation, which are cornerstones of organizational speed and flexibility. By cascading responsibility down the hierarchy, leaders not only improve quality and speed of operational decisions and employees' interest and motivation, but also free themselves from micromanagement and devote their time to larger issues. Modern organizations cannot be solely managed by one person sitting atop a hierarchical pyramid, with hundreds of rigid procedures regulating all aspects of internal life. Change leaders are needed at all levels. 'Distributed' leadership makes for high performance organizations. Empowerment and delegation must gradually replace command, control and compartmentalization as key principles of organizational architecture.

- Information has always been regarded as a sacred source of power in Russian organizations. It has been secretly collected, stored, classified and traded for very high stakes, including human lives. These practices migrated from the Soviet to new Russian companies, which created enormous barriers to information flow in the form of sophisticated control instruments. The real challenge is to destroy them and create information systems that support data and best practice sharing, and strengthen corporate values. Visionary leaders such as Ruben Vardanian have already dismantled them; the majority of businesses still have to undertake this task.

- All around the globe, organizations are becoming flatter, decentralized, and de-bureaucratized. Hierarchy will be increasingly replaced by networks, virtual or otherwise. Likewise, in Russia hierarchical multi-layer structures with stone walls between departments and power struggles between executives must give way to flatter organizations with intensive horizontal communication. Such instruments as cross-functional projects, job rotation, geographical moves, and so on should encourage employee cooperation at all levels.

- And last, but not least, the challenge is to open up Russian organizations toward the outside world, transforming them from a mindset of fortresses besieged by enemy armies into open systems giving and taking from an ever-changing environment. Exchanges with competitors, customers, suppliers and other industries should be constantly searched for, analysed and used as an important source of organizational learning. Coupled with effective internal information networks, an open-system organizational philosophy should ensure competitiveness in the long run. Knowledge management will be par for the course. Many Russian business leaders have successfully done it for themselves, now they need to make continuous learning and development a part of their organizations.

Adapting a new organizational model will require abandoning some of the long-time practices and behaviors of executives, middle managers and employees. This fundamental transformation needs strong leadership from the top and effective change agents at all organizational levels. Successful entrepreneurs turned corporate executives will likely provide high-level leadership. Knowing their personal capability to embrace progressive concepts, sense opportunities and learn new techniques, one can bet that it would be a strong push. However, even they will need strong allies within their organizations, who can successfully operate in a new model and pass their skills and attitudes on to others. Several groups could play such a role: Western executives and professionals, who more and more often work for Russian organizations; so-called hybrids, Russian managers with Western experience returning home; and Russian graduates of Western business schools. However, a new organizational model will only flourish and bring tangible benefits with the overhaul of the Russian managers' skill-set. For that Russia needs a well-functioning modern system of management education.

The country doesn't have a strong tradition of management education, but one can hardly underestimate its significance for development of competitive organizations anywhere, including Russia. Even though today there are many institutions offering management education, with almost every college having a business or management department, the content and scope of this education doesn't usually meet the existing challenge. It is primarily directed toward undergraduate and graduate students, often leaving practicing managers who are struggling with such key functional areas as marketing, consumer behavior, production management, international finance, business strategy, human resource management, and organizational development out in the cold.

There are some encouraging signs, with a small number of business schools offering various executive education programs, experimenting with methods of instruction and attracting accomplished faculty. However, in the new market economy, not only people at the top of the pyramid but people at all levels of an organization need to be exposed to a spectrum of management expertise. The handful of existing Russian business schools is not capable of delivering that. The business organizations themselves have to take on this task. The learning process can be accelerated via the exchange of 'best practices' – in other words, via benchmarking with successful companies, both nationally and internationally. While there is no tradition of benchmarking in Russia – given the Communist era's legacy of secrecy and information hoarding – it is a tool that holds great promise. Furthermore, like in many Western companies, company 'business universities' can take on the challenge of dealing with continuous and discontinuous change with the company's leadership taking on the role of coach.

LIGHT AT THE END OF THE TUNNEL?

Previous generations of leaders have largely failed to provide the Russian people with positive direction and a productive organizational environment. They have led them into bloody wars and revolutions, devastating political and economic experiments, intellectual oppression and physical destruction. Now, as the center of gravity in Russian society moves from politics towards economics, new business leaders are emerging as a principal force shaping the society and its future. Are these people who built their wealth and influence on the ruins of the Soviet empire capable of leading their nation to prosperity, civil society, personal freedom and openness?

The signals are mixed so far as traditional behavior and attitudes still act as a strong undertow. However, some trends are encouraging and probably determinant. Quick to learn Western business models and concepts, and adapt Western lifestyles for themselves (almost naively quick, in some cases) the new Russian leaders recognize the importance of a well-functioning government, a healthy market economy and democratic institutions. And as the leaders in this book show, when they want something they usually get it done.

It is too early to know what the new Russian society and the business organizations supporting it will look like. A simple replication of Western management systems will not work here, as history has already proved. Unique systems building on international experience, but compatible with the Russian character, must be found or developed. Likewise, only those leadership practices that resonate with Russian culture and values should be adopted. However, any organization system or leadership practice selected must make people management a priority. In this information age, human capital is the scarcest resource.

The French philosopher Jean Paul Sartre once said, 'Hell is other people'. Russians know all too well the meaning of this statement. Generations of people in Russia have lived through this kind of hell. But now they are poised on the brink of change. Russia has a great opportunity to find a unique and powerful place in the world. It could become a beacon for budding entrepreneurs. It could also break down into an 'Upper Volta with nuclear missiles', as a Russian Parliament deputy called it once. The future is in the hands of the 'heroes for a new Russia'.

NOTES

1. Josephson, M. (1934, 1962), *The Robber Barons, The Great American Capitalists, 1861–1901*, New York: Harcourt, Brace & World, Inc.
2. Chamberlain, J. (1963), *The Enterprising Americans: A Business History of the United States*, New York: Harper Colophon Books, p. 151.
3. Jones, P. d'Arcy (1968), *The Robber Barons Revisited*, Lexington, MA: D.C. Heath and Company, p. vii.
4. Klein, M. (1998), 'Russian tycoons are more robber than baron', *Wall Street Journal*, New York, 10 September, p. 1.
5. Klein, M. (1998), 'Russian tycoons are more robber than baron', *Wall Street Journal*, New York, 10 September, p. 1.
6. Mellow, C. (1997), 'Russia's robber barons', *Fortune*, 3 March, **135**, (4), 120–26.
7. The 2015 Club is an informal group of Russian business professionals and entrepreneurs concerned with the need for businessmen to take a socially responsible position. It was formed after the 1998 Russian financial crisis. The philosophy of the Club is to be an independent broadminded organization, and membership is based – in contrast to party discipline and majority rule – on strict professional and ethical criteria, personal freedom of every member, common sense and a desire to contribute to socially oriented programs implemented by the Club members.

Index

inertia 298
introspection 25
irrationality 4
mir mentality 15–17
mood swings 48, 49–50
'moral upbringing' 18–20
multiethnicity 44
nature, impact of 14–15
Oblomovism 26
order and chaos, oscillation between 19
paranoia 29–30
passive resistance 22
personal space 15
polychronic view of time 31–2
public humiliation 18, 23
reality, avoidance of 30–31
reporting phenomenon 53
seasonal affective disorder (SAD) 15
sense of externality 18
sense of impotence 19
social defenses 27
space 7
suffering 10–11
swaddling 17–18, 19
violence 10–11, 49
Russian Orthodox Church 10, 30, 50–51, 280
Russian Standard
brand 124–5
leadership style 139
and Roustam Tariko 124–46
Russian Standard Bank 125–7, 129
recruitment 133
services 126
Russian Standard Company 125
Russian Standard group of companies, recruitment and staffing 133–6
Russian Standard On-line 127–8
Russian Standard Vodka 122–4
advertising campaign 130
exports 123
launch 123
profit sharing 136
Russian Union of Industrialists and Entrepreneurs (RSPP) 76, 159, 298, 299–300
Bureau 234, 251, 255

Samaraenergo 243
SAP 206

Sberbank 193, 240
Schein, E. 7
Schneider, S. 6
Scientific Management 63, 64
seasonal affective disorder (SAD) 15
self, public and private 20–21, 22–3
'self-actualization' 165
self-efficacy 63, 64
sense of externality 18
sense of impotence 19
sequential planning processes 115
serfdom 51–2
service sector 295, 299
Sibneft, merger with Yukos Oil 147, 166
Sistema 179, 182, 185, 186–7, 189
Slavo 204, 206, 207
Slavo, in Russia
early years 205–206
foundation 205
problems in France 206–207
software implementation projects 206
'sleeping bears' 229
Sloutsker, Olga 259, 264–8, 279–82, 293
as charismatic leader 273
early life 260–61, 281
leadership style 273–4, 280–81
management style 270–72
and World Class fitness centres 259–82
SOCAP 202, 207
bonuses 217
career development 213–14
client contact consultants 212–13
compensation issues 216
consulting department 218–19
director of consulting 219
director of marketing 218
internal development project 215–16
and Maria Ilyina 202–21
merger of departments 217
mission statement 203, 216–17
name changed to Frontstep CIS 222–3
and Pavel Karaulov 218
personalized training 217–18
poaching of staff 214
professional development of employees 216
project organization 216
promotion structure 210–12
recruitment 214, 222–3